Opening Prayer

رَبَّنَآ ءَاتِنَا فِى ٱلدُّنْيَا حَسَنَةً
وَفِى ٱلْـَٔاخِرَةِ حَسَنَةً
وَقِنَا عَذَابَ ٱلنَّارِ

Our Lord, give us in this world [that which is]
good and in the Hereafter [that which is]
good and protect us from the punishment of the Fire.

– 2:201 –

Title: Recitation of the Glorious Qur'an

ISBN: 978-1-952306-16-7 | PAPERBACK

978-1-952306-19-8 | HARDBACK

FIRST EDITION | MAY 2023

Author: ʿABDULLAH SIRĀJ AL-DĪN AL-ḤUSAYNĪ

Translator: JAVED IQBAL

Proofreader: WORDSMITHS

Typesetting: IGPCONSULTANTS

www.imamghazalipublishing.com

Recitation of the Glorious Qur'an

ITS VIRTUES, ETIQUETTES, AND SPECIALTIES

By the Polymath Imam

ʿABDULLĀH SIRĀJ AL-DĪN AL-ḤUSAYNĪ
(1923-2002 CE)

Translated by
Javed Iqbal

Arabic Edited by
Abd al-Rahman Sha'ar

Imam Ghazali
PUBLISHING

Contents

Publisher's Message 11
The life & Legacy of the Shaykh 13
Recitation of the Glorious Qur'an 16

The Noble Qur'an is Literally the Speech of Allah Most High – From Him it Emanated and to Him it Returns 16

The Magnificence of Allah's Speaking the Revelation and the Awe of the Angels عَلَيْهِمُ السَّلَامُ 22

Allah Most High Preserving the Noble Qur'an 30

Allah Most High Preserving the Tablet Wherein it is Written and Enclosed 32

Allah Most High Preserving His Mighty Book and Safeguarding it Against Tampering 34

The Divine Command and the Prophetic Command to Recite the Noble Qur'an 70

The Command to Keep Revising the Qur'an Lest One Forget it 74

Warning Against Turning Away From the Qur'an and Forgetting it 74

The Merit of Reciting the Noble Qur'an 76

Regularly Completing One Recital After the Other is the Most Beloved Action to Allah Most High 84

Recitation of the Noble Qur'an is the Best Act of Worship 86

The Reciter is Rewarded With One Reward For Every Letter and the Reward is Multiplied Tenfold – be it With Or Without Understanding 86

The People of the Qur'an are Allah's People and His Chosen Ones 88

The Proficient Reciter of the Qur'an Will be With the Honourable and Virtuous Angel-Scribes 88

The Reciter of the Qur'an Speaks to Their Lord and Secretly Converses With Him 90

Whoever Loves the Qur'an, Allah and His Messenger صَلَّى ٱللَّهُ عَلَيْهِ وَعَلَىٰ آلِهِ وَسَلَّمَ Love Them 90

The Qur'an is the Banquet of Allah Most High; Whoever Enters it is Safe 92

The House In Which the Qur'an is Recited is Attended By the Angels and Becomes ....

Expansive For its Occupants 92

The House in Which the Qur'an is Recited Shines to the People of the Heavens 94

The Recitation of the Qur'an Contains Abundant Goodness 96

Reciting the Qur'an Makes the Reciter Pleasant 96

The Recitation of the Noble Qur'an Polishes the Hearts 98

Reciting the Noble Qur'an Benefits the Reciter and Their Parents 98

The Best of People are Those Who Have Learnt the Most Qur'an 100

The Most Well-Versed in the Qur'an is Given Precedence Over Others According to the Sacred Law 100

Honouring the People of the Qur'an is Part of Honouring the Symbols of Allah Most High 102

Honouring the One Who Has Memorized the Qur'an is Part of Exalting Allah Most High 104

The Reciter Will Not be Frightened by the Supreme Horror of the Day of Judgement 106

The Intercession of the Noble Qur'an for its Reciter 108

The Reciter Will Continue Ascending in Ranks on the Day of Judgement 110

Reciting the Noble Qur'an Benefits the Listeners With Fragrance and it Exudes the Scent of Musk 112

The Merit of Reciting in Prayer Over Reciting Outside of Prayer 112

Reciting From the *Muṣḥaf* is Multiplied [In Reward] 114

One of the Greatest Honours Allah Most High Will Bestow Upon the People of Paradise is That He Most Glorified Will Recite the Qur'an to Them 118

Serenity and Angels Descending Upon the Recitation of the Noble Qur'an 120

The Houses in Which the Qur'an is Recited Shine With Lights 124

The Most Inferior and Contemptible House is One in Which the Book of Allah Most High is Not Recited 124

The Angels Protect the Reciter of the Qur'an 126

Allah Most High Loves Those Who Recite His Book at Night 126

Reciting the Noble Qur'an Brings Down Blessings 128

The House in Which the Qur'an is Not Recited Has Little Goodness and Much Evil 128

The Person Who Recites the Qur'an to People Receives a Share in the Honour of Conveying On Behalf of the Messenger of Allah ﷺ 128

Allah Most High Loves the Slave Who Recites His Verses At Night Whilst Their Companions Asleep 130

The Merit of Gathering to Recite the Noble Qur'an and Studying it 132

CONTENTS

The Virtue of Memorizing the Noble Qur'an....... 142

Memorizing the Qur'an is the Greatest of Allah's Favours Upon His Slaves 146

The Most Noble People of This Ummah Are the Bearers of the Noble Qur'an....... 146

The Richest of People are the Bearers of the Noble Qur'an....... 148

The Protection of the Bearer of the Noble Qur'an 148

The Honour of the Bearer of the Noble Qur'an....... 148

The Bearer of the Noble Qur'an is the Flagbearer of Islam 150

The Bearer of the Noble Qur'an Benefits From Their Intellect 150

The Bearers of the Noble Qur'an are the Friends of Allah Most High....... 150

The Bearers of the Noble Qur'an will be in the Shade of Allah Most High 152

The Intercession of the Bearer of the Noble Qur'an....... 152

Allah Most High Will Not Punish a Heart Which Retained the Qur'an 152

The Bearers of the Qur'an Will be the Directors of the People of Paradise....... 154

The Bearer of Allah's Book Should be Honoured According to the Sacred Law 154

The Bearers of the Qur'an are Surrounded By Allah's Mercy & Acquire the Light of Allah 156

The Bearer of the Qur'an Has an Accepted Supplication....... 158

The Etiquette of the Bearer of the Noble Qur'an....... 158

The Etiquette and Requirements of Recitation 160

The Counsel of al-Ṣiddīq al-Akbar (The Great Truthful One) 182

Some Concise Words Regarding the Saying of Allah Most High: "We Have Surely Revealed to You a Book, in Which There is Your Mention. Will You Not Then Understand?" and What a Muslim's Stance Towards the Qur'an Should be and the Story of Aḥnaf Ibn al-Qays in That Regard 184

The Stations (*Maqāmāt*) of the Qur'an Reciters....... 190

The Pious Predecessors Liked to Recite Verses Repeatedly for the Sake of Contemplation....... 194

The Desirability of Beautifying the Voice When Reciting the Qur'an....... 208

The Desirability of Seeking Good Recitations and Listening to Them 212

Illuminating Gatherings With the Noble Qur'an 220

The Merit of Listening to the Recitation of the Noble Qur'an 222

The Etiquette and Requirements of Listening to the Noble Qur'an 224

The Merit of Learning and Teaching the Noble Qur'an 230

The Encouragement to Teach Young Children How to Recite the Noble Qur'an 232

The Importance Given by the Prophet ﷺ to Teaching the Noble Qur'an and Disseminating it ... 236

A Muslim Adopting a Litany of Recitation from the Noble Qur'an ... 240

The Habits of the Predecessors in Completing the Noble Qur'an ... 244

The Desirability of Being Regular in a Litany of Qur'anic Recitation in the Middle of the Night ... 248

The Ruling of a Person Who Oversleeps and Misses Their Litany ... 252

One Should Recite the Qur'an Abundantly in the Month of Ramadan ... 252

The Desirability of Reciting Loudly in the Middle of the Night as Long as it Does Not Trouble Others ... 258

The Etiquette of Completing the Noble Qur'an ... 260

It is Part of the Etiquette of Completing the Noble Qur'an to do so at the Beginning of the Day or Night ... 264

The Desirability of Attending the Gathering of the Completion of the Qur'an and its Immense Virtue ... 266

The Desirability of Supplicating Upon Completion Due to it Being Accepted ... 268

The Rulings of the Prostration of Recitation (*Sajdah al-Tilāwah*) ... 274

The Method of the Prostration of Recitation ... 276

The Remembrances for the Prostration of Recitation ... 278

The Divine Counsel and the Prophetic Counsel to Follow the Book and Sunnah and Firmly Abide by Them ... 278

Whomsoever the Qur'an Reaches is as Though They Have Seen the Messenger of Allah ﷺ and Heard From Him ... 288

Warning Muslims Against Not Acting Upon the Noble Qur'an ... 290

Warning Against Disconnecting the Sunnah From the Qur'an and Claiming There is No Need For it ... 290

Warning the Muslim Against Neglecting the Qur'anic Commands ... 294

Warning the Muslim Against Considering Unlawful Matters of the Qur'an As Lawful ... 296

Amongst the Worst of People are Those Who Recite the Qur'an But Do Not Repent ... 296

Whoever Does Not Act Upon the Noble Qur'an, Their Punishment Will Begin in the Realm of *Barzakh* (I.e., the Grave) Until the Resurrection and Beyond ... 298

The Qur'an Disputing With the Person Who Does Not Act Upon it and Defending the Person Who Acts Upon it ... 300

The Qur'an Will be a Proof With Allah Most High ... 302

CONTENTS

The Specialities of Certain *Sūrahs* and Verses and the Encouragement to Recite Them **306**

Sūrah al-Fātiḥah it is the Greatest Sūrah in the Noble Qur'an 308

Sūrah al-Fātiḥah is the Most Virtuous Part 308

Sūrah al-Fātiḥah is the Essence of the Noble Qur'an 310

Sūrah al-Fātiḥah is Called the Chapter of Secretly Conversing (*Sūrah al-Munājāh*) 312

It is Called the Curer (*al-Shāfiyah*) and the Incantation (*al-Ruqyah*) 312

It is Called the Cure (*al-Shifā'*) 314

It is Called the Opener of the Book (*Fātiḥah al-Kitāb*) 314

It is the Most Virtuous Sūrah In the Noble Qur'an 316

The Virtues of *Sūrah al-Baqarah* in General and the Specific Virtues of Certain Verses *Sūrah al-Baqarah* is the Peak of the Qur'an 316

Sūrah al-Baqarah is a Fortress Against the Devils 318

Sūrah al-Baqarah is the Battle Cry of the Fighters and the Camp of Those Who do Actions 318

Ten Verses of *Sūrah al-Baqarah* are a Protection From Every Disliked Thing 320

Āyah al-Kursī is the Leader of the Qur'an 320

Āyah al-Kursī is the Greatest Verse in the Book of Allah Most High 320

Āyah al-Kursī Comprises the Greatest Name (*al-Ism al-A 'ẓam*) 322

Āyah al-Kursī is a Fortified Fortress 324

Reciting *Āyah al-Kursī* After the Prayers is One of the Greatest Good Deeds 326

The Final Verses of *Sūrah al-Baqarah* are From a Treasure Under the Throne 326

The Conclusion of *Sūrah al-Baqarah* is a Supplication Allah Most High Has Taught His Slaves and He Has Guaranteed He Will Accept it 328

The Virtues Mentioned for *Sūrah al-Baqarah* and *Sūrah Āl 'Imrān* 330

The Verse "Allah [Himself] is a Witness That There is No God [Worthy of Worship] Except Him" is the Greatest Testimony in the Book of Allah Most High 332

The Verse "Say, [O Prophet,] "O Allah! Lord Over All Authorities!" 334

The Verse "But if They Turn Away, Then Say, [O Prophet,] 'Allah is Sufficient For Me. There is no God [Worthy of Worship] Except Him. In Him I Put My Trust. and He is the Lord of the Mighty Throne.'" 336

Sūrah al-Isrā' 336

The Last Verse of *Sūrah al-Isrā'* 338

Sūrah al-Kahf 340

Sūrah Ṭāhā 344

Sūrah al-Sajdah (Alif Lām Mīm) 344

Sūrah Yāsīn 346

The Virtue of the *Ḥawāmīm* 346

Ḥa Mīm Dukhān 348

Sūrah al-Raḥmān 348

Sūrah al-Wāqi 'ah 350

The *Musabbiḥāt* 350

Sūrah Tabārak 352

A Qur'anic and Prophetic Invocation 354

The Virtue of Reciting *Sūrah al-Bayyinah* 356

The Specialities of Reciting *Sūrah al-Kāfirūn* and the Subsequent *Sūrahs* When on a Journey 360

The Encouragement to Recite *Sūrah al-Ikhlāṣ* and its Virtue 360

Reciting *Sūrah al-Ikhlāṣ* Before Sleeping 364

The Virtue of Reciting *Sūrah al-Ikhlāṣ* Frequently 364

Reciting *Sūrah al-Ikhlāṣ* When Entering the Home 366

Reciting *Sūrah al-Ikhlāṣ* Ten Times After the Prayer 366

The Virtue of Reciting the *Mu 'awwidhatān* and Their Specialities 368

Reciting the *Mu 'awwidhāt* After the Obligatory Prayers 372

Reciting the *Mu 'awwidhāt* Seven Times After the Friday Prayer 372

Respecting the Muṣḥafs 374

Respect of the Noble Qur'an Requires a Number of Things 380

The *Muṣḥaf* is to be Revered and Honoured – Even if it Wears Out and its Pages Split 382

People Used to Kiss the *Muṣḥaf* and Wipe it on Themselves 388

They Used to Like Looking Into the Muṣḥaf in the Morning 392

Being Sincere to the Book of Allah Most High is Incumbent and it Has its Requirements 394

Publisher's Message

BELOVED READER, it is an immense honour to present to you "*Recitation of the Glorious Qur'an*" by the esteemed Knower of Allah, the polymath Imam, ʿAbdullāh Sirāj al-Dīn al-Ḥusaynī, a book that embodies a world of knowledge about the Qur'an, its recitation, and the profound values it imprints upon the hearts of those who engage with it.

Imam ʿAbdullāh Sirāj al-Dīn al-Ḥusaynī is a name that commands immense respect and recognition in Islamic scholarship. He is an intellectual giant who left an indelible mark on the academic landscape of the 20th and early 21st centuries. With a prodigious memory that held thousands upon thousands of hadith narrations, he was an encyclopaedic scholar par excellence who inspired an entire generation of scholars, not just in Syria, but also here regionally in the West and beyond.

His scholarly expertise and profound wisdom are reflected in this excellent work, "*Recitation of the Glorious Qur'an*". This book is a comprehensive work that goes beyond the mere act of discussing the recitation of the Qur'an; it delves into the conceptual realities and unique characteristics of the Qur'an. It outlines the virtues of the Qur'an, the benefits of its recitation and memorisation, and the proper etiquette for its handling and recitation. The book also highlights the practices of the the Companions of the Prophet Muhammad ﷺ and our pious predecessors, thereby serving as a bridge that connects contemporary readers with the rich traditions of the past.

We at Imam Ghazali Publishing have taken meticulous care to ensure the quality of this translation and overall effort. This edition of "*Recitation of the Glorious Qur'an*" comes with parallel English and Arabic text on facing pages, making it a universal resource for seekers of knowledge around the globe. The Arabic text has been reviewed and edited on the commission of this publishing house and includes full vowels for ease of reading by the Syrian scholar Shaykh Abd al-Rahman Sha'ar. The English translation, the work of the accomplished translator Ustadh Javed Iqbal, is clear, precise, and accessible to all readers, irrespective of their familiarity with Islamic terminology.

One of the remarkable aspects of this book is its extensive documentation. Nearly every paragraph is supported by a verse from the Qur'an, a hadith narration, or a statement from a righteous scholar, grounding the book's content firmly in the rich tradition of Islamic scholarship. Hundreds of footnotes, provided in English and Arabic, facilitate a deeper understanding of the sources and references used.

We believe this book is more than just a guide to the recitation of the Qur'an. It is a guide to understanding the Qur'an, respecting it, and allowing its profound teachings to shape our lives. It is a testament to the legacy of Shaykh ʿAbdullāh Sirāj al-Dīn al-Ḥusaynī and his remarkable contribution to Islamic scholarship.

In publishing "*Recitation of the Glorious Qur'an*", we hope to make this precious legacy accessible to people across the globe. We trust that it will serve as an invaluable resource for anyone seeking to deepen their understanding of the Qur'an, connect with its timeless teachings, and discover the spiritual treasures it holds.

As you embark on this journey of discovery, we pray that your engagement with the Qur'an becomes deeper, more meaningful, and immensely rewarding.

MUHAMMAD ADNAAN SATTAUR
Publisher, Imam Ghazali Publishing

The Life and Legacy of the Shaykh

SHAYKH ʿABDULLĀH ibn Muhammad Najīb Sirāj al-Dīn al-Ḥusaynī al-Ḥalabī was an eminent Islamic scholar, spiritual master, and *ḥāfiẓ* recognized for his profound knowledge, unparalleled piety, and dedicated service to Islam. Born in 1923 CE into a prestigious and devout family during the twilight of the Ottoman Caliphate, Shaykh ʿAbdullāh's spiritual journey was shaped by a nurturing environment rooted in Islamic values and scholarship.

The early years of Shaykh ʿAbdullāh's education were guided by his father, the esteemed Shaykh Muhammad Najīb Sirāj al-Dīn al-Ḥusaynī, who in his own right was a renowned scholar and spiritual guide. As a young man, Shaykh ʿAbdullāh was fortunate to study under a number of distinguished scholars of his time, including Imam Muhammad Ibrāhīm al-Salqīnī, Shaykh ʿĪsā al-Bayānūnī, Shaykh ʿUmar Masʿūd al-Ḥarīrī, Shaykh Fayḍullāh al-Ayyubī al-Kurdī, Shaykh Aḥmad al-Shammāʾ, and the highly respected historian of Aleppo, Shaykh Muhammad Rāghib al-Ṭabbākh. The latter, who recognized Shaykh ʿAbdullāh's intellect and devotion, would ultimately become his mentor.

Shaykh ʿAbdullāh's knowledge and spiritual insight led him to become an influential figure in the Islamic world, and his teachings produced a generation of scholars, such as Shaykh Dr. Aḥmad Sirāj al-Dīn, Shaykh Dr. Nūr al-Dīn ʿItr, Shaykh Dr. Sāmir al-Naṣṣ, and Shaykh Muhammad ʿAwwāmah, all of whom have carried forward his scholarly legacy.

The Shaykh's spiritual life was marked by extraordinary moments. His profound connection with the Prophet Muhammad ﷺ, as manifested in his dreams and visions, was a testament to his spiritual stature. Shaykh ʿAbdullāh had a deep-seated love for al-Madinah al-Munawwarah, the city of the Prophet ﷺ, where he stayed for a significant period teaching, writing, and worshipping. His numerous visits to the Mosque of the Prophet ﷺ, fervent prayers, and respect for the sacred space were indicative of his unwavering devotion.

Despite his towering accomplishments, Shaykh ʿAbdullāh was a man of profound humility. He was known to conduct his lessons with an emphasis on dhikr (remembrance of Allah) and good manners. He treated others with the utmost level of respect and kindness, thereby demonstrating the Islamic values he espoused. His humility notwithstanding his spiritual and scholarly stature – was stunning and exemplary. In one story, those accompanying him noted his refusal to let a caretaker of the Ḥaram kiss his hand, citing the sanctity of the land of the Prophet ﷺ, thereby epitomizing his humble nature. This humility, combined with his scholarly prowess and spiritual depth, made him a revered figure, both during his lifetime and beyond.

In 2002, after a surgical operation, Shaykh ʿAbdullāh's health rapidly declined; he tragically passed away on the 4th of March during the same year. His passing was a significant loss for the Muslim world, casting a veil of sorrow across communities that revered him. He was laid to rest in the Shaʿbāniyyah complex, next to the graves of its Ottoman founders, ultimately marking the end of an era of spiritual enlightenment.

Shaykh ʿAbdullāh ibn Muhammad Najīb Sirāj al-Dīn al-Ḥusaynī al-Ḥalabī's life and legacy continue to be an inspiration for many. His profound understanding of Islamic jurisprudence, exceptional scholarship of Hadith, and brilliant exegesis of the Qur'an remain relevant in the domain of contemporary Islamic thought. His teachings continue to guide scholars and spiritual seekers alike, making him a timeless beacon in the ocean of Islamic wisdom.

Selected List of the Shaykh's Works

- *Ḥawla Tafsīr Sūrah al-Fātiḥah*
- *Ḥawla Tafsīr Sūrah al-Ḥujurāt*
- *Ḥawla Tafsīr Sūrah Qāf*
- *Ḥawla Tafsīr Sūrah al-Mulk*
- *Ḥawla Tafsīr Sūrah al-Insān*
- *Ḥawla Tafsīr Sūrah al- ʿAlaq*
- *Ḥawla Tafsīr Sūrah al-Kawthar*
- *Ḥawla Tafsīr Sūrah al-Ikhlāṣ*
- *Hadī al-Qur'ān al-Karīm ilā Ḥujjah al-Burhān*
- *Hadī al-Qur'ān ilā Ma ʿrifah al- ʿUlūm wa al-Tafakkur*
- *Tilāwah al-Qur'ān al-Majīd*
- *al-Taqarrub ilā Allāh Ta ʿālā*
- *Shahādah Lā Ilāha Illā Allāh, Muḥammad Rasūl Allāh*
- *Sayyidunā Muḥammad Rasūl Allāh*
- *al-Hadī al-Nabawī wa al-Irshādāt al-Muḥamadiyyah*
- *al-Ṣalāh fī al-Islām*
- *al-Ṣalāh ʿalā al-Nabī*
- *Ṣu ʿūd al-Aqwāl wa-Raf ʿ al- ʿAmāl*
- *al-Du ʿā'*
- *al-Imān bi- ʿAwalim al-Ukhrā wa-Mawāqifuhā*
- *al-Ad ʿiyyah wa al-Adhkār al-Wāridah*
- *Ada ʿiyyah al-Ṣabāḥ wa al-Masā'*
- *Manāsik al-Ḥajj wa al- ʿUmrah*
- *al-Isrā' wa al-Mi ʿraj*
- *Hijrah Rasūl Allāh*

Recitation of the Glorious Qur'an

Its Virtues, Etiquettes, and Specialties

Shaykh ʿAbdullāh Sirāj al-Dīn al-Husaynī

THE NOBLE QUR'AN IS LITERALLY THE SPEECH OF ALLAH MOST HIGH – FROM HIM IT EMANATED AND TO HIM IT RETURNS

Allah Most High said, "And if anyone from the polytheists asks for your protection [O Prophet], grant it to them so they may hear the Word of Allah."[1]

He Most High said, "And indeed, you [O Prophet] are receiving the Qur'an from the One [Who is] All-Wise, All-Knowing."[2] Thus, the Noble Qur'an comes from the All-Wise, All-Knowing.[3] He Most High said, "We will soon send upon you a weighty discourse."[4]

Thus, it is the Word of Allah which He revealed to His Messenger – our

---

(1) *Al-Tawbah*, 6.

(2) *Al-Naml*, 6.

(3) *Al-Naml*, 6.

(4) *Al-Muzzammil*, 5.

تِلَاوَةُ القُرْآنِ الْمَجِيْدِ
فَضَائِلُهَا - آدَابُهَا - خَصَائِصُهَا

بقلم الشيخ
عبد الله سراج الدين

القرآنُ الكريمُ كلامُ الله تعالى على الحقيقةِ
منه بدأ وإليه يعود

قال اللهُ تعالى: {وَإِنْ أَحَدٌ مِنَ الْمُشْرِكِينَ اسْتَجَارَكَ فَأَجِرْهُ حَتَّى يَسْمَعَ كَلامَ اللَّهِ} [1] الآية. وقال تعالى: {وَإِنَّكَ لَتُلَقَّى الْقُرْآنَ مِن لَّدُنْ حَكِيمٍ عَلِيمٍ} [2]. فالقرآنُ الكريمُ صادرٌ {مِن لَّدُنْ حَكِيمٍ عَلِيمٍ} [3]. وقال تعالى: {إِنَّا سَنُلْقِي عَلَيْكَ قَوْلًا ثَقِيلًا} [4].

---

(١) التوبة: ٦.

(٢) النمل: ٦.

(٣) النمل: ٦.

(٤) المزمل: ٥.

master Muhammad ﷺ – through the medium of Jibrīl the Trustworthy.

Abū Saʿīd al-Khudrī narrated that the Messenger of Allah ﷺ said, "The Lord Most Blessed and High said, 'Whoever is preoccupie d by the Qur'an from supplicating Me, I grant him the best of what I grant those who supplicate. The merit of the Speech of Allah Most High over all other speech is like the merit of Allah over His creation."(1) Tirmidhī and Dārimī narrated it.

The Leader of the Believers (*Amīr al-Mu'minīn*) ʿAlī narrated that the Messenger of Allah ﷺ said, "Hold firm to the Qur'an and take it as a leader and guide, because it is the Speech of the Lord of all worlds – it is from Him and returns to Him. So, believe in its elusive verses and take lessons from its examples."(2) Ibn Shāhīn narrated it in *al-Sunnah*, and also Ibn Mardawayh, Ibn Lāl and Daylamī – as stated in *al-Jāmiʿ al-Ṣaghīr* and its commentary.

Dārimī narrated in his *Sunan* from Ibn ʿAṭiyyah that the Messenger of Allah ﷺ said, "There is no speech greater in the sight of Allah than His Speech, and the slaves do not draw near to Allah with any speech more beloved to Him than His Speech."(3)

Tirmidhī narrated on the authority of Jābir that the Messenger of Allah ﷺ would present himself to the people during the Hajj season and say, "Is there any man who can take me to his people so that I can convey the Speech of my Lord? Because the Quraysh have stopped me from conveying the speech of my Lord."(4)

Saʿīd ibn Jubayr said, "The Messenger of Allah ﷺ set out on an expedition and encountered the enemy. The Muslims picked out a man from the polytheists and pointed their spears towards him, to which the man said, 'Lift your weapons from me and let me hear the Speech of Allah

---

(1) *Tirmidhī* (2926).

(2) *Daylamī* (4023).

(3) *Dārimī* (3353).

(4) *Tirmidhī* (2925).

فهو قولُ اللهِ تعالى ألقاهُ على رسولِهِ سيِّدِنا محمدٍ ﷺ بواسطةِ جبريلَ الأمينِ.

عن أبي سعيد الخُدريّ رضي الله عنه قال: قال رسولُ اللهِ ﷺ: يقولُ الرَّبُّ تبارك وتعالى: «مَنْ شَغَلَهُ القُرْآنُ عَنْ مَسْأَلَتِي أَعْطَيْتُهُ أَفْضَلَ مَا أُعْطِي السَّائِلِينَ، وَفَضْلُ كَلَامِ اللهِ تَعالى عَلَى سَائِرِ الكَلَامِ كَفَضْلِ اللهِ عَلَى خَلْقِهِ»[1]. رواه الترمذيُّ والدارميُّ.

وعن أميرِ المؤمنينَ عليٍّ رضي اللهُ عنه قال: قال رسولُ الله صلى الله عليه وآلهِ وسلَّم: «عليكُمْ بالقرآنِ فاتَّخِذوهُ إماماً وقائداً؛ فإنَّهُ كلامُ ربِّ العالمينَ، الذي هو منهُ وإليه يعود، فآمِنوا بمُتشابِهِه، واعتبروا بأمثالِه»[2]. رواه ابنُ شاهين في (السُّنّة)، وابنُ مَرْدَوَيْه، وابنُ لال، والدَّيلميُّ، كما في (الجامع الصغير) وشرحِه.

وروى الدارميُّ في (سُننهِ) عن عطيّةَ رضي الله عنه أنّهُ قال: قال رسولُ الله ﷺ: «ما مِنْ كلامٍ أعظمُ عند اللهِ مِن كلامِه، وما ردَّ - أي: ما تقرَّبَ - العبادُ إلى اللهِ كلاماً أحبَّ إليه من كلامِه»[3].

وروى الترمذيُّ عن جابرٍ رضي الله عنه قال: كان رسولُ الله ﷺ يَعرِضُ نفسَهُ في الموسمِ على النّاسِ في الموقفِ، فيقول: «ألَا هل مِنْ رجلٍ يحملُني إلى قومِه حتى أُبلِّغَ كلامَ ربِّي؛ فإنّ قريشاً منعوني أن أُبلِّغَ كلامَ ربِّي»[4].

وعن سعيدِ بنِ جُبَيرٍ رحمه الله تعالى قال: (خرج رسولُ اللهِ صلى الله عليه وآله وسلَّمَ غازياً، فلقيَ العدوَّ، فأخرجَ المسلمون رجلاً من المشركين، وأشرعوا فيه الأَسِنَّةَ، فقال الرَّجلُ:

---

(١) أخرجه الترمذي (٢٩٢٦).

(٢) أخرجه الديلمي (٤٠٢٣).

(٣) أخرجه الدارمي (٣٣٥٣).

(٤) أخرجه الترمذي (٢٩٢٥).

Most High.'"[1] Bayhaqī narrated it and said it is a sound (*ḥasan*) *mursal*[2] narration. Dārimī narrated with his chain on the authority of Ibn ʿUmar ﷺ, as a hadith attributed to the Prophet ﷺ (i.e., a *marfū* ʿ[3] narration), "The Qur'an is more beloved to Allah Most High than the Heavens, the Earth, and everything within."[4]

Bayhaqī narrated with his chain that when the verses "*Alif Lām Mīm.* The Romans have been defeated in a nearby land"[5] were revealed, Abū Bakr al-Ṣiddīq ﷺ read them to the Quraysh. They asked him, "Is this your speech or your companion's speech?" He replied, "It is neither my speech nor that of my companion, but rather it is the Speech of Allah Almighty and Exalted."[6]

ʿUmar ibn al-Khaṭṭāb ﷺ said, "Indeed, this Qur'an is the Speech of Allah Most High, so let not your desires towards which you incline it deceive you."[7] What he meant by this was to seek direction from the Noble Qur'an and not divert it towards one's erroneous desires. This is how it is explained by Imam Aḥmad's narration in *al-Zuhd* with his chain from ʿUmar ﷺ who said, "Indeed, this Qur'an is the Speech of Allah, so place it in its rightful place and do not follow your desires regarding it."[8] Bayhaqī narrated with his chain that ʿUthmān ibn ʿAffān ﷺ said, "If our hearts were pure, they would never get enough of the Speech of our Lord. I dislike for even one day to pass without looking into the *muṣḥaf*."[9]

Ṭabarānī narrated on the authority of Ḥakam ibn ʿUmayr ﷺ – as cited

---

(1) Bayhaqī in *al-Asmā' wa al-Ṣifāt*, vol. 1, pg. 307.

(2) Translator's note: A hadith in which the link of the Companion is missing.

(3) Translator's Note: A *marfū* ʿ narration is one in which a statement, action, approval, or quality is attributed to the Prophet ﷺ.

(4) *Dārimī* (3224).

(5) *Al-Rūm*, 1-3.

(6) Bayhaqī in *al-Asmā' wa al-Ṣifāt*, vol. 1, p. 585.

(7) *Dārimī* (3355).

(8) Aḥmad in *al-Zuhd* (191).

(9) Bayhaqī in *Shu ʿab al-Īmān* (2149).

ارفعوا عنّي سلاحَكمْ، وأسمعوني كلامَ اللهِ تعالى) [1]. رواه البيهقيُّ، وقال: مرسَلٌ حسَنٌ.

وروى الدارميُّ بإسناده عن ابنِ عمرَ رَضِيَ اللَّهُ عَنْهُمَا مرفوعاً: «القرآنُ أحبُّ إلى اللهِ تعالى من السّمواتِ والأرضِ ومَن فيهنّ» [2]. وروى البيهقيُّ بإسناده عن أبي بكرٍ الصّديقِ رضي اللهُ عنه (أنّهُ لمّا نزلَتْ: { الم (١) غُلِبَتِ الرُّومُ (٢) فِي أَدْنَى الْأَرْضِ} [3] الآية، قرأَها على قريشٍ، فقالوا لأبي بكرٍ رَضِيَ اللَّهُ عَنْهُ: كلامُكَ أمْ كلامُ صاحبِكَ؟ فقال: ليس بكلامي ولا كلامِ صاحبي، ولكنْ كلام اللهِ عَزَّوَجَلَّ) [4].

وقال عمرُ بنُ الخطّابِ رَضِيَ اللَّهُ عَنْهُ: (إنَّ هذا القرآنَ كلامُ اللهِ تعالى، فلا يَغُرَّنَّكُمْ ما عطَفْتُموهُ على أهوائِكم) [5]. يعني بذلك: ابتغوا هَدْيَ القرآنِ الكريمِ، ولا تَميلوا به إلى أهوائِكمُ المنحرفةِ، كما تُفسِّرُهُ روايةُ الإمامِ أحمدَ في كتاب (الزُّهد) بسندهِ عنِ عمرَ رضي اللهُ عنه أنّه قال: (إنَّ هذا القرآنَ كلامُ اللهِ عزَّ وجل، فضعوهُ على مواضِعِه، ولا تتَّبِعوا فيه أهواءَكم) [6]. وروى البيهقيُّ بإسناده عن عثمانَ بنِ عفّانَ رَضِيَ اللَّهُ عَنْهُ أنه قال: (لو أنَّ قلوبَنا طَهُرَتْ ما شَبِعَتْ من كلامِ ربِّنا، وإنّي لَأَكرَهُ أنْ يأتيَ عليَّ يومٌ لا أنظرُ فيه في المصحفِ) [7].

---

(١) أخرجه البيهقي في الأسماء والصفات (٣٠٧/١).

(٢) أخرجه الدارمي (٣٢٢٤).

(٣) الروم: ١-٣.

(٤) أخرجه البيهقي في الأسماء والصفات (٥٨٥/١).

(٥) أخرجه الدارمي (٣٣٥٥).

(٦) أخرجه أحمد في الزهد (١٩١).

(٧) أخرجه البيهقي في شعب الإيمان (٢١٤٩).

in *al-Jāmiʿ al-Ṣaghīr* and *al-Fatḥ* – that the Prophet ﷺ said, "Take blessings from the Qur'an, because it is the Speech of Allah Most High."[1]

Muhammad ibn Naṣr narrated in *Qiyām al-Layl* that Khabbāb ibn al-Aratt رضي الله عنه would address himself and say, "O you! Draw near to Allah Most High as much as you can, but you will never be able to draw near to Him with anything more beloved to Him than His Speech."

Abū Dharr رضي الله عنه narrated that the Messenger of Allah ﷺ said, "Indeed, you cannot return to Allah (i.e., you cannot draw near to Allah) with anything better than what has come (i.e., initiated) from Him (i.e., the Qur'an)."[2]

Ḥāfiẓ al-Mundhirī said, "Ḥākim narrated and authenticated it, and Abū Dāwūd narrated it in his *Marāsīl* from Jubayr ibn Nufayr."

THE MAGNIFICENCE OF ALLAH'S SPEAKING THE REVELATION AND THE AWE OF THE ANGELS عليهم السلام

Allah Most High said, "*Ḥā-Mīm. ʿAyn Sīn Qāf.* And so you [O Prophet] are sent Revelation, just like those before you, by Allah – the Almighty, All-Wise. To Him belongs whatever is in the Heavens and whatever is on the Earth. And He is the Most High, the Greatest. The Heavens nearly burst, one above the other, [in awe of Him]. And the Angels glorify the praises of their Lord, and seek forgiveness for those on Earth. Surely Allah alone is the All-Forgiving, Most Merciful."[3]

In these noble verses, Allah Most Glorified informed us of the magnificence of the Revelation coming from Him; that He Most Glorified is the Almighty and nothing is like Him; and that He is All-Wise in sending Revelation to His Messengers. His Revelation to His Messengers has taken care of people's best interests and their felicity in this life and the next.

Thereafter, He Most Glorified said, "To Him belongs whatever is in the

(1) Al-Muttaqī al-Hindī in *Kanz al- ʿUmmāl* (2364).

(2) *Ḥākim* (2039).

(3) *Al-Shūrā*, 1-5.

وروى الطبرانيُّ عن الحكَمِ بنِ عُميرٍ رَضِيَ اللهُ عَنْهُ أنَّ النبيَّ صلى الله عليه وآله وسلم قال: «تبرَّكْ بالقرآنِ، فهو كلامُ اللهِ تعالى»[1]. كما في (الجامع الصغير) و(الفتح).

وروى محمّدُ بنُ نصرٍ في (قيامِ اللّيلِ) عن خبّابِ بنِ الأَرَتِّ رَضِيَ اللهُ عَنْهُ أنّهُ كان يُخاطِبُ نفسَهُ فيقول: (يا هَنَتاهُ تقرَّبْ إلى اللهِ تعالى ما استطعتَ؛ فإنّكَ لن تقرَّبَ إلى اللهِ بشيءٍ أحبَّ إليه من كلامِه).

وعن أبي ذرٍّ رَضِيَ اللهُ عَنْهُ قال: قال رسولُ صلى الله عليه وآله وسلم: «إنّكم لا تَرجعونَ إلى اللهِ تعالى - أي: لا تتقرَّبونَ إلى اللهِ تعالى- بشيءٍ أفضلَ ممّا خرجَ منهُ»[2] أي: بدأَ منه، - يعني: القرآنَ -. قال الحافظُ المنذريُّ: رواهُ الحاكمُ وصحّحهُ، ورواهُ أبو داودَ في (مراسيلِهِ) عن جُبَيرِ بنِ نُفَيرٍ. اهـ.

عظمةُ الكلامِ الإلهيّ بالوحي وهيبةُ الملائكةِ عليهِمُ السّلام

قال اللهُ تعالى: {حم (١) عسق (٢) كَذَٰلِكَ يُوحِي إِلَيْكَ وَإِلَى الَّذِينَ مِن قَبْلِكَ اللَّهُ الْعَزِيزُ الْحَكِيمُ (٣) لَهُ مَا فِي السَّمَاوَاتِ وَمَا فِي الْأَرْضِ ۖ وَهُوَ الْعَلِيُّ الْعَظِيمُ (٤) تَكَادُ السَّمَاوَاتُ يَتَفَطَّرْنَ مِن فَوْقِهِنَّ ۚ وَالْمَلَائِكَةُ يُسَبِّحُونَ بِحَمْدِ رَبِّهِمْ وَيَسْتَغْفِرُونَ لِمَن فِي الْأَرْضِ ۗ أَلَا إِنَّ اللَّهَ هُوَ الْغَفُورُ الرَّحِيمُ}[3].

ففي هذه الآياتِ الكريمةِ يُخبِرُ سبحانَهُ عن عظمةِ صدورِ الوحيِ مِن لَدُنْهُ، وأنّهُ

---

(١) أخرجه المتقي الهندي في كنز العمال (٢٣٦٤).

(٢) أخرجه الحاكم (٢٠٣٩).

(٣) الشورى: ١-٥.

Heavens and whatever is on the Earth." In other words, He informed us that all of this belongs to Him as His property and kingdom. To Him Most Glorified belong the creation and the command; there is neither anyone besides Him who owns all of this, nor is there any king besides Him within the creation. He is the One Who administers and acts freely in His property with His wisdom. He is Most High, the Greatest, Who can neither be defeated nor can anything come anywhere near His strength or power. Rather, Allah's Will always prevails.

Then by saying "The Heavens nearly burst, one above the other", He Most Glorified informed us of how the lofty Heavens are affected and overawed by the impact of the divine Command coming from above. Despite their colossal size and vastness, they are on the verge of splitting out of fear and reverence – due to the magnificence and awe of Revelation.

He Most Glorified also informed us of the fear and awe of the Angels, due to the impact of the Revelation and divine Speech. He says, "No intercession will be of any benefit with Him, except by those granted permission by Him. [At last,] when the dread is relieved from their hearts, they ask [the Angels], 'What has your Lord [just] said?' The Angels reply, 'The truth! And He is the Most High, All-Great.'"(1)

The explanation of this noble verse and the great news it comprises about this great matter have come from the Truthful (*al-Ṣādiq*) and the Trustworthy (*al-Amīn*) ﷺ – the most noble amongst the progeny of ʿAdnān – whom Allah Most High taught the Qur'an as well as the explanation of the Qur'an. He Most Glorified said, "It is certainly upon Us to [make you] memorize and recite it. So once We have recited a Revelation [through Gabriel], follow its recitation [closely]. Then it is surely upon Us to make it clear [to you]."(2) In other words, it is Our responsibility to explain this Qur'an to you. Allah Most High did explain the Qur'an to him and said to him, "And We have sent down to you [O Prophet] the Reminder, so that

(1) *Saba'*, 23.

(2) *Al-Qiyāmah*, 17-19.

سبحانه هو العزيزُ الذي ليسَ كمثلِه شيءٌ، وأنّهُ الحكيمُ في وحيِهِ إلى رُسُلِهِ، فقد تكفَّلَ وحيُهُ إلى رُسُلِهِ بمصالحِ العبادِ، وسعادتِهم في الدّنيا والآخرةِ.

ثُمَّ يُخبرُ سبحانه بقولِه: {لَهُ مَا فِي السَّمَاوَاتِ وَمَا فِي الْأَرْضِ} أي: إنّ جميعَ ذلك له مِلكاً ومُلكاً، فهو سبحانه له الخَلقُ وله الأمرُ، فلا مالكَ لذلك غيرُه، ولا مَلِكَ في ذلك غيرُه، فهو المدبِّرُ والمتصرِّفُ في مِلكهِ بحكمتِه، وهو العليُّ العظيمُ الذي لا يُغالَبُ ولا يُقارَبُ في قوَّتِهِ وقدرتِه، بل هو الغالِبُ على أمرِه.

ثُمَّ يُخبِرُ سبحانه بقوله: {تَكَادُ السَّمَاوَاتُ يَتَفَطَّرْنَ مِن فَوْقِهِنَّ} يخبِرُ بذلك عن تأثُّرِ السّمواتِ العُلى، ورَهبتِها من سُلطانِ الأمرِ الإلهيّ النّازلِ مِن فوقِهنّ، حتّى إنّها مع عِظَمِ جرمِها، ومدى سَعَتِها تكادُ تنشقُّ خشيةً ورهبةً من عظمةِ الوحيِ وهيبتِه.

وقد أخبرَ سبحانه عن خشيةِ الملائكةِ وهيبتِها من سلطانِ الوحيِ والكلامِ الإلهيّ فقال: {وَلَا تَنفَعُ الشَّفَاعَةُ عِندَهُ إِلَّا لِمَنْ أَذِنَ لَهُ حَتَّىٰ إِذَا فُزِّعَ عَن قُلُوبِهِمْ قَالُوا مَاذَا قَالَ رَبُّكُمْ قَالُوا الْحَقَّ وَهُوَ الْعَلِيُّ الْكَبِيرُ}[1].

وجاء البيانُ عن هذه الآيةِ الكريمةِ، وما فيها من الخبرِ العظيمِ عن ذلك الأمرِ العظيمِ، جاء ذلك البيانُ عن الصّادقِ الأمينِ أشرفِ ولدِ عدنانَ، الذي علّمهُ اللهُ تعالى القرآنَ، وعلّمهُ البيانَ عن القرآنِ، حيثُ قال سبحانه: {إِنَّ عَلَيْنَا جَمْعَهُ وَقُرْآنَهُ (١٧) فَإِذَا قَرَأْنَاهُ فَاتَّبِعْ قُرْآنَهُ (١٨) ثُمَّ إِنَّ عَلَيْنَا بَيَانَهُ}[2] أي: علينا أنْ نبيّنَ لك هذا القرآنَ، وقد بيّنَ اللهُ تعالى له ذلك، وقال له: {وَأَنزَلْنَا إِلَيْكَ الذِّكْرَ لِتُبَيِّنَ لِلنَّاسِ مَا نُزِّلَ إِلَيْهِمْ}[3] الآية.

---

(١) سبأ: ٢٣.

(٢) القيامة: ١٧- ١٩.

(٣) النحل: ٤٤.

you may explain to people what has been revealed for them."[1]

In explanation of the saying of Allah Most High "When the dread is relieved from their hearts", the Prophet ﷺ – as reported by Bukhārī from Abū Hurayrah ؓ – said, "When Allah decrees a command in the Heavens, the Angels flap their wings in submission to what He said, like the [sound of] a chain on a boulder. When the dread is relieved from their hearts, they say, 'What did your Lord say?' They say regarding what He said, 'The truth. And He is the Most High, All-Great.' The eavesdropping jinn – one on top of the other – then hear it." Sufyān [one of the narrators] described it with his hand, turning it and spreading out his fingers. "They hear something and convey it to the one below them, then they convey it to those below them, until they convey it to the sorcerer or soothsayer.

At times, a meteor strikes the jinn before they can convey it, but sometimes they convey it before being struck, in which case they mix a hundred lies with it. It is said, 'He told us such-and-such on such-and-such day.' They are thus considered truthful due to this one thing which was heard from the Heavens."[2]

This is why Ibn Mas'ūd ؓ said, "When Allah Most High speaks the Revelation and the inhabitants of the Heavens hear His Speech, they tremble with awe until they are overcome with a condition similar to fainting."

It is established that the first to be informed of and to hear the command which Allah Most High reveals are the carriers of the Throne (*'Arsh*). They are overcome with humility and awe, and then those who follow them. This is proven by the hadith of Muslim in his *Ṣaḥīḥ* and Aḥmad in his *Musnad* - and the wording here is that of Aḥmad - from Ibn 'Abbās ؓ that the Messenger of Allah ﷺ was sitting with a group of his Companions. 'Abd al-Razzāq's narration states they were from the Helpers (*Anṣār*). A shooting star appeared and lit up, so he ﷺ said, "What did you say when

(1) *Al-Naḥl*, 44.

(2) *Bukhārī* (4800); *Tirmidhī* (3223); *Ibn Mājah* (194).

فقال ﷺ في بيانِ معاني قولِه تعالى: {حَتَّىٰٓ إِذَا فُزِّعَ عَن قُلُوبِهِمۡ} الآيةَ، كما رواهُ البخاريُّ عندَ تفسيرِ هذه الآيةِ عن أبي هريرةَ رَضِيَ اللَّهُ عَنْهُ قال: إنَّ نبيَّ اللهِ ﷺ قال: «إذا قضى اللهُ الأمرَ في السّماءِ ضَرَبَتِ الملائكةُ بأجنحتِها خُضْعاناً لقولِه، كأنّهُ سِلْسِلَةٌ على صَفوانٍ، فإذا فُزِّعَ - أي: زال الفزعُ - عن قلوبِهم، قالوا: ماذا قال ربُّكم؟ قالوا للذي قال: الحقُّ، وهو العليُّ الكبيرُ، فيسمَعُها مُسْتَرِقُ السَّمْعِ، ومُسترِقُ السّمعِ، هكذا بعضُه فوقَ بعضٍ»، -ووصفَ سفيانُ بيدِهِ فحرَّفها -أي: أمالَها -، وبدَّدَ - أي: فرّقَ بين أصابِعه - «فيسمَعُ الكلمةَ فيُلْقيها إلى مَن تحتَهُ، ثمّ يُلقيها الآخَرُ إلى مَن تحتَه، حتى يُلقيَها على يدِ السّاحرِ أو الكاهنِ».

قال: «فربّما أدركَهُ الشّهابُ قبل أنْ يُلقيَها - أي: الكلمةَ التي سَمِعَها -، وربّما ألقاها قبلَ أنْ يُدرِكَهُ، فيكذبُ معها مائةَ كذبةٍ، فيُقال: قد قال لنا يومَ كذا وكذا: كذا وكذا، فيصدَّقَ بتلك الكلمةِ التي سُمِعَتْ من السّماء»[1].

ومِن هنا قال ابنُ مسعودٍ رَضِيَ اللَّهُ عَنْهُ: (إذا تكلَّمَ اللهُ تعالى بالوحي، وسمعَ أهلُ السّمواتِ كلامَهُ سبحانَه أُرعِدوا مِن الهيبةِ، حتى يلحقَهم مثلُ الغشيِّ).

ومِنَ المعلومِ أنَّ أوّلَ مَن يبلُغُه الأمرُ الذي يوحيه اللهُ تعالى، وأوّلَ مَنْ يسمعُ ذلك هم حَمَلةُ العرشِ، فتأخذُهُمُ الخَشْعَةُ والرَّهبَةُ، ثمّ الذين يَلونَهم، كما دلَّ عليه حديثُ مسلمٍ في (صحيحِه)، وأحمدَ في (مسندِه) واللّفظُ له، عنِ ابنِ عبّاسٍ رضي اللهُ عنهما قال: كان رسولُ الله ﷺ جالساً في نفرٍ من أصحابِهِ - قال عبدُ الرّزّاقِ: مِنَ الأنصارِ - فرُمِيَ بنجمٍ فاستنارَ، فقال ﷺ: «ما كنتُم تقولونَ إذا كان مثلُ هذا في الجاهليةِ»؟، قالوا: كنّا نقول: يولَدُ عظيمٌ أو يموتُ عظيمٌ، قلتُ للزُّهريّ: أكانَ يُرمَى بها في الجاهليّة؟ قال:

(١) أخرجه البخاري (٤٨٠٠)، والترمذي (٣٢٢٣)، وابن ماجه (١٩٤).

something like this happened in the [pre-Islamic] era of ignorance?" They said, "We used to say that a great person will be born or a great person will die." I asked Zuhrī, "Were there shooting stars in the era of ignorance also?" He said, "Yes, but they became more frequent when the Prophet ﷺ was sent."

Ibn ʿAbbās said that the Messenger of Allah ﷺ said, "They do not appear on the death or life of anyone. Rather, when our Lord Most Blessed and Most High decrees a matter, the bearers of the Throne glorify Him, then the people of the Heavens below them glorify Him - until the glorification reaches this lowest Heaven. The people of the Heavens below the bearers of the Throne ask them, 'What did your Lord say?' So, they tell them, and the people of every Heaven inform the Heaven below, until the news reaches this Heaven. The jinn eavesdrop and they are struck with shooting stars. Whatever they bring in its original form is true, but they cast things into it and add more."(1)

It is thus evident from the above that when the Lord of Glory speaks the Revelation, and the Angels hear it, fear seizes them and they are overcome with unconsciousness, until this condition clears from them. It is also reported that when they hear it, they are left stunned and fall into prostration before Allah Most High.

Ṭabarānī and Ibn Mardawayh narrated - and the wording is Ibn Mardawayh's - from Nawwās ibn Samʿān that the Messenger of Allah ﷺ said, "When Allah wants to reveal His command, He speaks the Revelation. When He speaks, the Heavens tremble intensely out of fear of Allah Most High. When the people of the Heavens hear it, they faint and fall prostrate to Allah. The first to raise their head is Jibrīl. Allah then speaks to him of His Revelation what He wishes, and then Jibrīl passes it on to the Angels. Every time he passes by one of the Heavens, the Angels there ask him, 'What did our Lord say, O Jibrīl?' He says, 'The truth, and He is the Most High, the Great.' They then say as Jibrīl said, and Jibrīl then

(1) *Muslim* (2229); *Tirmidhī* (3224); *Aḥmad* (1882).

نعم، ولكنْ غُلِّظَتْ - أي: أُكثِرَتْ - حين بُعِثَ النّبيُّ صلى الله عليه وآله وسلَّمَ.

قال ابنُ عبّاسٍ رَضِيَ اللَّهُ عَنْهُمَا: قال رسول الله صلى الله عليه وآله وسلَّمَ: «فإنّها لا يُرمَى بها لموتِ أحدٍ ولا لحياتِه؛ ولكنَّ ربَّنا تَبَارَكَ وَتَعَالَى إذا قضى أمراً سبَّحَ حَمَلَةُ العرشِ، ثمَّ سبَّحَ أهلُ السّماءِ الذينَ يلونَهم، حتّى يَبلُغَ التّسبيحُ هذه السَّماءَ الدُّنيا، ثمّ يستخبِرُ أهلُ السّماءِ الذين يَلُونَ حَمَلَةَ العرشِ، فيقول الذين يَلُونَ حملةَ العرشِ لحملةِ العرشِ: ماذا قال ربُّكم؟ فيُخبِرونَهم، ويُخبِرُ أهلُ كلِّ سماءٍ سماءً حتى ينتهيَ الخبرُ إلى هذه السّماءِ، فتخطَفُ الجِنُّ السَّمعَ، فيُرمَونَ - أي: بالشُّهبِ - فما جاؤوا به على وجهِهِ فهو حقٌّ؛ ولكنّهم يَقذِفونَ فيه ويزيدون»[1]. فتبيَّنَ ممّا سبقَ أنَّ ربَّ العزّةِ إذا تكلَّمَ بالوحيِ، وسَمِعَتِ الملائكةُ ذلك أخذَتْهُمُ الخَشيةُ، واعترَتْهُمُ الغَشيةُ، حتّى ينجليَ عنهم ذلك.

وورد أيضاً أنّهم إذا سَمِعوا ذلك صُعِقوا وخَرّوا للهِ تعالى سُجّداً.

فقد روى الطبرانيُّ وابنُ مَرْدَوَيْه - واللّفظُ له - عن النّواسِ بنِ سمعانَ رضي اللهُ عنه قال: قال رسولُ الله صلى الله عليه وآلِه وسلم: «إذا أرادَ اللهُ أنْ يوحيَ بأمرِهِ تكلَّمَ بالوحيِ، فإذا تكلَّمَ أخذتِ السّمواتُ منهُ رجفةً - أو قال: رِعدةً - شديدةً من خوفِ اللهِ تعالى، فإذا سمعَ بذلك أهلُ السّمواتِ صُعِقوا وخَرّوا لله سُجَّداً، فيكونُ أوّلَ مَن يرفعُ رأسَهُ جبريلُ عَلَيْهِ السَّلَامُ، فيُكلِّمُهُ اللهُ من وحيِهِ ممّا أراد، فيمضي به جبريلُ على الملائكةِ كلَّما مَرَّ بسماءٍ سألهُ ملائكتُها: ماذا قال ربُّنا يا جبريلُ؟ فيقول: قال الحقَّ، وهو العليُّ الكبيرُ، فيقولون مثلَ ما قال جبريلُ، فينتهي جبريلُ بالوحي حيثُ أمرَهُ اللهُ تعالى من السّماءِ والأرضِ»[2]. قال الحافظُ في (الفتحِ): وقد روى ابنُ مَرْدَوَيْه مِن حديثِ ابنِ مسعودٍ

(١) أخرجه مسلم (٢٢٢٩)، والترمذي (٣٢٢٤)، وأحمد (١٨٨٢).

(٢) أخرجه الطبري في (تفسيره) (٣٩٧/٢٠)، وابن خزيمة في (التوحيد) (٣٤٨/١)، وابن نصر

takes this Revelation wherever in the Heavens or the Earth Allah Most High commanded him."[1]

Ḥāfiẓ [Ibn Ḥajar] said in *al-Fatḥ* that Ibn Mardawayh narrated from the hadith of Ibn Mas'ūd, as a hadith attributed to the Prophet ﷺ, "When Allah Most High speaks the Revelation, the people of the Heavens hear a clanging like the clanging of a chain on a rock, and they become frightened and think it to be the final Hour." He then recited, 'When the dread is relieved from their hearts.'[2]"[3]

ALLAH MOST HIGH PRESERVING THE NOBLE QUR'AN

It is incumbent upon every intelligent person to believe that Allah Most High preserved this Noble Qur'an in many different ways – this is proven through decisive evidences.

He preserved its locus and the tablet wherein it is written in the Higher Assembly (*al-Mala' al-A'lā*). He preserved the route of its Revelation to His noble Messenger, our master Muhammad ﷺ. He preserved its texts, words and letters from additions, deletions, and changes. He preserved its meanings from distortions. He also prepared people who will preserve its letters from additions and deletions, preserves its meanings from distortions and changes, and He Most Glorified guaranteed that these people will continue and remain until the Day of Requital.

Hereunder are the details for all of the above.

(1) Ṭabarī in his commentary, vol. 20, p. 397; Ibn Khuzaymah in al-Tawḥīd, vol. 1, p. 348; Ibn Naṣr al-Marwazī in *Ta'ẓīm Qadr al-Ṣalāh* (216), and Ṭabarānī, as stated in *Majma' al-Zawā'id* of al-Haythamī, vol. 7, p. 97.

(2) *Saba'*, 23.

(3) It states in *al-Fatḥ* (vol. 8, p. 413) that this hadith is narrated primarily in Abū Dāwūd (4725) and Bukhārī has brought it without a chain.

رفَعَه: «إذا تكلَّمَ اللهُ تعالى بالوحي سمِعَ أهلُ السَّمواتِ صَلصلةً كصلصلةِ السِّلسلةِ على الصَّفوانِ، فيفزَعونَ ويَرونَ أنَّه من أمرِ السَّاعةِ، وقرأ {حَتَّىٰ إِذَا فُزِّعَ عَن قُلُوبِهِمْ} الآية»(2).

حفظُ اللهِ تعالى لهذا القرآنِ الكريمِ

إنَّ من الواجبِ على العاقلِ أن يعتقدَ أنَّ اللهَ تعالى حفِظَ هذا القرآنَ الكريمَ بأنواعٍ من الحفظِ، وقد ثَبَتَ ذلك بالأدلَّةِ القطعيَّةِ. فقد حَفِظَ محلَّهُ ولوحَ كتابتِه في الملأِ الأعلى، وحَفِظَ طريقَ نزولِه ووحيِه إلى رسولِه الأكرمِ سيِّدِنا محمَّدٍ صلى الله عليه وآله وسلم، وحَفِظَ نصوصَه وكلماتِه وحروفَه من الزِّيادةِ والنُّقصانِ والتَّبديلِ، وحَفِظَ معانيَه من التَّحريفِ، وأقامَ له مَن يَحفَظُ حروفَهُ من الزِّيادةِ والنُّقصانِ، ويَحفظُ معانيَه من التَّحريفِ والتَّغييرِ، وتكفَّلَ سبحانه باستمرارِهم وبقائِهم إلى يومِ الدِّينِ. وإليكَ تفاصيلُ ذلك كلِّه.

---

(1) المروزي في (تعظيم قدر الصلاة) (216)، والطبراني كما في (مجمع الزوائد) للهيثمي (7/97). سبأ: 23.

(2) قال في الفتح (8/413): وأصله عند أبي داود (4725) وغيره، وعلقه المصنف - البخاري - موقوفا، ويأتي في كتاب التوحيد. قال الخطابي: الصلصلة: صوت الحديد إذا تحرك وتداخل.

ALLAH MOST HIGH PRESERVING THE TABLET WHEREIN IT IS WRITTEN AND ENCLOSED

Allah Most High said, "In fact, this is a glorious Qur'an, recorded in a Preserved Tablet."[1]

Allah Most High described the locus of this Noble Qur'an and the Tablet wherein it is written - which is in the Higher Assembly - as being protected from the reach of the devils or their tampering. This indicates that the contents of this Tablet are protected all the more certainly - the outer shell is preserved for the sake of the pearl it contains, and so the Tablet is preserved all the more certainly for the sake of protecting what is written on the Tablet.

This noble verse is sufficient proof that Allah Most High protected the routes through which the Qur'an would come down to the Messenger of Allah ﷺ and that Allah Most High protected its words and letters. It is unthinkable of the wisdom of Allah - the All-Knowing, All-Wise, Who preserved the Tablet of this Noble Qur'an, and preserved it in the Higher Assembly - that He would step back from preserving the route through which it come down and after it had come down to this world. It is unthinkable that He would make it prone to loss, tampering, additions,

(1) *Al-Burūj*, 21-22.

حِفظُ اللهِ تعالى لوحَ كتابتِهِ وصَدفَ جوهرِهِ

قال اللهُ تعالى: {بَلْ هُوَ قُرْآنٌ مَّجِيدٌ (٢١) فِي لَوْحٍ مَّحْفُوظٍ}[1].

فلقد وصف اللهُ تعالى محَلَّ هذا القرآنِ الكريمِ، ولوحَ كتابتِه الذي هو في الملأِ الأعلى، وصفَ ذلك بأنّهُ محفوظٌ من أنْ تَصِلَ إليه الشّياطينُ، أو تتلاعبَ فيه، وفي هذا إشارةٌ إلى أنَّ ما فيه فهو محفوظٌ من بابٍ أَولى وأَحقّ؛ فإنَّ حِفْظَ صَدفةِ الجواهرِ يُرادُ منه حِفظُ ما في الصَّدَفةِ من الجواهرِ، وإنَّ حِفظَ اللّوحِ يُرادُ منه من بابٍ أَولى حِفظُ ما لاحَ وكُتِبَ في اللّوحِ.

ويكفيكَ دليلاً بهذه الآيةِ الكريمةِ على حفظِ اللهِ تعالى لهذا القرآنِ في طُرُقِ تنزُّلاتِهِ بالوحي إلى رسولِ اللهِ ﷺ، وعلى حِفظِ اللهِ تعالى لنُصوصِ كلماتِه وحروفِه؛ فإنَّ اللهَ تعالى الحكيمَ العليمَ الذي حَفِظَ لوحَ هذا القرآنِ الكريمِ، وحَفِظَ هذا القرآنَ الكريمَ في الملأِ الأعلى، حاشاهُ بمقتضى حِكمتِه أنْ يتخلّى عن حِفظِهِ له في طريقِ نزولِه، وبعد نزولِه إلى هذا العالَمِ، ويُعرِّضَهُ للضّياعِ والتّلاعبِ فيه، والزّيادةِ والنُّقصانِ،

(١) البروج: ٢١- ٢٢.

deletions, distortions, or changes. Hence, He Most Glorified guaranteeing the preservation of its Tablet and the preservation of its words in the Higher Assembly proves that He has guaranteed to protect it also in the Lower Assembly.

This is why Allah Most High proclaimed that He will preserve the Qur'an specifically, not the other divine Books. This constant everlasting guarantee is where He Most Glorified said, "It is certainly We Who have revealed the Reminder, and it is certainly We Who will preserve it."(1) In bringing the word *lahū* before its associate (*muta ʿalliq*) there is proof that preservation is restricted specifically to the Qur'an and not the other divine Books – as we shall explain later on, if Allah wishes.

He Most High said, "And indeed, it is – in the Master Record with Us – highly esteemed, rich in wisdom."(2) He Most Glorified informed us here regarding the magnificent status of this Noble Qur'an in the Higher Assembly, and that it is on a standing of majesty, magnificence, and grandeur – "with Us" as He Most Glorified informed.

ALLAH MOST HIGH PRESERVING HIS MIGHTY BOOK AND SAFEGUARDING IT AGAINST TAMPERING

Allah Most High revealed this Noble Qur'an upon our master, the Prophet Muhammad ﷺ – the Truthful and Trustworthy – through the medium of the Trustworthy Spirit, Jibrīl ﷺ. He Most Glorified preserved the route through which it came down from the tampering and interference of the devils. Thus, He filled the Heavens with a heavy guard of noble Angels – strong and mighty – and with many large burning meteors. Allah Most High informs of this in *Sūrah al-Jinn* where He Most Glorified, relating the statement of the jinn, said, "[Earlier] we tried to reach heaven [for news], only to find it filled with stern guards and shooting stars. We used to take

(1) *Al-Ḥijr*, 9.

(2) *Al-Zukhruf*, 4.

والتَّحريفِ والتبديلِ، فكَفالَتُهُ سبحانه بحفظِ لوحِهِ، وحِفظِ كلماتِه ثَمَّةَ في الملأِ الأعلى دليلٌ على كفالتِهِ بحفظِهِ له أيضاً في الملأِ الأدنى. ولذلك أعلنَ اللهُ تعالى كفالتَهُ بحفظِ هذا القرآنِ الخاصّةَ به دونَ سائرِ الكتبِ الإلهيّة، تلك الكفالةُ الدّائمةُ الباقيةُ حيثُ قال سبحانه: {إِنَّا نَحْنُ نَزَّلْنَا الذِّكْرَ وَإِنَّا لَهُ لَحَافِظُونَ}[1]، وفي تقديمِ كلمةِ {له} على متعلَّقِها دليلُ التخصيصِ بالحِفظِ لهذا القرآنِ دونَ ما سِواهُ من الكتبِ الإلهيّة، كما سنوضِّحُ ذلك فيما يأتي إن شاء اللهُ تعالى. وقال تعالى: {وَإِنَّهُ فِي أُمِّ الْكِتَابِ لَدَيْنَا لَعَلِيٌّ حَكِيمٌ}[2] فقد أخبرَ سبحانه عن عظيمِ شأنِ هذا القرآنِ الكريمِ في الملأِ الأعلى، وأنّهُ في مقامِ الإجلالِ والإعظامِ والإكبارِ، مقامِ {لدينا} كما أخبرَ سبحانه.

حفظُ اللهِ تعالى كتابَه العزيزَ وصيانتُه من التّلاعُبِ فيه

إنَّ اللهَ تعالى أنزل هذا القرآنَ الكريمَ على سيّدِنا محمّدٍ ﷺ الصادقِ الأمينِ، بواسطةِ الرُّوحِ الأمينِ جبريلَ عليه السّلام، وقد حَفِظَ سبحانه طريقَ نزولِه من تلاعُبِ الشّياطينِ ومشاغبَتِهم، فمَلأَ السّماءَ حَرَساً شديداً من الملائكةِ الكرامِ، الأقوياءِ العِظامِ، وشُهُباً كبيرةً كثيرةً مُحرِقةً، كما أخبر اللهُ تعالى عن ذلك في سورةِ الجِنّ حيثُ قال سبحانه مُخبِراً عن الجِنّ: {وَأَنَّا لَمَسْنَا السَّمَاءَ فَوَجَدْنَاهَا مُلِئَتْ حَرَسًا شَدِيدًا وَشُهُبًا (٨) وَأَنَّا كُنَّا نَقْعُدُ مِنْهَا مَقَاعِدَ لِلسَّمْعِ}[3] أي: كان ذلك قبلَ بعثةِ النّبيّ ﷺ، وبَدءِ نزولِ القرآنِ عليه

---

(١) الحجر: ٩.

(٢) الزخرف: ٤.

(٣) الجن: ٨- ٩.

up positions there for eavesdropping."[1] This was before the Prophet ﷺ was sent and the Revelation of the Qur'an began. "But whoever dares eavesdrop now (i.e., after he ﷺ has been sent) will find a flare lying in wait for them."[2]

Thus, the great Qur'an was revealed from the Lord of Honour upon the heart of the Prophet ﷺ, whilst being fully protected and preserved. Moreover, the Angel with whom it was sent is the trustworthy Spirit, along with a large convoy of Angels to surround it and guard it. Furthermore, the one to whom it was revealed is the Truthful and Trustworthy, the Imam of all the Prophets and Messengers – may Allah send blessings and peace on him and all of them. The route of its Revelation is also protected and fortified. He Most High said, "The trustworthy Spirit brought it down into your heart [O Prophet] – so that you may be one of the warners – in a clear Arabic tongue. And it has indeed been [foretold] in the Scriptures of those before."[3] In other words, this Qur'an has been discussed and informed of in all previous Books.

Allah Most High refuted the claim of those who said this Qur'an is sorcery or soothsaying. He established that it is His Speech which He sent down upon His true Messenger Muhammad ﷺ through the medium of the trustworthy Spirit. He Most High said, "It was not the devils who brought this [Qur'an] down; it is not for them [to do so], nor are they able to [do this], for they are strictly barred from [even] overhearing [it]."[4] This verse conclusively and decisively refutes the opponents, leaving no scope for any interpretation.

The meaning is: This Noble Qur'an was brought down by the trustworthy Spirit, accompanied by a group of honourable Angels. "It was not the devils who brought this [Qur'an] down." In other words, it is neither the business

---

(1) *Al-Jinn*, 8-9.

(2) *Al-Jinn*, 9.

(3) *Al-Shu'arā'*, 193-196.

(4) *Al-Shu'arā'*, 210-212.

{فَمَن يَسْتَمِعِ الْآنَ} أي: بعدما بُعِثَ {يَجِدْ لَهُ شِهَابًا رَّصَدًا}.

فنزل القرآنُ العظيمُ من حضرةِ ربِّ العزَّةِ على قلبِ النّبيِّ مَصوناً محفوظاً، وإنَّ الذي نزلَ به هو الرُّوحُ الأمينُ في جمعٍ حافلٍ من الملائكةِ يحفُّونَهُ ويَحرِسونَهُ، والمُنَزَّلُ عليه هو الصّادقُ الأمينُ إمامُ الأنبياءِ والمرسلينَ، صلى اللهُ عليه وعليهم أجمعينَ، وطريقُ نزولِه مَصونٌ وحصينٌ. قال تعالى: {نَزَلَ بِهِ الرُّوحُ الْأَمِينُ (١٩٣) عَلَىٰ قَلْبِكَ لِتَكُونَ مِنَ الْمُنذِرِينَ (١٩٤) بِلِسَانٍ عَرَبِيٍّ مُّبِينٍ (١٩٥) وَإِنَّهُ لَفِي زُبُرِ الْأَوَّلِينَ}[1] يعني: إنَّ هذا القرآنَ مُحدَّثٌ عنه، ومُخبَرٌ به في الكتبِ السّابقةِ كلِّها.

وقد أبطلَ اللهُ تعالى دعوى مَنِ ادَّعى أنَّ هذا القرآنَ هو مِن بابِ السِّحريّاتِ أو الكَهاناتِ، وأثبتَ أنَّهُ كلامُهُ أنزلَهُ على رسولِه الحقِّ محمدٍ ﷺ بواسطةِ الرّوحِ الأمينِ؛ قال تعالى: {وَمَا تَنَزَّلَتْ بِهِ الشَّيَاطِينُ (٢١٠) وَمَا يَنبَغِي لَهُمْ وَمَا يَسْتَطِيعُونَ (٢١١) إِنَّهُمْ عَنِ السَّمْعِ لَمَعْزُولُونَ}[2] وفي هذه الآيةِ ردودٌ قاطعةٌ مُفحِمَةٌ للخصمِ لا تحتمِلُ التأويلَ. والمعنى: أنَّ هذا القرآنَ الكريمَ نزل به الرُّوحُ الأمينُ، ومعه طائفةٌ من ملائكةِ اللهِ المُكرَمين {وَمَا تَنَزَّلَتْ بِهِ الشَّيَاطِينُ، وَمَا يَنبَغِي لَهُمْ} يعني: أنّهُ ليس مِن شأنِ الشّياطينِ أنْ تَنزِلَ بهذا القرآنِ الكريمِ، ولا مِن سَجيَّتِهِم؛ لأنهم شاطِنون - أي: بعيدون - عن كلِّ خيرٍ وبرٍّ، وعن كلِّ كمالٍ وفضيلةٍ، بل إنَّ شأنَهم وشاكِلَتَهم كلُّ فسادٍ وشرٍّ، وقبيحةٍ ورذيلةٍ، هذا طَبْعُهم، وهذا وَضْعُهم، وهذا وَصْفُهم.

فكيف يُتَصوَّرُ لدى العقولِ أنْ تنزلَ الشّياطينُ التي من شأنِها وطبعِها السّوءُ والشّرُّ والأذى والضرُّ؟ كيف تنزلُ بهذا القرآنِ الكريمِ، الجامعِ لكلِّ خيرٍ وبرٍّ، وكلِّ كمالٍ

---

(١) الشعراء: ١٩٣-١٩٦.

(٢) الشعراء: ٢١٠-٢١٢.

of the devils to bring down this Noble Qur'an nor their nature, because they are far removed (*shāṭin*) from all goodness, righteousness, perfection, and virtue. Rather, their nature and way is all forms of corruption, evil, obnoxiousness, and lowliness. This is their nature, this is their condition, and this is their character.

How is it then conceivable that the devils - whose very nature is disposed to evil and harm - bring down this Noble Qur'an, the Book which encompasses all goodness, righteousness, perfection, beauty, excellence, grace, excellent manners, and lofty characteristics? These two neither come together nor are they compatible with one another. Rather, they are diametrically opposed. The only thing suited to the Noble Qur'an is that the trustworthy Spirit bring it down in the midst of a group of honourable Angels. Furthermore, how is it conceivable that the devils bring this Qur'an down when "they are strictly barred from [even] overhearing [it]"? In other words, they are repelled and barred from hearing it from the Heavens - even through eavesdropping. The guard of the Angels and the burning meteors lie in wait for them, so how can they possibly grasp it completely and bring it down in its entirety? And how is it conceivable that the devils bring it down when they are incapable of bearing it and conveying it? They have no power or strength to do this. "Nor are they able to do this." Bearing it and acquiring it, followed by revealing it and conveying it, require a great amount of strength from Allah Most High and support through His mercy. This is because the Qur'an comprises lofty and sacred points of knowledge, and sublime knowledge and fine points of wisdom. If even a portion of these noble verses were to be revealed upon the peak of towering mountains, they would split and crumble. He Most High said, "Had We sent down this Qur'an upon a mountain, you would have certainly seen it humbled and torn apart in awe of Allah. We set forth such comparisons for people, [so] perhaps they may reflect."(1) He Most High said, "We will soon send upon you a weighty Revelation."(2)

(1) *Al-Ḥashr*, 21.

(2) *Al-Muzzammil*, 5.

وجمالٍ، وإحسانٍ وإفضالٍ، وآدابٍ فاضلةٍ، وأخلاقٍ عاليةٍ؛ فإنَّ ذَينك لا يلتقيانِ ولا يتناسبانِ ولا يجتمعان، بل هما ضِدّانِ ونقيضانِ؛ وإنّما المناسِبُ لهذا القرآنِ الكريمِ أنْ ينزلَ به الرُّوحُ الأمينُ في حفلٍ من الملائكةِ المُكْرَمين.

ثمّ كيف يُتصوَّرُ لدى العقولِ أنْ تنزلَ الشّياطينُ بهذا القرآنِ الكريمِ في حينِ {إِنَّهُمْ عَنِ السَّمْعِ لَمَعْزُولُونَ}؟ أي: مطرودونَ، وممنوعونَ عنِ الاستماعِ إليه من السّمواتِ ولو بالاستراقِ، فإنَّ حَرَسَ الملائكةِ، وشُهُبَ النّيرانِ تترصَّدُهم، فأنّى لهم أن يتلقّوهُ تامّاً ويتنزّلوا به كاملاً؟

ثمّ إنه كيف يُتصوَّرُ لدى العقولِ أنْ تنزلَ به الشّياطينُ في حينِ أنّهم عاجزون عن تحمُّلِهِ وتأْدِيَتِه، فإنّهم لا قوّةَ ولا طاقةَ لهم بذلك {وَمَا يَسْتَطِيعُونَ}؛ فإنَّ تحمُّلَ ذلك وتَلَقّيهِ, ثُمَّ إلقاءَهُ وتأديتَهُ يحتاج ذلك إلى قوّةٍ قويّةٍ مِن عند اللهِ تعالى، وتأييدٍ بروحٍ من اللهِ تعالى؛ لأنَّ فيه المعارفَ العلويّةَ، والمعارفَ القدسيّةَ، والعلومَ السَّنيّةَ، والحِكَمَ السّاميةَ، بحيثُ إنَّ طائفةً من تلكَ الآياتِ الكريمةِ لو أُنزِلَتْ على صُمّ الجبالِ الشّامخاتِ لتشقّقتْ وتصدَّعَتْ. قال تعالى: {لَوْ أَنزَلْنَا هَٰذَا الْقُرْآنَ عَلَىٰ جَبَلٍ لَّرَأَيْتَهُ خَاشِعًا مُّتَصَدِّعًا مِّنْ خَشْيَةِ اللَّهِ ۚ وَتِلْكَ الْأَمْثَالُ نَضْرِبُهَا لِلنَّاسِ لَعَلَّهُمْ يَتَفَكَّرُونَ}[1]، وقال تعالى: {إِنَّا سَنُلْقِي عَلَيْكَ قَوْلًا ثَقِيلًا}[2].

وروى الإمامُ أحمدُ والحاكمُ وغيرُهما عن السّيدةِ عائشةَ رَضِيَ اللهُ عَنْهَا: (أنَّ النبيَّ صَلَّى اللهُ عَلَيْهِ وَسَلَّمَ كان إذا أُوحيَ إليه وهو على ناقتِه وَضَعَتْ جِرانها - هو باطنُ العُنُقِ - فما تستطيعُ أن

(١) الحشر: ٢١.

(٢) المزمل: ٥.

Imam Aḥmad, Ḥākim, and others narrated on the authority of Sayyidah ʿĀ'ishah ﷺ that when the Prophet ﷺ would be receiving Revelation whilst on his camel, the camel would put its neck down and not be able to move until the Revelation stopped. She then recited, "We will soon send upon you a weighty Revelation."(1) In the two *Ṣaḥīḥ* collections, ʿĀ'ishah ﷺ narrated, "I saw Revelation coming down on him on a bitterly cold day. The Revelation would come to an end but his forehead would be dripping with perspiration."(2) Zayd ibn Thābit ﷺ said, "Revelation came down upon the Messenger ﷺ whilst his thigh was upon my thigh, and my thigh was about to break."(3)

Nobody had the strength for the Revelation, and to acquire and bear it, except for the greatest Messenger and the most honoured Beloved (*Ḥabīb*) ﷺ, whom Allah had helped, prepared, strengthened, and gifted.

Furthermore, Allah Most High refuted these false claims and erroneous fabrications in another way: He explained the compatibility of the devils with those upon whom they descend. He Most High said, "Shall I inform you of whom the devils [actually] descend upon? They descend upon every sinful liar, who gives an [attentive] ear [to half-truths], mostly passing on sheer lies."(4) This style of refutation dumbfounds the liars, decisively refutes those who reject and deny, and makes them swallow the bitter pill of abandonment. It contains glaring evidences and decisive proofs regarding our master Muhammad ﷺ, namely that he is the Messenger of Allah upon whom the Angels of Allah descend. There cannot be any second opinion in this regard.

The first aspect of the refutation explains the nobility, holiness, and trustworthiness of the one bringing this Noble Qur'an; it is undisputedly Jibrīl the Trustworthy and it is impossible for the devils to interfere in this.

---

(1) *Ḥākim* (3865).

(2) *Bukhārī* (2); *Muslim* (2333); *Tirmidhī* (3634).

(3) *Bukhārī* (4592).

(4) *Al-Shuʿarā'*, 221-223.

تتحرَّكَ حتى يُسرَّى عنه). وتلَتْ رضي اللهُ عنها: {إِنَّا سَنُلْقِي عَلَيْكَ قَوْلًا ثَقِيلًا} [1] [2].

وفي (الصّحيحينِ) عن عائشةَ رضي الله عنها قالت: (ولقد رأيتُهُ صلى الله عليه وآله وسلم ينزلُ عليه الوحيُ في اليومِ الشّديدِ البردِ فيُفصَمُ عنه، وإنَّ جبينَهُ ليَتفصَّدُ عرَقاً) [3].

وقال زيدُ بنُ ثابتٍ رضي الله عنه: (أُنزِلَ على رسولِ الله صلى الله عليه وآله وسلم - أي: القرآنُ - وفَخِذُهُ على فَخِذي، فكادتْ ترُضُّ فَخِذي) [4] الحديثَ كما في البخاريِّ وغيرِه.

فلا يقوى لنزولِ القرآنِ وتَلقّيه وتحمُّلِه إلّا هذا الرّسولُ الأعظمُ، والحبيبُ الأكرمُ صلى الله عليه وآله وسلم الذي أمدَّهُ اللهُ تعالى، وأعدَّهُ، وقوّاهُ، وأعطاه.

ثمَّ إنَّ اللهَ تعالى ردَّ تلك الدّعاويَ الباطلةَ، والافتراءاتِ الضالّةَ بوجهٍ آخرَ بيَّنَ فيه وجوهَ المناسبةِ بيْنَ الشّياطينِ، وبيَّنَ مَن تتنزَّلُ عليه، فقال تعالى: {هَلْ أُنَبِّئُكُمْ عَلَىٰ مَن تَنَزَّلُ الشَّيَاطِينُ (٢٢١) تَنَزَّلُ عَلَىٰ كُلِّ أَفَّاكٍ أَثِيمٍ (٢٢٢) يُلْقُونَ السَّمْعَ وَأَكْثَرُهُمْ كَاذِبُونَ} [5]. وفي هذا اللّونِ مِنَ الرّدِّ: إفحامٌ للمفترين، وخصمٌ قاطعٌ للجاحدينَ المنكرينَ، وإلقامُهم حَجَرَ الخُذلانِ، وفيه الحُجَجُ السّاطعةُ، والبَيّناتُ القاطعةُ على قضيّةِ سيّدِنا محمّدٍ صلى الله عليه وآله وسلم، وهي أنّهُ رسولُ اللهِ صلى الله عليه وآله وسلم، تنزَّلُ عليه ملائكةُ اللهِ تعالى لا يحتمِلُ أمرُهُ غيرُ ذلك.

ففي الوجهِ الأوّلِ من الرّدِّ: بيانُ شرفِ النّازلِ بهذا القرآنِ الكريمِ، وقداستِه، وأمانتِه، وأنّهُ جبريلُ الأمينُ قطعاً، وأنَّ مِنَ المستحيلِ أنْ تتدخَّلَ الشّياطينُ في ذلك.

---

(١) المزمل: ٥.

(٢) أخرجه الحاكم (٣٨٦٥).

(٣) أخرجه البخاري (٢)، ومسلم (٢٣٣٣)، والترمذي (٣٦٣٤).

(٤) أخرجه البخاري (٤٥٩٢).

(٥) الشعراء: ٢٢١- ٢٢٣.

The second aspect of the refutation explains the nobility, purity, cleanliness, inerrancy, and trustworthiness of the one upon whom it is revealed. It explains the impossibility of the devils gathering around him, affecting him, or coming down upon him, because there is absolutely no compatibility here. It is an established fact that compatibility is the foundation for things to come together and harmonize.

The explanation of this is that the devils have evil souls, and are corrupt and evil by nature. There is no compatibility between them and the nature of Muhammad ﷺ – this pleasant, pure, pristine, and immaculate nature, attributed with qualities of virtue and perfection, traits of nobility and generosity, and with noble characteristics and excellent actions. What compatibility is there between him and the devils that they should come down upon him? Birds of a feather flock together and souls settle with other souls of a similar nature. The devils are flagrant liars in what they say, and sinful and treacherous in their actions and dealings.

As for our master Muhammad ﷺ, he was neither a liar nor sinful. Rather, he was truthful in all his statements and trustworthy in all his deeds and actions. This is attested to by his friends and enemies alike, as they all knew his truthfulness, trustworthiness, chastity, and immaculacy. Therefore, there is absolutely no compatibility between him and the devils. His compatibility is only affirmed and established with the Angels of Allah Most High, who are trustworthy, pious, and near to Him. They descend upon him, bringing the commands of Allah Most High and His Revelation. Their leader and head is Jibrīl عليه السلام, as he is the one who brought down the Qur'an from the presence of the Sovereign, the Recompenser. "The trustworthy Spirit brought it down into your heart",[1] O Truthful and Trustworthy ﷺ. It is established according to the scholars and those who introduce people to others that compatibility is the cause for things to assemble and gather; nothing assembles and gathers with another thing except due to compatibility between them.

---

(1) *Al-Shu'arā'*, 193-194.

وأما الوجهُ الثاني من الرَّدِّ: ففيه بيانُ شرفِ المُنزَلِ عليه، وطهارتِه، ونَقائِه، وعِصمتِه، وأمانتِه، وبيانُ إحالةِ قُربِ الشّياطينِ حولَهُ، أو نيلِها منه، أو تنزُّلِها عليه؛ لأنّهُ لا مناسبةَ في ذلك أصلاً، ومن المقرَّرِ أنَّ المناسبةَ هي أساسٌ في الاجتماعِ والانسجامِ.

وبيانُ ذلك: أنَّ الشّياطينَ ذَووا نفوسٍ شرّيرةٍ، وطبائعَ فاسدةٍ قبيحةٍ، لا مناسبةَ بينها وبينَ نَفسيَّةِ محمّدٍ ﷺ تلك النفسيّة الطيّبة الزَّكيَّة التقيَّة النقيَّة المتَّصفة بصفاتِ الفضلِ والكمالِ، وخصائلِ المجدِ والنّوالِ، ومكارمِ الأخلاقِ، ومحاسنِ الأفعال، فأيُّ مناسَبةٍ بينهُ وبين الشّياطينِ حتّى تنزلَ عليه؛ فإنَّ الطّيورَ على أشكالِها تقعُ، والأرواحَ عند أشباهِها تضعُ، فالشّياطينُ أفّاكونَ كذّابونَ فيما يقولون، وآثمونَ فاجرونَ خائنونَ فيما يعملونَ ويعامِلون.

وأما سيّدُنا محمّدٌ رسولُ اللهِ ﷺ فهو ليس بأفّاكٍ ولا أثيمٍ؛ بل هو الصّادقُ في جميعِ أقوالِه، الأمينُ في جميعِ أفعالِه وأعمالِه، باعترافِ أحبابِه وأعدائِه؛ فإنّهم كلَّهم يعلمونَ صِدقَهُ، وأمانتَهُ، وعِفّتَهُ، وحَصانتَهُ، فلا مناسبةَ قطعاً بينهُ وبينَ الشّياطينِ.

وإنّما ثبتَتْ مناسبتُه وحقّتْ مع ملائكةِ اللهِ تعالى الأمناءِ، الأتقياءِ، الأصفياءِ، فهم يتنزّلونَ عليه بأوامرِ اللهِ تعالى ووحيِهِ، وقائدُهم ورئيسُهم جبريلُ عليه السلام، فهو الذي نَزلَ بالقرآنِ مِن حضرةِ المَلِكِ الدَّيّانِ {نَزَلَ بِهِ الرُّوحُ الْأَمِينُ (١٩٣) عَلَى قَلْبِكَ}[1] يا أيُّها الأمينُ الصّادقُ ﷺ.

وقد تقرَّرَ لدى العلماءِ والعُرَفاءِ: أنَّ المناسَبةَ هي عِلّةُ الضَّمِّ والجَمعِ، فلا يَنضَمُّ شيءٌ إلى شيءٍ، ولا يجتمعُ شيءٌ إلى شيءٍ إلّا بمناسَبةٍ بينَهما.

---

(١) الشعراء: ١٩٣- ١٩٤.

ALLAH MOST HIGH ETERNALLY PRESERVING THIS GREAT QUR'AN FROM DISTORTIONS, CHANGES, ADDITIONS, AND DELETIONS

As for Allah Most High preserving this Noble Qur'an from changes, distortions, additions, and deletions, it is decisively established by His clear statement, "And We have sent down to you [O Prophet] the Reminder, so that you may explain to people what has been revealed for them."(1)

In this verse, Allah Most Glorified informed of two significant matters.

The first is that He Most Glorified is the One Who sent down this Reminder – the Noble Qur'an – and not anyone besides Him. In other words, this Qur'an is most assuredly from Allah Most High, not from anyone besides Him. This is because nobody besides Allah has the strength to bring it. And nobody can produce anything like it – neither in terms of its text and its inimitability, nor in the perfection of its verses and the rulings of its Sacred Law (Shariah), and nor in its informing of unseen matters and encompassing some of the knowledge that He brought in His Book.

The second is that He Most Glorified Who sent down the Qur'an is

(1) *Al-Hijr*, 9.

حِفْظُ اللهِ تعالى لهذا القرآنِ العظيمِ من التّحريفِ والتّبديلِ والزّيادةِ والنّقصانِ أبدَ الآبِدين

وأمّا حِفْظُ اللهِ تعالى لهذا القرآنِ الكريمِ من التّبديلِ والتّحريفِ، والزّيادةِ والنّقصانِ فإنّهُ ثابتٌ قطعاً بنَصِّ قولِه تعالى: {إِنَّا نَحْنُ نَزَّلْنَا الذِّكْرَ وَإِنَّا لَهُ لَحَافِظُونَ}[1].

فأَخبرَ سبحانه في هذه الآيةِ عن أمرَينِ عظيمَينِ:

الأوّل: أنّهُ سبحانه هو الّذي نزَّلَ هذا الذِّكرَ، أي: القرآنَ الكريمَ، لا غيرُه، يعني: أنَّ هذا القرآنَ هو مِن عندِ اللهِ تعالى قطعاً لا مِن عندِ غيرِ اللهِ تعالى؛ لأنَّ غيرَ اللهِ تعالى لا يَقْدِرُ على الإتيانِ به، ولا يستطيعُ أنْ يأتيَ بمِثلِهِ، لا نصّاً ولا إعجازاً، ولا إحكاماً لآياتِه، ولا أحكاماً لشريعتِهِ، ولا إخباراً عن المغيَّباتِ، ولا إحاطةً ببعض تلك العلومِ والمعارفِ التي جاء بها في كتابِهِ.

الثاني: أنّه سبحانه الذي أنزلَ هذا القرآنَ هو تكفَّلَ أنْ يحفظَهُ من التّلاعبِ

---

(١) الحجر: ٩.

the One Who undertook to preserve it from tampering, additions, and deletions. Therefore, just as one must firmly believe that Allah Most High sent down this Qur'an, one must also firmly believe that Allah is the One Who most definitely preserves this Qur'an. This is from the distinctive features of the Noble Qur'an, because He Most Glorified did not guarantee to preserve any of the Books He sent down to His previous Messengers. He did not guarantee that He will preserve the Torah, the Evangel, the Psalms, or any other Book. Rather, He entrusted its preservation to the rabbis and priests. He Most High said, "Indeed, We revealed the Torah, containing guidance and light, by which the Prophets, who submitted themselves to Allah, made judgements for Jews. So too did the rabbis and scholars judge according to Allah's Book, with which they were entrusted."(1) Allah Most High entrusted them to preserve their Books. However, they were unable to preserve them against additions, deletions, and distortions.

As for this great Qur'an, Allah personally undertook its protection. He said, "And We have sent down to you [O Prophet] the Reminder, so that you may explain to people what has been revealed for them."(2) Thus, no changes, distortions, additions, or deletions have affected it, and never will it be affected by such. This is because Allah – the Protector, the All-Knowing – personally undertook its preservation, and there is a world of difference between preservation by the Creator and that by the creation. He Most Glorified said, "Indeed, those who deny the Reminder after it has come to them [are doomed], for it is truly a mighty Book. Falsehood cannot approach it from any angle. [It is] a Revelation from the [One Who is] All-Wise, Praiseworthy."(3)

From these verses, it becomes very clear to the intelligent person that this Noble Qur'an is protected against the distortion of those who seek to distort it and the tampering of those who wish to tamper with it. It is protected from deletions, additions, changes, and alterations. This is a

---

(1) *Al-Mā'idah*, 44.

(2) *Al-Hijr*, 9.

(3) *Fuṣṣilat*, 41-42.

والزّيادةِ والنّقصانِ، فكما يجبُ الإيمانُ قطعاً بأنَّ هذا القرآنَ أنزلَهُ اللهُ تعالى، يجبُ الإيمانُ قطعاً بأنَّ اللهَ هو حافِظٌ لهذا القرآنِ قطعاً، وهذا من خصائصِ القرآنِ الكريمِ، فإنّه سبحانه لم يتكفَّلْ بحفظِ أيِّ كتابٍ أنزلَهُ على رُسُلِهِ السّابقين، فلم يتكفَّلْ بحفظِ التّوراةِ والإنجيلِ، ولا الزّبورِ وغيرِها، بل وَكَلَ حِفْظَها للرّبّانيّينَ والأَحْبارِ؛ قال تعالى: {إِنَّا أَنزَلْنَا التَّوْرَاةَ فِيهَا هُدًى وَنُورٌ ۚ يَحْكُمُ بِهَا النَّبِيُّونَ الَّذِينَ أَسْلَمُوا لِلَّذِينَ هَادُوا وَالرَّبَّانِيُّونَ وَالْأَحْبَارُ}، أي: يحكمونَ بذلك و{بِمَا اسْتُحْفِظُوا مِن كِتَابِ اللَّهِ وَكَانُوا عَلَيْهِ شُهَدَاءَ}[1] الآيةَ. فلقد استحفَظَهُمُ اللهُ تعالى إيّاها فما اسطاعوا أن يحفظوها من الزّيادةِ والنّقصانِ والتّحريف.

أمّا هذا القرآنُ العظيمُ فقد تولّى اللهُ حِفظَهُ حيثُ قال: {إِنَّا نَحْنُ نَزَّلْنَا الذِّكْرَ وَإِنَّا لَهُ لَحَافِظُونَ}[2]؛ فلم ينَلْهُ تبديلٌ ولا تحريفٌ، ولا زيادةٌ ولا نَقصٌ، ولنْ ينالَهُ ذلك أبداً؛ لأنَّ اللهَ تعالى الحفيظَ العليمَ هو بنفسِهِ تولّى حِفظَه، وشتّانَ بين حِفظِ الخالقِ وحِفظِ المخلوقِ. ومن ثَمَّ قال سبحانه: {إِنَّ الَّذِينَ كَفَرُوا بِالذِّكْرِ لَمَّا جَاءَهُمْ ۖ وَإِنَّهُ لَكِتَابٌ عَزِيزٌ (٤١) لَّا يَأْتِيهِ الْبَاطِلُ مِن بَيْنِ يَدَيْهِ وَلَا مِنْ خَلْفِهِ ۖ تَنزِيلٌ مِّنْ حَكِيمٍ حَمِيدٍ}[3].

ومِن هذه الآياتِ التي ذكرناها يتّضِحُ للعاقلِ جَليّاً أنَّ هذا القرآنَ الكريمَ هو مَصُونٌ عن عَبَثِ العابِثينَ، وتَلاعُبِ المتَلاعِبين، محفوظٌ من النَّقصِ، والزّيادةِ، والتّبديلِ، والتّغييرِ، وهذا أمرٌ يجبُ الإيمانُ به جزماً، والاعتقادُ به قطعاً؛ وذلك لأمورٍ متعدّدةٍ:

(١) المائدة: ٤٤.

(٢) الحجر: ٩.

(٣) فصلت: ٤١- ٤٢.

matter one must have faith in with conviction and believe firmly, for a number of reasons.

One: If alterations, changes, additions or deletions could occur in the Qur'an, Allah's informing that "it is certainly We Who will preserve it" would be invalid. Furthermore, He Most High would not be true to His promise to preserve this great Qur'an – highly exalted is He above that. Allah Most High does not break His promise, and what He informs of is true and definitely occurs. "And whose word is more truthful than Allah's?"[1] "And whose promise is truer than Allah's?"[2] His statement is never false, His promise never fails, and His guarantee never breaks. In Allah's saying "it is certainly We Who will preserve it", there is an assured guarantee from Allah Most High, emphatic information and an inevitable promise; anyone who contemplates will realize this. He Most High said, "[This is] a blessed Book which We have revealed to you [O Prophet] so that they may contemplate its verses, and people of reason may be mindful."[3]

Two: If alterations, changes, additions, or deletions could occur in the Qur'an, that would negate and contradict His saying: "Falsehood cannot approach it from any angle. [It is] a Revelation from the [One Who is] All-Wise, Praiseworthy." Allah Most High informed that falsehood cannot approach this Qur'an or seep into it – neither in its text nor in its meaning. It cannot neither be opposed or contradicted, nor can it be increased or decreased. Any addition to it would be falsehood that is not part of it, and any deletion from it would be falsifying that which is rightly part of it and which proves the truth.

Thus, His saying, "Falsehood cannot approach it from any angle" is evidence for its being safeguarded and preserved against tampering, additions, and deletions.

This information given by the Qur'an cannot falter or change. Falsehood

(1) *Al-Nisā'*, 122.

(2) *Al-Tawbah*, 111.

(3) *Ṣād*, 29.

١- لو جرى على هذا القرآنِ تبديلٌ أو تغييرٌ، أو زيادةٌ أو نقصٌ لَمَا صحَّ الخبرُ في قولِه تعالى: {وَإِنَّا لَهُ لَحَافِظُونَ}، ولَمَا صدقَ اللهُ تعالى وعدَهُ بالحفظِ لهذا القرآنِ العظيمِ، وتعالى اللهُ عن ذلك عُلوّاً كبيراً؛ فإنَّ اللهَ تعالى لا يُخلِفُ وعدَهُ، وإنَّ خبرَهُ صادقٌ مُحتَّمُ الوقوعِ {وَمَنْ أَصْدَقُ مِنَ اللَّهِ قِيلًا}[1]، {وَمَنْ أَوْفَىٰ بِعَهْدِهِ مِنَ اللَّهِ}[2]. فإنّهُ سبحانه لا يَكذِبُ خبرُهُ، ولا يتخلَّفُ وعدُهُ، ولا تُنقَضُ كفالَتُهُ؛ فإنَّ في قوله تعالى: {وَإِنَّا لَهُ لَحَافِظُونَ} كَفالةً من اللهِ تعالى موثَّقةً، وخبراً مؤكَّداً، ووعداً مُحتَّماً، يعرفُ ذلك مَنْ تدبَّرَ. قال تعالى: {كِتَابٌ أَنزَلْنَاهُ إِلَيْكَ مُبَارَكٌ لِّيَدَّبَّرُوا آيَاتِهِ وَلِيَتَذَكَّرَ أُولُو الْأَلْبَابِ}[3].

٢- أنّهُ لو جرى على هذا القرآنِ الكريمِ تبديلٌ، أو زيادةٌ، أو نَقصٌ، لكان ذلك مُنافِياً ومُعارِضاً لقولِه تعالى: {لَّا يَأْتِيهِ الْبَاطِلُ مِن بَيْنِ يَدَيْهِ وَلَا مِنْ خَلْفِهِ ۖ تَنزِيلٌ مِّنْ حَكِيمٍ حَمِيدٍ}؛ فإنَّ اللهَ تعالى أخبرَ أنَّ الباطلَ لا يأتي هذا القرآنَ، ولا يتسرَّبُ إليه، لا في نُصوصِهِ ولا في معانيه، فهو لا يُعارَضُ ولا يُناقَضُ، ولا يُزادُ فيه ولا يُنقَصُ منه؛ لأنَّ الزّيادةَ فيه باطلةٌ ليستْ منه، والنّقصَ منه هو إبطالٌ لِما هو منه حقّاً دالّاً على حقٍّ.

فقولُه تعالى: {لَّا يَأْتِيهِ الْبَاطِلُ مِن بَيْنِ يَدَيْهِ وَلَا مِنْ خَلْفِهِ} دليلُ صيانتِه، وحِفظِه من التّلاعُبِ والزّيادةِ والنّقصِ.

وهذا الخبرُ القرآنيُّ لا يتخلَّفُ، ولا يتبدَّلُ؛ فإنَّ الباطلَ لا يمكنُ أن يتسرَّبَ إلى هذا القرآنِ الكريمِ قطعاً، لا في نصوصِ كلماتِه بزيادةٍ أو نقصٍ، ولا في معانيه بتكذيبٍ أو نقصٍ.

---

(١) النساء: ١٢٢.

(٢) التوبة: ١١١.

(٣) ص: ٢٩.

can never seep into the Qur'an – neither in its wording through additions or deletions, nor in its meanings through denial or contradiction.

Three: If distortion, additions, or deletions could occur in the Qur'an, this would negate and oppose His saying: "And this Qur'an has been revealed to me so that, with it, I may warn you and whoever it reaches."[1] This is because Allah Most High commanded His Prophet: "Ask [them, O Prophet], 'Who is the best witness?' Say, 'Allah is! He is a Witness between me and you. And this Qur'an has been revealed to me so that, with it, I may warn you and whoever it reaches.'"[2] Thus the best witness – whose testimony to our master Muhammad ﷺ being the Messenger of Allah is the best testimony – is Allah, Most High, the Great. He openly testified that Muhammad is the Messenger of Allah, through the cosmic signs of the Heavens and the Earth, and in trees, water, food, drink and so forth. These signs are the miracles that Allah Most High manifested upon the hands of the Prophet ﷺ, as testimony to his being the Messenger ﷺ. Amongst the heavenly signs are the splitting of the Moon, the clouds raining down, and so forth.

Likewise, He Most Glorified informed His slaves of His testimony that Muhammad is the Messenger of Allah in the verses compiled in the Qur'an. He Most High said, "He is the One Who has sent His Messenger with [right] guidance and the religion of truth, making it prevail over all others. And sufficient is Allah as a Witness. Muhammad is the Messenger of Allah."[3] This is the meaning of His saying: "Ask [them, O Prophet], 'Who is the best witness?' Say, 'Allah is! He is a Witness between me and you.'"

Thereafter, He Most Glorified said, "And this Qur'an has been revealed to me so that, with it, I may warn you and whoever it reaches." In other words, say to them, O Muhammad, that "this Qur'an has been revealed to me so

(1) *Al-An'ām*, 19.

(2) *Al-An'ām*, 19.

(3) *Al-Fatḥ*, 28-29.

٣- لو جرى على هذا القرآنِ الكريمِ تحريفٌ أو زيادةٌ أو نقصٌ لكان ذلك مُنافياً ومخالِفاً لقولِه تعالى: {وَأُوحِيَ إِلَيَّ هَٰذَا الْقُرْآنُ لِأُنذِرَكُم بِهِ وَمَن بَلَغَ}[1] الآيةَ، وذلك أنَّ اللهَ تعالى أمَرَ نبيَّهُ ﷺ بقولِه: {قُلْ أَيُّ شَيْءٍ أَكْبَرُ شَهَادَةً ۖ قُلِ اللَّهُ ۖ شَهِيدٌ بَيْنِي وَبَيْنَكُمْ ۚ وَأُوحِيَ إِلَيَّ هَٰذَا الْقُرْآنُ لِأُنذِرَكُم بِهِ وَمَن بَلَغَ}[2]، فأكبرُ شاهدٍ: شهادتُه أكبرُ شهادةٍ لسيّدِنا محمدٍ ﷺ أنّهُ رسولُ اللهِ ﷺ، هو اللهُ العليُّ الكبيرُ الذي أعلنَ شهادتَهُ بأنَّ محمّداً رسولُ اللهِ ﷺ في الآياتِ التكوينيّةِ السّماويّةِ، والأَرضيّةِ، والشَّجريّةِ، والمائيّةِ، والطّعامِ، والشّرابِ، وغيرِ ذلك، وهي المعجزاتُ التي أجراها اللهُ تعالى على يديهِ ﷺ شهادةً له بأنّهُ رسولُ اللهِ تعالى ﷺ، ومن الآياتِ السّماويّةِ: انشقاقُ القمرِ، وإمطارُ السُّحُبِ، ونحوُ ذلك.

كما أنّهُ سبحانه أعلمَ عبادَهُ بشهادَتِهِ أنَّ محمّداً رسولُ اللهِ ﷺ في آياتِهِ التدوينيّةِ القرآنيّةِ؛ قال تعالى: {هُوَ الَّذِي أَرْسَلَ رَسُولَهُ بِالْهُدَىٰ وَدِينِ الْحَقِّ لِيُظْهِرَهُ عَلَى الدِّينِ كُلِّهِ ۚ وَكَفَىٰ بِاللَّهِ شَهِيدًا مُّحَمَّدٌ رَّسُولُ اللَّهِ}[3]، فهذا معنى قولِه تعالى: {قُلْ أَيُّ شَيْءٍ أَكْبَرُ شَهَادَةً ۖ قُلِ اللَّهُ ۖ شَهِيدٌ بَيْنِي وَبَيْنَكُمْ}.

ثمَّ قال سبحانه: {وَأُوحِيَ إِلَيَّ هَٰذَا الْقُرْآنُ لِأُنذِرَكُم بِهِ وَمَن بَلَغَ} أي: قلْ لهم يا محمّد صلى اللهُ عليه آله وسلم: {وَأُوحِيَ إِلَيَّ هَٰذَا الْقُرْآنُ لِأُنذِرَكُم بِهِ} أيُّها النّاسُ، أي: الذين بلَّغتُكُم وشافَهتُكُم، {وَمَن بَلَغَ} أي: وأنذِرْ به كلَّ مَن بَلَغَهُ هذا القرآنُ الكريمُ إلى يومِ القيامةِ.

---

(١) الأنعام: ١٩.

(٢) الأنعام: ١٩.

(٣) الفتح: ٢٨-٢٩.

that, with it, I may warn you" O mankind, i.e., those to whom I conveyed and directly addressed, "and whoever it reaches", i.e., I am warning all to whom this Noble Qur'an will reach until the Day of Judgement.

Allah Most High ordained that he ﷺ warn the first, the middle and the last of this ummah equally. In this regard, he ﷺ said, "Whomsoever this Qur'an reaches, it is as though I have spoken it to him directly."(1) Ibn Mardawayh, Abū Nuʿaym, and Khaṭīb narrated it from Ibn ʿAbbās ﷺ. Ibn Abī Shaybah, Ibn al-Mundhir, and others narrated the same from Muhammad ibn Kaʿb al-Quraẓī, as cited in the exegeses of Ibn Kathīr, al-Qurṭubī, and al-Ālūsī.

Thus, Allah Most High made the Noble Qur'an a proof for the Messenger of Allah ﷺ against all people and a message from Him to all His slaves until the Day of Return. He ﷺ is a universal Messenger sent to both men and jinn until the Day of Judgement. For this reason, divine wisdom necessitates that the Book which Allah Most High revealed to Him remain preserved until the Day of Judgement. This is to ensure the proof is established against all the slaves, they find guidance to the right path, and the last of this ummah convey it just as he ﷺ conveyed it to the first of them.

If it was possible for any distortions, additions, or deletion to occur in the Qur'an, the Prophet's warning through the Qur'an to those coming after him would not be realized in the same way he warned the people in his era – whereas the verse informs of his warning the people of his era and those after him equally.

Four: If distortions, additions, or deletions could occur in the Qur'an, it would lead to distrust of the Qur'an and people not believing its contents with conviction. How is it possible for it not to be trusted and for its contents not to be firmly believed when Allah Most High clearly told His slaves that this Book – with all its verses – is trusted and decisively true, and that falsehood or discrepancies cannot make their way into it from

---

(1) Khaṭīb al-Baghdādī in *Tārīkh Baghdād*, vol. 2, p. 49.

فقد أمرَهُ اللهُ تعالى أنْ يُنذِرَ به أوَّلَ هذه الأمّةِ ووسطَها وآخرَها على حدٍّ سواء. وفي ذلك يقولُ ﷺ: «مَنْ بلغهُ القرآن فكأنّما شافهْتُهُ به»، ثُمَّ قرأ {وَأُوحِيَ إِلَيَّ هَٰذَا الْقُرْآنُ لِأُنذِرَكُم بِهِ وَمَن بَلَغَ}[1]. رواه ابنُ مَرْدَوَيْه، وأبو نُعيم، والخطيبُ عن ابنِ عباسٍ رضي الله عنهما، وروى ابنُ أبي شيبةَ، وابنُ المنذِرِ، وغيرُهما نحوَ ذلك عن محمّدِ بنِ كعبٍ القرظيِّ، كما في (تفسيرِ) ابنِ كثيرٍ والقرطبيّ والألوسيِّ.

فقد جعل اللهُ تعالى القرآنَ الكريمَ حُجّةً لرسولِ اللهِ ﷺ وعلى جميعِ العبادِ، وبلاغاً عنه لكافّةِ العبادِ إلى يومِ المعاد؛ فإنّهُ ﷺ صاحبُ الرِّسالةِ العامّةِ للثَّقلينِ إلى يومِ القيامة، ولذلك اقتضتِ الحكمةُ الإلهيّةُ أن يبقى كتابُهُ الذي أَنزله اللهُ تعالى عليه يبقى محفوظاً إلى يومِ الدِّين؛ لتقومَ الحُجّةُ على العبادِ، وليهتدوا به إلى سبيلِ الرَّشاد، ويبلِّغُهُ آخرُ هذه الأمّةِ كما بلَّغَهُ ﷺ لأوَّلِها.

فلو جاز أن يجريَ عليه تحريفٌ أو زيادةٌ أو نقصٌ لَمَا تحقَّقَ إنذارُه ﷺ بالقرآنِ لِمَن يأتي مِن بعدِه، كما أنذرَ الذين في عصرِه، في حينِ أنَّ الآيةَ تُخبِرُ بإنذاره ﷺ لِمَن في عصرِهِ ومَن بعدَهُ على حدٍّ سواء.

٤- لو جرى على هذا القرآنِ الكريمِ تحريفٌ، أو زيادةٌ، أو نقصٌ لأدّى ذلك إلى ذهابِ الثِّقةِ به، ولأدّى ذلك إلى عدمِ الإيمانِ الجازمِ بما جاء به، وكيف لا يُوثَقُ به ولا يُقطَعُ جزماً بما جاء به، مع أنَّ اللهَ تعالى بيَّنَ لعباده أنَّ هذا الكتابَ الذي هو بجميعِ آياتِهِ موثوقٌ به، ومقطوعٌ بحقيقته لا يتطرَّقُ الباطلُ ولا الخَلَلُ إلى جانبٍ من جوانبه، قال تعالى: {لَّا يَأْتِيهِ الْبَاطِلُ مِن بَيْنِ يَدَيْهِ وَلَا مِنْ خَلْفِهِ ۖ تَنزِيلٌ مِّنْ حَكِيمٍ حَمِيدٍ}، فإنَّ فحوى هذه الآيةِ ونصَّها يُناديانِ العبادَ، ويُخبِرانِهم أنَّ الثِّقةَ كلَّ الثِّقةِ، واليقينَ كلَّ

---

(١) أخرجه الخطيب البغدادي في تاريخ بغداد (٤٩/٢).

any angle? He Most High said, "Falsehood cannot approach it from any angle. [It is] a Revelation from the [One Who is] All-Wise, Praiseworthy." The purport and the wording of this verse proclaim and clearly informs the slaves that complete and utmost trust, conviction, and truth is in this mighty Book to which falsehood, mistakes, lies, fabrications, tampering, and anything of this nature can find no way.

Thus, if distortion, additions, or deletions could occur therein, trust and belief in it would not remain.

As for distrust regarding what has been added, it needs no explanation.

With respect to distrust regarding that to which things have been added, the intelligent person will say, "Perhaps there is an addition here also, so how do we know if any of this is genuine?"

And with respect to distrust in the case of deletions, it is because there is a link – in meaning, rulings, information, and so forth – between the original text from which the deletion was made and the deletion itself. If deletions were to occur, it would lead to distrust in both the deletion and that from which it has been deleted. No Muslim would have any trust in their religion: it is possible some of the prayers have been abrogated, their times have been changed, or something has been added to them. Likewise, *zakāh* (alms-tax) or its measures may have been abrogated. Fasting may have been abrogated, increased in some way, or replaced with something else. Hajj may have been abrogated. Forbidden things like alcohol or gambling may have been made lawful, or certain lawful things may have been prohibited. In this manner, nobody would perform any act of worship except that they would be doubtful regarding it, and nobody would intend a lawful action or desist from an unlawful action except that they would be in doubt. Where then would there be any faith and conviction in Allah's Sacred Law? We seek Allah's refuge.

In such a state, firm belief would be impossible and the need would arise for Allah to send a new Prophet to clarify to the people what has been deleted or added. However, there is no Prophet after our master Muhammad, the last of the Prophets ﷺ. He Most High said, "Muhammad is not the father of any of your men, but is the Messenger of Allah and the

تِلاوَةُ القُرآنِ المَجيدِ

اليقينِ، والحقُّ كلَّ الحقِّ في هذا الكتابِ العزيزِ الذي لا يجدُ الباطلُ والوهمُ، والكذبُ والافتراءُ، والتّلاعُبُ، وما شابه ذلكَ لا يجدُ إلى الكتابِ سبيلاً أصلاً.

فلو جرى عليه تحريفٌ أو زيادةٌ أو نقصٌ لذهبَتِ الثّقةُ واليقينُ به. أمّا ذهابُ الثّقةِ بالمزيدِ: فالأمرُ بيِّنٌ. وأمّا ذهابُ الثّقةِ بالمزيدِ عليهِ: فإنَّ العاقلَ يقول: لعلَّ في هذا الأصلِ زيادةً أيضاً، فما يُدرينا أنَّها كلَّها أصلٌ؟

وأما ذهابُ الثّقةِ به حالةَ النَّقصِ: فذلك لأنَّ بينَ الأصلِ المنقوصِ عنه، والشّيءِ النّاقصِ منه ارتباطاً في المعاني، والأحكامِ، والأخبارِ، وغيرِ ذلك، ولو جرى عليه النَّقصُ لأدّى ذلك إلى عدمِ الثِّقةِ بالنَّاقصِ والمنقوصِ منه، فلا يكونُ أحدٌ من المسلمينَ على ثقةٍ بدينه؛ لاحتمالِ نسخِ بعضِ الصّلواتِ، أو تغييرِ أوقاتِها، أو الزّيادةِ عليها، أو نسخِ الزّكاةِ أو مقاديرِها، أو نسخِ الصّيامِ أو الزّيادةِ فيه، أو بتبديلِهِ بغيرِهِ، أو نسخِ الحجِّ، أو تحليلِ الخمرِ والمَيسِرِ ونحوِها من المحرَّمات، أو تحريمِ بعضِ أنواعٍ من الحلال، وبذلك لا يكونُ أحدٌ من النّاسِ على عبادةٍ إلّا وهو على شكٍّ منها، ولا يُقدِمُ على حلالٍ، ولا يُحجِمُ عن حرامٍ إلّا وهو متشكِّكٌ، فأينَ الإيمانُ والجزمُ بشرعِ اللهِ تعالى! - نعوذُ باللهِ تعالى-.

وحينئذٍ لا يمكنُ الإيمانُ الجازمُ به والحالةُ هذه، وحينئذٍ لا بُدَّ من نبيٍّ يبعثهُ اللهُ تعالى يُبيِّنُ للنّاسِ ما نقصَ منه أو ما زيدَ فيه، ولا نبيَّ بعد نبيِّ اللهِ تعالى سيِّدِنا محمّدٍ ﷺ خاتمِ النّبيينَ. قال تعالى: {مَّا كَانَ مُحَمَّدٌ أَبَا أَحَدٍ مِّن رِّجَالِكُمْ وَلَٰكِن رَّسُولَ اللَّهِ وَخَاتَمَ النَّبِيِّينَ ۗ وَكَانَ اللَّهُ بِكُلِّ شَيْءٍ عَلِيمًا}[1] فهو سبحانه يَعلمُ بعلمِهِ القديمِ الذي لا أوَّلَ له أنَّ ختمَ النّبواتِ لا يليقُ به إلّا سيِّدُنا محمّدٌ ﷺ، وقال ﷺ

---

(١) الأحزاب: ٤٠.

seal of the Prophets. And Allah has [perfect] knowledge of all things."[1] He Most Glorified knew pre-eternally that the seal of Prophethood only befits our master Muhammad ﷺ. He ﷺ stated in a lengthy hadith, "I am the last of the Prophets; there is no Prophet after me."[2]

This is why we see that due to the previous divine Books being prone to distortions, additions, and deletions, Allah's divine wisdom required that He send Prophets successively one after the other. One Prophet would go, only to be replaced by another. At times, there would be a number of Prophets together in one era. He Most High said, "Then We sent Our Messengers in succession: whenever a Messenger came to his people, they denied him."[3] The purpose behind this (i.e., sending Prophets) was to explain to people what had been revealed to them from their Lord and to remove any doubt regarding their religion, so that they have full conviction regarding their Book and sacred law. In this manner, Allah's proof against the slaves is established. "So humanity should have no excuse before Allah after [the coming of] the Messengers."[4]

As for the Book which our master Muhammad ﷺ brought from Allah Most High, it shall remain until the Day of Judgement - preserved and protected against all changes, distortions, additions, and deletions. In conclusion, the message of Muhammad ﷺ is everlasting.

At this juncture, there are two major points that are mutually indispensable:

Firstly, he ﷺ is a Messenger for all men and jinn until the Day of Judgement. Secondly, Allah Most High has preserved His Book which He revealed to the Prophet ﷺ and will keep it safe from tampering until the Day of Judgement.

Therefore, criticizing any one of these two is criticizing the other,

---

(1) *Al-Aḥzāb*, 40.

(2) *Tirmidhī* (2219).

(3) *Al-Mu'minūn*, 44.

(4) *Al-Nisā'*, 165.

في حديثٍ طويلٍ: «وأنا خاتَمُ النّبيّينَ، ولا نبيَّ بعدي»[1] ﷺ.

ولذلك نرى أنَّ الكتبَ السّماويةَ السّابقةَ لمّا كانتْ في مَعرِضِ التّحريفِ والزّيادةِ والنّقصِ اقتضتْ حكمةُ اللهِ تعالى أن يُتابعَ ويُوالِيَ بينَ بعثةِ الأنبياءِ، بحيثُ ما يذهبُ نبيٌّ إلّا يبعثُ اللهُ تعالى نبيّا آخرَ، وربّما اجتمع في زمانٍ واحدٍ عدّةٌ مِنَ الأنبياءِ، قال تعالى: {ثُمَّ أَرْسَلْنَا رُسُلَنَا تَتْرَىٰۖ كُلَّ مَا جَاءَ أُمَّةً رَّسُولُهَا كَذَّبُوهُ}[2]؛ وذلك لأجل أنْ يُبيّنوا للنّاسِ ما نُزِّلَ إليهم من ربّهم، ويُبعدوهم عن الشّكِّ في دينِهم، بحيثُ يكونون على يقينٍ في كتابِهم وشريعتِهم، وبذلك تقومُ حُجّةُ اللهِ تعالى على العبادِ؛ {لِئَلَّا يَكُونَ لِلنَّاسِ عَلَى اللَّهِ حُجَّةٌ بَعْدَ الرُّسُلِ}[3].

وأما الكتابُ الذي جاء به سيّدُنا محمّدٌ ﷺ مِن عندِ اللهِ تعالى فهو باقٍ إلى يومِ القيامةِ، محفوظٌ مَصونٌ عن التغييرِ والتحريفِ، والزّيادةِ والنّقصِ. فرسالةُ سيّدِنا محمّدٍ صلى الله عليه وسلم باقيةٌ.

فهاهنا أمرانِ عظيمانِ متلازمانِ لا ينفكّانِ عن بعضِهما:

الأوّلُ: عمومُ رسالتِهِ ﷺ إلى جميعِ الثّقلينِ إلى يومِ الدّينِ.

الثّاني: حِفظُ اللهِ تعالى كتابَهُ النّازلَ عليه ﷺ، وإبقاؤُهُ مصوناً عن التّلاعبِ فيه إلى يومِ الدّينِ.

فالطّعنُ في أحدِ هذينِ الأمرينِ هو طعنٌ في الأمرِ الآخرِ؛ لأنّهما مرتبِطان ببعضِهما، وكما أنَّ عمومَ رسالتِه ﷺ ثابتٌ بالنّصوصِ القطعيّةِ، نحو قولِهِ تعالى: {قُلْ

---

(١) أخرجه الترمذي (٢٢١٩).

(٢) المؤمنون: ٤٤.

(٣) النساء: ١٦٥.

because they are interconnected. His being a universal Messenger is established through decisive texts, such as His saying, "Say [O Prophet]: "O humanity! I am Allah's Messenger to you all."[1] And His Saying, "We have sent you [O Prophet] only as a deliverer of good news and a warner to all of humanity."[2] And His saying, "...so that, with it, I may warn you and whoever it reaches."[3] And His saying, "We have sent you [O Prophet] only as a mercy for the whole world."[4] Likewise, Allah's preserving the Book which He sent down to him ﷺ is also established through decisive evidence that dumbfounds the intellect, as has come before.

Amongst this evidence is the saying of Allah Most High, "Blessed is the One Who sent down the Standard to His servant, so that he may be a warner to the whole world."[5] He Most Glorified has clarified in this verse that the role of our master Muhammad ﷺ – His slave and His Messenger – is to warn to the whole world until the Day of Judgement; this is not confined just to his era. This must inevitably occur, because it is from Allah Most High. "And whose word is more truthful than Allah's?"[6] So how has that occurred? Has it transpired or not? The answer is that it has certainly transpired, as Allah Most High stated, "And this Qur'an has been revealed to me so that, with it, I may warn you and whoever it reaches."[7] In other words, I am warning everyone to whom this Qur'an will reach until the Day of Judgement, because this Qur'an will remain preserved by the Lord of all worlds until the Day of Judgement.

Five: Allah Most High mentions the Torah with praise and esteem, whereafter He mentions the Evangel. He then mentions the Noble Qur'an, and clarifies its position amongst all the divine Books, its loftiness over

---

(1) *Al-A 'rāf*, 158.

(2) *Saba'*, 28.

(3) *Al-An 'ām*, 19.

(4) *Al-Anbiyā'*, 107.

(5) *Al-Furqān*, 1.

(6) *Al-Nisā'*, 122.

(7) *Al-An 'ām*, 19.

يا أَيُّهَا النَّاسُ إِنِّي رَسُولُ اللَّهِ إِلَيْكُمْ جَمِيعًا}[1] الآية، وقولِهِ تعالى: {وَمَا أَرْسَلْنَاكَ إِلَّا كَافَّةً لِّلنَّاسِ بَشِيرًا وَنَذِيرًا}[2] الآية، وقولِه تعالى: {لِأُنذِرَكُم بِهِ وَمَن بَلَغَ}[3]، وقولِهِ تعالى: {وَمَا أَرْسَلْنَاكَ إِلَّا رَحْمَةً لِّلْعَالَمِينَ}[4]، فكذلك أيضاً حِفظُ كتابِهِ النّازِلِ عليه صلى الله عليه وآله وسلم، ثابتٌ بالأدلّةِ القطعيّةِ المُفحِمَةِ للعقولِ، كما تقدَّم.

ومِن ذلك أيضاً قولُهُ تعالى: {تَبَارَكَ الَّذِي نَزَّلَ الْفُرْقَانَ عَلَىٰ عَبْدِهِ لِيَكُونَ لِلْعَالَمِينَ نَذِيرًا}[5] فقد بيَّنَ سبحانه في هذهِ الآيةِ أنَّ وظيفةَ سيّدِنا محمّدٍ صلى الله عليه وآله وسلم عبدِ اللهِ ورسولِهِ أنْ يُنذِرَ العالمينَ إلى يومِ الدّينِ، دون أن يقتصرَ على أهلِ زمانِهِ فحسب. ولا بُدَّ لهذا الخبرِ أنْ يتحقّقَ وقوعُهُ؛ لأنّهُ مِنَ اللهِ تعالى {وَمَنْ أَصْدَقُ مِنَ اللَّهِ قِيلًا}[6] فكيف كان ذلك؟ هل تحقّقَ أم لا؟

نعم كان ذلك حقّاً، كما بيَّنَ اللهُ تعالى في قولِهِ: {وَأُوحِيَ إِلَيَّ هَٰذَا الْقُرْآنُ لِأُنذِرَكُم بِهِ وَمَن بَلَغَ}[7]، أي: وأُنْذِرُ كلَّ مَن بلغَهُ هذا القرآنُ إلى يومِ الدّينِ؛ لأنَّ هذا القرآنَ باقٍ كما هو إلى يومِ الدّينِ بحفظِ ربِّ العالمين.

٥- لقد ذكر اللهُ تعالى بالمدحِ والتّعظيمِ التّوراةَ، ثمَّ ذكرَ الإنجيلَ، ثمَّ ذكر هذا

---

(١) الأعراف: ١٥٨.

(٢) سبأ: ٢٨.

(٣) الأنعام: ١٩.

(٤) الأنبياء: ١٠٧.

(٥) الفرقان: ١.

(٦) النساء: ١٢٢.

(٧) الأنعام: ١٩.

all other Books, and that it is an authority over the Heavenly scriptures sent down before it. He Most High said, "Indeed, We revealed the Torah, containing guidance and light."[1] He Most High then said, "Then in the footsteps of the Prophets, We sent Jesus, son of Mary, confirming the Torah revealed before him. And We gave him the Gospel containing guidance and light."[2] He Most High then said, "We have revealed to you [O Prophet] this Book with the truth, as a confirmation of previous Scriptures and a supreme authority (*muhaymin*) on them."[3]

Allah Most Glorified informed of the position of this magnificent Book in relation to all the previous Books: it confirms what they have brought from Allah Most High and it is a supreme authority on all previous Books.

Imam Bukhārī writes in his *Ṣaḥīḥ*: "Chapter on how the Revelation came down and the first of it to come down. Ibn ʿAbbās ﷺ said *muhaymin* is a protector, and the Qur'an protects all previous Books."

Thus, this Noble Qur'an is a protector and judge over every Book before it. It affirms the truth they contain and negates whatever has been distorted thereof and anything false that has been interpolated into it.

It is also narrated that Ibn ʿAbbās ﷺ said *muhaymin* means witness. In another narration from him, he interpreted *muhaymin* in this place as judge. All of these meanings are similar and interrelated. Hence, this Noble Qur'an is a protector, witness, and judge over previous Books.

When the relationship of the Qur'an with the previous Books is that it is a protector over them and a judge over their contents, it is impossible for any of its word to be distorted, or for any word to be added or deleted – in that case, it would also require a further protector over it and a judge to pass judgement on its contents. This is one way of looking at it.

From another perspective, if it were possible for any word to be distorted, or for a word to be added to or deleted from the Qur'an, it

---

(1) *Al-Mā'idah*, 44.

(2) *Al-Mā'idah*, 46.

(3) *Al-Mā'idah*, 48.

القرآنَ الكريمَ، وبيَّنَ منزلتَهُ من بين الكتبِ الإلهيّةِ، ورِفعةَ رُتبتِهِ على جميعِ الكتبِ، وأنّه المهيمنُ على الكتبِ السماويّةِ التي نزلَتْ قبلَهُ. قال تعالى: {إِنَّا أَنزَلْنَا التَّوْرَاةَ فِيهَا هُدًى وَنُورٌ}[1] الآيةَ، ثمّ قال تعالى: {وَقَفَّيْنَا عَلَىٰ آثَارِهِم بِعِيسَى ابْنِ مَرْيَمَ مُصَدِّقًا لِّمَا بَيْنَ يَدَيْهِ مِنَ التَّوْرَاةِ وَآتَيْنَاهُ الْإِنجِيلَ فِيهِ هُدًى وَنُورٌ}[2] الآيةَ. ثمّ قال تعالى: {وَأَنزَلْنَا إِلَيْكَ الْكِتَابَ بِالْحَقِّ مُصَدِّقًا لِّمَا بَيْنَ يَدَيْهِ مِنَ الْكِتَابِ وَمُهَيْمِنًا عَلَيْهِ}[3].

فقد أخبر سبحانَهُ عن رتبةِ هذا الكتابِ العزيزِ بالنّسبةِ لجميعِ الكتبِ قبلَهُ بأنّه مصدِّقٌ لِما جاءتْ به مِن عندِ اللهِ تعالى، وأنّهُ المهيمنُ على جميعِ الكتبِ قبلَهُ.

قال الإمامُ البخاريُّ رحمه اللهِ في (صحيحِه): باب «كيف نزلَ الوحيُ وأوّلُ ما نزل» قال ابنُ عبّاسٍ رضي اللهُ عنهما: المهيمِنُ: الأمينُ، والقرآنُ أمينٌ على كلِّ كتابٍ قبلَه. اهـ.

فهذا القرآنُ الكريمُ هو الأمينُ الحَكَمُ على كلِّ كتابٍ قبلَه، يُحِقُّ ما فيها من حقٍّ، ويُبطِلُ ما حُرِّفَ منها، وأُدخِلَ عليها من باطلٍ.

ورويَ عن ابنُ عبّاسٍ رَضِيَ اللَّهُ عَنْهُمَا أنّهُ قال: المهيمِنُ: هو الشّاهدُ.

وفي روايةٍ عنه فسّرَ المهيمِنَ هنا: بمعنى الحاكمِ، وكلُّها متقاربةٌ ومتلازمةٌ، فهذا القرآنُ الكريمُ هو الأمينُ على الكتبِ قبلَهُ، والشّاهدُ والحاكمُ.

فإذا كان أمرُ القرآنِ وموقفُهُ مع الكتبِ قبلَهُ هو أنّهُ الأمينُ عليها، والحاكمُ على ما فيها فلا يمكنُ أن يجريَ عليه تحريفٌ في كلمةٍ، أو زيادةٌ أو نقصٌ؛ لأنّهُ حينئذٍ يحتاجُ إلى

---

(١) المائدة: ٤٤.

(٢) المائدة: ٤٦.

(٣) المائدة: ٤٨.

would mean Allah Most High has appointed an unreliable protector and an untrustworthy judge over His previous Books – Highly exalted is Allah, All-Wise, All-Knowing, above this.Rather, deeming this Noble Qur'an a protector and judge over the previous Books is His testimony to the protection and trustworthiness of this Qur'an, and that He has preserved it from tampering, additions, and deletions.

That is why it is entitled to be an authority over the previous divine Books, a judge over them, and a witness and protector. It affirms the truth they contain, and negates whatever has been distorted thereof and anything false that has been interpolated into them.

Six: Indeed, the Noble Qur'an has been distinguished amongst the other divine Books by its inimitability (*iʿjāz*). All the divine Books are books that invite the slaves to Allah Most High and explain those matters that will ensure their felicity in this world and the Hereafter.

But the Qur'an is a Book that invites to Allah Most High and clarifies, as well as being a inimitable Book of evidence. It is thus a Book of invitation and proof simultaneously. These two aspects – inviting to Allah and explaining that which contains felicity in one's worldly and religious life, and proof through its inimitable nature and its clear evidence – are inseparable. Therefore, its invitation and its explanation are dependent on its inimitable nature and evidence; the latter cannot be separated from the former.

This is why the proof and miracle of the Noble Qur'an are the greatest and most powerful of miracles and proofs. The Qur'an is the greatest miracle whereby Allah Most High testified to the veracity of the Prophethood of our master Muhammad ﷺ and it is the greatest miracle with which Allah Most High aided him. He also kept it as a lasting proof against all the worlds until the Day of Judgement, as has come in *Ṣaḥīḥ al-Bukhārī* and other works on the authority of Abū Hurayrah ؓ that the Prophet ﷺ said, "There is no Prophet amongst the Prophets except that he was given such signs because of which people would believe in him. That which I have been given is Revelation which Allah revealed to me. And I hope to have

أمينٍ عليه، وحكمٍ آخرَ يحكمُ فيه، هذا من وجهٍ.

ومن وجهٍ آخرَ: فإذا جاز على هذا القرآنِ تحريفُ كلمةٍ، وزيادةٌ أو نقصانٌ فيه فإنَّ اللهَ تعالى يكون قد نصبَ على كتبهِ السّماويّةِ السّابقةِ أميناً غيرَ مضمونٍ، وحَكَماً غيرَ مأمونٍ، تعالى اللهُ الحكيمُ العليمُ عن ذلك علوّاً كبيراً.

بل إنَّ في جعلِ اللهِ تعالى هذا القرآنَ الكريمَ أميناً، وحَكَماً على الكتبِ قبلَه شهادةً منه سبحانه بضمانةِ وأمانةِ هذا القرآنِ، وحفظِهِ من التّلاعبِ فيه، والزّيادةِ والنّقصِ.

ولذلك حُقَّ له أن يكونَ مهيمِناً على الكتبِ السّماويّةِ قبلَه، حاكماً عليها، وشاهداً، وأميناً، يُحِقُّ ما فيها من حقٍّ، ويُبطِلُ ما حُرِّفَ منها، وزِيدَ فيها من باطل.

٦- إنَّ هذا القرآنَ الكريمَ قد خصَّهُ اللهُ تعالى من بينِ سائرِ الكتبِ الإلهيّةِ بالإعجازِ، فجميعُ الكتبِ الإلهيّةِ هي كتبُ دعوةِ العبادِ إلى الله تعالى، وبيان ما فيه سعادتُهُم في الدّنيا والآخرةِ.

وأمّا هذا القرآنُ فهو كتابُ دعوةٍ إلى اللهِ تعالى وبيانٍ، وكتابُ إعجازٍ وبرهانٍ، فهو كتابُ دعوةٍ وحُجّةٍ معاً لا ينفكّانِ: دعوةٍ إلى اللهِ تعالى, وبيانِ ما فيه سعادةُ الدنيا والدين، وحجةٍ بإعجازِه وبرهانِه المبينِ، فدعوتُهُ وبيانُهُ قائمان على الإعجازِ والبرهانِ لا ينفكُّ عن الدّعوةِ والبيان.

ولذلك كانت حُجّةُ القرآنِ الكريمِ ومعجزتُهُ هي أكبرُ المعجزاتِ وأقوى الحُجَجِ، هي أكبرُ المعجزاتِ التي شهد اللهُ تعالى بها بصدقِ نبوّةِ سيّدِنا محمدٍ ﷺ، وهي أكبرُ معجزةٍ أيّدهُ اللهُ تعالى بها، وأبقاها حجّةً على العالمينَ كلِّهم إلى يومِ الدين، كما جاء في (صحيح) البخاريّ وغيرِه عن أبي هريرةَ رَضِيَ اللهُ عَنْهُ قال: قالَ النبيُّ ﷺ: «ما مِنَ الأنبياءِ نبيٌّ إلا أُعطيَ من الآياتِ ما مِثلَهُ آمنَ عليه البشرُ، وإنّما كان الذي أوتيتُهُ وحياً أوحاهُ

the most followers amongst them on the Day of Judgement."[1]

The expert scholars say the meaning of this hadith is that the miracles of the Prophets ﷺ came to an end with the end of their respective eras and that only those who were present in their eras witnessed those miracles. As for the miracle of the Qur'an, it is everlasting and continuous until the Day of Judgement, and its phenomenal style, eloquence, and foretelling unseen matters is unending. Hence, no era passes except that some of what the Noble Qur'an said will happen transpires therein. Thus, its being phenomenal in these various aspects proves the validity of its claim, the veracity of the one upon whom it was sent down, and the fact that he is truly the Messenger of Allah ﷺ.

Furthermore, the past miracles were perceptible and could be physically seen, like the camel of Ṣāliḥ ﷺ, the staff of Mūsā ﷺ, and the dead being revived by ʿĪsā ﷺ. The miracle of the Noble Qur'an, however, can be observed by both the physical eye and the intellect. In this way, his followers are greater in number. This is because that which is observed by the physical eye ends with the demise of its observer. On the other hand, that which is observed through the eye of the intellect and the light of cognizance is everlasting and can be observed by everyone who comes after him until the Day of Judgement. It is inimitable Speech and nobody is able to produce anything like it – not even a *sūrah* like it. This is a fact attested to by every person of intellect and prudence.

On this basis, it is not possible to add or delete anything from the Qur'an. This is because that to which something is added cannot be inimitable, and that which has been deleted would disrupt the inimitable nature of the rest with respect to its construction, style, and interconnection. In this manner, it would cease to be inimitable – an impossibility considering that the attribute of being inimitable cannot part from it, as it is Allah Most High Who has made it inimitable. Allah Most High made the Qur'an in Arabic. He Most High said, "Certainly, We have made it a Qur'an in Arabic so

---

(1) *Bukhārī* (7274); *Muslim* (152) with a slight difference.

اللهُ إليَّ، فأرجو أنْ أكونَ أكثرَهم تابعاً يومَ القيامةِ»(١).

قال المحقّقونَ من العلماءِ: المرادُ من هذا الحديثِ أنَّ معجزاتِ الأنبياءِ صلواتُ اللهِ عليهم قد انقرضَتْ بانقراضِ أعصارِهم، فلم يُشاهِدْها إلّا مَن حضرَها، وأمّا معجزةُ القرآنِ فهي باقيةٌ مستمرّةٌ إلى يومِ القيامة، وخَرْقُهُ للعادةِ في أسلوبِهِ وبلاغتِهِ، وفي إخبارِهِ بالمغيَّباتِ مستمرٌّ فلا يمرُّ عصرٌ من الأعصارِ إلّا ويظهرُ فيه شيءٌ ممّا أخبرَ به القرآنُ الكريمُ أنّه سيكون.

فخَرْقُهُ للعادةِ بتلك الوجوهِ المتعدِّدَةِ يدلُّ على صحّةِ دعواهُ، وصِدقِ الذي أُنزِلَ عليه صلواتُ اللهِ وسلامُه عليه، وأنّهُ حقّاً رسولُ اللهِ ﷺ.

كما أنَّ المعجزاتِ الماضيةَ كانت حسيّةً تشاهَدُ بالأبصارِ، كناقةِ صالحٍ، وعصا موسى، وإحياءِ الموتى على يدِ عيسى عليه الصّلاةُ والسّلامُ، وأمّا معجزةُ القرآنِ الكريمِ فإنَّها تُشاهَدُ بالبصرِ والبصيرةِ، فيكون مَن يتّبِعُهُ ﷺ أكثر؛ لأنَّ الذي يُشاهَدُ بعينِ الرَّأسِ ينقرضُ بانقراضِ مُشاهِدِهِ، وأمّا الذي يُشاهَدُ بعينِ البصيرةِ ونورِ العقلِ فهو باقٍ، يُشاهِدُهُ مَن جاء بعدَهُ إلى يومِ الدِّينِ، فإنّهُ كلامٌ مُعجِزٌ لا يَقدِرُ أحدٌ أن يأتيَ بمثلِهِ، ولا بسورةٍ مثلِهِ، يشهدُ بذلك كلُّ ذي عقلٍ ورويّةٍ.

وبناءً على ذلك فلا يمكن أن يُزادَ فيه أو أن يُنقصَ؛ لأنَّ المزيدَ فيه ليس بمعجِزٍ، والنّاقصَ منه يُخِلُّ بإعجاز الباقي بتركيبِهِ، وأسلوبِهِ، ومناسَبَتِهِ، وبذلك يخرجُ عن كونِهِ معجِزاً، وهذا مستحيلٌ؛ لأنَّ صفةَ الإعجاز لا تُفارِقُهُ؛ لأنَّ الإعجازَ هو جَعلُ اللهِ تعالى إيّاهُ معجِزاً، فكما أنّه تعالى جَعَلَ القرآنَ عربياً قال تعالى: {إِنَّا جَعَلْنَاهُ قُرْآنًا عَرَبِيًّا

---

(١) أخرجه البخاري (٧٢٧٤)، ومسلم (١٥٢) باختلاف يسير.

perhaps you will understand."[1] It is impossible to void it of being Arabic. Likewise, He made the Qur'an inimitable; thus, it is impossible to void it of its inimitability. It is totally inconceivable for the Qur'an to ever be imitable, just as it is inconceivable for it to ever be non-Arabic. Moreover, this making (i.e., of the Qur'an) is not in terms of creating, but rather in terms of decreeing (*taqdīr*) – as pointed out by the expert scholars – because the Qur'an is uncreated in both its essence and its attribute.

If it were possible for any addition, deletion, distortion, or change to occur in the Qur'an, this greatest miracle – which Allah Most High has kept until the Day of Judgement as a proof for the Messenger ﷺ against all the creation and as evidence for his veracity – would become unreliable, distrusted, and unprotected. In fact, interpolations would enter it, and falsities and deviances would find their way into it. In that case, what proof and evidence would there remain for him in the Noble Qur'an? Exalted is Allah above that. Thus, all of these various evidences decisively prove that the Noble Qur'an is preserved by Allah Most High from distortion, change, and tampering.

Seven: The Noble Qur'an is the main foundation and central pillar of the Sacred Law of Muhammad ﷺ, which comprises matters of faith, along with practical and verbal rulings. The Prophetic Sunnah – consisting of his statements, actions, and confirmations – explains the matters of faith and rulings of the Sacred Law that are in the Qur'an. He Most High said, "And We have sent down to you [O Prophet] the Reminder, so that you may explain to people what has been revealed for them."[2] The Prophet explained the beliefs contained in the Noble Qur'an and also the rulings – commands, prohibitions, lawful and unlawful matters, and so forth – contained therein. So, if it were possible for any additions, deletions, distortions, or changes to occur in the Qur'an, it would lead to discrepancies and nullities in the Sacred Law of Muhammad ﷺ which

(1) *Al-Zukhruf*, 3.

(2) *Al-Naḥl*, 44.

لَّعَلَّكُمْ تَعْقِلُونَ}[1]، ولا يمكنُ تجريدُهُ عن العربيّة، كذلك جعلَ القرآنَ مُعجزاً، فلا يمكنُ تجريدُهُ عن صفةِ الإعجازِ، فلا يُتصوَّرُ القرآنُ بحالٍ من الأحوالِ غيرَ مُعجزٍ، كما لا يُتصوَّرُ بحالٍ من الأحوالِ غيرَ عربيٍّ، وليس هذا الجَعلُ تخليقياً؛ بل هو جَعلُ التّقديرِ، كما نبَّهَ عليه المحقّقونَ؛ فإنَّ القرآنَ غيرُ مخلوقٍ أصلاً ولا وصفاً.

على أنّهُ لو أمكنَ أن يجريَ على القرآنِ زيادةٌ أو نقصٌ، أو تحريفٌ أو تبديلٌ لكانت هذه المعجزةُ الكبرى التي أبقاها اللهُ تعالى حُجّةً إلى يومِ الدّينِ مصدِّقةً لرسول الله ﷺ على العباد كلِّهم، وبيّنةً على صِدقهِ ﷺ لكانت تلك الحجّةُ غيرَ موثوقةٍ، ولا مضمونةٍ، ولا مَصونةٍ، بل يدخلُها الدَّخيلُ، وتتسرَّبُ إليها الأباطيلُ والأضاليلُ، فأيُّ حُجّةٍ وبينّةٍ له ﷺ باقيةٌ بعدُ حينئذٍ بالقرآنِ الكريمِ؟ تعالى اللهُ عن ذلك.

فهذه الوجوهُ من الأدلّةِ كلِّها تُحتِّمُ وتوجِبُ القطعَ أنَّ القرآنَ الكريمَ محفوظٌ بحفظِ اللهِ تعالى عن التّحريفِ، والتّبديلِ، والتّلاعُبِ.

٧- إنَّ القرآنَ الكريمَ هو الأصلُ الأصيلُ، والرُّكنُ الرَّكينُ في الشّريعةِ المحمّديّةِ المشتملةِ على القضايا الإيمانيّةِ، والأحكامِ العمليّةِ والقوليّةِ على صاحبِها أفضلُ الصّلاةِ والسّلامِ، وقد جاءتِ السُّنّةُ النبويّةُ المحمّديةُ المشتمِلةُ على أقوالِه وأفعالِه ﷺ وتقريراتِه بياناً للقضايا الإيمانيّةِ، والأحكامِ الشرعيّةِ التي جاء بها القرآنُ؛ قال تعالى: {وَأَنزَلْنَا إِلَيْكَ الذِّكْرَ لِتُبَيِّنَ لِلنَّاسِ مَا نُزِّلَ إِلَيْهِمْ وَلَعَلَّهُمْ يَتَفَكَّرُونَ}[2].

وقد بيَّنَ ﷺ ما جاء في القرآنِ الكريمِ من العقائدِ الإيمانيّةِ، وبيَّنَ ما جاء فيه أيضاً من الأحكامِ: الأوامرِ والمَناهي، والحلالِ والحرامِ، إلى ما وراءَ ذلك.

---

(١) الزخرف: ٣.

(٢) النحل: ٤٤.

must be followed and practiced until the Day of Judgement. And if any distortions or changes could occur in the Qur'an, it would lead to making unlawful things lawful, making lawful things unlawful, and discrepancies in the commands and prohibitions of the Noble Qur'an. It would hence cease to be a trusted sacred law that is full of wisdom and by which one must firmly abide until the Day of Judgement - an impossibility in light of the Sacred Law and from a factual and rational perspective.

This is because we see that the Prophet ﷺ ordained and advised to firmly abide by the Book and the Sunnah until the Day of Judgement, and to consider their lawful matters as lawful and their unlawful matters as unlawful - without deeming anything lawful or unlawful based on one's own desires. He ﷺ said, "So, when I am taken away, hold onto the Book of Allah Most High. Consider its lawful things as lawful and its unlawful things as unlawful."[1]

Ṭabarānī narrated with a good chain that Abū Shurayḥ al-Khuzā'ī ‎رضي الله عنه said, "The Messenger of Allah ﷺ came out to us and said, 'Rejoice and give glad tidings. Do you not testify that there is no deity besides Allah and that I am the Messenger of Allah?' They said, 'Of course.' He ﷺ said, 'Indeed, one end of this Qur'an is in Allah's Hand and its other end is in your hands. So, hold firmly to it, for you will never go astray or perish thereafter."[2]

Ṭabarānī narrated with a chain whose narrators are reliable that Abū Ayyūb al-Anṣārī ‎رضي الله عنه, "The Messenger of Allah ﷺ came out to us and said, 'Obey me as long as I am amongst you. And hold firm to the Book of Allah Most High. Consider its lawful things as lawful and its unlawful things as unlawful.'"[3]

Hence, if any distortion, additions, or deletions could occur in the Qur'an, this would result in discrepancies arising in the Sacred Law of the Prophet Muhammad ﷺ which Allah Most High has obliged the slaves to

(1) *Aḥmad* (6606)

(2) Ṭabarānī in *al-Mu'jam al-Kabīr* (2681).

(3) Ṭabarānī in *al-Mu'jam al-Kabīr* (65).

فلو جاز أن يجريَ على القرآنِ الكريمِ تحريفٌ أو تبديلٌ، أو زيادةٌ أو نقصٌ لأدّى ذلك إلى وقوعِ الخَلَلِ والعَبَثِ في الشّرعِ المحمّديّ الواجبِ اتّباعُهُ والعملُ به إلى يوم الدين، ولو جاز أنْ يجريَ على القرآنِ شيءٌ من التّحريفِ والتّبديلِ لأدّى ذلك إلى تحليلِ الحرامِ، وتحريمِ الحلال، والنَّقصِ في الأوامرِ والمناهي التي جاءت في القرآن الكريم، ويخرج حينئذٍ عن كونِهِ شرعاً حكيماً موثوقاً يجبُ التّمسُّكُ به إلى يومِ الدّين، وهذا مُحالٌ شرعاً وواقعاً وعقلاً؛ فإننا نرى أنَّ النبيَّ ﷺ قد أَمرَ وأوصى بالتمسُّكِ بالكتابِ والسُّنّةِ إلى يوم الدين، وأَمَرَ العبادَ بإحلالِ الحلالِ، وتحريمِ الحرامِ فيهما دونَ أن يُحِلّوا أو يُحرِّموا مِن تِلقاءِ أنفسِهم. قال ﷺ: «فإذا ذُهِبَ بي فعليكُم بكتابِ اللهِ تعالى، أَحِلُّوا حلالَهُ، وحَرِّمُوا حرامَه»[1].

وروى الطبرانيُّ بإسنادٍ جيّدٍ عن أبي شُرَيحٍ الخُزاعيّ رضي اللهُ عنه قال: خرج علينا رسولُ الله ﷺ فقال: «أليسَ تشهدون أنْ لا إلهَ إلاّ اللهُ، وأنّي رسولُ الله»؟ قالوا: بلى، قال: «إنَّ هذا القرآنَ طَرَفُهُ بيدِ اللهِ وطَرَفُهُ بأيديكم، فتمسَّكوا به؛ فإنّكُمْ لن تَضِلُّوا ولن تَهلِكُوا بعدَهُ أبداً»[2]. وروى الطبرانيُّ بسندٍ رُواتُهُ ثِقاتٌ عن أبي أيوب الأنصاريّ رضي اللهُ عنه قال: خرجَ علينا رسولُ الله ﷺ فقال: «أطيعوني ما كنتُ بين أَظهُرِكُمْ، وعليكمْ بكتابِ اللهِ أَحِلُّوا حلالَه، وحرِّموا حرامَه»[3]. فلو جاز أن يجريَ على القرآنِ تحريفٌ في كلمةٍ، أو زيادةٌ أو نقصٌ لأدّى ذلك إلى وقوعِ الخللِ في هذه الشّريعةِ المحمّديّةِ التي كلَّفَ اللهُ تعالى العبادَ أنْ يتمسّكوا بها إلى يومِ القيامةِ فلا

---

(١) أخرجه أحمد (٦٦٠٦).

(٢) أخرجه الطبراني في الكبير (٢٦٨١).

(٣) أخرجه الطبراني في الكبير (٦٥).

abide by firmly until the Day of Judgement. Therefore, it is inevitable that the Qur'an and the Sacred Law of Muhammad ﷺ will remain preserved in their entirety until the Day of Judgement – as the Prophet ﷺ said, "I have left you upon [hearts like] clear land whose night and day are the same. Nobody diverges therefrom except one doomed to perish."[(1)] Ibn Abī ʿĀṣim narrated it with a sound chain, and others have also narrated it with various chains.

THE DIVINE COMMAND AND THE PROPHETIC COMMAND TO RECITE THE NOBLE QUR'AN

Allah Most High said, "Say, [O Prophet,] 'I have only been commanded to worship the Lord of this city [of Mecca], Who has made it sacred, and to Him belongs everything. And I am commanded to be one of those who [fully] submit [to Him], and to recite the Qur'an.'"[(2)] He Most High said, "Recite what has been revealed to you of the Book and establish prayer. Indeed, [genuine] prayer should deter [one] from indecency and wickedness. The remembrance of Allah is [an] even greater [deterrent]. And Allah [fully] knows what you [all] do."[(3)] Allah Most High has commanded *tilāwah* of the Noble Qur'an. *Tilāwah* linguistically means to follow. From this is His saying, "By the sun and its brightness, and the moon as it follows it (*talāhā*)."[(4)]

Firstly, there is *tilāwah* through the tongue, which is to recite the words and letters of the Qur'an – and there are hadiths regarding its virtue. Amongst them is the hadith of Tirmidhī and others: "Whoever recites a letter of the Book of Allah receives a reward for it, and the reward is multiplied tenfold."[(5)]

---

(1) *Abū Dāwūd* (4607); *Tirmidhī* (2676); *Ibn Mājah* (42); *Aḥmad* (17144).

(2) *Al-Naml*, 91-92

(3) *Al- 'Ankabūt*, 45.

(4) *Al-Shams*, 1-2.

(5) *Tirmidhī* (2910).

بُدَّ وأنَّ هذا القرآنَ محفوظٌ، وأنَّ الشّريعةَ المحمّديّةَ محفوظةٌ باقيةٌ بتمامِها إلى يومِ الدّين، كما قال ﷺ: «تركتُكُمْ على مثلِ البَيضاءِ ليلُها كنهارِها لا يزيغُ عنها إلّا هالِكٌ»[1] رواهُ ابنُ أبي عاصمٍ في كتابِ (السّنّةِ) بإسنادٍ حسنٍ، ورواهُ غيرُهُ أيضاً بأسانيدَ متعدّدةٍ.

الأمرُ الإلهيُّ ثمّ النّبويُّ بتلاوةِ القرآنِ الكريم

قال الله تعالى: {إِنَّمَا أُمِرْتُ أَنْ أَعْبُدَ رَبَّ هَٰذِهِ الْبَلْدَةِ الَّذِي حَرَّمَهَا وَلَهُ كُلُّ شَيْءٍ ۖ وَأُمِرْتُ أَنْ أَكُونَ مِنَ الْمُسْلِمِينَ وَأَنْ أَتْلُوَ الْقُرْآنَ}[2] الآيةَ.

وقال تعالى: {اتْلُ مَا أُوحِيَ إِلَيْكَ مِنَ الْكِتَابِ وَأَقِمِ الصَّلَاةَ ۖ إِنَّ الصَّلَاةَ تَنْهَىٰ عَنِ الْفَحْشَاءِ وَالْمُنكَرِ ۗ وَلَذِكْرُ اللَّهِ أَكْبَرُ ۗ وَاللَّهُ يَعْلَمُ مَا تَصْنَعُونَ}[3].

فقد أمرَ اللهُ تعالى بتلاوةِ القرآنِ الكريمِ، والتّلاوةُ في أصلِ معناها اللُّغويّ: هي المتابعةُ، ومِن ذلك قولُه تعالى: {وَالشَّمْسِ وَضُحَاهَا (١) وَالْقَمَرِ إِذَا تَلَاهَا}[4] أي: تَبِعَها.

فهنالك تلاوةٌ باللِّسانِ: وهي قراءةُ كلماتِ القرآنِ وحروفِهِ، وقد جاءتِ الأحاديثُ في فضلِها، ومِن ذلك ما جاء في (صحيحِ) التّرمذيِّ وغيرِهِ: «مَن قرأَ حرفاً مِنْ كتابِ اللهِ تعالى فلَهُ به حسنةٌ، والحسنةُ بعشرِ أمثالِها»[5]. الحديثَ كما سيأتي في محلّه.

وهناك تلاوةٌ للقرآنِ بالأعمالِ والأقوالِ: وهي العملُ بمقتضى القرآنِ الكريمِ؛ ائتماراً

---

(١) أخرجه أبو داود (٤٦٠٧)، والترمذي (٢٦٧٦)، وابن ماجه (٤٢)، وأحمد (١٧١٤٤) باختلاف يسير.

(٢) النمل: ٩١-٩٢.

(٣) العنكبوت: ٤٥.

(٤) الشمس: ١-٢.

(٥) أخرجه الترمذي (٢٩١٠).

And then there is *tilāwah* through actions and statements, which is to act in accordance with the Noble Qur'an, fulfil its commands, refrain from its prohibitions, adopt its manners and characteristics, and so forth. Thus, rightful *tilāwah* of the Noble Qur'an encompasses all of this.

As for the Prophetic hadiths which command recitation of the Noble Qur'an, they are many. Amongst them is the hadith Muslim narrated on the authority of Abū Umāmah ﵁ who said he heard the Messenger of Allah ﷺ say, "Recite the Qur'an, as it will come as an intercessor for its reciters on the Day of Judgement."[1]

Abū Dharr ﵁ narrated, "I said, 'O Messenger of Allah, give me advice.' He said, 'Adopt consciousness of Allah (*taqwā*), as it is the essence of all affairs.' I said, 'O Messenger of Allah, advise me further.' He said, 'Hold fast to reciting the Qur'an, as it is a light for you in the Heavens and a provision for you on Earth.'"[2] Ibn Ḥibbān narrated it in his *Ṣaḥīḥ*.

Dārimī narrated with his chain that Ibn Mas'ūd ﵁ said, "Recite the Qur'an frequently before it is lifted." They said, "These *muṣḥafs* will be lifted, but what about that which is in people's hearts?" He said, "It will be taken by night and they will awake in the morning empty of it. They will forget *Lā ilāha ill Allāh* and start reading the sayings and poetry of [pre-Islamic] ignorance. That is when the word will be fulfilled against them."[3]

Ibn Mājah, Ḥākim, and Bayhaqī narrated, "Islam will wear out in the way embroidery on a cloth wears out, until fasting, prayer, pilgrimage, and charity become unknown.

The Book of Allah will be taken one night and not a single verse of it will remain on Earth. There will remain some people – old men and women – who will say, 'We found our forefathers saying this phrase, "*Lā ilāha ill Allāh*", so we also say it.'"[4]

---

(1) *Muslim* (804).

(2) *Ibn Ḥibbān* (361).

(3) *Dārimī* (3207).

(4) *Ibn Mājah* (4049).

بأمره, وانتهاءً عن نهيه، وتأدُّباً بآدابه, وتَخلُّقاً بأخلاقِهِ، إلى ما وراءَ ذلك، فتلاوةُ القرآنِ الكريمِ حقَّ تلاوتِه تشملُ ذلك كلَّه.

وأما الأحاديثُ النبويّةُ التي جاءت في الأمرِ بقراءةِ القرآنِ الكريمِ فهي كثيرةٌ، ومن ذلك ما رواهُ مسلمٌ عن أبي أُمامةَ رَضِيَ اللَّهُ عَنْهُ قال: سمعتُ رسولَ اللهِ صَلَّى اللَّهُ عَلَيْهِ وَسَلَّمَ يقول: «اقرؤوا القرآنَ؛ فإنّهُ يأتي يومَ القيامةِ شفيعاً لأصحابِه«[1]. الحديث.

وعن أبي ذرٍّ رَضِيَ اللَّهُ عَنْهُ أنه قال قلتُ: يا رسولَ اللهِ أوصني! فقال: «عليكَ بتقوى اللهِ فإنَّهُ رأسُ الأمرِ كلِّه». فقلتُ: يا رسول اللهِ زِدْني. قال: «عليك بتلاوةِ القرآنِ فإنَّهُ نورٌ لك في الأرضِ، وذُخرٌ لكَ في السّماءِ» [2]. رواهُ ابنُ حِبّان في (صحيحه).

وروى الدارميُّ بإسنادِهِ عن ابنِ مسعودٍ رضي اللهُ عنه أنّهُ قال: (أكثِروا تلاوةَ القرآنِ قبل أن يُرفَعَ، قالوا: هذه المصاحفُ تُرفَعُ، فكيف بما في صدورِ الرِّجال؟ فقال: يُسرى عليه ليلاً فيصبحونَ منه فقراءَ، وينسَونَ قولَ لا إلهَ إلا الله، ويقعون في قولِ الجاهليّةِ وأشعارِهم، وذلك حينَ يقعُ عليهمُ القولُ) [3].

وروى ابنُ ماجه والحاكمُ والبيهقيُّ: «يُدرَسُ الإسلامُ كما يُدرَسُ وشيُ الثّوبِ، حتّى لا يُدرى صيامٌ ولا صلاةٌ ولا نسكٌ ولا صدقةٌ، ويُسرى على كتابِ اللهِ تعالى في ليلةٍ فلا يبقى في الأرضِ منه آيةٌ، وتبقى طوائفُ من النّاسِ: الشّيخُ الكبيرُ والعجوزُ يقولون: أدركْنا آباءَنا على هذه الكلمةِ: لا إله إلا اللهُ، فنحن نقولُها»[4].

---

(١) أخرجه مسلم (٨٠٤).

(٢) أخرجه ابن حبان (٣٦١).

(٣) أخرجه الدارمي (٣٢٠٧).

(٤) أخرجه ابن ماجه (٤٠٤٩).

THE COMMAND TO KEEP REVISING THE QUR'AN LEST ONE FORGET IT

Bukhārī, Muslim, and Aḥmad narrated on the authority of Abū Mūsā ﷺ that the Prophet ﷺ said, "Keep revising the Qur'an. By the One in Whose Hand lies the soul of Muhammad, it escapes from the hearts of men quicker than camels escape from their tether."[1]

The meaning is that a believer should be particular about revising the Qur'an lest it escape from their memory and they forget it.

Bukhārī and Muslim narrated on the authority of Ibn ʿUmar ﷺ that the Messenger of Allah ﷺ said, "The example of someone who has memorized the Qur'an is like a tethered camel: If he keeps watch over it, he will retain it, but if he sets it free, it will go."[2]

WARNING AGAINST TURNING AWAY FROM THE QUR'AN AND FORGETTING IT

Tirmidhī narrated, and declared authentic, on the authority of Ibn ʿAbbās ﷺ that the Messenger of Allah ﷺ said, "The person who has no portion of the Qur'an in his heart is like a derelict house."[3]

Abū Dāwūd, Tirmidhī, and others narrated on the authority of Anas ﷺ that the Messenger of Allah ﷺ said, "The rewards of my ummah were presented to me – even litter that a person removes from the masjid – and the sins of my ummah were also presented to me. I did not see any sin greater than a *sūrah* or verse of the Qur'an which a person is granted but then forgets."[4]

Abū Dāwūd narrated on the authority of Saʿd ibn ʿUbādah ﷺ that the

(1) *Bukhārī* (5033); *Muslim* (1880).

(2) *Bukhārī* (5031); *Muslim* (790).

(3) *Tirmidhī* (2913).

(4) *Abū Dāwūd* (461); *Tirmidhī* (2916).

الأمرُ بتعاهدِ القرآنِ خوفَ النّسيان

روى الشّيخانِ والإمامُ أحمدُ عن أبي موسى رَضِيَ اللَّهُ عَنْهُ عن النبيّ صَلَّى اللَّهُ عَلَيْهِ وَآلِهِ وَسَلَّمَ قال: «تعاهَدوا هذا القرآنَ، فوالذي نفسُ محمّدٍ بيده لَهُوَ أشدُّ تفلُّتاً - وفي روايةٍ: تفصِّياً - مِنْ قلوبِ الرِّجالِ من الإبلِ مِن عُقُلِها»(١).

والمعنى: أنَّ المؤمنَ ينبغي له أن يُحافِظَ على تلاوةِ القرآن الكريم؛ خشيةَ أن يتفلَّتَ منه وينساه.

وروى الشّيخانِ عن ابنِ عمرَ رَضِيَ اللَّهُ عَنْهُمَا أنَّ رسولَ الله صَلَّى اللَّهُ عَلَيْهِ وَآلِهِ وَسَلَّمَ قال: «إنّما مَثَلُ صاحبِ القرآنِ كمَثَلِ الإبِلِ المُعقَّلَةِ، إنْ عاهدَ عليها أَمسَكَها، وإن أَطلَقَها ذَهَبَتْ»(٢).

التحذيرُ من الإعراضِ عن القرآنِ وتعريضِه للنِّسيان

روى الترمذي وصححهُ عن ابنِ عباسٍ رَضِيَ اللَّهُ عَنْهُمَا قال: قال رسولُ الله صَلَّى اللَّهُ عَلَيْهِ وَآلِهِ وَسَلَّمَ: «إنَّ الَّذي ليسَ في جوفِهِ شيءٌ مِنَ القرآنِ كالبَيتِ الخَرِبِ»(٣).

وروى أبو داودَ والترمذيُّ وغيرُهما عن أنسٍ رَضِيَ اللَّهُ عَنْهُ قال: قال رسولُ الله صَلَّى اللَّهُ عَلَيْهِ وَآلِهِ وَسَلَّمَ: «عُرِضتْ عليَّ أجورُ أمّتي حتّى القَذاةُ يُخرِجُها الرَّجلُ من المسجدِ، وعُرِضَتْ عليَّ ذنوبُ أمّتي فلم أَرَ فيها ذنباً أعظمَ مِنْ سورةٍ من القرآنِ أو آيةٍ أُوتيَها رجلٌ ثم نَسِيَها»(٤). وروى

---

(١) أخرجه البخاري (٥٠٣٣) ومسلم (١٨٨٠).

(٢) أخرجه البخاري (٥٠٣١) ومسلم (٧٩٠).

(٣) أخرجه الترمذي (٢٩١٣).

(٤) أخرجه أبو داود (٤٦١) والترمذي (٢٩١٦).

Messenger of Allah ﷺ said, "There is no person who learns the Qur'an then forgets it except that they will meet Allah on the Day of Judgement with leprosy." Leprosy is an illness with which the flesh disintegrates.

Most scholars opine that forgetting the Qur'an – whether all or part of it – is a major sin, as proven by the severe warning stated in this hadith. However, as Jalāl al-Bulqīnī, Zarkashī, and others stated, it is a major sin when one forgets out of laziness or neglect. If one forgets due to illness, old age or a similar reason, it will not fall under this ruling. This is as stated in the commentary of *al-Adhkār*.

Ḥāfiẓ al-Suyūṭī said in *al-Itqān*, "Forgetting the Qur'an is a major sin. Nawawī stated this in *al-Rawḍah*." He substantiated this through the severe warning in the previous hadiths.

THE MERIT OF RECITING THE NOBLE QUR'AN

Allah Most High said, "Surely those who recite the Book of Allah, establish prayer, and donate from what We have provided for them – secretly and openly – [can] hope for an exchange that will never fail, so that He will reward them in full and increase them out of His grace. He is truly All-Forgiving, Most Appreciative. The Book We have revealed to you [O Prophet] is the truth, confirming what came before it. Surely Allah is All-Aware, All-Seeing of His servants. Then We granted the Book to those We have chosen from Our servants. Some of them wrong themselves, some follow a middle course, and some are foremost in good deeds by Allah's Will. That is [truly] the greatest bounty."(1)

The first of these noble verses is called the verse of the reciters (*āyat al-qurrā'*). Qatādah said that when Muṭarrif 🙵 would recite this verse, he would say, "This is the verse of the reciters." In this verse, Allah Most High has praised the reciters who recite the Book and act upon it; thus, they pray, spend [in charity] and fulfil His commands. Thereafter, He has given

(1) *Al-Fāṭir*, 29-32.

أبو داودَ عن سعدِ بنِ عبادةَ رَضِيَ اللَّهُ عَنْهُ قال: قال رسولُ اللهِ ﷺ: «ما مِن امرئٍ يقرأُ القرآنَ ثمَّ ينساهُ إلّا لَقِيَ اللهَ يومَ القيامةِ أجذمَ»[1].

والأجذمُ: هو المصابُ بداءِ الجُذامِ، وهو داءٌ يتقطَّعُ به اللّحمُ.

وأكثرُ العلماءِ على أنَّ نسيانَ القرآنِ -كلِّه أو بعضِه- يُعتَبَرُ كبيرةً كما يدلُّ عليه الوعيدُ الشديدُ الواردُ في هذا الحديثِ؛ ولكنْ كما قال الجلالُ البُلْقينيُّ والزَّركَشيُّ وغيرُهما: إنَّ ذلك كبيرةٌ إذا كان عن تكاسلٍ أو تهاونٍ، وأمّا إذا كان النِّسيانُ بسببِ مرضٍ، أو كبرِ سِنٍّ، أو نحوِ ذلك فلا يدخلُ تحت هذا الحُكمِ. اهـ. كما في (شرحِ الأذكارِ).

وقال الحافظُ السّيوطيُّ في (الإتقانِ): نسيانُ القرآنِ كبيرةٌ، صرَّحَ به النّوويُّ في (الرَّوضةِ). اهـ. واستدلَّ على ذلك بما وردَ من الوعيدِ الشديدِ في الأحاديثِ السابقةِ.

فضل تلاوة القرآن الكريم

قال اللهُ تعالى: {إِنَّ الَّذِينَ يَتْلُونَ كِتَابَ اللَّهِ وَأَقَامُوا الصَّلَاةَ وَأَنفَقُوا مِمَّا رَزَقْنَاهُمْ سِرًّا وَعَلَانِيَةً يَرْجُونَ تِجَارَةً لَّن تَبُورَ (٢٩) لِيُوَفِّيَهُمْ أُجُورَهُمْ وَيَزِيدَهُم مِّن فَضْلِهِ ۚ إِنَّهُ غَفُورٌ شَكُورٌ وَالَّذِي أَوْحَيْنَا إِلَيْكَ مِنَ الْكِتَابِ هُوَ الْحَقُّ مُصَدِّقًا لِّمَا بَيْنَ يَدَيْهِ ۗ إِنَّ اللَّهَ بِعِبَادِهِ لَخَبِيرٌ بَصِيرٌ (٣١) ثُمَّ أَوْرَثْنَا الْكِتَابَ الَّذِينَ اصْطَفَيْنَا مِنْ عِبَادِنَا ۖ فَمِنْهُمْ ظَالِمٌ لِّنَفْسِهِ وَمِنْهُم مُّقْتَصِدٌ وَمِنْهُمْ سَابِقٌ بِالْخَيْرَاتِ بِإِذْنِ اللَّهِ ۚ ذَٰلِكَ هُوَ الْفَضْلُ الْكَبِيرُ}[2].

الآيةُ الأولى من هذه الآياتِ الكريمةِ تُسمّى آيةَ القُرّاءِ، كما قال قتادةُ: كان مُطرِّفٌ رحمه اللهُ تعالى إذا قرأ هذه الآيةَ يقول: هذه آيةُ القُرّاءِ؛ فقد أثنى اللهُ تعالى في تلك الآيةِ

---

(١) أخرجه أبو داود (١٤٧٦).

(٢) فاطر: ٢٩-٣٢.

them glad tidings of the immense reward and everlasting bliss He has promised them. He Most Glorified said, "…so that He will reward them in full," i.e., their reward in exchange for their actions. However, this is not their only reward, but rather there is further grace from Allah Most High: He shall grant them more and increase them from Himself. Moreover, the amount and measure of this extra grace is only known to Allah, the Lord of great bounty. The greatest grace that He shall bestow upon them – and it is the greatest increase in their reward and honour – is that He shall remove the veil from them so that they can see Him. This is as Muslim and others have narrated on the authority of Ṣuhayb ﷺ that the Messenger of Allah ﷺ said, "When the people of Paradise will enter Paradise, Allah Most High will say to them, 'Do you want me to grant you anything more?' They will say, 'Our Lord, have You not brightened our faces? Have You not entered us into Paradise? Have you not saved us from Hellfire?' The veil will then be removed. They will not be granted anything more beloved to them than seeing their Lord Most Blessed and High." Thereafter He read the verse, "Those who do good will have the finest reward and [even] more"(1) until the end of the verse.(2)

Thereafter, He Most Glorified mentioned the virtue of this mighty Book and the virtue of the one upon whom it was revealed. That is because this Qur'an is the truth which confirms the previous divine Books revealed to the Messengers – blessings be upon them and upon our Prophet. Also, He Most High is All-Aware and All-Seeing of His slaves. Hence, He knows which heart amongst the hearts of the Messengers is prepared to receive the Revelation of this Qur'an. Indeed, it is the heart of the most honoured Master ﷺ, whom Allah prepared and supported.

He Most High said, "The Trustworthy Spirit (Jibrīl) brought it down into your heart [O Prophet] – so that you may be one of the warners."

Thereafter, Allah Most High praised this ummah of Muhammad – may

---

(1) *Yūnus*, 26.

(2) *Muslim* (181).

الكريمةِ على القُرَّاءِ الذين يتلونَ الكتابَ ويعملون به، فيُصلُّونَ وينفقونَ، ويقومونَ بأوامرِهِ سبحانه، ثمَّ بشَّرهم بما وعدهم من الثّوابِ العظيمِ، والنّعيمِ المُقيمِ فقال سبحانه: {لِيُوَفِّيَهُمْ أُجُورَهُمْ}، أي: أجورَهم في مقابِلِ أعمالِهم؛ فإنَّ الأجرَ هو ما كان مقابَلًا بعملٍ، ولكنْ ليس هذا ثوابَهم فحسبُ، بل هناك الفضلُ من اللهِ تعالى بالزّيادة، ويزيدُهم بها مِنْ لَدُنْهُ، وهذه الزّيادةُ من فضلِهِ لا يَعلَمُ قَدرَها ومِقدارَها إلا اللهُ ذو الفضلِ العظيمِ، وأعظمُ الفضلِ الذي تفضَّلَ به عليهم -وهو أعظمُ الزّياداتِ في ثوابِهم وتكريمِهم- أنْ يَكشِفَ لهمُ الحجابَ حتى ينظروا إليه سبحانه، كما روى مسلمٌ وغيرُهُ عن صُهَيبٍ رضي الله عنه قال: قال رسول الله صلى الله عليه وآله وسلم: «إذا دخلَ أهلُ الجنّةِ الجنّةَ يقولُ اللهُ تعالى: أتريدونَ شيئاً أَزيدُكم؟ فيقولون: يا ربَّنا ألم تُبَيِّضْ وجوهَنا؟ ألم تُدخِلْنا الجنّةَ؟ ألم تُنجِنا منَ النّارِ؟ قال: فيُكشَفُ الحجابُ، فما أُعطوا شيئاً أحبَّ إليهم من النّظرِ إلى ربِّهم تبارك وتعالى»، ثمَّ قرأَ قولَ اللهِ تعالى: {لِّلَّذِينَ أَحْسَنُوا الْحُسْنَىٰ وَزِيَادَةٌ}(1) الآيةَ (2). اللّهمَّ اجعلنا منهم.

ثم ذكرَ سبحانه فضلَ هذا الكتاب العزيزِ، وفضلَ الذي أُنزِلَ عليه؛ وذلك أنَّ هذا القرآنَ هو الحقُّ مُصدِّقاً لِمَا سبَقَهُ من الكُتُبِ الإلهيّةِ النّازلةِ على الرُّسلِ صلواتُ اللهِ تعالى على نبيِّنا وعليهم، وأنّهُ تعالى بعبادِه خبيرٌ بصيرٌ، فهو يعلمُ القلبَ المستعِدَّ لنزولِ هذا القرآنِ عليه من بين قلوبِ الرُّسلِ، ألا وهو قلبُ السّيدِ الأكرمِ صلى الله عليه وآله وسلم، الذي أعدَّهُ اللهُ تعالى وأمدَّهُ.

قال تعالى: {نَزَلَ بِهِ الرُّوحُ الْأَمِينُ (١٩٣) عَلَىٰ قَلْبِكَ لِتَكُونَ مِنَ الْمُنذِرِينَ}(3).

---

(١) يونس: ٢٦.

(٢) أخرجه مسلم (١٨١).

(٣) الشعراء: ١٩٣-١٩٤.

the choicest blessings and peace be upon him – as being chosen amongst all other nations to inherit this mighty Book. And it behoves the best ummah to inherit the best Book from the best Messenger, who is the Imam of all the Prophets and Messengers – may Allah's blessings and peace upon him and all of them.

Then, with respect to holding onto the Book and firmly adhering to it, He Most Glorified categorized them into three groups.

He Most High said, "Some of them wrong themselves." They are those who leave a decisive command or commit a prohibited act that is unlawful. These are those who have mixed good actions with bad actions, as stated by the Predecessors.

Thereafter, He Most High said, "Some follow a middle course." They are those who fulfil the necessary actions, i.e., between them and their Creator, and also between them and the creation. Likewise are those who leave forbidden actions. These people are referred to as the People of the Right (*Aṣḥāb al-Yamīn*). They are also referred to as the Righteous (*Abrār*) when comparing them to the Nearest (*Muqarrabūn*).

He Most High then says, "And some are foremost in good deeds (*khayrāt*) by Allah's Will. That is [truly] the greatest bounty." They are those who fulfilled all the commands, refrained from all prohibitions, and were foremost in doing good deeds, i.e., additional (*nafl*) actions above and beyond obligatory actions. The good deeds in this noble verse are those to which the Prophet ﷺ indicated when replying to the question of Muʿādh ؓ, "Inform me of an action that will enter me into Paradise and distance me from Hellfire." He ﷺ replied, "You have asked regarding a great matter, but it is easy for the one for whom Allah makes it easy. Worship Allah and do not associate any partner with him, establish prayer, fast Ramadan, and perform Hajj of the House." He ﷺ then said, "Shall I not point to you the doors of goodness?" This refers to the additional actions which if you perform, the doors of divine goodness will be opened for you.

Thus, those who are foremost in good actions draw near to Allah Most High through additional actions, attaining a lofty rank in divine nearness. He Most High said, "And the foremost [in faith] will be the foremost [in

ثم أثنى اللهُ تعالى على هذه الأمّةِ المحمّديّةِ على رسولِها أفضلُ الصلاة والسلام بأنّها المُصطَفاةُ من بين الأممِ المخصوصةِ بوِراثةِ هذا الكتابِ العزيز، وحُقَّ لأفضلِ أمّةٍ أن ترثَ أفضلَ كتابٍ عن أفضلِ رسولٍ ﷺ، الذي هو إمامُ الأنبياءِ والمرسَلينَ صلواتُ اللهِ تعالى وسلامُهُ عليه وعليهم أجمعين.

ثم صنَّفهم سبحانه إلى ثلاثةِ أصنافٍ بالنّسبةِ لأخذِهِمْ بالكتابِ وتمسُّكِهِم به فقال تعالى: {فَمِنْهُمْ ظَالِمٌ لِّنَفْسِهِۦ}، وهو: التّاركُ لأمرٍ مُحتَّمٍ، أو فاعلٌ لمنهيٍّ عنه مُحرَّمٍ، وهؤلاءِ المُخلِّطونَ الذين خَلَطوا عملاً صالحاً وآخرَ سيئاً، كما قالَه السَّلفُ.

ثم قال تعالى: {وَمِنْهُم مُّقْتَصِدٌ}، وهو: المُؤدِّي للواجباتِ، أي: ما بينَهُ وبينَ الخالقِ سبحانه، والواجباتِ ما بينه وبين المخلوقاتِ، والتّاركُ للمُحرَّماتِ كذلك، ويقال لهؤلاءِ: أصحابُ اليمين، ويُقال لهمُ: الأبرارُ عند مقابلتِهِمْ بالمُقرّبين.

ثمَّ قال تعالى: {وَمِنْهُمْ سَابِقٌۢ بِالْخَيْرَٰتِ بِإِذْنِ اللَّهِ ۚ ذَٰلِكَ هُوَ الْفَضْلُ الْكَبِيرُ}، وهؤلاءِ همُ الذين قاموا بجميعِ الأوامرِ، وتركوا جميعَ المناهي، وسبَقوا بفعلِ الخيراتِ وهي النّوافلُ فوقَ الفرائضِ وهذه «الخيرات» في الآيةِ الكريمةِ هي التي أشار إليها النّبيُّ ﷺ في جوابِهِ لمعاذٍ رَضِيَ اللَّهُ عَنْهُ حين قال: أخبِرني بعملٍ يُدخلني الجنّةَ، ويباعُدُني من النار، فقال له ﷺ: »لقد سألتَ عن عظيمٍ، وإنّه لَيسيرٌ على مَن يسّرهُ اللهُ عليه: تعبدُ اللهَ ولا تشركُ به شيئاً، وتقيمُ الصّلاةَ، وتُؤتي الزّكاةَ، وتصومُ رمضانَ، وتحجُّ البيتَ، ثمّ قال له ﷺ: «ألا أَدُلُّكَ على أبوابِ الخيرِ» [1]، أي: فعلِ الخيراتِ، وهي النّوافلُ التي إذا فعلتَها فُتِحتْ لك أبوابُ الخيرِ الإلهيّ.

فراح هؤلاءِ السّابقونَ بالخيراتِ يتقرّبونَ إلى اللهِ تعالى بالنّوافلِ، فنالوا مقاماً

---

(١) رواه الترمذي (١٦١٦).

Paradise]. They are the ones nearest [to Allah]."[1] The divine (*qudsī*) hadith states, "My slave continues to draw near to Me through additional actions until I love him."[2]

This is not the place to discuss the difference between these three categories in detail. Rather, you will find it in our book *Drawing Near to Allah Most High*[3].

(1) *Al-Wāqi'ah*, 10-11.

(2) *Bukhārī* (6502).

(3) This work has also been translated by Imam Ghazali Publishing.

عالياً في القُربِ؛ قال تعالى: {وَالسَّابِقُونَ السَّابِقُونَ (١٠) أُولَٰئِكَ الْمُقَرَّبُونَ}[١]. وفي الحديثِ القُدسيِّ: «ما يزالُ عبدي يتقرَّبُ إليَّ بالنّوافلِ حتّى أحبَّه»[٢]. الحديثَ كما في البخاريّ.

وتفصيلُ الكلامِ على الفرقِ بين الأصنافِ الثلاثةِ ليس هنا موضعُهُ، بل تجدُهُ في كتابِنا (التقرُّبُ إلى اللهِ تعالى).

---

(١) الواقعة: ١٠-١١.

(٢) رواه البخاري (٦٥٠٢).

REGULARLY COMPLETING ONE RECITAL AFTER THE OTHER IS THE MOST BELOVED ACTION TO ALLAH MOST HIGH

Tirmidhī narrated on the authority of Ibn ʿAbbās ﷺ that a man asked, "O Messenger of Allah, which action is most beloved to Allah Most High?" He said, "The one who reads from the beginning of the Qur'an until the end; whenever he dismounts, he proceeds."(1)

This means that they begin a new recital every time they complete one. This is why the scholars of the Qur'an have desirable for one completing the Qur'an to follow it with reciting *Sūrah al-Fātiḥah* and the beginning of *Sūrah al-Baqarah* until His saying, "And it is they who will be successful."(2) This is to realize his saying, "Whenever he dismounts, he proceeds."

This noble hadith contains clear guidelines for a person wanting to traverse the path of drawing near to the King of all kings, and that is for them to complete consecutive recitals [of the Qur'an].

This is dismounting and proceeding, and it results in attaining divine nearness and connection. This form of traversing is the quickest and safest,

(1) *Tirmidhī* (2948).

(2) *Al-Baqarah*, 5.

المواظبةُ على متابعةِ الخَتَماتِ
أحبُّ الأعمالِ إلى اللهِ تعالى

روى الترمذيُّ وغيرُه عن ابنِ عبّاسٍ رَضِيَ اللهُ عَنْهُمَا قال: قال رجلٌ: يا رسولَ اللهِ أيُّ الأعمالِ أحبُّ إلى اللهِ تعالى؟ قال: «الذي يضربُ - أي: يبدأُ - مِن أوَّلِ القرآنِ إلى آخرِه، كلَّما حَلَّ ارتحلَ»(1).

والمعنى: أنّهُ كلَّما ختمَ ختمةً شَرَعَ في غيرِها، ولذلك استحسَنَ علماءُ القرآنِ لِمَن يختِمُ الختمةَ أنْ يتبعَها بفاتحةِ الكتابِ وبفاتحةِ سورةِ البقرة إلى قولِهِ تعالى: {وَأُولَٰئِكَ هُمُ الْمُفْلِحُونَ}(2)؛ تحقيقاً لقولِهِ صَلَّى اللهُ عَلَيْهِ وَسَلَّمَ: «كلَّما حَلَّ ارتحلَ». وفي هذا الحديثِ الشّريفِ دليلٌ واضحٌ لِمَن يريدُ السَّيرَ والسُّلوكَ تقرُّباً إلى ملكِ الملوكِ، وذلك بأنْ يُتابِعَ تلاوةَ الختَماتِ؛ فإنَّ فيها حَلّاً وارتحالاً، ويُنتِجُ ذلك قرباً واتِّصالاً؛ لأنَّ هذا السَّيرَ هو السَّيرُ

---

(1) أخرجه الترمذي (٢٩٤٨).

(2) البقرة: ٥.

and there is no quicker way, as indicated by our master the Messenger of Allah ﷺ in this hadith.

RECITATION OF THE NOBLE QUR'AN IS THE BEST ACT OF WORSHIP

Bayhaqī narrated on the authority of Nuʿmān ibn Bashīr that the Prophet ﷺ said, "The best act of worship for my ummah is reciting the Qur'an."(1) Sijzī narrated in *al-Ibānah* from Anas , as a hadith attributed to the Prophet ﷺ, "The best act of worship is to recite the Qur'an."(2) Daylamī narrated on the authority of Abū Hurayrah that the Messenger ﷺ said, "The greatest of worshippers are those who recite the Qur'an the most."(3) In a narration of Marhabī from Yaḥyā ibn Abī Kathīr as a *mursal* narration, "The greatest of people in worship those who recite the Qur'an the most, and the greatest act of worship is supplication (*du ʿā*)."

THE RECITER IS REWARDED WITH ONE REWARD FOR EVERY LETTER AND THE REWARD IS MULTIPLIED TENFOLD – BE IT WITH OR WITHOUT UNDERSTANDING

Tirmidhī and others narrated that Ibn Masʿūd said he heard the Messenger of Allah ﷺ say, "Whoever recites a letter of the Book of Allah receives a reward for it, and the reward is multiplied tenfold. I am not saying *Alif Lām Mīm* is one letter, but rather *Alif* is one letter, *Lām* is one letter and *Mīm* is one letter."(4) This hadith proves that whoever recites the Qur'an – even without understanding it – will receive multiplied reward,

(1) Al-Quḍāʿī in *Musnad al-Shihāb* (1284); Bayhaqī in *Shu ʿab al-Īmān* (2022).

(2) Al-Muttaqī al-Hindī in *Kanz al- ʿUmmāl* (2356).

(3) Al-Muttaqī al-Hindī in *Kanz al- ʿUmmāl* (2260).

(4) *Tirmidhī* (2910).

السّريعُ المنيعُ، ولا أسرعَ منهُ كما أرشدنا إليه سيّدُنا رسولُ الله ﷺ في هذا الحديث.

تلاوةُ القرآنِ الكريمِ أفضلُ العبادات

روى البيهقيُّ عن النُّعمانِ بنِ بَشيرٍ رضي الله عنه عن النبيِّ ﷺ أنّه قال: «أفضلُ عبادةِ أُمَّتي تلاوةُ القرآنِ»[1]. وروى السِّجزيُّ في (الإبانةِ) عن أنسٍ رضي الله عنه مرفوعاً: «أفضلُ العبادةِ قراءةُ القرآنِ»[2]. وروى الدَّيلَميُّ عن أبي هريرةَ رضي الله عنه عن النبيِّ صلى الله عليه وآله وسلم قال: «أعبَدُ النّاسِ أكثرُهُمْ تلاوةً للقرآنِ»[3]. وفي روايةِ المرهبيِّ عن يحي بنِ أبي كثيرٍ مُرسَلاً: (أعبَدُ النّاسِ أكثرُهم تلاوةً للقرآن، وأفضلُ العبادةِ الدُّعاءُ).

يُؤجَرُ القارئُ بكلِّ حرفٍ حسنةً
والحسنةُ بعشرِ أمثالِها بفَهمٍ أو بغيرِ فَهمٍ

وروى الترمذيُّ وغيرُه عن ابنِ مسعودٍ رضي الله عنه قال: سمعتُ رسولَ الله ﷺ يقول: «مَن قرأَ حرفاً من كتابِ اللهِ تعالى فله بهِ حسنةٌ، والحسنةُ بعشرِ أمثالِها، لا أقولُ: الم حرفٌ، ولكن ألفٌ حرفٌ، ولامٌ حرفٌ، وميمٌ حرفٌ»[4].

---

(١) أخرجه القضاعي في (مسند الشهاب) (١٢٨٤)، والبيهقي في (شعب الإيمان) (٢٠٢٢) باختلاف يسير.

(٢) أخرجه المتقي الهندي في (كنز العمال) (٢٣٥٦).

(٣) أخرجه المتقي الهندي في (كنز العمال) (٢٢٦٠).

(٤) أخرجه الترمذي (٢٩١٠).

because most people who recite *Alif Lām Mīm* do not understand its meaning.

Imam Nawawī ﵀ said, "Know that the correct, chosen stance adopted by reliable scholars is that the recitation of the Qur'an is more virtuous than *tasbīḥ* (declaring Allah's purity by saying *Subḥān Allāh*), *taḥmīd* (praising Allah by saying *Al-ḥamd lillāh*), *tahlīl* (declaring Allah's Oneness by saying *Lā ilāha ill Allāh*), and other forms of remembrance." ʿAbdullāh (i.e., the author) says that the proof for this is the hadith of Tirmidhī from Anas ﵁ that the Prophet ﷺ said, "The merit of Allah's Speech over all other speech is like the merit of Allah over His creation."[1]

THE PEOPLE OF THE QUR'AN ARE ALLAH'S PEOPLE AND HIS CHOSEN ONES

Nasāʾī, Ibn Mājah, and Ḥākim narrated with a sound chain from Anas ﵁ that the Messenger of Allah said, "Indeed, Allah has His own people amongst mankind." They asked, "Who are they, O Messenger of Allah?" He [The Messenger] ﷺ said, "The people of the Qur'an. They are the people of Allah and His chosen ones."[2]

Thus, whoever wants to be from the people of Allah should hold fast to the Qur'an, for it is a path which truly takes one to Allah Most High, as attested to by the Messenger of Allah ﷺ. O Allah make us amongst the people of the Qur'an. *Āmīn.*

THE PROFICIENT RECITER OF THE QUR'AN WILL BE WITH THE HONOURABLE AND VIRTUOUS ANGEL-SCRIBES

Bukhārī and Muslim narrated on the authority of ʿĀ'ishah ﵂ that the

(1) *Tirmidhī* (2910).

(2) *Tirmidhī* (2926).

وفي هذا الحديثِ دليلٌ على أنَّ مَن قرأَ القرآنَ ولو بغيرِ فهمٍ فله ذلك الأجرُ المضاعَفُ؛ لأنَّ أكثرَ النّاسِ يقرأونَ {الم} ولا يعرفونَ معناها.

قال الإمامُ النوويُّ رَضِيَ اللهُ عَنْهُ: اعلم أنَّ المذهَبَ المختارَ الصّحيحَ الذي عليه مَن يُعتمَدُ من العلماءِ أنَّ قراءةَ القرآنِ أفضلُ من التّسبيحِ والتّهليلِ وغيرِهما من الأذكار. اهـ.

قال عبدُ الله: والدّليلُ على ذلك ما جاء في حديثِ الترمذيِّ عن أنسٍ رَضِيَ اللهُ عَنْهُ أنَّ النبيَّ صَلَّى اللهُ عَلَيْهِ وَآلِهِ وَسَلَّمَ قال: «وإنَّ فَضْلَ كلامِ اللهِ على سائرِ الكلامِ كفَضْلِ اللهِ على خَلقِهِ»(1).

أهلُ القرآنِ هم أهلُ اللهِ تعالى وخاصَّتُه

روى النَّسائيُّ وابنُ ماجه والحاكمُ بإسنادٍ حسنٍ عن أنسٍ رضي الله عنه قال: قال رسولُ الله صلى الله عليه وآله وسلم: «إنَّ للهِ أَهْلِينَ مِن النّاسِ، قالوا: مَن هم يا رسولَ الله؟ فقال صلى الله عليه وآله وسلم: «أهلُ القرآنِ هم أهلُ اللهِ وخاصَّتُه»(2).

أي: فمَن أراد أن يكونَ من أهلِ اللهِ فعليه بالقرآنِ، فهو طريقٌ موصِلٌ إلى اللهِ تعالى حقّاً، كما شَهِدَ بذلك رسولُ الله صَلَّى اللهُ عَلَيْهِ وَآلِهِ وَسَلَّمَ. اللّهمَّ اجعلنا من أهلِ القرآنِ. آمين.

الماهِرُ بالقرآنِ مع السَّفَرَةِ الكرامِ البَرَرَةِ

روى الشّيخانِ عن عائشةَ رَضِيَ اللهُ عَنْهَا قالت: قال رسولُ الله صَلَّى اللهُ عَلَيْهِ وَآلِهِ وَسَلَّمَ: «الماهرُ بالقرآنِ مع

---

(1) أخرجه الترمذي (٢٩٢٦).

(2) أخرجه الحاكم (١/ ٧٣٨) وابن ماجه (٢١٥).

Messenger of Allah ﷺ said, "The proficient reciter of the Qur'an will be with the honourable and virtuous Angel-scribes (*safarah*). As for the one who recites the Qur'an and struggles therein, finding it difficult, will have two rewards."(1) There is a difference of opinion regarding the meaning of *safarah*. Some scholars said it means the scribes amongst the noble Angels, because a scribe makes clear (*yusfiru*). Thus, a scribe is *sifr* and the plural is *safarah*. Others said the scribes are the Angels who carry the Preserved Tablet. Allah Most High said, "By the hands of Angel-scribes, honourable and virtuous."(2) They are called this because they copy the divinely-revealed Books to the Prophets; thus, they are like scribes. Others said the *safarah* are the Nearest Angels.

THE RECITER OF THE QUR'AN SPEAKS TO THEIR LORD AND SECRETLY CONVERSES WITH HIM

Anas ﷺ narrated that the Prophet ﷺ said, "If one of you wants to speaks to their Lord, they should recite the Qur'an."(3) *Sūrah al-Fātiḥah* is called the Chapter of Secret Conversation (*Munājāh*), as will come later, if Allah wills. ʿAllāmah al-Munāwī ﷺ said, "This (i.e., the reciter speaking to their Lord) is an implicit metaphor (*istiʿārah bi al-kināyah*). This is because the Noble Qur'an is a message from Allah Most High to His slaves. Hence, it is as though the reciter is saying, 'O my Lord, You have said such-and-such.' Thus, they are secretly conversing with Allah Most High."

WHOEVER LOVES THE QUR'AN, ALLAH AND HIS MESSENGER صَلَّىٰ ٱللَّٰهُ عَلَيْهِ وَعَلَىٰ آلِهِ وَسَلَّمَ LOVE THEM

Ṭabarānī narrated with a chain whose narrators are reliable from, Ibn Masʿūd ﷺ that the Messenger of Allah ﷺ said, "Whoever loves that they

---

(1) *Bukhārī* (4653); *Muslim* (798).

(2) *ʿAbasa*, 15-16.

(3) Al-Muttaqī al-Hindī in *Kanz al-ʿUmmāl* (2254).

السَّفَرَةِ الكرامِ البَرَرَةِ، والّذي يقرأُ القرآنَ ويُتَعْتِعُ فيه وهو عليه شاقٌّ له أجران»[1].

وقد اختُلِفَ في المراد «بالسَّفَرَةِ» هنا: فقال بعضُ العلماء: هُمُ الكَتَبَةُ من الملائكةِ الكرامِ؛ لأنَّ الكتابَ يُسفِرُ، أي: يُبَيِّنُ ما يُكتَبُ، فالكتابُ سِفرٌ، وهم سَفَرَةٌ.

وقال بعضُهم: السَّفرةُ همُ الملائكةُ الذين هم حَمَلةُ اللَّوحِ المحفوظِ، قال تعالى: {بِأَيْدِي سَفَرَةٍ (١٥) كِرَامٍ بَرَرَةٍ}[2]، وسُمُّوا بذلك: لأنَّهم يَنقلونَ الكُتُبَ الإلهيّةَ المُنزَّلةَ إلى الأنبياءِ، فكأنَّهم سَفَرَة. وقال بعضُهم: السَّفرةُ هم المقرَّبونَ من الملائكة.

قارئُ القرآنِ يُحَدِّثُ ربَّه تعالى ويُناجِيه

عن أنسٍ رَضِيَ اللهُ عَنهُ أنَّ النبيَّ صَلَّى اللهُ عَلَيهِ وَآلِهِ وَسَلَّمَ قال: «إذا أَحَبَّ أحدُكُمْ أنْ يُحَدِّثَ ربَّهُ فلْيقرَأِ القرآنَ»[3]. وتُسمَّى سورةُ الفاتحةِ سورةَ المناجاةِ، كما سيأتي إن شاء اللهُ تعالى. قال العلاّمةُ المناويُّ رحمه اللهُ تعالى: وهذا -أي معنى أنَّ القارئَ يُحَدِّثُ ربَّهُ- من بابِ الاستعارةِ بالكِناية؛ فإنَّ القرآنَ الكريمَ هو رسالةٌ من اللهِ تعالى لعبادِهِ، فكأنَّ القارئَ يقول: يا ربِّ قلتَ: كذا وكذا، فهو مناجٍ لله تعالى.

مَن أحبَّ القرآنَ فقد أحبَّهُ اللهُ ورسولُه صلى الله عليه وسلم

روى الطبرانيُّ بسندٍ رجالُهُ ثِقاتٌ عن ابنِ مسعودٍ رضي اللهُ عنه قال: قال رسولُ الله صلى الله عليه وآله وسلم: «مَن أحبَّ أنْ يُحِبَّهُ اللهُ ورسولُهُ فلْينظرْ،

---

(١) أخرجه البخاري (٤٦٥٣) ومسلم (٧٩٨).

(٢) عبس: ١٥-١٦.

(٣) أخرجه المتقي الهندي في (كنز العمال) (٤٢٢٥).

should be loved by Allah and His Messenger should think: If they love the Qur'an, then they love Allah and His Messenger ﷺ."[1]

THE QUR'AN IS THE BANQUET OF ALLAH MOST HIGH; WHOEVER ENTERS IT IS SAFE

Dārimī narrated with his chain from Ibn Mas'ūd ﷺ that the Prophet ﷺ said, "Recite the Qur'an, for Allah does not punish the heart that has memorized the Qur'an. Indeed, this Qur'an is the banquet of Allah Most High; whoever enters it is safe, and whoever loves the Qur'an should rejoice."[2]

Ḥākim narrated and authenticated, and Dārimī also narrated on the authority of Ibn Mas'ūd ﷺ that the Prophet ﷺ said, "Indeed, this Qur'an is the banquet of Allah Most High, so accept His banquet as much as you can. Indeed, this Qur'an is the rope of Allah, the clear light, the beneficial cure, a protection for whoever holds firm to it, and a saviour for whoever follows it. It does not deviate for it to be reprimanded and it is not crooked for it to be straightened. Its wonders never cease and it does not wear out due to frequent repetition. Recite it, for Allah will reward you upon reciting each letter with ten rewards. I am not saying *Alif Lām Mīm* is one letter, but rather *Alif* is one letter, *Lām* is one letter, and *Mīm* is one letter."[3]

THE HOUSE IN WHICH THE QUR'AN IS RECITED IS ATTENDED BY THE ANGELS AND BECOMES EXPANSIVE FOR ITS OCCUPANTS

Imam Muhammad ibn Naṣr al-Marwazī narrated with his chain from Anas ﷺ as a hadith attributed to the Prophet ﷺ, "The house in which the

(1) *Majma' al-Zawā'id* of al-Haythamī, vol. 7, p. 168.

(2) *Dārimī* (3319).

(3) *Dārimī* (3315).

فإنْ كان يحبُّ القرآنَ فهو يُحِبُّ اللّٰهَ ورسولَهَ صلى الله عليه وسلم»[1].

القرآنُ مأْدُبَةُ اللهِ تعالى فمَن دخلَه فهو آمنٌ

روى الدارِميُّ بإسنادِهِ عن ابنِ مسعودٍ رضي اللّٰهُ عنه أنَّ النبيَّ ﷺ قال: «اقرؤوا القرآنَ؛ فإنَّ اللّٰهَ لا يعذِّبُ قلباً وعى القرآنَ، إنَّ هذا القرآنَ مأدُبَةُ اللهِ تعالى فمَن دخلَ فيه فهو آمِنٌ، ومَن أحبَّ القرآنَ فليُبشِرْ» [2]. أي: فليَستبشِر. وروى الحاكمُ وصحَّحهُ والدّارِميُّ أيضاً عن ابنِ مسعودٍ رَضِيَ اللهُ عَنْهُ عن النَّبيِّ ﷺ قال: «إنَّ هذا القرآنَ مأدُبةُ اللهِ تعالى فاقبَلوا مأدُبَتَهُ ما استطعتم، إنَّ هذا القرآنَ حبلُ اللّٰهِ، والنّورُ المبينُ، والشّفاءُ النّافعُ، عصمةٌ لِمَنْ تمسَّكَ به، ونجاةٌ لِمَنِ اتَّبعَه، ولا يَزِيغُ فيُستَعتَبُ، ولا يَعْوجُ فيقوَّمُ، ولا تنقضي عجائبُهُ، ولا يَخلَقُ على كثرةِ الرَّدِّ، اتلوه فإنَّ اللّٰهَ يأجُرُكم على تلاوتِهِ كلَّ حرفٍ عشرَ حسناتٍ، إنِّي لا أقولُ: {الم} حرفٌ، ولكن ألفٌ حرفٌ، ولامٌ حرفٌ، وميمٌ حرفٌ»[3].

البيتُ الذي يُقرأُ فيه القرآنُ
تَحضُرُهُ الملائكةُ ويتَّسِعُ على أهله

روى الإمامُ محمّدُ بنُ نصرٍ المِروزيُّ بإسنادِهِ عن أنسٍ رَضِيَ اللهُ عَنْهُ مرفوعاً: «إنَّ البيتَ إذا

---

(١) أخرجه الهيثمي في (مجمع الزوائد) (١٦٨/٧).

(٢) أخرجه الدارمي (٣٣١٩).

(٣) أخرجه الدارمي (٣٣١٥).

Qur'an is recited is attended by the Angels, the devils move away from it, it becomes expansive for its occupants, its goodness increases, and its evil decreases. The house in which the Qur'an is not recited is attended by the devils, the Angels move away from it, it is tight upon its occupants, its goodness decreases, and its evil increases."(1)

He said that there is also a narration of Abū Hurayrah ﷺ as a *mawqūf*(2) narration and from Ibn Sīrīn in this regard.

I (i.e., the author) say that the narration of Abū Hurayrah ﷺ has been narrated by Dārimī.

Dāraquṭnī narrated in *al-Afrād* from Anas and Jābir ﷺ that the Prophet ﷺ said, "Recite the Qur'an frequently in your homes, because the house in which the Qur'an is not recited has little goodness, much evil, and becomes tight for its occupants."(3)

THE HOUSE IN WHICH THE QUR'AN IS RECITED SHINES TO THE PEOPLE OF THE HEAVENS

Bayhaqī narrated on the authority of Sayyidah 'Ā'ishah ﷺ that the Messenger ﷺ said, "The house in which the Qur'an is recited appears to the people of the Heavens like the stars appear to the people of the Earth."(4)

Abū Nu'aym narrated in *al-Ma'rifah* from Abū Juḥayfah ﷺ, as a hadith attributed to the Prophet ﷺ, "The house in which Allah is remembered shines to the people of the Heavens like the stars shine to the people of the Earth."(5)

Ḥakīm al-Tirmidhī narrated on the authority of Abū Hurayrah and

---

(1) Al-Muttaqī al-Hindī in *Kanz al- 'Ummāl* (2434).

(2) Translator's Note: A *mawqūf* narration is one in which a statement or action is attributed to a Companion.

(3) Al-Muttaqī al-Hindī in *Kanz al- 'Ummāl* (41486).

(4) Al-Muttaqī al-Hindī in *Kanz al- 'Ummāl* (2288).

(5) Al-Muttaqī al-Hindī in *Kanz al- 'Ummāl* (1818).

قُرِئَ فيه القرآنُ حَضرتْهُ الملائكةُ، وتنكبَّتْ - أي: تباعَدَتْ - عنه الشّياطينُ، واتَّسَعَ على أهلِهِ، وكَثُرَ خيرُهُ وقلّ شرُّه، وإنَّ البيتَ إذا لم يُقرَأْ فيه القرآنُ حضَرَتْهُ الشّياطينُ، وتنكَّبَتْ عنه الملائكةُ، وضاقَ على أهلِهِ، وقلَّ خيرُه وكَثُرَ شرُّه»[1].

وقال: وفي البابِ عن أبي هريرةَ رَضِيَ اللهُ عَنْهُ موقوفاً وعن ابنِ سيرين. اهـ.

قلتُ: وأثَرُ أبي هريرةَ رَضِيَ اللهُ عَنْهُ رواهُ الدارِميُّ.

وروى الدارَقُطنيُّ في (الأفرادِ) عن أنسٍ وجابرٍ رَضِيَ اللهُ عَنْهُمَا عن النبي صَلَّى اللهُ عَلَيْهِ وَآلِهِ وَسَلَّمَ قال: «أكثِروا من تلاوةِ القرآنِ في بيوتِكم؛ فإنَّ البيتَ الذي لا يُقرأُ فيه القرآنُ يَقِلُّ خيرُهُ، ويَكثُرُ شرُّهُ، ويَضيقُ على أهلِه»[2].

البيتُ الذي يُقرأُ فيه القرآنُ يُضيءُ لأهلِ السّماء

روى البيهقيُّ عن السيدةِ عائشةَ رَضِيَ اللهُ عَنْهَا عن النبيّ صَلَّى اللهُ عَلَيْهِ وَآلِهِ وَسَلَّمَ قال: «البيتُ الذي يُقرأُ فيه القرآنُ يَتراءى لأهلِ السّماءِ كما تتراءى النُّجومُ لأهلِ الأرضِ»[3].

وروى أبو نُعيمٍ في (المعرفةِ) عن أبي جُحيفةَ الجُمَحيّ رَضِيَ اللهُ عَنْهُ رفَعَه: «إنَّ البيتَ الذي يُذكَرُ اللهُ فيه لَيُضيءُ لأهلِ السّماءِ كما تُضيءُ النُّجومُ لأهلِ الأرضِ»[4].

وروى الحكيمُ الترمذيُّ عن أبي هريرةَ وأبي الدرداءِ رَضِيَ اللهُ عَنْهُمَا مرفوعاً: «إنَّ بُيوتاتِ المؤمنينَ لَمصابيحُ إلى العرشِ، يعرفها مُقرَّبو السّمواتِ السّبعِ، يقولون: هذا النّورُ من

---

(١) أخرجه المتقي الهندي في (كنز العمال) (٢٤٣٤).

(٢) أخرجه المتقي الهندي في (كنز العمال) (٤١٤٨٦).

(٣) أخرجه المتقي الهندي في (كنز العمال) (٢٢٨٨).

(٤) أخرجه المتقي الهندي في (كنز العمال) (١٨١٨).

Abū al-Dardā' ﷺ, as a hadith attributed to the Prophet ﷺ, "The houses of the believers are lanterns to the Throne. The Nearest ones of the seven Heavens say, 'This is the light of the believers' houses in which the Qur'an is being recited.'"[1]

Abū Nuʿaym narrated in *al-Ḥilyah* from Ibn ʿAmr ﷺ, as a hadith attributed to the Prophet ﷺ, "Every verse in the Qur'an is a rank in Paradise and a lantern in your homes."[2]

THE RECITATION OF THE QUR'AN CONTAINS ABUNDANT GOODNESS

Imam Muslim narrated on the authority of ʿUqbah ibn Āmir ﷺ who said, "The Prophet ﷺ came out whilst we were in the *Ṣuffah*[3] (portico). He said, 'Which one of you would like to go every day to Buṭḥān (a valley in Medina) or ʿAqīq and bring back two large-humped camels, without incurring any sin or breaking ties of kinship?' We said, 'O Messenger of Allah, all of us would like that.' He said, 'Can any of you not go to the masjid and learn or read two verses of the Book of Allah Most High? That is better than two camels, three verses are better than three camels, four verses are better than four camels, and so forth."[4]

RECITING THE QUR'AN MAKES THE RECITER PLEASANT

Bukhārī and Muslim narrated on the authority of Abū Mūsā al-Ashʿarī ﷺ that the Prophet ﷺ said, "The example of a believer who recites the Qur'an is like a citron; its scent is pleasant and its taste is pleasant. The example of

(1) Al-Muttaqī al-Hindī in *Kanz al- 'Ummāl* (2481).

(2) Al-Muttaqī al-Hindī in *Kanz al- 'Ummāl* (2308).

(3) Translator's Note: This was a portico next to the Prophet's Masjid where a number of homeless Companions would live. They were known as the *Ahl al-Ṣuffah* (the People of the Portico).

(4) *Muslim* (806).

بُيوتاتِ المؤمنينَ التي يُتلى فيها القرآنُ»[1].

وروى أبو نُعيمٍ في (الحليةِ) عن ابنِ عمرٍو رَضِيَ اللَّهُ عَنْهُمَا مرفوعاً: «كلُّ آيةٍ في القرآنِ درجةٌ في الجنّةِ، ومصباحٌ في بيوتكم»[2].

قراءةُ القرآن فيها الخيرُ الكثيرُ

روى الإمامُ مسلمٌ عن عُقبةَ بنِ عامرٍ رَضِيَ اللَّهُ عَنْهُ قال: خرج النبيُّ صَلَّى اللَّهُ عَلَيْهِ وَآلِهِ وَسَلَّمَ ونحنُ في الصُّفّةِ فقال: «أيُّكُم يُحِبُّ أنْ يغدوَ كلَّ يومٍ إلى بُطحانَ أو إلى العقيقِ ويأتيَ بناقتين كَوماوَين - أي: عظيمتَي السَّنامِ - من غيرِ إثمٍ، ولا قطيعةِ رحمٍ؟، - أي: من طريقٍ سهلٍ حلالٍ- قلنا: يا رسولَ اللهِ كلُّنا يحبُّ ذلك، فقال: أفلا يغدو أحدُكم إلى المسجدِ فيتعلّمَ أو يقرأَ آيتينِ من كتابِ اللهِ تعالى فهو خيرٌ له من ناقتين، وثلاثٌ خيرٌ له من ثلاثٍ، وأربعٌ خيرٌ له من أربعٍ، ومِن أعدادِهنَّ من الإبل»[3].

تلاوةُ القرآنِ تُطيّبُ القارئَ

روى الشّيخانِ - واللّفظُ لمسلمٍ - عن أبي موسى الأشعريّ رَضِيَ اللَّهُ عَنْهُ عن النبيّ صَلَّى اللَّهُ عَلَيْهِ وَآلِهِ وَسَلَّمَ قال: «مَثَلُ المؤمنِ الذي يقرأُ القرآنَ مَثَلُ الأُتْرُجّةِ ريحُها طيّبٌ وطعمُها طيّبٌ؛

ومَثَلُ المؤمنِ الذي لا يقرأُ القرآنَ مَثَلُ التَّمرةِ لا ريحَ لها وطعمُها حلوٌ؛ ومَثَلُ المنافقِ الذي يقرأُ القرآنَ مَثَلُ الرَّيحانةِ ريحُها طيّبٌ وطعمُها مُرٌّ، ومَثَلُ المنافقِ الذي لا

---

(١) أخرجه المتقي الهندي في (كنز العمال) (٢٤٨١).

(٢) أخرجه المتقي الهندي في (كنز العمال) (٢٣٠٨).

(٣) أخرجه مسلم (٨٠٦). بُطْحَانَ: وَادٍ بِالمَدِيْنَةِ. الكَوْمَاءُ: النَّاقَةُ العَظِيْمَةُ السَّنَامِ.

a believer who does not recite the Qur'an is like a date; it has no scent but its taste is pleasant. The example of the hypocrite who recites the Qur'an is like basil; its scent is pleasant but its taste is bitter. The example of the hypocrite who does not recite the Qur'an is like that of a colocynth; it has no scent and its taste is bitter."[1]

THE RECITATION OF THE NOBLE QUR'AN POLISHES THE HEARTS

Ibn ʿUmar ﷺ narrated that the Messenger of Allah ﷺ said, "The hearts rust just like iron rusts when water touches it." He was asked, "O Messenger of Allah, what is the polish for that?" He replied, "Remembering death often and reciting the Qur'an."[2]

RECITING THE NOBLE QUR'AN BENEFITS THE RECITER AND THEIR PARENTS

Abū Dāwūd narrated on the authority of Sahl ibn Muʿādh ﷺ that the Messenger of Allah ﷺ said, "Whoever recites the Qur'an and acts upon it, Allah will crown their parents with a crown whose light is more radiant than the sun, were it in one of the houses of this world. So, what do you think about the one who acted upon it?"[3]

In other words: if the parents of the reciter are going to be crowned with such a luminous crown, then how great a reward will the reciter themselves be granted, and what a great crown of honour will they be given. Their reward and honour will most assuredly be greater than that. May Allah Most High make us amongst them. *Āmīn*.

---

(1) *Muslim* (799).

(2) Bayhaqī in *Shuʿab al-Īmān* (2014).

(3) *Abū Dāwūd* (1453).

يقرأُ القرآنَ كمَثَلِ الحَنظَلةِ ليس لها ريحٌ وطعمُها مُرٌّ»[1].

تلاوةُ القرآنِ الكريمِ جلاءٌ للقلوب

روي عن ابنِ عمرَ رَضِيَ اللهُ عَنْهُمَا أنّه قال: قال رسولُ الله صَلَّى اللهُ عَلَيْهِ وَآلِهِ وَسَلَّمَ:

«إنَّ هذه القلوبَ تَصدَأُ كما يَصدأُ الحديدُ إذا أصابه الماءُ»، قيل: يا رسولَ الله وما جلاؤها؟ قال: «كثرةُ ذِكرِ الموتِ وتلاوةُ القرآنِ»[2].

تلاوةُ القرآنِ الكريم تنفعُ القارئَ ووالديه

روى أبو داودَ عن سهلِ بنِ معاذٍ رَضِيَ اللهُ عَنْهُ أنَّ رسولَ الله صَلَّى اللهُ عَلَيْهِ وَآلِهِ وَسَلَّمَ قال: «مَن قرأ القرآنَ وعَمِلَ به أَلبسَ اللهُ والديه تاجاً يومَ القيامةِ ضَوؤهُ أحسنُ من ضوءِ الشَّمسِ في بيتٍ من بيوتِ الدُّنيا لو كانت فيه، فما ظنُّكم بالذي عَمِلَ به»؟[3].

والمعنى:

أنه إذا كان والِدَا القارئِ يُلبَسانِ هذا التاجَ الوضّاءَ فماذا يُعطى القارئُ مِنَ الأجر؟ وماذا يُلبَسُ من تيجانِ الكرامة؟

نعم إنَّ ثوابَه وإكرامَه لَأَعظمُ من ذلك. جعلنا اللهُ تعالى منهم. آمين.

---

(١) أخرجه مسلم (٧٩٩).

(٢) أخرجه البيهقي في شعب الإيمان (٢٠١٤).

(٣) أخرجه أبو داود (١٤٥٣).

THE BEST OF PEOPLE ARE THOSE WHO HAVE LEARNT THE MOST QUR'AN

Imam Aḥmad and Ṭabarānī narrated on the authority of Durrah ﷺ that the Prophet ﷺ said, "The best of people are those who are most well-versed in the Qur'an, most knowledgeable regarding Allah's religion, most conscious of Allah, foremost in commanding the good and forbidding the evil, and in maintaining ties of kinship."(1)

THE MOST WELL-VERSED IN THE QUR'AN IS GIVEN PRECEDENCE OVER OTHERS ACCORDING TO THE SACRED LAW

Imam Muslim and others narrated on the authority of Ibn Masʿūd ﷺ that the Prophet ﷺ said, "The people will be led in prayer by the most well-versed amongst them regarding the Book of Allah Most High."(2)

Imam Aḥmad narrated in his *Musnad* from Ibn Masʿūd ﷺ that the Prophet ﷺ said, "The people will be led in prayer by the most well-versed amongst them regarding the Book of Allah Most High. If they are equal with respect to the Qur'an, then the most knowledgeable of them regarding the Sunnah. If they are equal with respect to the Sunnah, then the first of them to migrate. If they are equal with respect to migration, then the eldest of them. A person should not be led in prayer in his own house or where he holds authority, and nor should anyone sit in his house in his special seat except with his permission."(3)

Bukhārī and others narrated that the Prophet ﷺ would combine two men from the martyrs of Uḥud (when burying) and ask which of them had learnt the most Qur'an. If any of them was pointed out, he would place

---

(1) *Aḥmad* (27474).

(2) *Muslim* (2373).

(3) *Aḥmad* (17901).

خيرُ النّاسِ أقرؤُهم

روى الإمامُ أحمدُ والطّبرانيُّ عن درّةَ رَضِيَ اللَّهُ عَنْهَا أنَّ النبيَّ صَلَّى اللَّهُ عَلَيْهِ وَآلِهِ وَسَلَّمَ قال: «خيرُ النّاسِ أقرؤُهم وأفقهُهم في دينِ الله، وأتقاهُم لله، وآمَرُهم بالمعروف، وأنهاهُم عن المنكرِ، وأوصَلُهم للرَّحِم»[1].

يُقدَّمُ الأقرأُ على غيرِه شرعاً

روى الإمامُ مسلمٌ وغيرُه عن ابنِ مسعودٍ رَضِيَ اللَّهُ عَنْهُ أنَّ النبيَّ صَلَّى اللَّهُ عَلَيْهِ وَآلِهِ وَسَلَّمَ قال: «يؤمُّ القومَ أقرؤُهم لكتابِ اللهِ تعالى»[2].

وفي روايةِ أحمدَ في (مسنده) عن ابن مسعودٍ رَضِيَ اللَّهُ عَنْهُ أنَّ النبيَّ صَلَّى اللَّهُ عَلَيْهِ وَآلِهِ وَسَلَّمَ قال: «يؤمُّ القومَ أقرؤُهم لكتابِ اللهِ تعالى، فإن كانوا في القرآنِ سواءً فأعلَمُهم بالسُّنّةِ، فإن كانوا في السُّنّةِ سواءً فأقدَمُهم هجرةً، فإن كانوا في الهجرةِ سواءً فأقدَمُهم سِنّاً، ولا يُؤَمَّنَّ الرَّجلُ في أهلِهِ، ولا في سلطانِهِ، ولا يُقعَدُ في بيتِهِ على تكرمَتِهِ إلا بإذنِهِ»[3].

وروى البخاريُّ وغيرُه أنَّ النبيَّ صَلَّى اللَّهُ عَلَيْهِ وَآلِهِ وَسَلَّمَ كان يجمعُ بين الرَّجلينِ مِن قتلى أُحُدٍ، ثم يقول: «أيُّهما أكثرُ أخذاً للقرآن»؟ فإنْ أُشيرَ إلى أحدِهم قدّمه في اللَّحدِ[4].

وروى أصحابُ السُّننِ عن هشامِ بنِ عامرٍ رَضِيَ اللَّهُ عَنْهُ أنَّ النبيَّ صَلَّى اللَّهُ عَلَيْهِ وَآلِهِ وَسَلَّمَ قال: «احفِروا،

---

(١) أخرجه أحمد (٢٧٤٧٤).

(٢) أخرجه مسلم (٢٣٧٣).

(٣) أخرجه أحمد (١٧٠٩١).

(٤) أخرجه البخاري (١٣٤٣).

them in the grave first.[1]

The authors of the *Sunan* collections narrated on the authority of Hishām ibn 'Āmir ﷺ that the Prophet ﷺ said, "Dig [the graves], and make them deep and wide. Bury two or three in a grave and place the one who was most well-versed amongst them regarding the Qur'an first."[2]

Ibn 'Abbās ﷺ narrated that it was the Qur'an reciters who would sit in the gathering of 'Umar ﷺ and whom he would consult, regardless of whether they were old or young.

HONOURING THE PEOPLE OF THE QUR'AN IS PART OF HONOURING THE SYMBOLS OF ALLAH MOST HIGH

Allah Most High said, "And whoever honours the symbols of Allah, it is certainly out of the piety of the heart."[3] The symbols of Allah Most High are the symbols of His religions and the bearers of His sacred law. Thus, the symbols of His religion include the Qur'anic *muṣḥafs*, masjids designated for prayer, Hajj rites, and so forth.

The bearers of His sacred law include scholars and reciters. Imam Nawawī ﷺ used this noble verse to substantiate the necessity of honouring the people of the Qur'an, because they are amongst the symbols of Allah Most High. Likewise, it is necessary to honour the scholars who are the bearers of Allah's religion. It is not permissible to harm them, look down upon them, or belittle them, because harming and belittling them is a sign of hypocrisy and an evil ending – we seek Allah's refuge therefrom.

Imam Nawawī has reported from the two illustrious imams, Abū Ḥanīfah ﷺ and Shāfi'ī ﷺ, that they said, "If the scholars are not the friends of Allah, then Allah has no friends."

---

(1) *Bukhārī* (1343).

(2) *Tirmidhī* (1713); *Nasā'ī* (2010).

(3) *Al-Ḥajj*, 32.

وأعمِقوا، وأوسِعوا، وادفِنوا الاثنينِ والثّلاثةَ في قبرٍ واحدٍ وقدِّموا أكثرَهم قرآناً»[1].

وعن ابنِ عبّاسٍ رضي اللهُ عنهما قال: كان القُرّاءُ أصحابَ مجلسِ عمرَ رَضِيَ اللَّهُ عَنْهُ ومشاورته كهولاً كانوا أو شبّاناً.

إكرامُ أهلِ القرآنِ من تعظيمِ شعائرِ اللهِ تعالى

قال اللهُ تعالى: {وَمَن يُعَظِّمْ شَعَائِرَ اللَّهِ فَإِنَّهَا مِن تَقْوَى الْقُلُوبِ}[2].

شعائرُ اللهِ تعالى: هي معالِمُ دينِهِ، وحمَلَةُ شريعتِهِ.

فمعالِمُ الدّينِ: تشمَلُ المصاحفَ القرآنيّةَ، ومساجدَ الصّلواتِ، ومناسكَ الحجّ، إلى ما وراءَ ذلك.

وحمَلَةُ شريعتِه: تشمل العلماءَ والقُرّاءَ، وقد استدلَّ الإمامُ النّوويُّ رَضِيَ اللَّهُ عَنْهُ بهذه الآيةِ الكريمةِ على وجوبِ إكرامِ أهلِ القرآنِ؛ لأنّهم من شعائرِ اللهِ تعالى، كما يجبُ تعظيمُ العلماءِ الذين هم حمَلَةُ دينِ الله تعالى، ولا يجوز إيذاؤهم ولا تحقيرُهم، ولا الاستهانةُ بهم؛ فإنَّ إيذاءَهم والاستهانةَ بهم علامةٌ على النّفاقِ، وسوءِ الخاتمةِ والعياذُ بالله تعالى.

وقد نقلَ الإمامُ النوويُّ عن الإمامينِ الكبيرينِ أبي حنيفةَ والشّافعيِّ رضي الله تعالى عنهما أنّهما قالا: إنْ لم يكنِ العلماءُ أولياءَ اللهِ تعالى فليس للهِ تعالى وليٌّ. اهـ.

كما نُقل أيضاً عن الحافظِ ابن عساكرَ أنّه قال: اعلم يا أخي - وفّقنا اللهُ تعالى وإيّاك لمرضاتِه، وجعلنا ممَّنْ يخشاه ويتّقيه حقَّ تُقاتِه-: أنَّ لحومَ العلماءِ مسمومةٌ، وعادةُ اللهِ تعالى في هتكِ أستارِ مُنتَقِصِيهم معلومةٌ، وأنَّ مَن أطلقَ لسانَهُ في العلماءِ بالثّلبِ،

---

(١) أخرجه الترمذي (١٧١٣)، والنسائي (٢٠١٠).

(٢) الحج: ٣٢.

It is also reported that Ḥāfiẓ Ibn ʿAsākir ﷺ said, "Know my brother – may Allah Most High enable you and us to what pleases Him and make us amongst those who fear Him and are mindful of Him as He deserves – that the flesh of scholars is poisonous and the habit of Allah in exposing those who disparage them is well-known. Whoever lets their tongue loose regarding the scholars, He Most High afflicts them before their [physical] death with death of the heart. 'So let those who disobey his orders beware, for an affliction may befall them, or a painful torment may overtake them.'[(1)]"

Ṭabarānī narrated on the authority of Abū Umāmah ﷺ that the Prophet ﷺ said, "There are three people whom only a hypocrite disparages: an elderly Muslim, a person of knowledge, and a just leader."[(2)]

Abū al-Shaykh narrated on the authority of Jābir ﷺ that the Prophet ﷺ said, "There are three people whom only an open hypocrite disparages: an elderly Muslim, a just leader, and one who teaches good things."[(3)]

HONOURING THE ONE WHO HAS MEMORIZED THE QUR'AN IS PART OF EXALTING ALLAH MOST HIGH

Abū Dāwūd narrated on the authority of Abū Mūsā al-Ashʿarī ﷺ that the Messenger of Allah ﷺ said, "Part of exalting Allah Most High is to honour an elderly Muslim, the one who has memorized the Qur'an and neither exceeds the bound nor neglects it, and a person of authority who is just."[(4)] Sayyidah ʿĀ'ishah ﷺ narrated, "The Messenger of Allah ﷺ commanded us to treat people according to their rank."[(5)] Abū Dāwūd narrated it and Muslim mentioned it in the introduction to his *Ṣaḥīḥ*.

(1) *Al-Nūr*, 63.

(2) *Ṭabarānī* (7819)

(3) Abū al-Shaykh in *al-Thawāb*, and Iṣbahānī, as stated in *Itḥāf al-Khiyarah al-Maharah*, vol. 8, p. 184.

(4) *Abū Dāwūd* (4843).

(5) *Abū Dāwūd* (4842).

ابتلاهُ تعالى قبلَ موتِهِ - جسماً -، بموتِ القلبِ، {فَلْيَحْذَرِ الَّذِينَ يُخَالِفُونَ عَنْ أَمْرِهِ أَن تُصِيبَهُمْ فِتْنَةٌ أَوْ يُصِيبَهُمْ عَذَابٌ أَلِيمٌ}(١).

روى الطبرانيُّ عن أبي أمامةَ رَضِيَ اللهُ عَنْهُ أنَّ النبيَّ ﷺ قال: «ثلاثةٌ لا يَستخِفُّ بحقِّهم إلا منافقٌ: ذو الشَّيبةِ في الإسلامِ، وذو العلمِ، وإمامٌ مُقسِطٌ»(٢).

وروى أبو الشّيخِ عن جابرٍ رَضِيَ اللهُ عَنْهُ عن النبيِّ ﷺ قال: «ثلاثةٌ لا يستخِفُّ بحقِّهم إلّا منافقٌ بَيِّنُ النِّفاقِ: ذو الشَّيبةِ في الإسلامِ، والإمامُ المُقسِطُ، ومعلِّمُ الخيرِ»(٣).

إكرامُ حاملِ القرآنِ من إجلالِ اللهِ تعالى

روى أبو داودَ عن أبي موسى الأشعريِّ رضي الله تعالى عنه قال: قال رسولُ الله صلى الله عليه وآله وسلم: «إنَّ مِن إجلالِ اللهِ تعالى إكرامَ ذي الشَّيبةِ المسلمِ، وحاملِ القرآنِ غيرِ الغالي فيه والجافي عنه، وإكرامَ ذي السُّلطانِ المقسِطِ»(٤). وعن السيدة عائشةَ رضي الله عنها قالت: أمَرَنا رسولُ الله ﷺ أنْ نُنزِلَ النّاسَ منازلَهم(٥). رواه أبو داودَ وذكرَهُ مسلمٌ في مقدّمةِ (صحيحه).

---

(١) النور: ٦٣.

(٢) أخرجه الطبراني (٧٨١٩).

(٣) أخرجه أبو الشيخ في (الثواب) والأصبهاني كما في (إتحاف الخيرة المهرة) للبوصيري (١٨٤/٨).

(٤) أخرجه أبو داود (٤٨٤٣). الغُلُوُّ في الدِّينِ: التَّشْدِيدُ فِيهِ وَمُجَاوَزَةُ الحَدِّ. وَمِنْهُ حَامِلُ الْقُرْآنِ غَيْرُ الْغَالِي فِيهِ. وَالجَافِي فِيهِ: الَّذِي لَا يَتَعَاهَدُهُ وَيَبْعُدُ عَنْ تِلَاوَتِهِ كَمَا فِي النِّهَايَةِ. وَيُفْهَمُ مِنْهَا أَنَّ الْغَالِيَ الَّذِي يُبَالِغُ فِي سُرْعَةِ قِرَاءَتِهِ، وَالْمَطْلُوبُ الْوَسَطُ.

(٥) أخرجه أبو داود (٤٨٤٢).

THE RECITER WILL NOT BE FRIGHTENED BY THE SUPREME HORROR OF THE DAY OF JUDGEMENT

Ṭabarānī narrated with a chain that is acceptable from Ibn ʿUmar ﷺ that the Messenger of Allah ﷺ said, "There are three people who will neither be frightened by the Supreme Horror (*al-Fazaʿ al-Akbar*) nor will they be taken to account, and they will be on mounds of musk until the whole creation has been reckoned. [They are] a person who learnt the Qur'an for the pleasure of Allah Most High and led the people in prayer whilst they were pleased with him; a caller to prayer (*mu'adhdhin*) who calls towards the prayers for the pleasure of Allah; and a slave who is excellent in his conduct with his Lord and in his conduct with his masters."[1]

(1) Ṭabarānī in *al-Muʿjam al-Kabīr* (1116).

القارئُ لا يهولُهُ الفَزَعُ الأكبرُ يومَ القيامة

روى الطبرانيُّ بإسنادٍ لا بأسَ به عن ابنِ عمرَ رَضِيَ اللهُ عَنْهُمَا قال: قال رسولُ الله صَلَّى اللهُ عَلَيْهِ وَآلِهِ وَسَلَّمَ: «ثلاثةٌ لا يهولُهُمُ الفزعُ الأكبرُ، ولا ينالهُمُ الحسابُ، وهم على كثبٍ من المسكِ حتّى يُفرغَ من حسابِ الخلائقِ: رجلٌ قرأَ القرآنَ ابتغاءَ وجهِ اللهِ تعالى وأمَّ قوماً وهم به راضون، وداعٍ - أي: مؤذِّنٌ - يدعو إلى الصّلواتِ ابتغاءَ وجهِ الله، وعبدٌ أحسنَ فيما بينَهُ وبين ربّهِ وفيما بينَه وبينَ مَواليه»[1].

(١) أخرجه الطبراني في (المعجم الصغير) (١١١٦).

THE INTERCESSION OF THE NOBLE QUR'AN FOR ITS RECITER

Muslim narrated on the authority of Abū Umāmah رضي الله عنه that the Messenger of Allah ﷺ said, "Recite the Qur'an, as it will come as an intercessor for its reciters on the Day of Judgement."(1) Jābir رضي الله عنه narrated that the Prophet ﷺ said, "The Qur'an is an intercessor whose intercession will be accepted and a witness whose testimony will be considered true. Whoever puts it in front of them, it will lead them to Paradise. But whoever puts it behind them, it will drag them to Hellfire."(2)

The intercession of the Qur'an for its reciter will in some cases be through sins being forgiven, and in other cases, it will be through elevation of ranks and being adorned with excellence. The first is proven by the narration of Tirmidhī, Abū Dāwūd, and others on the authority of Abū Hurayrah رضي الله عنه that the Prophet ﷺ said, "Indeed, a *sūrah* of the Qur'an consisting of 30 verses interceded for a person until Allah forgave them. It is, 'Blessed is the One in Whose Hand lies all authority (i.e., *Sūrah al-Mulk*).'"(3)

---

(1) *Muslim* (804).

(2) *Ibn Ḥibbān* (124).

(3) *Abū Dāwūd* (1400); *Tirmidhī* (2891).

شفاعةُ القرآنِ الكريمِ لقارئه

روى مسلمٌ عن أبي أُمامةَ رَضِيَ اللهُ عَنْهُ أنَّ رسولَ الله صَلَّى اللهُ عَلَيْهِ وَآلِهِ وَسَلَّمَ قال: «اقرؤوا القرآنَ؛ فإنّه يأتي يومَ القيامةِ شفيعاً لأصحابِهِ»[1]. والحديثُ يأتي بتمامِه.

وعن جابرٍ رضي اللهُ عنه عن النبيّ صَلَّى اللهُ عَلَيْهِ وَآلِهِ وَسَلَّمَ قال: «القرآنُ شافعٌ ومشفَّعٌ، وماحِلٌ مصدَّقٌ، من جَعلَهُ أمامَه قادَهُ إلى الجنّةِ، ومَن جعله خلفَه ساقَه إلى النّار»[2]. رواهُ ابنُ حِبّان في (صحيحِه). وشفاعةُ القرآنِ للقارئِ قد تكون بمغفرةِ الذُّنوبِ، وقد تكون برفعِ الدَّرجاتِ والحليةِ بالكمالات. فالأُولى: يدلُّ عليها ما رواهُ الترمذيُّ وأبو داودَ وغيرُهما عن أبي هريرةَ رَضِيَ اللهُ عَنْهُ عن النبيِّ صَلَّى اللهُ عَلَيْهِ وَآلِهِ وَسَلَّمَ قال: «إنَّ سورةً من القرآنِ ثلاثون آيةً شفَعَتْ

---

(١) أخرجه مسلم (٨٠٤).

(٢) أخرجه ابن حبان (١٢٤). الماحل: الشاهد.

The second is proven by the narration of Tirmidhī on the authority of Abū Hurayrah ﷺ that the Messenger of Allah ﷺ said, "The one who memorized the Qur'an will come on the Day of Judgement and the Qur'an will say, 'O my Lord, adorn him.' So he will be given a crown of honour. The Qur'an will then say, 'O Allah, give him more.' He will then be clothed in a suit of honour (i.e., a long noble garment that will be a sign of people honoured in the sight of Allah Most High). The Qur'an will then say, 'O Allah, be pleased with him.' He will thus be pleased with him. Thereafter, it will be said to the reciter, 'Read and rise.' And he will receive an extra reward for every verse."(1)

Abū Hurayrah ﷺ narrated that the Prophet ﷺ said, "The fast and the Qur'an will intercede for the slave on the Day of Judgement. The fast will say, 'O my Lord, I stopped him from eating and drinking during the day, so accept my intercession for him.' The Qur'an will say, 'O my Lord, I stopped him from sleeping at night, so accept my intercession for him.' Thus, their intercession will be accepted."(2) Imam Aḥmad narrated it.

THE RECITER WILL CONTINUE ASCENDING IN RANKS ON THE DAY OF JUDGEMENT

Tirmidhī narrated on the authority of Ibn ʿUmar ﷺ that the Messenger of Allah ﷺ said, "It will be said to the one who had memorized the Qur'an, 'Recite and rise, and recite diligently as you used to in the world, for your rank will be at the last verse you recite.'"(3)

Ibn Mardawayh narrated on the authority of Anas ﷺ that the Messenger of Allah ﷺ said, "The levels of Paradise are equal in number to the verses of the Qur'an. Thus, whoever enters Paradise amongst those who had

(1) *Tirmidhī* (2915).

(2) Aḥmad in his *Musnad* (6626).

(3) *Abū Dāwūd* (1464); *Nasāʾī* (8056); *Tirmidhī* (2915).

لرجلٍ حتّى غفرَ اللهُ له، وهي {تَبَارَكَ الَّذِي بِيَدِهِ الْمُلْكُ}[1]»[2]. والثانيةُ: يدلُّ عليها ما رواهُ الترمذيُّ عن أبي هريرةَ رَضِيَ اللَّهُ عَنْهُ أنَّ رسولَ اللهِ ﷺ قال: «يجيءُ صاحبُ القرآنِ يومَ القيامةِ، فيقولُ القرآنُ: يا ربِّ حَلِّهِ، فيُلبَسُ تاجَ الكرامةِ، ثمّ يقول القرآنُ: يا ربِّ زِدْهُ، فيُلبَسُ حُلَّةَ الكرامةِ» - أي: ثوباً سابغاً كريماً، شعارَ أهلِ الكرامةِ عند الله تعالى - ثمّ يقولُ القرآنُ: «يا ربِّ ارضَ عنه، فيرضى عنه، فيُقال للقارئِ: اقرأْ وارقَ، ويزدادُ بكلِّ آيةٍ حسنةً»[3]. وعن أبي هريرةَ رضي اللهُ عنه عن النبيِّ ﷺ قال: «الصّيامُ والقرآنُ يشفعانِ للعبدِ يومَ القيامة، يقولُ الصّيامُ: ربِّ إنّي منعتُهُ الطّعامَ والشّرابَ بالنّهارِ، فشَفِّعني فيه، ويقولُ القرآنُ: ربِّ إنّي منعتُهُ النّومَ باللّيلِ، فشفِّعني فيه، فيُشفَّعانِ»[4]. رواهُ الإمامُ أحمدُ.

القارئُ لا يزال يترقَّى في المنازلِ يومَ القيامة

روى الترمذيُّ عن ابنِ عمرَ رَضِيَ اللَّهُ عَنْهُمَا قال: قال رسولُ الله ﷺ: «يُقالُ لصاحبِ القرآنِ: اقرأْ وارقَ ورتِّلْ كما كنتَ تُرتِّلُ في الدّنيا، فإنَّ منزلتَكَ عندَ آخرِ آيةٍ تقرؤُها»[5].

وروى ابنُ مَرْدَوَيْه عن أنسٍ رَضِيَ اللَّهُ عَنْهُ عن النبيِّ ﷺ أنّه قال: «عددُ دَرَجِ الجنّةِ

---

(١) الملك: ١.

(٢) أخرجه أبو داود (١٤٠٠)، والترمذي (٢٨٩١).

(٣) أخرجه الترمذي (٢٩١٥).

(٤) أخرجه أحمد في مسنده (٦٦٢٦).

(٥) أخرجه أبو داوود (١٤٦٤) والنسائي (٨٠٥٦) والترمذي (٢٩١٤).

memorized the Qur'an will not find anyone above them."(1) Thus, the person who memorized the Qur'an will not stop reciting, even in Paradise. They will recite, and continue ascending in ranks and increasing in rewards, as already stated: "It will be said to the reciter, 'Read and rise.' Thus, he will receive an extra reward for every verse."(2)

RECITING THE NOBLE QUR'AN BENEFITS THE LISTENERS WITH FRAGRANCE AND IT EXUDES THE SCENT OF MUSK

ʿUthmān ibn ʿAffān ﵁ narrated that the Prophet ﷺ said, "The Qur'an is like a bag of musk whose mouth has been tied.

If you open it, the fragrance of musk will exude. If you leave it, it will be musk that is put away. This is like the Qur'an: if you recite it [it exudes], otherwise it is in your chest."(3) Ḥakīm al-Tirmidhī narrated it, as stated in *al-Fatḥ al-Kabīr*.

THE MERIT OF RECITING IN PRAYER OVER RECITING OUTSIDE OF PRAYER

It is narrated on the authority of Sayyidah ʿĀ'ishah ﵂ that the Messenger of Allah ﷺ said, "Reciting the Qur'an in prayer is better than outside of prayer; reciting the Qur'an outside of prayer is better than *tasbīḥ* and *takbir*; *tasbīḥ* is better than (additional) charity; charity is better than (additional) fasting; and fasting is a shield against Hellfire."(4)

---

(1) Al-Muttaqī al-Hindī in *Kanz al- 'Ummāl* (2269).

(2) *Tirmidhī* (2915).

(3) Al-Muttaqī al-Hindī in *Kanz al- 'Ummāl* (2320).

(4) Al-Muttaqī al-Hindī in *Kanz al- 'Ummāl* (2300).

عددُ آيِ القرآنِ، فمَن دخلَ الجنّةَ ممَّنْ قرأَ القرآنَ لم يكنْ فوقَه أحدٌ»[1]. فصاحبُ القرآنِ لا ينقطعُ عن قراءتِهِ في الجنّةِ، فهو يقرأُ ويترقّى في الدّرجاتِ، ويزدادُ من الحسناتِ كما تقدَّم: «يُقالُ للقارئِ: اقرأْ وارقَ، ويزدادُ بكلِّ آيةٍ حسنةً»[2]. الحديثَ.

تلاوةُ القرآنِ الكريمِ
تنفحُ السّامعينَ بالطِّيبِ وتتضوَّعُ بالمسك

عن عثمانَ بنِ عفّانَ رَضِيَ اللهُ عَنْهُ عن النبيِّ صَلَّى اللهُ عَلَيْهِ وَآلِهِ وَسَلَّمَ قال: «إنَّ القرآنَ مَثَلُهُ كمَثَلِ جِرابٍ فيه مسكٌ قد رَبَطْتَ فاهُ، فإنْ فتحتَهُ فاحَ ريحُ المسكِ، وإن تركتَهُ كان مِسكاً موضوعاً، مثل القرآنِ إن قرأْتَهُ وإلّا فهو في صدرِكَ»[3]. رواهُ الحكيمُ الترمذيُّ، كما في (الفتحِ الكبيرِ).

فضلُ القراءةِ في الصلاة على غيرِها

روي عن السيدة عائشةَ رَضِيَ اللهُ عَنْهَا أنَّ النبيَّ صَلَّى اللهُ عَلَيْهِ وَآلِهِ وَسَلَّمَ قال: «قراءةُ القرآنِ في الصّلاةِ أفضلُ من قراءةِ القرآنِ في غير الصّلاةِ، وقراءةُ القرآنِ في غيرِ الصّلاةِ أفضلُ من التّسبيحِ والتّكبيرِ، والتَّسبيحُ أفضلُ من الصَّدَقةِ - أي: النّافلةِ -، والصّدقةُ أفضلُ من الصّومِ - أي: النفل -، والصّومُ جُنّةٌ من النّار»[4].

---

(١) أخرجه المتقي الهندي في (كنز العمال) (٢٢٦٩).

(٢) أخرجه الترمذي (٢٩١٥).

(٣) أخرجه المتقي الهندي في (كنز العمال) (٢٣٢٠).

(٤) أخرجه المتقي الهندي في (كنز العمال) (٢٣٠٠).

RECITING FROM THE MUṢḤAF IS MULTIPLIED [IN REWARD]

Aws ibn Aws narrated that the Prophet said, "A person's reciting from other than the *muṣḥaf* is 1000 ranks, and reciting from the *muṣḥaf* is multiplied more than that to 2000 ranks."(1)

Ibn Mas'ūd narrated, as a hadith attributed to the Prophet, "Whoever it pleases to be loved by Allah and His Messenger should recite in the *muṣḥaf*."(2)

Ibn Mardawayh narrated on the authority of 'Amr ibn Aws, as a hadith attributed to the Prophet, "Your reciting from the *muṣḥaf* is multiplied in reward over your reciting from memory, just as the obligatory prayer has merit over the additional prayer."(3)

Bayhaqī and Ḥakīm al-Tirmidhī narrated on the authority of Abū Sa'īd, as a hadith attributed to the Prophet, "Give your eyes their share of worship: looking into the *muṣḥaf*, contemplating over it, and pondering over its wonders."(4)

Ibn Abi Dāwūd narrated on the authority of Ibn 'Abbās that when 'Umar ibn al-Khaṭṭāb would enter his house, he would open his *muṣḥaf* and recite from it.(5) Imam Aḥmad narrated in *Kitāb al-Zuhd* that 'Uthmān ibn 'Affān said, "I do not like for a day or night to pass by except that I have looked into the Book of Allah Most High (i.e., looking into the *muṣḥaf*)."(6) Bayhaqī has narrated with a good chain that Ibn Mas'ūd

(1) Al-Muttaqī al-Hindī in *Kanz al- 'Ummāl* (2301).

(2) Ibn 'Adī in *al-Kāmil fi al-Ḍu 'afā'*, vol 2, p. 449; Abū Nu'aym in *Ḥilyah al-Awliyā'*, vol. 7, p. 209; Bayhaqī in *Shu 'ab al-Īmān* (2219).

(3) Al-Muttaqī al-Hindī in *Kanz al- 'Ummāl* (2302).

(4) Abū al-Shaykh in *al- 'Aẓamah*, vol. 1, p. 225; Bayhaqī in *Shu 'ab al-Īmān* (2222); Daylamī in *al-Firdaws* (352) with a slight difference.

(5) Al-Muttaqī al-Hindī in *Kanz al- 'Ummāl* (2302).

(6) *Mawsū 'ah Āthār al-Ṣaḥābah* (3763).

مضاعفةُ القراءةِ في المصحفِ على غيرِها

عن أوسِ بنِ أوسٍ رَضِيَ اللَّهُ عَنْهُ عن النبيِّ ﷺ أنّه قال: «قراءةُ الرَّجلِ في غيرِ المصحفِ ألفُ درجةٍ، وقراءتُهُ في المصحفِ تُضعَّفُ على ذلكَ إلى ألفي درجةٍ»[1]. وعن ابنِ مسعودٍ رَضِيَ اللَّهُ عَنْهُ مرفوعاً: «مَن سرَّهُ أنْ يحبَّ اللهَ ورسولَهَ فلْيقرأْ في المصحفِ»[2]. وروى ابن مَرْدَوَيْه عن عمرِو بنِ أوسٍ مرفوعاً: «قراءَتُكَ نَظَراً تضاعَفُ على قراءتِكَ ظاهراً كفضلِ المكتوبةِ على النّافلةِ»[3]. وروى البيهقيُّ والحكيمُ الترمذيُّ عن أبي سعيدٍ رضي الله عنه مرفوعاً: «أَعطُوا أعينَكُمْ حظَّها مِن العبادةِ: النّظرِ في المصحفِ، والتفكُّرِ فيه، والاعتبارِ عند عجائبِهِ»[4]. وروى ابنُ أبي داودَ عن ابنِ عبّاسٍ رَضِيَ اللَّهُ عَنْهُمَا قال: (كان عمرُ بنُ الخطّابِ رَضِيَ اللَّهُ عَنْهُ إذا دخلَ البيتَ نشرَ المصحفَ فقرأَ فيه)[5]. وروى الإمامُ أحمدُ في كتاب (الزُّهدِ) عن عثمانَ بنِ عفّانَ رَضِيَ اللَّهُ عَنْهُ أنه قال: (ما أحبُّ أن يأتيَ عليَّ يومٌ ولا ليلةٌ إلا أنظُرُ في كتابِ اللهِ تعالى)[6]. يعني: القراءةَ في المصحفِ. وروى البيهقيُّ بسندٍ

---

(١) أخرجه المتقي الهندي في (كنز العمال) (٢٣٠١).

(٢) أخرجه ابن عدي في (الكامل في الضعفاء) (٢/٤٤٩)، وأبو نعيم في (حلية الأولياء) (٧/٢٠٩) واللفظ له، والبيهقي في (شعب الإيمان) (٢٢١٩).

(٣) أخرجه المتقي الهندي في (كنز العمال) (٢٣٠٢).

(٤) أخرجه أبو الشيخ في (العظمة) (١/٢٢٥)، والبيهقي في (شعب الإيمان) (٢٢٢٢) واللفظ لهما، والديلمي في (الفردوس) (٣٥٢) باختلاف يسير.

(٥) أخرجه المتقي الهندي في (كنز العمال) (٤١٠٨).

(٦) ينظر (موسوعة آثار الصحابة) (٣٧٦٣).

said, "Keep looking into the *muṣḥaf*."[1]

Ibn Sa'd narrated that Nāfi' was asked what 'Abdullāh ibn 'Umar ﷺ would do at home. He said, "You cannot do it; *wuḍū'* for every prayer and [reading] the *muṣḥaf* in between." Nāfi' related that when Ibn 'Umar ﷺ would open the *muṣḥaf* to recite, he would start by saying, "O Allah, You guided me, but had You not wished, I would not have been guided. Do not deviate my heart after You have guided me and grant me Your mercy. Surely You are the Giver of all bounties."

Imam Nawawī – may Allah have mercy on him and benefit us through him – said, "Reciting the Qur'an from the *muṣḥaf* is better than reciting it from memory, because looking at the *muṣḥaf* is an act of worship in itself – in this way reciting and looking are combined.

This is what al-Qāḍī Ḥusayn from our [Shāfi'ī] scholars, Abū Ḥāmid al-Ghazālī, and many of the Predecessors said."

Thereafter, Imam Nawawī ﷺ explained that it would be good to say there is detail in this, namely that it varies according to the individual. Thus, whichever of the two recitations is closer to veneration and contemplation will be more virtuous. He said, "It is clear that the discussion and practice of the Predecessors will be interpreted according to this explanation."

Ḥāfiẓ [Ibn Ḥajar] said in *al-Fatḥ*, "Many scholars have clearly stated that reciting from the *muṣḥaf* is better than reciting from memory." He further said, "Abū 'Ubayd narrated from the path (*ṭarīq*) of 'Abdullāh ibn 'Abd al-Raḥmān from one of the Companions of the Prophet ﷺ, as a hadith attributed to the Prophet ﷺ, 'The merit of reciting looking in over reciting from memory is like the merit of the obligatory prayer over the additional prayer.'"[2]

Ḥāfiẓ further said in *al-Fatḥ*, "Its chain is weak. From the same path [Abū 'Ubayd narrated] from Ibn Mas'ūd ﷺ as a *mawqūf* narration, 'Keep looking into the *muṣḥaf*.' Its chain is authentic (*ṣaḥīḥ*)."

---

(1) Bayhaqī in *Shu'ab al-Īmān* (2220)

(2) *Fatḥ al-Bārī*, vol 9, p. 78.

حسنٍ عن ابنِ مسعودٍ رَضِيَ اللَّهُ عَنْهُ أنّه قال: (أديموا النَّظرَ في المصحفِ) [1].

وروى ابنُ سعدٍ أنه قيلَ لنافعٍ: ما كان يصنعُ عبدُ اللهِ بنُ عمرَ رَضِيَ اللَّهُ عَنْهُمَا في منزله؟ فقال: لا تطيقونَه: الوضوءَ لكلِّ صلاةٍ، والمصحفَ فيما بينَهما. وقال نافعٌ: كان ابنُ عمرَ رضي اللهُ عنهما إذا افتتحَ المصحفَ لِيقرأَ بدأَ فقال: اللّهمَّ أنتَ هديتَني ولو شئتَ لم أهتدِ، لا تُزِغْ قلبي بعدَ إذ هديتَني، وهَبْ لي من لَدُنكَ رحمةً إنّكَ أنتَ الوهّابُ. قال الإمامُ النوويُّ رحمه اللهُ تعالى ونفَعَنا به: قراءةُ القرآنِ في المصحفِ أفضلُ من القراءةِ عن ظهرِ قلبٍ؛ لأنَّ النَّظرَ في المصحفِ عبادةٌ مطلوبةٌ، فتجتمعُ القراءةُ والنّظرُ، هكذا قاله القاضي حسينٌ من أصحابِنا، وأبو حامدٍ الغزاليُّ، وجماعاتٌ من السَّلف.

ثمَّ بيَّنَ الإمامُ النّوويُّ رحمه اللهُ تعالى أنّه لو قيلَ بالتفصيلِ لكان القولُ حسناً؛ وذلك أنّه يختلفُ باختلافِ الأشخاصِ فأيّةُ القراءتينِ أقربُ إلى الخشوعِ والتدبُّرِ فهي أفضلُ. قال: والظاهرُ من كلامِ السَّلفِ وفعلِهم محمولٌ على هذا التَّفسيرِ اهـ.

وقال الحافظُ في (الفتح): وقد صرَّحَ كثيرٌ من العلماءِ بأنَّ القراءةَ منَ المُصحَفِ نظراً أفضلُ من القراءةِ عن ظهرِ قلبٍ. قال: وأخرجَ أبو عُبيدٍ من طريقِ عبدِ اللهِ بنِ عبدِ الرَّحمنِ عن بعضِ أصحابِ النبيِّ صَلَّى اللَّهُ عَلَيْهِ وَسَلَّمَ رفَعَهُ قال: «فضلُ قراءةِ القرآنِ نظراً على مَن يقرؤُهُ ظهراً كفضلِ الفريضةِ على النّافلةِ» [2]. قال الحافظُ في (الفتح): وإسنادُه ضعيفٌ، قال: ومِن طريقه - أي: روى أبو عُبيدٍ - من طريقِ ابنِ مسعودٍ رضي اللهُ عنه موقوفاً: (أديموا النَّظرَ في المصحفِ). قالَ: وإسنادُهُ صحيحٌ. اهـ.

---

(١) أخرجه البيهقي في (شعب الإيمان) (٢٢٢٠).

(٢) ينظر (فتح الباري) (٧٨/٩).

ONE OF THE GREATEST HONOURS ALLAH MOST HIGH WILL BESTOW UPON THE PEOPLE OF PARADISE IS THAT HE MOST GLORIFIED WILL RECITE THE QUR'AN TO THEM

Ḥakīm al-Tirmidhī narrated on the authority of Buraydah ﷺ that the Prophet ﷺ said, "The people of Paradise will enter upon the Supreme in Might (al-Jabbār) twice a day and He will recite the Qur'an to them. Each person amongst them will be sitting in their own exclusive seat upon pulpits of pearls, rubies, emeralds, gold, and silver - according to their actions. They will not be joyous about anything as they will about that, and they will not have heard anything more magnificent or better than that. They will then return to their homes and their source of joy, blissfully happy until the same on the following day."(1)

This will be amongst the greatest pleasures and the greatest forms of honour. Their ears will experience such enjoyment that they have never experienced anything like it before - not even a fraction of it. This is as Sijzī narrated in *al-Ibānah* from Anas ﷺ, as a hadith attributed to the Prophet ﷺ, "It will be as though the people had never [previously] heard the Qur'an when Allah recites to them in Paradise."(2)

The author of *al-Firdaws* narrated on the authority of Abū Hurayrah ﷺ that the Prophet ﷺ said, "It will be as though the creation had never before heard the Qur'an when they will hear the Most Compassionate recite it to them on the Day of Judgement."(3)

It is evident that these people honoured with hearing the Speech of Allah Most High from Him twice daily are amongst the highest-ranking people in Paradise. As for others, they will all have a share according to their status. This is proven by the narration in *Sunan al-Tirmidhī* and the

---

(1) Abū Nu'aym in *Ṣifah al-Jannah* (270); Ḥakīm al-Tirmidhī in *Nawādir al-Uṣūl* (156).

(2) Al-Muttaqī al-Hindī in *Kanz al- 'Ummāl* (39335).

(3) Al-Muttaqī al-Hindī in *Kanz al- 'Ummāl* (39336).

مِن أعظمِ إكرامِ اللهِ تعالى لأهلِ الجنّةِ أنْ يُسمِعَهمُ القرآنَ منه سبحانه

روى الترمذيُّ الحكيمُ عن بُريدةَ رَضِيَٱللَّهُعَنْهُ عن النبيِّ ﷺ قال: «إنَّ أهلَ الجنّةِ يدخلونَ على الجبّارِ كلَّ يومٍ مرَّتينِ فيقرأُ عليهِمُ القرآنَ، وقد جلسَ كلُّ امرئٍ منهم مجلِسَهُ الذي هو مجلِسُهُ على منابرِ الدُّرِّ والياقوتِ، والزُّمُردِ، والذَّهبِ، والفضَّةِ بالأعمالِ، فلا تقرُّ أعينُهم قطُّ كما تقرُّ بذلك، ولم يسمعوا شيئاً أعظمَ منه ولا أحسنَ منه، ثمَّ ينصرفونَ إلى رحالِهم، وقرَّةُ أعينِهم ناعمين إلى مثلِهِ من الغد»[1].

وهذا من أعظمِ النَّعيمِ، وأجلِّ أنواعِ التكريمِ، وتعتريهم لذّةٌ في سماعِهم ما ذاقوا لها من قبلُ مثيلاً، ولا معشاراً منها ولا فتيلاً، كما روى السِّجزيُّ في (الإبانة) عن أنسٍ رضي الله عنه مرفوعاً: «كأنَّ النّاسَ لم يسمعوا القرآنَ حين يتلوهُ اللهُ عليهم في الجنّة»[2].

وروى صاحبُ الفردوسِ عن أبي هريرةَ رضي اللهُ عنه عن النبيِّ ﷺ قال: «كأنَّ الخَلقَ لم يسمعوا القرآنَ حين يسمعونَهُ من الرَّحمنِ يتلوهُ عليهم يومَ القيامةِ»[3].

والذي يظهرُ أنَّ هؤلاءِ المكرَّمينِ - الذين يسمعونَ كلامَ اللهِ تعالى من الحقِّ كلَّ يومٍ مرَّتين - هم من أعلى أهلِ الجنّةِ منزلةً، وأمّا غيرُهم فلكلٍّ منهم نصيبٌ حسَبَ مقامِه، يدلُّ على ذلك ما جاء في (سُنَنِ الترمذيّ) و(المُسنَدِ) وغيرِهما - واللَّفظُ للترمذيّ - عن ابنِ عمرَ رَضِيَٱللَّهُعَنْهُمَا أنَّ النبيَّ ﷺ قال: «إنَّ أدنى أهلِ الجنّةِ منزلةً لَمَن ينظرُ إلى

---

(١) أخرجه أبو نعيم في صفة الجنة (٢٧٠), والحكيم الترمذي في (نوادر الأصول) (١٥٦).

(٢) أخرجه المتقي الهندي في (كنز العمال) (٣٩٣٣٥).

(٣) أخرجه المتقي الهندي في (كنز العمال) (٣٩٣٣٦).

Musnad, amongst other works, on the authority of Ibn ʿUmar ﷺ that the Prophet ﷺ said, "The lowest of the people of Paradise is one who will look towards his gardens, wives, bounties, servants and couches for 1000 years (the narration of *Musnad* states 2000 years). The furthest of them will be just as visible to him as the closest of them."(1)

He ﷺ said, "The most honourable amongst them in Allah's sight are those who will look towards His noble Countenance every morning and evening."(2)

It is narrated that Allah Most High will recite *Sūrah al-Raḥmān* to all the people of Paradise, so that they attest to His grace and favour.

SERENITY AND ANGELS DESCENDING UPON THE RECITATION OF THE NOBLE QUR'AN

Imam Muslim narrated in a lengthy hadith on the authority of Abū Hurayrah ﷺ that the Messenger of Allah ﷺ said, "No people gather in one of the houses of Allah Most High – reciting the Book of Allah Most High and studying it amongst themselves – except that serenity descends upon them, mercy covers them, the Angels surround them, and Allah mentions them to those by Him."(3)

In the narration of *al-Ḥilyah* on the authority of Abū Hurayrah ﷺ, the Prophet ﷺ said, "Serenity descends upon the gatherings of remembrance (the best of them being the gatherings of the Qur'an), the Angels surround them, mercy covers them, and Allah mentions them on His Throne."(4)

Bukhārī narrated that whilst Usayd ibn Ḥuḍayr ﷺ was reciting *Sūrah al-Baqarah* one night with his horse tied near him, his horse suddenly became quite disturbed. He became quiet and the horse also calmed down.

---

(1) *Tirmidhī* (2553).

(2) Aḥmad in his *Musnad* (5317).

(3) *Muslim* (2699).

(4) Abū Nuʿaym in *Ḥilyah al-Awliyā'*, vol. 2, p. 215.

جِنانِهِ، وأزواجِه، ونِعَمِه، وخَدَمِه، وسررُه مسيرةَ ألفِ سنةٍ» [1] - وفي روايةِ (المسند): ألفي سنةٍ - «يُرى أقصاهُ كما يُرى أدناهُ»[2].

قال ﷺ: «وأكرمُهم على اللهِ تعالى مَن ينظرُ إلى وجهِهِ الكريمِ غُدوّاً وعشيّةً» [3].

وقد رويَ أنَّ اللهَ تعالى يقرأُ على جميعِ أهلِ الجنّةِ سورةَ الرّحمنِ؛ لِيُقرُّوا له بالفضلِ والامتنانِ.

نزولُ السَّكينةِ وتنزُّلُ الملائكةِ لقراءةِ القرآنِ الكريم

روى الإمامُ مسلمٌ في حديثٍ طويلٍ عن أبي هريرةَ رَضِيَ اللَّهُ عَنْهُ، وفيه: قال رسولُ اللهِ ﷺ: «وما اجتمعَ قومٌ في بيتٍ من بيوتِ اللهِ تعالى يتلونَ كتابَ اللهِ تعالى ويتدارَسونَهُ بينَهم إلّا نزلَتْ عليهِمُ السّكينةُ، وغَشِيَتهُمُ الرَّحمةُ، وحفَّتْهمُ الملائكةُ، وذَكَرَهُمُ اللهُ فيمَن عندَهُ»[4].

وفي روايةِ (الحليةِ) عن أبي هريرةَ رَضِيَ اللَّهُ عَنْهُ أنَّ النبيَّ ﷺ، قال: «مجالِسُ الذِّكرِ - أي: وأفضلُها مجالسُ القرآنِ - تنزلُ عليهم السّكينةُ، وتحفُّ بهمُ الملائكةُ، وتغشاهُمُ الرَّحمةُ، ويذكرهم على عرشِهِ» [5].

وروى البخاريُّ عن أُسَيدِ بنِ حُضيرٍ رَضِيَ اللَّهُ عَنْهُ قال: (بينما هو يقرأُ من اللّيلِ سورةَ

---

(١) أخرجه الترمذي (٢٥٥٣).

(٢) أخرجه أحمد في مسنده (٥٣١٧).

(٣) أخرجه الترمذي (٣٣٨٦).

(٤) رواه مسلم (٢٦٩٩).

(٥) أخرجه أبو نعيم في (حلية الأولياء) (٢/٢١٥).

He then recited and the horse became disturbed again, so he became quiet and it calmed down. He read again and the horse became disturbed again. His son Yaḥyā was near the horse, so he turned and moved him back. He then lifted his head towards the sky to something resembling a cloud containing what seemed like lanterns. In the morning, he related this to the Prophet ﷺ, who said to him, "Do you know what that was?" He said, "No." The Prophet ﷺ said, "Those were Angels who came close to [hear] your voice. If you had carried on reciting, the people would have clearly seen them in the morning and they would not have concealed themselves from them."(1) In other words, they would not have remained hidden, but rather all of them would have seen the Angels. A narration of Muslim states, "I saw something like a cloud containing what seemed like lights rising up in the air until I could no longer see them. He ﷺ said, 'Those were Angels who came close to [hear] your voice.'" Another narration states, "Those were Angels who were listening to you."(2)

A narration of Ḥākim states, "Those were Angels who came down for the recitation of the Qur'an. Had you continued [reciting], you would have seen wonders."(3)

Bukhārī narrated on the authority of Barā' ﷺ that a man was reciting *Sūrah al-Kahf* with his horse next to him, tied with two ropes. A cloud suddenly covered him and started approaching him whilst his horse was trying to break loose. In the morning, he went to the Prophet ﷺ and related this to him. The Prophet ﷺ said, "That was serenity descending due to the Qur'an."(4) In the narration of Tirmidhī, it states, "It descended with (or upon) the Qur'an."(5)

---

(1) *Bukhārī* (5018).

(2) *Muslim* (796).

(3) Ḥākim in *al-Mustadrak*.

(4) *Bukhārī* (5011); *Muslim* (795).

(5) *Tirmidhī* (2885).

البقرةِ وفرسُهُ مربوطةٌ عنده إذ جالتِ الفرسُ - أي: اضطربت -، فسكتَ - أي: أمسكَ عن القراءةِ -، فسكنتِ الفرسُ، فقرأَ فجالَت، فسكتَ فسكنَتِ الفرسُ، ثمّ قرأَ فجالَتْ، وكان ابنُه يحيى قريباً منها فانصرفَ فأخَّره، ثمَّ رفعَ رأسَه إلى السّماءِ فإذا مثلُ الظُّلَّةِ - السّحابةِ - فيها أمثالُ المصابيحِ، فلمّا أصبحَ حدَّثَ النبيَّ ﷺ)، فقال ﷺ: «وتدري ما ذاك»؟ قال: لا، فقال ﷺ: «تلكَ الملائكةُ دَنَتْ لصوتِكَ، ولو قرأتَ لأصبحتَ ينظرُ إليها النّاسُ لا تتوارى منهم»[1]. أي: لا تختفي عنهم؛ بل كلُّهم يرونَ الملائكةَ. وفي روايةٍ لمسلمٍ: «فرأيتُ مثلَ الظُّلّةِ فيها أمثالُ السُّرُجِ، عرجَتْ في الجوِّ حتّى ما أراها! فقال ﷺ: «تلكَ الملائكةُ دنَتْ لصوتِك». وفي روايةٍ: «تلكَ الملائكةُ تستمعُ لكَ»[2]. وفي روايةٍ للحاكمِ: «تلكَ الملائكةُ نزلت لقراءةِ القرآنِ، أمَا إنَّكَ لو مضَيتَ - أي: لو بَقِيتَ على قراءَتِكَ - لرأيتَ العجائبَ»[3].

وروى البخاريُّ عن البراءِ رضي الله عنه قال: كان رجلٌ يقرأُ سورةَ الكهفِ، وإلى جانبِهِ حصانٌ مربوطٌ بشَطَنَينِ - أي: حبلين - فتغشَّتْهُ سحابةٌ، فجعلتْ تدنو وتدنو - أي: تقرُبُ من مكانِ القارئِ - وجعلَ فرسُه ينفرُ، فلمّا أصبحَ أتى النبيَّ ﷺ، فذكر ذلك له، فقال النبي ﷺ: «تلكَ السّكينةُ تنزَّلَتْ للقرآنِ»[4]، وفي روايةِ الترمذيِّ: «نزلَتْ مع القرآنِ، أو على القرآنِ»[5].

---

(١) أخرجه البخاري (٥٠١٨).

(٢) أخرجه مسلم (٧٩٦).

(٣) أخرجه الحاكم في المستدرك (٢٠٣٥).

(٤) أخرجه البخاري (٥٠١١)، ومسلم (٧٩٥).

(٥) أخرجه الترمذي (٢٨٨٥).

THE HOUSES IN WHICH THE QUR'AN IS RECITED SHINE WITH LIGHTS

Bayhaqī has narrated on the authority of Anas ﷺ that the Prophet ﷺ said, "Illuminate your houses with prayer and recitation of the Qur'an."(1) It has already passed in the hadiths that the houses in which the Qur'an is recited shine for the people of the Heavens.

Abū ʿUbayd narrated from a *mursal* path that someone said to the Prophet ﷺ, "Did you not see that the house of Thābit ibn Qays ibn Shammās was glowing with lanterns all last night?" The Prophet ﷺ said, "Perhaps he recited *Sūrah al-Baqarah*?" Thābit ﷺ was asked, to which he replied that he had recited *Sūrah al-Baqarah*. This is cited in the exegesis of Ibn Kathīr and other works.

THE MOST INFERIOR AND CONTEMPTIBLE HOUSE IS ONE IN WHICH THE BOOK OF ALLAH MOST HIGH IS NOT RECITED

Nasāʾī narrated in *ʿAmal al-Yawm wa al-Laylah* on the authority of Ibn Masʿūd ﷺ that the Messenger of Allah ﷺ said, "Let me not find any of you with one foot over the other singing, whilst leaving the recitation of al-Baqarah, because the devil flees from the house in which *Sūrah al-Baqarah* is recited. The most inferior house is the one bereft and empty of the Book of Allah Most High."(2)

(1) Bayhaqī in *Shuʿab al-Īmān* (1974).

(2) Nasāʾī in al-*Sunan al-Kubrā* (8015).

البيوتُ التي يُقرأُ فيها القرآنُ تضيءُ بالأنوار

روى البيهقيُّ عن أنسٍ رضي اللهُ عنه عن النبيِّ صلى اللهُ عليه وآله وسلَّم قال: «نوِّروا منازلَكُمْ بالصّلاةِ، وقراءةِ القرآنِ» (١). وتقدَّمَ في الأحاديثِ أنَّ بيوتَ القرآنِ تضيءُ لأهلِ السّماواتِ.

وروى أبو عُبيدٍ من طريقٍ مرسَلَةٍ: قيل للنبي ﷺ: ألم ترَ لثابتِ بنِ قيسِ بن شماسٍ لم تزلْ دارُهُ البارحةَ تُزهِرُ مصابيحَ؟ فقال النبيُّ ﷺ: «فلعلَّهُ قرأَ سورةَ البقرةِ»؟ (٢)، فسُئِلَ ثابتٌ فقال: قرأتُ سورةَ البقرةِ. كما في (تفسيرِ ابنِ كثيرٍ) وغيره.

أصغرُ البيوتِ وأحقرُها بيتٌ لا يُتلى فيه كتابُ اللهِ تعالى

روى النَّسائيُّ في (عملِ اليومِ واللّيلةِ)، عنِ ابنِ مسعودٍ رضي اللهُ عنه أنَّ رسولَ اللهِ صلى اللهُ عليهِ وآلهِ وسلم قال: «ولا أُلفِينَّ -أي: لا أجدَنَّ- أحدَكم يضعُ إحدى رجليه على الأُخرى يتغنَّى ويَدَعُ - أي: يتركُ - البقرةَ يقرؤها؛ فإنَّ الشّيطانَ ينُفُرُ من البيتِ الذي تُقرأُ فيه سورةُ البقرةِ، وإنَّ أصغرَ البيوتِ الجوفُ الصِّفرُ - أي: الخاليةُ - من كتاب اللهِ تعالى» (٣).

---

(١) أخرجه البيهقي في (شعب الإيمان) (١٩٧٤).

(٢) ينظر (فتح الباري) (٨/٦٧٤).

(٣) أخرجه النسائي في (السنن الكبرى) (٨٠١٥).

THE ANGELS PROTECT THE RECITER OF THE QUR'AN

Tirmidhī narrated on the authority of Shaddād ibn Aws ﵁ that the Messenger of Allah ﷺ said, "There is no Muslim who retires to bed and then recites a *sūrah* from the Book of Allah Most High except that Allah appoints an Angel over him. Nothing harmful can approach him until whenever he awakes from his sleep."(1)

Aḥmad narrated it with the following wording: "Allah sends an Angel to protect him from every harmful thing until whenever he wakes up."(2)

Mundhirī said that the narrators of Aḥmad are all narrators of the *Ṣaḥīḥ* collections.

ALLAH MOST HIGH LOVES THOSE WHO RECITE HIS BOOK AT NIGHT

Tirmidhī narrated on the authority of Ibn Mas'ūd ﵁ that the Prophet ﷺ said, "Three people are loved by Allah Almighty and Exalted: a man who stands at night reciting the Book of Allah; a man who gives charity with

(1) *Tirmidhī* (3407).

(2) Aḥmad in his *Musnad* (17132).

حفظُ الملائكةِ لقارئِ القرآن

روى الترمذيُّ عن شدَّادِ بنِ أوسٍ رَضِيَ اللَّهُ عَنْهُ قال: قال رسولُ اللهِ صَلَّى اللَّهُ عَلَيْهِ وَآلِهِ وَسَلَّمَ: «ما مِن مسلمٍ يأخُذُ مضجعَهُ فيقرأُ سورةً من كتابِ اللهِ تعالى إلّا وَكَّلَ اللهُ له ملَكاً، فلا يقرَبُهُ شيءٌ يؤذيهِ حتّى يهبَّ من نومِه متى هبَّ» [1].

ورواهُ أحمدُ بلفظِ: «بعثَ اللهُ له مَلَكاً يحفظُهُ مِن كلِّ شيءٍ يُؤذيهِ حتّى يهبَّ متى هَبَّ» [2]. قال المنذريُّ: ورواةُ أحمدَ رواةُ الصّحيحِ. اهـ.

اللهُ تعالى يحبُّ مَن يتلو كتابَه في اللَّيل

روى الترمذيُّ عن ابنِ مسعودٍ رضي الله تعالى عنه أنَّ النبيَّ صَلَّى اللَّهُ عَلَيْهِ وَآلِهِ وَسَلَّمَ قال: «ثلاثةٌ يحبُّهُمُ اللهُ عزَّ وجلَّ: رجلٌ قام من اللَّيلِ يتلو كتابَ اللهِ، ورجلٌ تصدَّقَ صدقةً بيمينِهِ يُخفِيها

(١) أخرجه الترمذي (٣٤٠٧).

(٢) أخرجه أحمد في مسنده (١٧١٣٢).

the right hand whilst concealing it from the left hand; and a man who went out in battle, and after his companions were defeated, faced the enemy [alone]."(1)

RECITING THE NOBLE QUR'AN BRINGS DOWN BLESSINGS

Ṭabarānī narrated on the authority of Ḥakam ibn 'Umayr, as a hadith attributed to the Prophet ﷺ, "Take blessings from the Qur'an, because it is the Speech of Allah Most High."(2)

THE HOUSE IN WHICH THE QUR'AN IS NOT RECITED HAS LITTLE GOODNESS AND MUCH EVIL

Dāraquṭnī narrated in *al-Afrād* on the authority of Anas and Jābir ﷺ that the Prophet ﷺ said, "Recite the Qur'an frequently in your homes, because the house in which the Qur'an is not recited has little goodness, much evil, and becomes tight for its occupants."(3) Therefore, frequently recite the Qur'an in your house, O Muslim, so that your character and sustenance become more accommodating, and your life becomes pleasant.

THE PERSON WHO RECITES THE QUR'AN TO PEOPLE RECEIVES A SHARE IN THE HONOUR OF CONVEYING ON BEHALF OF THE MESSENGER OF ALLAH ﷺ

Bukhārī narrated on the authority of Ibn 'Amr ﷺ that the Messenger of Allah ﷺ said, "Propagate on my behalf, even if it be one verse. Relate from the Children of Israel; there is no harm in that. And whoever lies against

(1) *Tirmidhī* (2567).

(2) Al-Muttaqī al-Hindī in *Kanz al- 'Ummāl* (2364).

(3) Al-Muttaqī al-Hindī in *Kanz al- 'Ummāl* (41486).

عن شمالِهِ، ورجلٌ كان في سَريّةٍ فانهزمَ أصحابُهُ فاستقبلَ العدوَّ»[1].

تلاوةُ القرآنِ الكريمِ تُنزِّلُ البركةَ

روى الطبرانيُّ عن الحَكَمِ بنِ عُمَيرٍ مرفوعاً: «تبرَّكْ بالقرآنِ فهو كلامُ اللهِ تعالى»[2].

البيتُ الذي لا يُقرَأُ فيه القرآنُ قليلُ الخيرِ، كثيرُ الشَّرِّ

روى الدارَقطنيُّ في (الأفرادِ) عن أنسٍ وجابرٍ رضي الله عنهما أنَّ النبيَّ صلى الله عليه وآله وسلم قال: «أكثِروا من تلاوةِ القرآنِ في بيوتِكُمْ، فإنَّ البيتَ الذي لا يُقرَأُ فيه القرآنُ يقِلُّ خيرُه ويَكثُرُ شرُّهُ، ويضيقُ على أهلِهِ»[3].

فأكثِر أيُّها المسلمُ من تلاوةِ القرآنِ الكريمِ في بيتِكَ؛ ليتَّسِعَ خُلُقُكَ، ورزقُكَ، وليَطيبَ عَيشُكَ.

تالي القرآنِ على النّاسِ ينالُ حظَّهُ من شرفِ التّبليغِ عن رسولِ اللهِ صلى الله عليه وسلم

روى البخاريُّ عن ابنِ عمرٍو قال: قال رسولُ اللهِ صلى الله عليه وآله وسلم: «بلّغوا عنّي ولو آيةً، وحَدِّثوا عن بني إسرائيلَ ولا حرجَ، ومَن كَذَبَ عليَّ متعمِّداً فليَتبَوَّأْ مَقعدَهُ من النّارِ»[4].

---

(١) أخرجه الترمذي (٢٥٦٧).

(٢) أخرجه المتقي الهندي في كنز العمال (٢٣٦٤).

(٣) أخرجه المتقي الهندي في (كنز العمال) (٤١٤٨٦).

(٤) أخرجه البخاري (٣٤٦١).

me deliberately should prepare their abode in Hellfire."[1] Tirmidhī and Aḥmad have narrated it. Therefore, the person who recites the Words of Allah Most High to His slaves should intend to draw near to Allah Most High thereby and to convey on behalf of the Messenger of Allah ﷺ, in fulfilment of his command.

ALLAH MOST HIGH LOVES THE SLAVE WHO RECITES HIS VERSES AT NIGHT WHILST THEIR COMPANIONS ASLEEP

Tirmidhī and Nasā'ī narrated on the authority of Abū Dharr ؓ that the Messenger of Allah ﷺ said, "There are three whom Allah loves and three whom Allah hates. As for those whom Allah loves, they are: a man who came to some people and begged of them in Allah's name – not because of any relationship between him and them – but they refused him. Then another man withdrew from them (i.e., moved away from them and hid) and gave him something secretly; no one knew of his gift besides Allah and the one to whom he gave. Then are a people who travelled all night until sleep was dearer to them than anything else that could be compared with it. They put their heads down, but one of them stood imploring Me and reciting My verses. Then is a man who was in an expedition which faced the enemy and was defeated, yet he proceeded straight ahead until he was killed or given victory. The three whom Allah hates are an old man who commits fornication, a poor person who is arrogant, and a rich man who is oppressive."[2]

(1) *Bukhārī* (3461).

(2) *Tirmidhī* (2568); *Nasā'ī* (2570); *Aḥmad* (21393).

ورواهُ الترمذيُّ والإمامُ أحمدُ. فينبغي لِمَن يتلو كلامَ اللهِ على عبادِ اللهِ أن يقصِدَ بذلك التقرُّبَ إلى اللهِ تعالى، والتَّبليغَ عن رسولِ الله ﷺ ممتثلاً أمرَهُ ﷺ بذلك.

اللهُ تعالى يحبُّ العبدَ يتلو آياتِهِ في اللّيلِ وقد نامَ أصحابُهُ

روى الترمذيُّ والنَّسائيُّ عن أبي ذرٍّ الغفاريِّ رضي اللهُ عنه أنَّ رسولَ الله ﷺ قال: «ثلاثةٌ يحبُّهُمُ اللهُ، وثلاثةٌ يبغضُهُمُ اللهُ، فأمّا الذينَ يحبُّهُمُ اللهُ: فرجلٌ أتى قوماً فسألَهم باللهِ - ولم يسألْهُمُ القرابةَ بينَهُ وبينَهم - فمنعوه، فتخلَّفَ رجلٌ بأعقابِهم - أي: تأخَّرَ عنهم وتوارى - فأعطاهُ سرّاً لا يعلمُ بعطيَّتِهِ إلّا اللهُ والذي أعطاه، وقومٌ ساروا ليلَتَهم حتّى إذا كان النَّومُ أحبَّ إليهم ممّا يُعدَلُ به - أي: أحبَّ مِن كلِّ شيءٍ من الدُّنيا - فوضعوا رؤوسَهم، فقام أحدُهم يتملَّقُني ويتلو آياتي، ورجلٌ كان في سَرِيّةٍ فلقِيَ العدوَّ فهُزِموا فأقبلَ بصدرِهِ حتّى يُقتَلَ أو يُفتحَ له، والثلاثةُ الذين يُبغِضُهُمُ اللهُ: فالشَّيخُ الزّاني، والفقيرُ المُختالُ، والغنيُّ الظَّلومُ»[1].

---

(١) أخرجه الترمذي (٢٥٦٨)، والنسائي (٢٥٧٠)، وأحمد (٢١٣٩٣).

THE MERIT OF GATHERING TO RECITE THE NOBLE QUR'AN AND STUDYING IT

Imam Muslim narrated on the authority of Abū Hurayrah ﷺ that the Prophet ﷺ said, "Whoever alleviates a worldly calamity from a believer, Allah will alleviate from them one of the calamities of the Day of Judgement. Whoever creates ease for a person in difficulty, Allah will create ease for them in this world and the Hereafter. Whoever conceals the faults of a Muslim, Allah will conceal their faults in this world and in the Hereafter. Allah continues helping a person as long as a person continues helping their brother. Whoever treads a path in order to seek knowledge, Allah will make easy for them a path to Paradise thereby. No people gather in one of the houses of Allah in order to recite the Book of Allah and study it among themselves, except that serenity descends upon them, mercy covers them, the Angels surround them, and Allah mentions them to those who are by Him. Whoever is kept behind by their deeds cannot be taken forward by their lineage."(1)

This noble hadith contains comprehensive words of the Prophet ﷺ which combine many aspects of knowledge and wisdom. It contains

(1) *Muslim* (2699).

فضلُ الاجتماعِ على تلاوةِ القرآنِ الكريمِ ومدارَسَتِهِ

روى الإمامُ مسلمٌ عن أبي هريرةَ رَضِيَ اللهُ عَنْهُ عن النبيِّ ﷺ قال: «مَن نفَّسَ عن مؤمنٍ كُربَةً من كُرَبِ الدُّنيا نفَّسَ اللهُ عنه كُربةً من كُرَبِ يومِ القيامةِ، ومَن يسَّرَ على مُعسِرٍ يسَّرَ اللهُ عليه في الدُّنيا والآخرةِ، ومَن سترَ مسلماً سترهُ اللهُ في الدُّنيا والآخرةِ، واللهُ في عَونِ العبدِ ما كان العبدُ في عَونِ أخيه، ومَن سَلَكَ طريقاً يلتَمِسُ فيه علماً سهَّلَ اللهُ له به طريقاً إلى الجنّةِ، وما اجتمعَ قومٌ في بيتٍ من بيوتِ اللهِ يتلونَ كتابَ اللهِ، ويتدارَسونَهُ بينَهم إلّا نزلَتْ عليهِمُ السَّكينةُ، وغَشِيَتْهُمُ الرَّحمةُ، وحفَّتْهُمُ الملائكةُ، وذَكَرَهُمُ اللهُ فيمَن عنده، ومَن بطَّأَ به عمَلُهُ لم يُسرِعْ به نسَبُهُ» (١).

وفي هذا الحديثِ الشّريفِ جوامِعُ من كَلِمِهِ ﷺ الجامعةُ لأنواعٍ من العلومِ والحِكَمِ، فيها الإرشاداتُ والتّوجيهاتُ، وبيانُ مراتبِ جُمَلٍ من البرِّ والإحسانِ، ومِنَ القُرُباتِ والطّاعاتِ، وبيانٌ لمقابِلاتِها وأجزيَتِها:

---

(١) رواه مسلم (٢٦٩٩).

instructions and guidelines, explaining the rank of numerous acts of righteousness, excellence, obedience, and divine nearness, and stating their corresponding rewards.

The first point encourages alleviating calamities from those who are distressed. A calamity (*kurbah*) is a colossal difficulty that lands the afflicted person in distress. Alleviating it is to lighten its severity from the afflicted if one is unable to remove it entirely. However, removing it entirely is greater, whereby their worry and grief dissipates. Hence, the reward for alleviating someone's calamity is one's own calamity being alleviated, and the reward of removing someone's calamity is one's own calamity being removed. This is as stated in the hadith of Ṭabarānī on the authority of Kaʿb ibn ʿUjrah رضي الله عنه that the Prophet ﷺ said, "Whoever alleviates one of the calamities of a believer, Allah will alleviate from them one of the calamities of the Day of Judgement. Whoever conceals the faults of a believer, Allah will conceal their faults. Whoever removes the calamity of a believer, Allah will remove their calamity."[1]

The second point is encouragement to make things easy for a person in difficulty: "Whoever creates ease for a person in difficulty, Allah will create ease for them in this world and the Hereafter." This proves that on the Day of Judgement there will be people at ease and also people in difficulty.

Creating ease for people in this world, in financial terms, is by giving respite to them until a time of ease – this is obligatory, due to His saying, "If it is difficult for someone to repay a debt, postpone it until a time of ease."[2] Alternatively, it is through foregoing the debt if they are the creditor, or by giving them that with which removes their financial difficulty.

The third point is encouraging concealing a Muslim's faults. "Whoever conceals the faults of a Muslim, Allah will conceal their faults in this world and in the Hereafter." Ibn Mājah narrated on the authority of Ibn ʿAbbās رضي الله عنهما that the Prophet ﷺ said, "Whoever conceals the faults of his Muslim

---

(1) Ṭabarānī in *al-Muʿjam al-Awsaṭ* (178).

(2) *Al-Baqarah*, 280.

الأُولى: الحثُّ على تنفيسِ الكُرَبِ عن المكروبين، والكُربَةُ هي: الشِّدَّةُ العظيمةُ توقعُ صاحبَها في الكَربِ، وتنفيسُها هو: أنْ يخفِّفَ عن المكروبِ من شِدَّتِها إن لم يستطعْ إزالتَها وتفريجَها عنه؛ فإنَّ التفريجَ أعظمُ، وهو أنْ يُزيلَ الكُربةَ عن المكروبِ، وبذلك يزولُ همُّهُ وغمُّهُ، فجزاءُ التَّنفيسِ هو التَّنفيسُ، وجزاءُ التَّفريجِ هو التَّفريجُ، كما جاءَ في الحديثِ الذي رواهُ الطَّبرانيُّ عن كعبِ بنِ عُجرةَ رَضِيَ اللَّهُ عَنْهُ عن النبيِّ صَلَّى اللَّهُ عَلَيْهِ وَآلِهِ وَسَلَّمَ قال: «مَن نفَّسَ عن مؤمنٍ كُربةً من كُرَبِهِ نفَّسَ اللهُ عنه كُربَةً مِن كُرَبِ يومِ القيامةِ، ومَن سترَ على مؤمنٍ عَورَتَهُ سترَ اللهُ عَورَتَهُ، ومَن فرَّجَ عن مؤمنٍ كُربَةً فرَّجَ اللهُ عنه كُربتَهُ»[(١)].

الثانيةُ: الحثُّ على التيسيرِ على المعسِر، «ومَن يسَّر على معسِرٍ يسَّرَ اللهُ عليه في الدُّنيا والآخرةِ»، وفي هذا دليلٌ على أنَّ يومَ القيامةِ فيه مَن هو ذو يُسرٍ، ومَن هو ذو عُسرٍ.

والتيسيرُ على المعسرِ في الدُّنيا من جهةِ المالِ: هو إمّا بانتظارِهِ إلى المَيسَرَةِ، وذلك واجبٌ؛ لقولِه تعالى: {وَإِن كَانَ ذُو عُسْرَةٍ فَنَظِرَةٌ إِلَىٰ مَيْسَرَةٍ}[(٢)]، وإمّا بالوضعِ عنه إن كان غَريماً، وإلّا فبإعطائِهِ ما يزولُ به إعسارُهُ.

الثالثةُ: الحثُّ على سَترِ المسلمِ «ومَن سترَ مسلماً سترهُ اللهُ في الدُّنيا والآخرةِ».

وروى ابنُ ماجه عن ابنِ عبّاسٍ رضي اللهُ عنهما أنَّ النبيَّ صَلَّى اللَّهُ عَلَيْهِ وَآلِهِ وَسَلَّمَ قال: «مَن سترَ عَورةَ أخيه المسلمِ سترَ اللهُ عَورتَهُ يومَ القيامةِ، ومَن كشفَ عورةَ أخيهِ المسلمِ كشفَ

---

(١) أخرجه الطبراني في (المعجم الأوسط) (١٧٨).

(٢) البقرة: ٢٨٠.

brother, Allah will conceal their faults on the Day of Judgement. Whoever exposes the faults of his Muslim brother, Allah will expose their faults, to the extent that He will humiliate them as a result within their houses."[1]

Fourthly, it encourages helping other Muslims: "Allah continues helping a person as long as a person continues helping their brother." Ṭabarānī narrated on the authority of ʿUmar ﷺ, as a hadith attributed to the Prophet ﷺ, "The best of actions is to make a believer happy – you conceal his fault, remove his hunger or fulfil his need."[2]

Fifthly, it encourages a person to tread the path of knowledge: "Whoever treads a path in order to seek knowledge, Allah will make easy for them a path to Paradise thereby."

ʿAllāmah Ibn Rajab al-Ḥanbalī ﷺ said, "The meaning of this could be that Allah facilitates and makes easy for him the knowledge which he has seeking and whose path he has taken. This is similar to the saying of Allah Most High, 'And We have certainly made the Qur'an easy to remember. So is there anyone who will be mindful?'[3] It could also mean that Allah makes it easy for the seeker of knowledge, when through seeking it they intend to please Allah Most High, benefit from it and act accordingly. Hence, it becomes a cause for their guidance, and consequently, their entry into Paradise. At times, Allah Most High facilitates for this seeker of knowledge other branches of knowledge from which they benefit and which lead them to Paradise. It is said, 'Whoever acts upon their knowledge, Allah grants them knowledge of that which they did not know.'"

He then said, "Included in this also is facilitating the best path to Paradise on the Day of Judgement – namely the Bridge (*Ṣirāṭ*) and the horrors before and after it on the Day of Judgement. It is thus made easy for the seeker of knowledge, because they benefit from it, as knowledge leads the way to Allah Most High through the closest and easiest route. Whoever treads the

(1) *Ibn Mājah* (2546)

(2) Ṭabarānī in *al-Muʿjam al-Awsaṭ* (5081)

(3) *Al-Qamar*, 22.

اللهُ عورَتَهُ حتّى يفضَحَهُ بها في بيتِه»[1].

الرابعةُ: الحثُّ على إعانةِ المسلمينَ «واللهُ في عَونِ العبدِ ما كان العبدُ في عَونِ أخيهِ».

وقد روى الطَّبرانيُّ من حديثِ عمرَ رَضِيَ اللهُ عَنْهُ مرفوعاً: «أفضلُ الأعمالِ إدخالُ السُّرورِ على المؤمنِ: كَسَوتَ عورَتَهُ، أو أشبَعْتَ جوعَتَهُ، أو قضَيتَ له حاجةً»[2].

الخامسةُ: الحثُّ على سلوكِ طريقِ العلمِ «ومَن سلكَ طريقاً يلتمسُ فيه علماً سهَّلَ اللهُ له به طريقاً إلى الجنّةِ».

قال العلاّمةُ ابنُ رجبٍ الحنبليّ رحمهُ اللهُ تعالى: قد يُرادُ بذلك أنَّ اللهَ يُسهِّلُ له العِلمَ الذي طلبَهُ وسلكَ طريقَهُ ويُيسِّره عليه؛ فإنَّ العلمَ طريقٌ يوصِّلُ إلى الجنّةِ، وهذا كقولِه تعالى: {وَلَقَدْ يَسَّرْنَا الْقُرْآنَ لِلذِّكْرِ فَهَلْ مِن مُّدَّكِرٍ}[3].

وقد يُراد أيضاً أنَّ اللهَ تعالى يُيَسِّرُ لطالبِ العلمِ إذا قصدَ بطلَبِهِ وجهَ اللهِ تعالى، والانتفاعَ به والعملَ بمقتضاه فيكونُ سبباً لهدايتِهِ، ولدخولِ الجنّةِ بذلك، وقد يُيسِّرَ اللهُ تعالى لطالبِ العلمِ علوماً أُخَرَ ينتفعُ بها، وتكونُ موصِلَةً إلى الجنّةِ كما قيل: مَن عَمِلَ بما عَلِمَ أورثَهُ اللهُ عِلْمَ ما لم يَعلَمْ.

ثمَّ قال: وقد يدخلُ في ذلك أيضاً تسهيلُ طريقُ الجنّةِ الحُسنى يومَ القيامةِ، وهو الصِّراطُ وما قبلَهُ وما بعدَهُ من الأهوالِ، فيُيَسَّر ذلك على طالبِ العلم للانتفاعِ به؛ فإنَّ العلمَ يدلُّ على اللهِ تعالى من أقربِ الطُّرقِ إليه، فمَن سلكَ طريقَهُ ولم يعوجَ عنه وصلَ

---

(١) أخرجه ابن ماجه (٢٥٤٦).

(٢) أخرجه الطبراني في الأوسط (٥٠٨١).

(٣) القمر: ٢٢.

path of knowledge and does not deviate from it reaches Allah Most High and Paradise through the closest and easiest route. All the paths leading to Paradise in this world and the Hereafter become easy for them. This is because there is no path to recognition of Allah, attaining His pleasure, and successfully acquiring His nearness and His proximity except through beneficial knowledge with which Allah sent His Messengers and revealed His Books. Knowledge is what leads towards Him, and through it is one guided in the darkness of ignorance, misgivings, and doubts. He Most High said, "There certainly has come to you from Allah a light and a clear Book through which Allah guides those who seek His pleasure to the ways of peace, brings them out of darkness and into light by His Will, and guides them to the Straight Path."(1)

Sixthly, it encourages studying the Book of Allah Most High and gathering to recite it. He ﷺ said, "No people gather in one of the houses of Allah in order to recite the Book of Allah and study it among themselves, except that serenity descends upon them, mercy covers them, the Angels surround them and Allah mentions them to those who are by Him."

This proves that it is desirable to sit in the masjids to recite and study the Qur'an. This includes gathering to learn and teach the Qur'an, just as it includes to study the Qur'an in general (by oneself).

Ibn 'Abbās ﷺ was asked, "What is the best action?" He said, "Remembering Allah Most High. No people gather in one of the houses of Allah Most High - engaging in and studying the Book of Allah amongst themselves - except that the Angels shade them with their wings. They remain the guests of Allah for as long as they are in that state, until they engage in some other topic."(2) This has been narrated, as a hadith attributed to the Prophet ﷺ, but the *mawqūf* narration is more authentic, as pointed out by 'Allāmah Ibn Rajab al-Ḥanbalī.

He said that Yazīd al-Raqāshī narrated on the authority of Anas ﷺ that

---

(1) *Al-Mā'idah*, 15-16.

(2) *Dārimī* (368).

إلى اللهِ تعالى وإلى الجنّةِ من أقربِ الطُّرُقِ وأسهلِها، فسهُلَتْ عليه الطُّرُقُ الموصِلَةُ إلى الجنّةِ كلُّها في الدُّنيا والآخرةِ، فلا طريقَ إلى معرفةِ اللهِ، وإلى الوصولِ إلى رضوانه، والفوزِ بقُربِهِ، ومجاورتِهِ في الآخرةِ إلّا بالعلمِ النّافعِ الذي بعثَ اللهُ به رُسُلَهُ وأنزلَ به كتُبَهُ، فهو الدَّليلُ عليه، وبه يُهتدَى في ظلماتِ الجهلِ والشُّبَهِ والشُّكوكِ، قال تعالى: {قَدْ جَاءَكُم مِّنَ اللَّهِ نُورٌ وَكِتَابٌ مُّبِينٌ (١٥) يَهْدِي بِهِ اللَّهُ مَنِ اتَّبَعَ رِضْوَانَهُ سُبُلَ السَّلَامِ وَيُخْرِجُهُم مِّنَ الظُّلُمَاتِ إِلَى النُّورِ بِإِذْنِهِ وَيَهْدِيهِمْ إِلَىٰ صِرَاطٍ مُّسْتَقِيمٍ}[١].

السادسةُ: الحثُّ على مُدارسةِ كتابِ اللهِ تعالى، والاجتماعِ على تلاوتِهِ قال ﷺ: «وما اجتمعَ قومٌ في بيتٍ من بيوتِ اللهِ تعالى يتلونَ كتابَ اللهِ، ويتدارسونَهُ بينَهم إلّا نزلتْ عليهِمُ السَّكينةُ، وغَشِيَتْهُمُ الرَّحمةُ، وحفَّتْهُمُ الملائكةُ، وذكَرَهُمُ اللهُ فيمَن عندَه».

وهذا يدلُّ على استحبابِ الجلوسِ في المساجدِ؛ لتلاوةِ القرآنِ ومدارستِه، وهذا يشملُ الاجتماعَ على تعلُّمِ القرآنِ وتعليمِه، ويشملُ الاجتماعَ في المساجدِ على دراسةِ القرآنِ مطلقاً.

وقد سُئلَ ابنُ عبّاسٍ رَضِيَ اللهُ عَنْهُما: أيُّ العملِ أفضلُ؟ قال: (ذكرُ اللهِ تعالى، وما جلسَ قومٌ في بيتٍ من بيوتِ اللهِ تعالى يتعاطَونَ فيه كتابَ اللهِ فيما بينَهم، ويتدارسونَهُ إلّا أظلَّتْهُمُ الملائكةُ بأجنحتِها، وكانوا أضيافَ اللهِ ما داموا على ذلك حتّى يخوضوا في حديثٍ غيرِهِ)[٢]. وروي هذا مرفوعاً، والموقوفُ أصحُّ، كما نبَّهَ عليه العلاّمةُ ابنُ رجبٍ الحنبليُّ.

قال: وروى يزيدُ الرَّقاشيُّ عن أنسٍ رَضِيَ اللهُ عَنْهُ قال: كانوا إذا صلَّوا الغَداةَ قعدوا

---

(١) المائدة: ١٥-١٦.

(٢) أخرجه الدارمي (٣٦٨).

when they would finish performing the morning prayer, they would sit in circles and recite the Qur'an, study the rulings of obligatory and sunnah actions, and remember Allah Most High.

ʿAṭiyyah narrated on the authority of Abū Saʿīd al-Khudrī ﵁ that the Prophet ﷺ said, "No people perform the morning prayer then remain seated in their place, engaging in and studying the Book of Allah, except that Allah appoints Angels to seek forgiveness on their behalf, until they engage in some other topic."[1]

Ibn Rajab ﵀ said, "This proves it is desirable to gather after the morning prayer to study the Qur'an. However, ʿAṭiyyah has some weakness in him.

Ḥarb al-Kirmānī narrated with his chain that Awzāʿī was asked regarding studying after the morning prayer.

He said, 'Ḥassān ibn ʿAṭiyyah informed me that the first person to initiate this practice in the masjid of Damascus was Hishām ibn Ismāʿīl al-Makhzūmī, and so people adopted this.'

With his chain he narrates that Saʿīd ibn ʿAbd al-ʿAzīz and Ibrāhīm ibn Sulaymān used to teach the Qur'an after the morning prayer in Beirut whilst Awzāʿī was in the masjid. He would not correct them or criticize them.

Ḥarb mentioned that he saw that the people of Damascus, Homs, Mecca, and Basra would gather for the Qur'an after the morning prayer. However, the people of the Levant (Shām) would all recite the Qur'an collectively from one *sūrah* in a loud voice. The people of Basra and Mecca would get together, with each of them reciting ten verses whilst the rest of the people remained silent. Then the next person would recite ten verses until they all finished. Ḥarb said all of this is excellent and good."

(1) *Daylamī* (6118).

حلقاً حلقاً، يقرأونَ القرآنَ، ويتعلَّمونَ الفرائضَ والسُّنَنَ، ويذكرونَ اللهَ تعالى.

قال: وروى عطيّةُ عن أبي سعيدٍ الخدريّ رَضِيَ اللهُ عَنهُ عن النبيّ صَلَّى اللهُ عَلَيهِ وَآلِهِ وَسَلَّمَ قال: «ما من قوم صلَّوا صلاةَ الغَداةِ ثمَّ قعدوا في مُصلَّاهم يتعاطونَ كتابَ اللهِ، ويتدارسونَهُ إلّا وَكَّلَ اللهُ تعالى بهمُ الملائكةَ يستغفرونَ لهم حتّى يخوضوا في حديثٍ غيرِهِ»[1].

قال رحمهُ اللهُ تعالى: وهذا يدلُّ على استحبابِ الاجتماعِ بعد صلاةِ الغَداةِ لمدارسةِ القرآن، ولكنَّ عطيّةَ فيه ضعفٌ.

وقد روى حَربٌ الكرمانيُّ بإسنادِهِ عن الأوزاعيّ أنَّهُ سُئِلَ عن المُدارسةِ بعد صلاةِ الصُّبحِ؟

فقال: أخبَرني حسَّانُ بنُ عطيَّةَ: أنَّ أوَّلَ مَن أحدَثَها في مسجدِ دمشقَ هشامُ بنُ إسماعيلَ المخزوميُّ، فأخذَ النّاسُ بذلك.

وبإسنادِهِ عن سعيدِ بنِ عبدِ العزيزِ، وإبراهيمَ بنِ سُليمانَ أنّهما كانا يُدرِّسانِ القرآنَ بعد صلاةِ الصُّبحِ ببيروت، والأوزاعيُّ في المسجدِ لا يُغيِّرُ ولا يُنكِرُ عليهم.

وذكر حربٌ أنّه رأى أهلَ دمشقَ وحمصَ وأهلَ مكَّةَ وأهلَ البصرةِ يجتمعونَ على القرآنِ بعد صلاةِ الصُّبحِ، ولكنَّ أهلَ الشّامِ يقرأونَ القرآنَ كلَّهم جملةً واحدةً، من سورةٍ واحدةٍ بأصواتٍ عاليةٍ، وأهلَ البصرةِ وأهلَ مكَّةَ يجتمعون فيقرأُ أحدُهم عشرَ آياتٍ والنّاُس يُنصِتونَ، ثمَّ يقرأُ آخَرُ عشرَ آياتٍ حتى يفرُغوا، قال حربٌ: كلُّ ذلك حسنٌ جميلٌ. اهـ. كلام ابن رجبٍ رَحِمَهُ اللهُ تَعَالَى.

---

(١) أخرجه الديلمي (٦١١٧).

THE VIRTUE OF MEMORIZING THE NOBLE QUR'AN

Indeed, one of the greatest divine favours with which Allah Most High has distinguished this ummah – may the choicest blessings and peace, and the most sublime greetings be upon their Messenger – is that He Most Glorified has made the hearts of this ummah containers for His Speech. He has made their bosoms *muṣḥafs* to preserve His verses. It cannot be washed away by a current of water or erased by the scheming of the enemies. Allah Most High said, "But this [Qur'an] is [a set of] clear Revelations [preserved] in the hearts of those gifted with knowledge. And none denies Our Revelations except the [stubborn] wrongdoers."(1)

As for the evidence that it cannot be washed away with water, there is a hadith of Muslim on the authority of 'Iyāḍ ﷺ that the Prophet ﷺ said, "My Lord commanded me to teach you that which you do not know from what He has taught me today: All wealth I have given the slave is lawful. I created My slaves as sincerely devout [to Allah]. The devils then came to them and turned them away from their religion, making unlawful for them what I made lawful for them and commanding them to associate with Me that for which I did not send down any authority. Indeed, Allah

(1) *Al-'Ankabūt*, 49.

فضيلةُ استظهارِ القرآنِ الكريمِ

إنَّ مِن أعظمِ المِنَنِ الإلهيّةِ التي خصَّ اللهُ تعالى بها هذه الأمّةَ على رسولِها أفضلُ الصّلاةِ والسّلامِ، وأطيبُ التحيّةِ - ولم يُعْطِها أحداً من الأممِ القبليّةِ - أنّه سبحانه جعل قلوبَ هذه الأمّةِ أوعيةً لكلامِهِ، وجعل صدورَها مصاحفَ لحفظِ آياتِهِ، لا يغسِلُهُ من قلوبِهم تيّارُ الماءِ، ولا يمحوهُ من صدورِهِمْ كيدُ الأعداء. قال اللهُ تعالى: {بَلْ هُوَ آيَاتٌ بَيِّنَاتٌ فِي صُدُورِ الَّذِينَ أُوتُوا الْعِلْمَ ۚ وَمَا يَجْحَدُ بِآيَاتِنَا إِلَّا الظَّالِمُونَ}[1].

أما الدليلُ على أنّهُ لا يغسِلُهُ الماءُ: ففي (صحيح مسلم) عن عياضٍ رَضِيَ اللهُ عَنْهُ، أنَّ النبيَّ صَلَّى اللهُ عَلَيْهِ وَآلِهِ وَسَلَّمَ قال: «إنَّ ربِّي أمَرَني أنْ أعلِّمَكم ما جَهِلْتُم ممّا علَّمني يومي هذا: كلُّ مالٍ نَحَلتُهُ - أي: أعطيتُهُ - عبداً حلالٌ، وإنّي خَلقْتُ عبادي حنفاءَ كلَّهم - أي: على المِلَّةِ الحنيفيّةِ - وإنّهم أتتهمُ الشّياطينُ فاجتالَتْهم عن دينِهم، وحرَّمَتْ عليهم ما أحللْتُ لهم، وأمَرَتْهم أن يُشركوا بي ما لم أُنزِلْ به سلطاناً، وإنَّ اللهَ تعالى نظرَ إلى أهلِ الأرضِ فمقتَهم،

---

(١) العنكبوت: ٤٩.

looked towards the inhabitants of the Earth and despised them – Arabs and non-Arabs alike – except for some remnants from the People of the Book." Allah Most High said, "I only sent you to test you and to test [others] through you. I sent down to you a Book which water cannot wash away; you can read it whilst asleep and awake."(1)

As for the evidence for the nobility of this ummah by making their bosoms *muṣḥafs* for the verses of the Noble Qur'an, Abū Nuʿaym narrated in *al-Dalā'il* with his chain on the authority of Anas ﷺ that the Messenger of Allah ﷺ said, "When I had finished with what Allah commanded me regarding the matters of the Heavens and the Earth, I said (on the night of the Ascension), 'O my Lord, there is no Prophet before me except that You honoured them. You took Ibrāhīm as a close friend (*khalīl*) and Mūsā as an interlocutor (*kalīm*). You subjugated the mountains for Dāwūd and the wind and jinn for Sulaymān. You revived the dead for ʿĪsā. What have you given me?' He said, 'Did I not give you better than all of this? I am not remembered except that you are remembered alongside Me. I made the bosoms of your ummah scrolls (i.e., *muṣḥafs*); they recite the Qur'an from memory, and no other ummah was given this. I granted you a treasure from the treasures of my Throne: *Lā ḥawla wa lā quwwata illā bi Allāh al-ʿAliyy al- ʿAẓīm*."(2) Others besides Abū Nuʿaym have also narrated it, such as Ibn Kathīr in his exegesis, and others.

Ṭabarānī narrated on the authority of Ibn Masʿūd ﷺ that the Prophet ﷺ said, "My attribute is Aḥmad the Reliant (al-Mutawakkil). He is neither cruel nor hard-hearted. He repays good with good and does not reciprocate evil. He will be born in Mecca and his place of migration will be Ṭaybah. His ummah are those who praise abundantly (*al-ḥammādūn*). They wear their lower garment to halfway down the shins, and they perform *wuḍū'* of their arms and feet. Their scrolls are in their bosoms. They stand in rows for prayer just as they stand in rows to fight. Their sacrifice through which

(1) *Muslim* (2865)

(2) Ibn Kathīr in *al-Bidāyah wa al-Nihāyah*, vol. 6, p. 288.

عربَهم وعجمَهم إلّا بقايا من أهلِ الكتابِ»، وقال اللهُ تعالى: «إنّما بعثتُكَ لأبتليَكَ وأَبتليَ بك، وأنزَلتُ عليك كتاباً لا يَغْسِلُهُ الماءُ، تقرأه نائماً ويقظاناً» (١) الحديثَ.

وأما الدَّليلُ على شرفِ هذه الأمّةِ بجعل صدورِها مصاحفَ لآياتِ القرآن الكريم:

فقد روى أبو نُعيمٍ في (الدَّلائلِ) بإسنادِهِ عن أنسٍ رَضِيَ اللَّهُ عَنْهُ قال: قال رسولُ الله صلى الله عليه وآله وسلم: «لمّا فرَغتُ ممّا أمرَني اللهُ به من أمرِ السّمواتِ والأرضِ قلتُ: - أي: ليلةَ المعراجِ - يا ربِّ إنّه لم يكنْ نبيٌّ قبلي إلّا وقد كرَّمته: جعلتَ إبراهيمَ خليلاً، و موسى كليماً، وسخَّرتَ لداودَ الجبالَ، ولسُليمانَ الرّيحَ والشّياطينَ، وأحيَيتَ لعيسى الموتى، فما جعلتَ لي؟ قال: أوَليسَ أعطيتُكَ أفضلَ من ذلك كلِّهِ: إنّي لا أُذْكَرُ إلا ذُكِرْتَ معي، وجعلتُ صدورَ أمّتِكَ أناجيلَ - أي: مصاحفَ - يقرؤونَ القرآنَ ظاهراً، ولم أُعطِها أمّةً - أي: مِن قبلِك -. وأعطيتُكَ كنزاً من كنوزِ عرشي: لا حولَ ولا قوّةَ إلّا باللهِ العليّ العظيمِ» (٢). ورواهُ غيرُ أبي نُعيم، كما في (تفسيرِ) ابنِ كثيرٍ وغيرِه.

وروى الطّبرانيُّ عن ابنِ مسعودٍ رضي اللهُ عنه أنَّ النبيَّ صَلَّى اللَّهُ عَلَيْهِ وَآلِهِ وَسَلَّمَ قال: «صِفَتي: أحمدُ المتوكِّلُ، ليس بفظٍّ ولا غَليظٍ، يَجزي بالحسنةِ الحسنةَ، ولا يكافِئُ بالسّيئةِ، مَولِدُهُ بمكّةَ، ومهاجَرُهُ طيبةُ، وأمّتُهُ الحمّادونَ، يأتَزِرونَ على أنصافِهِم، ويوضّئونَ أطرافَهم، أناجيلُهم في صدورِهم، يصفّونَ للصّلاةِ كما يصفّونَ للقتالِ، قُربانُهم الذي يتقرّبونَ به إليّ

(١) أخرجه مسلم (٢٨٦٥).

(٢) أخرجه ابن كثير في (البداية والنهاية) (٢٨٨/٦).

they draw near to Me is their blood. They are worshippers by night and lions by day."[1]

As for honouring this ummah by making their hearts containers for the Noble Qur'an, Abū Umāmah ؓ narrated that the Prophet ﷺ said, "Recite the Qur'an, for Allah Most High will not punish the heart that has memorized the Qur'an."[2]

Imam Aḥmad narrated on the authority of ʿUqbah ibn ʿĀmir ؓ that the Prophet ﷺ said, "If the Qur'an were to be placed in a skin, fire would not burn it." Abū ʿUbayd said that by skin he meant the heart of the believer and his insides which have retained the Qur'an.

MEMORIZING THE QUR'AN IS THE GREATEST OF ALLAH'S FAVOURS UPON HIS SLAVES

Bayhaqī narrated, and Bukhārī in his *Tarīkh*, on the authority of Rajā' al-Ghanawī as a *mursal* narration that the Prophet ﷺ said, "Whoever Allah granted memorization of His Book but thought someone else was given something better than what they were given has erred."[3] Another narration states, "He has belittled the greatest bounty". Another narration states, "He has disparaged the greatest bounty."

THE MOST NOBLE PEOPLE OF THIS UMMAH ARE THE BEARERS OF THE NOBLE QUR'AN

Ṭabarānī and Bayhaqī narrated on the authority of Ibn ʿAbbās ؓ that the Prophet ﷺ said, "The most noble people of my ummah are the bearers of the Qur'an and the people of the night (i.e., those who are regular in

---

(1) Ṭabarānī in *al-Kabīr* (9907).

(2) *Dārimī* (3319).

(3) Aḥmad in al-*Musnad* (1716).

دماؤُهم، رهبانٌ بالليل لُيوثٌ بالنَّهار» (١). وأما تشريفُ هذه الأمّةِ بجعل قلوبها أوعيةً للقرآنِ الكريمِ: فعن أبي أُمامةَ رَضِيَ اللَّهُ عَنْهُ أنَّ النبيَّ صَلَّى اللَّهُ عَلَيْهِ وَآلِهِ وَسَلَّمَ قال: «اِقرؤوا القرآنَ؛ فإنَّ اللهَ تعالى لا يعذِّبُ قلباً وعى القرآنَ» (٢).

وروى الإمامُ أحمدُ عن عقبةَ بنِ عامرٍ رضي اللهُ عنه عن النبيِّ صَلَّى اللَّهُ عَلَيْهِ وَآلِهِ وَسَلَّمَ أنّه قال: «لو كان القرآنُ في إهابٍ ما أكَلَتْهُ النّارُ» (٣).

قال أبو عُبيدٍ: أراد بالإهابِ قلبَ المؤمنِ، وجوفَهُ الذي قد وعي القرآنَ. اهـ.

حفظُ القرآنِ أعظمُ نعمِ اللهِ تعالى على العبادِ

روى البيهقيُّ والبخاريُّ في (تاريخِهِ) عن رجاءَ الغنويِّ مُرسَلاً عن النبيِّ صَلَّى اللَّهُ عَلَيْهِ وَآلِهِ وَسَلَّمَ أنّهُ قال: «مَن أعطاهُ اللهُ تعالى حفظَ كتابِهِ فظنَّ أنَّ أحداً أُعطيَ أفضلَ ممّا أُعطيَ فقد غَلِطَ» (٤). وفي روايةٍ: «فقد صغَّرَ أعظمَ النِّعَمِ»، وفي روايةٍ: «فقد غَمَطَ أعظمَ النِّعَمِ».

أشرافُ الأمّةِ حَمَلَةُ القرآنِ الكريمِ

روى الطبرانيُّ والبيهقيُّ عن ابنِ عبّاسٍ رَضِيَ اللَّهُ عَنْهُمَا عن النبيِّ صَلَّى اللَّهُ عَلَيْهِ وَآلِهِ وَسَلَّمَ أنّه قال: «أشرافُ أمّتي حَمَلَةُ القرآنِ، وأصحابُ اللّيلِ» (٥)، أي: المواظبونَ على قيامِ اللّيلِ.

---

(١) أخرجه الطبراني في الكبير (٩٩٠٧).

(٢) أخرجه الدارمي (٣٣١٩).

(٣) أخرجه أحمد في المسند (١٧١٦).

(٤) أخرجه البيهقي في (شعب الإيمان) (٢٣٥٢).

(٥) أخرجه الطبراني في الكبير (١٢٦٦٢).

praying at night)."(1)

'Allāmah Munāwī ﵀ said, "The bearers of the Qur'an are those who have memorized it, carrying it in their bosoms, knowing how to recite it, and acting upon its requirements. The people of the night are those who stay awake at night in various acts of worship.

'Allāmah Ṭībī said, 'Attributing people to the night is due to their abundantly standing in prayer therein, just as an *ibn al-sabīl* (literally the son of the path) is used to refer to a person who is constantly travelling.'"

THE RICHEST OF PEOPLE ARE THE BEARERS OF THE NOBLE QUR'AN

Ibn 'Asākir narrated on the authority of Anas ﵁, as a hadith attributed to the Prophet ﷺ, "The richest of people are the bearers of the Qur'an."(2)

THE PROTECTION OF THE BEARER OF THE NOBLE QUR'AN

Daylamī narrated in *Musnad al-Firdaws* on the authority of 'Uthmān ibn 'Affān ﵁ that the Prophet ﷺ said, "The bearer of the Qur'an is protected."(3) 'Allāmah Munawi ﵀ said, "*Mūqā* is a passive participle, i.e., protected from Hellfire and from harm."

THE HONOUR OF THE BEARER OF THE NOBLE QUR'AN

Ibn 'Umar ﵁ narrated that the Prophet ﷺ said, "Honour the bearers of the Qur'an, for whoever honours them has honoured me, and whoever honours me has honoured Allah Most High. Listen carefully! Do not

---

(1) Ṭabarānī in *al-Kabīr* (12662).

(2) Al-Muttaqī al-Hindī in *Kanz al- 'Ummāl* (4036).

(3) *Daylamī* (2690).

قال العلّامةُ المناويُّ رحمه الله تعالى: حمَلَةُ القرآنِ هم حُفّاظُه الحاملونَ له في صدورِهم، العالِمونَ تلاوتَه، العاملونَ بمقتضاه، وأصحابُ اللّيلِ هم الذين يُحيونَهُ بأنواعِ العبادة.

قال: وقال العلّامة الطّيبيُّ: إضافةُ الأصحابِ إلى اللّيلِ لكثرةِ مباشرةِ القيامِ والصَّلاةِ فيه، كما يُقال: ابنُ السَّبيلِ لِمَن يواظِبُ على السُّلوكِ فيه. اهـ.

أغنى النّاسِ حملَةُ القرآنِ الكريمِ

روى ابنُ عساكرَ عن أنسٍ رضي اللهُ عنه مرفوعاً: «أغنى النّاسِ حملَةُ القرآنِ» [1].

وِقايةُ حاملِ القرآنِ الكريم

روى الدَّيلميُّ في (مسندِ الفِردَوسِ) عن عثمانَ بنِ عفّانَ رضي الله عنه عن النبيِّ صلى الله عليه وآله وسلم أنّهُ قال: «حاملُ القرآنِ مُوقًى» [2].

قال العلّامةُ المناويُّ رحمه الله تعالى: مُوقًى: مبنيٌّ للمفعول، أي: محفوظٌ من النّارِ، ومن الأذى.

كرامةُ حاملِ القرآنِ الكريمِ

عن ابنِ عمرَ رضي اللهُ عنهما عن النبيِّ صلى اللهُ عليه وآله وسلم قال: «أكرِموا حمَلَةَ

---

(١) أخرجه المتقي الهندي في (كنز العمال) (٤٠٣٦).

(٢) أخرجه الديلمي (٢٦٩٠).

deprive the bearers of the Qur'an of their rights, because they have a status with Allah."(1)

THE BEARER OF THE NOBLE QUR'AN IS THE FLAGBEARER OF ISLAM

Abū Umāmah ؓ narrated, as a hadith attributed to the Prophet ﷺ, "The bearer of the Qur'an is the flagbearer of Islam. Whoever honours him has honoured Allah Most High. And whoever humiliates him, then may Allah's curse be upon him."(2)

THE BEARER OF THE NOBLE QUR'AN BENEFITS FROM THEIR INTELLECT

Ibn ʿAdī narrated on the authority of Anas ؓ, as a hadith attributed to the Prophet ﷺ, "Whoever gathers (i.e., memorizes) the Qur'an, Allah will allow them to benefit from their intellect until they die."(3)

THE BEARERS OF THE NOBLE QUR'AN ARE THE FRIENDS OF ALLAH MOST HIGH

Ibn al-Najjār narrated on the authority of ʿAbdullāh ibn ʿUmar ؓ, as a hadith attributed to the Prophet ﷺ, "The bearers of the Qur'an are the friends of Allah. Whoever despises them despises Allah, and whoever befriends them befriends Allah Most High."(4)

---

(1) Al-Muttaqī al-Hindī in *Kanz al- 'Ummāl* (2271).

(2) Al-Muttaqī al-Hindī in *Kanz al- 'Ummāl* (2291).

(3) Al-Muttaqī al-Hindī in *Kanz al- 'Ummāl* (2318).

(4) Al-Muttaqī al-Hindī in *Kanz al- 'Ummāl* (2292).

القرآنِ، فمَن أكرمَهم فقد أكرمَني، ومَن أكرمَني فقد أكرمَ اللهَ تعالى، ألاَ فلا تَنقُصوا حملةَ القرآنِ حقوقَهم؛ فإنّهم منَ اللهِ بمكانةٍ»[(١)].

حاملُ القرآنِ الكريمِ حاملُ رايةِ الإسلامِ

عن أبي أُمامةَ رضي اللهُ عنه مرفوعاً: «حاملُ القرآنِ حاملُ رايةِ الإسلامِ، مَن أكرَمَهُ فقد أكرمَ اللهَ تعالى، ومَن أهانه فعليهِ لعنةُ اللهِ»[(٢)].

حاملُ القرآنِ الكريمِ ممتَّعٌ بعقلِهِ

روى ابنُ عَديٍّ عن أنسٍ رضي اللهُ عنه مرفوعاً: «مَن جمعَ القرآنَ متَّعهُ اللهُ تعالى بعقلِهِ حتّى يموتَ»[(٣)].

حملةُ القرآنِ الكريمِ أولياءُ اللهِ تعالى

روى ابنُ النَّجّارِ عن عبدِ اللهِ بنِ عمرَ رضي اللهُ عنهما مرفوعاً: «حَمَلَةُ القرآنِ أولياءُ اللهِ، فمَن عاداهم عادى اللهَ، ومَن والاهم فقد والى اللهَ تعالى»[(٤)].

---

(١) أخرجه المتقي الهندي في (كنز العمال) (٢٢٧١).

(٢) أخرجه المتقي الهندي في (كنز العمال) (٢٢٩١).

(٣) أخرجه المتقي الهندي في (كنز العمال) (٢٣١٨).

(٤) أخرجه المتقي الهندي في (كنز العمال) (٢٢٩٢).

THE BEARERS OF THE NOBLE QUR'AN WILL BE IN THE SHADE OF ALLAH MOST HIGH

In *Musnad al-Firdaws*, it is narrated on the authority of the Leader of the Believers (*Amīr al-Mu'minīn*) 'Alī ﵁ that the Prophet ﷺ said, "Indeed, the bearers of the Qur'an will be in the shade of Allah Most High on the day there shall be no shade besides His, along with His Prophets and chosen slaves."(1)

THE INTERCESSION OF THE BEARER OF THE NOBLE QUR'AN

Tirmidhī and others narrated on the authority of 'Alī ﵁ that the Prophet ﷺ said, "Whoever recites the Qur'an and memorizes it, deeming its lawful matters as lawful and its unlawful matters as unlawful, Allah will enter them into Paradise and grant them the right to intercede on behalf of ten such family members for whom Hellfire had become binding."(2)

ALLAH MOST HIGH WILL NOT PUNISH A HEART WHICH RETAINED THE QUR'AN

Ḥāfiẓ Ibn Ḥajar states in *al-Fatḥ* that Ibn Abī Dāwūd narrated with an authentic chain on the authority of Abū Umāmah ﵁, "Recite the Qur'an and do not be deceived by these *muṣḥafs* that are hanging, because Allah does not punish a heart that has retained the Qur'an."(3)

---

(1) Al-Muttaqī al-Hindī in *Kanz al- 'Ummāl* (45401).

(2) *Tirmidhī* (2905); *Ibn Mājah* (221).

(3) *Dārimī* (3319).

حملةُ القرآنِ الكريمِ في ظلِّ اللهِ تعالى

جاء في (مسندِ الفردَوسِ) عن أميرِ المؤمنينَ عليٍّ كرَّمَ اللهُ تعالى وجهَه عن النبيِّ ﷺ قال: «إنَّ حملةَ القرآنِ في ظلِّ اللهِ تعالى يومَ لا ظِلَّ إلا ظِلُّهُ مع أنبيائِهِ وأصفيائِهِ»[1]. الحديث.

شفاعةُ حاملِ القرآنِ الكريم

روى الترمذيُّ وغيرُهُ عن عليٍّ رضي الله عنه أنَّ النبيَّ ﷺ قال: «مَن قرأَ القرآنَ فاستظهرَه - أي: حَفِظَه - فأحلَّ حلالَه، وحرَّم حرامَهُ أدخلَهُ اللهُ تعالى الجنّةَ، وشفَّعَهُ في عشرةٍ مِن أهلِ بيتِهِ، كلُّهم قد وجبَتْ له النّارُ»[2].

لا يُعذِّبُ اللهُ تعالى قلباً وعى القرآنَ

قال الحافظُ ابنُ حجرٍ في (الفتح): أخرج ابنُ أبي داودَ بإسنادٍ صحيح عن أبي أُمامةَ رضي اللهُ عنه أنّه قال: «اقرؤوا القرآنَ ولا تغرَّنَّكم هذه المصاحفُ المعلَّقةُ، فإنَّ اللهَ تعالى لا يعذِّبُ قلباً وعى القرآنَ»[3].

---

(١) أخرجه المتقي الهندي في (كنز العمال) (٤٥٤٠١).

(٢) أخرجه الترمذي (٢٩٠٥) وابن ماجه (٢٢١).

(٣) أخرجه الدارمي (٣٣١٩).

THE BEARERS OF THE QUR'AN WILL BE THE DIRECTORS OF THE PEOPLE OF PARADISE

Ṭabarānī narrated on the authority of Ḥusayn ibn ʿAlī ﷺ, as a hadith attributed to the Prophet ﷺ, "The bearers of the Qur'an will be the directors of the people of Paradise on the Day of Judgement."[1]

Note: It states in *Sharḥ al-Munyah* that to memorize that amount [of the Qur'an] whereby prayer is valid is an individual obligation (*farḍ ʿayn*) upon every accountable person, to memorize *Sūrah al-Fātiḥah* and another *sūrah* is necessary (*wājib*), and to memorize the entire Qur'an is a communal obligation (*farḍ kifāyāh*). Moreover, an individual *sunnah* is better than additional prayer." ʿUmar ibn al-Khaṭṭāb wrote to Abū Mūsā al-Ashʿarī ﷺ to fix a stipend for those who had memorized the Qur'an in Basra that will cover their needs.

THE BEARER OF ALLAH'S BOOK SHOULD BE HONOURED ACCORDING TO THE SACRED LAW

Imam Bukhārī stated in his *Ṣaḥīḥ*: "Chapter on reciting from memory." Thereafter he narrated with his chain on the authority of Sahl ibn Saʿd ﷺ that a woman came to the Messenger of Allah ﷺ and said, "O Messenger of Allah, I have come to give myself to you." But, when the woman saw that he has not decided anything regarding her, she sat down. One of his Companions then stood and said, "O Messenger of Allah, if you have no need for her, marry her to me." He ﷺ asked him, "Do you have anything with you?" He said, "No, by Allah." He said, "Go to your family and see if you can find something." He went but returned saying, "No, by Allah, O Messenger. I could not find anything." He ﷺ said, "Look, even if it be an iron ring." He then went again but came back and said, "No, by Allah, O Messenger, not even an iron ring. However, this is my lower garment." The

(1) Ṭabarānī in *al-Kabīr* (2899).

حملةُ القرآنِ عرفاءُ أهلِ الجنّةِ

روى الطَّبرانيُّ عن الحُسين بنِ عليٍّ رَضِيَ اللهُ عَنْهُمَا مرفوعاً: «حملَةُ القرآنِ عُرَفاءُ أهلِ الجنّةِ يومَ القيامةِ»[1].

تنبيه: قال في (شرحِ المُنيَةِ): إنَّ حِفظَ ما تجوزُ به الصّلاةُ فرضُ عينٍ على كلِّ مكلَّفٍ، وحِفظَ فاتحةِ الكتابِ وسورةٍ واجبٌ، وحِفظَ سائرِ القرآنِ فرضُ كفايةٍ, وسنّةُ عينٍ أفضلُ من صلاةِ النَّفلِ. اهـ.

وقد كتبَ عمرُ بنُ الخطّابِ إلى أبي موسى الأشعريِّ رَضِيَ اللهُ عَنْهُمَا: أن يَفرِضَ لحفّاظِ القرآنِ في البصرةِ ما يفي بحاجَتِهم.

حاملُ كتابِ اللهِ تعالى يُكرَمُ شرعاً

قال الإمامُ البخاريُّ في (صحيحه): «بابُ القراءةِ عن ظهرِ قلبٍ» ثمَّ أسندَ عن سهلِ بنِ سعدٍ أنَّ امرأةً جاءتْ رسولَ اللهِ صَلَّى اللهُ عَلَيْهِ وَآلِهِ وَسَلَّمَ فقالت: يا رسولَ الله جئتُ لأهبَ لكَ نفسي، فلمّا رأتِ المرأةُ أنّه لم يقضِ فيها شيئاً جلسَتْ، فقام رجلٌ من أصحابِه فقال: يا رسولَ اللهِ إنْ لم يكنْ لكَ بها حاجةٌ فزوِّجْنِيها، فقال له صَلَّى اللهُ عَلَيْهِ وَسَلَّمَ: «هل عندكَ من شيءٍ»؟، فقال: لا واللهِ يا رسولَ اللهِ. قال: «اذهبْ إلى أهلِكَ فانظرْ هل تجدُ شيئاً»، فذهبَ ثمَّ رجع فقال: لا واللهِ يا رسول اللهِ ما وجدتُ شيئاً، قال: «انظُر ولو خاتماً مِن حديدٍ»، فذهبَ ثمَّ رجعَ، فقال: لا واللهِ يا رسولَ اللهِ، ولا خاتماً من حديدٍ! ولكنْ هذا إزاري!، فقال رسولُ اللهِ صَلَّى اللهُ عَلَيْهِ وَسَلَّمَ: «ما تصنعُ بإزارِكَ؟ إن لَبِسْتَهُ لم يكن عليها منه شيءٌ، وإن لَبِسَتْهُ

(١) أخرجه الطبراني في الكبير (٢٨٩٩).

Messenger of Allah ﷺ said, "What will she do with your lower garment? If you wear it, no part of it will be on her, and if she wears it, no part of it will be on you." The man then sat for a long time before standing to leave. The Messenger of Allah ﷺ saw him leaving and called him back. When he came, he ﷺ said to him, "What portion of the Qur'an do you have with you?" He said, "I have such-and-such *sūrahs* (enumerating them)." He ﷺ said, "Do you read them from memory?" He said, "Yes." The Prophet ﷺ said, "Go, for I have made her yours in exchange for whatever Qur'an you have with you."

THE BEARERS OF THE QUR'AN ARE SURROUNDED BY ALLAH'S MERCY & ACQUIRE THE LIGHT OF ALLAH

It states in *al-Mirqāh* – the commentary of *Mishkāh* – that the Leader of the Believers 'Alī ؓ said, "The Qur'an is better than everything besides Allah Most High. So, whoever respects it has respected Allah Most High, and whoever does not respect it has slighted the right of Allah Most High. The Qur'an is an intercessor whose intercession is accepted and a truthful witness. For whomsoever the Qur›an intercedes, its intercession will be accepted. And for whomsoever the Qur'an testifies, its testimony will be accepted. Whoever puts the Qur'an in front of them, it will lead them to Paradise. Whoever puts the Qur'an behind them, it will drag them to Hellfire. The bearers of the Qur'an are surrounded by the mercy of Allah Most High, acquire the light of Allah Most High, and learn the Speech of Allah Most High. Whoever despises them has despised Allah Most High, and whoever befriends them has befriended Allah Most High. O bearers of Allah's Book! Respond to Allah by respecting His Book: He shall increase you in love and make you beloved to His creation. The evil of this world is repelled from the person who listens to the Qur'an, and the calamity of the Hereafter is repelled from the reciter of the Qur'an. Listening to a verse of the Book of Allah Most High is better for the listener than Ṣīr (the name of a mountain) in gold, and reciting a verse from the Book of Allah Most High is better than whatever is beneath the sky. There is a *sūrah* of

لم يكن عليكَ شيءٌ، فجلس الرَّجلُ حتّى طال مجلِسُهُ ثمّ قامَ، فرآهُ رسولُ اللهِ ﷺ مُوَلِّياً - أي: ذاهباً - فأمرَ بهِ فدُعيَ، فلمّا جاء قال له ﷺ: «ماذا معكَ منَ القرآنِ»؟، قال: معي سورةُ كذا، وسورةُ كذا، وسورةُ كذا - عدَّها -، فقال ﷺ: «أتقرؤُهُنَّ عن ظهرِ قلبِك»؟، فقال: نعم. قال: «اذهبْ فقد ملَّكْتُكَها بما معكَ منَ القرآنِ».

حملَةُ القرآنِ همُ المحفوفونَ برحمةِ اللهِ المكتسبونَ نورَ اللهِ تعالى

جاءَ في (المرقاةِ شرح المشكاةِ)، عن أميرِ المؤمنينَ عليّ كرَّمَ اللهُ تعالى وجهَهُ أنّهُ قال: إنَّ القرآنَ أفضلُ من كلِّ شيءٍ دونَ اللهِ تعالى، فمَن وقَّرَ القرآنَ فقد وقَّرَ اللهَ تعالى، ومَن لم يوقِّرِ القرآنَ فقد استخفَّ بحقِّ اللهِ تعالى، والقرآنُ شافعٌ مشفَّعٌ وماحِلٌ مصدَّقٌ، مَن شفَعَ له القرآنُ شُفِّعَ، ومَن محل به القرآنُ صُدِّقَ، ومَن جعل القرآنَ أمامَه قادَهُ إلى الجنّةِ، ومَن جعلَهُ خلفَهُ ساقَهُ إلى النّارِ، وحملَةُ القرآنِ هم المحفوفونَ برحمةِ اللهِ تعالى، المكتسبونَ نورَ اللهِ تعالى، المتعلّمونَ كلامَ اللهِ تعالى، مَن عاداهم فقد عادى اللهَ تعالى، ومَن والاهم فقد والى اللهَ تعالى، يا حمَلَةَ كتابِ اللهِ استجيبوا للهِ تعالى بتوقيرِ كتابِهِ يَزِدْكُم حبّاً ويحبِّبْكُمْ إلى خَلقِهِ، يُدفَعُ عن مستمِعِ القرآنِ سوءُ الدّنيا، ويدفعُ عن تالي القرآنِ بلوى الآخرةِ، ومستمِعُ آيةٍ من كتابِ اللهِ تعالى خيرٌ له من صِيرٍ - اسم جبل - ذهباً، وتالي آيةٍ من كتابِ اللهِ تعالى خيرٌ له ممّا تحتَ أديمِ السّماءِ، وإنَّ من القرآنِ لسورةً عظيمةً عندَ اللهِ تعالى يُدعى صاحبُها الشّريفُ عندَ اللهِ، يشفعُ صاحبُها يومَ القيامةِ في أكثرَ من ربيعةَ ومُضَر، وهي سورةُ يس. اهـ.

the Qur'an which is great in the sight of Allah Most High. The one who has memorized it is called noble (*sharīf*) in the court of Allah and will intercede on the Day of Judgement for more people than Rabīʿah and Muḍar. It is *Sūrah Yāsīn*."

THE BEARER OF THE QUR'AN HAS AN ACCEPTED SUPPLICATION

Imam Muslim narrated on the authority of Abū Umāmah ﷺ that the Prophet ﷺ said, "The bearer of the Qur'an has an accepted supplication."

THE ETIQUETTE OF THE BEARER OF THE NOBLE QUR'AN

Ibn ʿUmar ﷺ narrated that the Messenger of Allah ﷺ said, "Whoever recites (i.e., memorizes) the Qur'an has gathered Prophethood between his ribs – except that Revelation does not come to them. It does not behove the person of the Qur'an to become angry along with those who become angry, and to behave ignorantly along with the ignorant, whilst the Speech of Allah Most High is in his chest."[1]

The Prophet ﷺ addressed the bearers of the Qur'an and guided them to the requirements and manners which they should implement.

Bayhaqī narrated in *Shu ʿab al-Īmān* that the Prophet ﷺ said, "O people of the Qur'an, do not make the Qur'an into a pillow. Rather, recite it as it should be recited in the hours of the night and day. Spread it, recite it melodiously, and ponder over its contents so that you may be successful. Do not seek its reward in advance, for it has a great reward."[2]

The meaning is: seek the pleasure of Allah Most High and His everlasting reward, and do not hastily seek the reward of this life and its perishing

---

(1) *Ḥākim*, vol. 1, p. 552.

(2) Bayhaqī in *Shu ʿab al-Īmān* (2210).

لحامِلِ القرآنِ دعوةٌ مستجابةُ

روى الإمامُ مسلمٌ عن أبي أُمامةَ رضي اللهُ عنه عن النبيِّ ﷺ قال: «لحامِلِ القرآنِ دعوةٌ مستجابةٌ» (١).

آدابُ حاملِ القرآنِ الكريمِ

عن ابنِ عمرَ رَضِيَ اللهُ عَنْهُمَا أنَّ رسولَ اللهِ ﷺ قال: «مَن قرأَ القرآنَ فقدِ استدرجَ النبوَّةَ بين جَنبَيهِ غيرَ أنّهُ لا يُوحَى إليه، لا ينبغي لصاحبِ القرآنِ أن يجدَ مع مَن وجَد، ولا يَجهلَ مع مَن جَهِلَ، وفي جَوفِهِ كلامُ اللهِ تعالى» (٢). رواهُ الحاكمُ، وقال: صحيحُ الإسناد.

وقد خاطبَ النبيُّ ﷺ حملةَ القرآنِ، وأرشدَهم إلى المطالِبِ والآدابِ التي ينبغي أنْ يتحقَّقوا بها.

فقد روى البيهقيُّ في (الشُّعَبِ) أنَّ النبيَّ ﷺ قال: «يا أهلَ القرآنِ لا تتوسَّدوا القرآنَ، واتلوهُ حقَّ تلاوتِهِ في آناءِ اللّيلِ والنَّهارِ، وأفشوهُ وتغنَّوهُ وتدبَّروا ما فيه لعلَّكم تفلحون، ولا تعَجَّلوا ثوابَه فإنَّ له ثواباً» (٣). والمعنى: فابتغوا وجهَ اللهِ تعالى وثوابَه الباقي، ولا تتعجَّلوا ثوابَ الدُّنيا وحُطامَها الفاني. ومعنى «لا تتوسَّدوا القرآنَ»: لا تجعلوهُ كالوسادةِ تَنامونَ عليه، وتغفلونَ عن حقوقِهِ؛ بل قوموا بواجبِ القرآنِ وطبِّقوا العملَ به، ومِن ذلك القيامُ به ليلاً، فإنَّ للقرآنِ حقّاً في اللّيلِ، وحقّاً في النّهار.

---

(١) أخرجه المتقي الهندي في (كنز العمال) (٢٣١٢).

(٢) أخرجه الحاكم (١/٥٥٢).

(٣) أخرجه البيهقي في (شعب الإيمان) (٢٢١٠).

vanities. The meaning of "do not make the Qur'an into a pillow" is do not treat it like a pillow that you sleep on and do not become heedless of its rights. Rather, fulfil the necessary rights of the Qur'an and put it into practice. And one of these rights is to recite it in prayer at night, because the Qur'an has a right during the night and a right during the day.

O Allah, make us amongst those who recite it as it should be recited, fulfil its rights and obligations, and ponder over its verses and words.

THE ETIQUETTE AND REQUIREMENTS OF RECITATION

Know – may Allah Most High grant you and us knowledge – that deeming an action or statement to be an act of Allah's worship, an act of drawing near to Allah Most High, or a good deed whose reward is sought with Allah requires evidence from the Sacred Law to establish the respective ruling. Otherwise, this ruling will be rejected in spite of its claimant. This is because describing a statement or action as an act of worship, an act of drawing near to Allah, or a good deed, is a revelatory (*tawqīfī*) matter, i.e., it is dependent upon being mentioned by the Sacred Law with consent to perform it.

Once you know this, then know that reciting the Noble Qur'an is amongst the greatest acts of worship, an act that draws a person extremely near to Allah Most High, and one of the most comprehensive good deeds. The evidence for this will follow.

As for it being an act of worship, Allah Most High has – in the context of acts of worship – commanded it and informed of it. He Most High said, "Recite what has been revealed to you of the Book and establish prayer."[1] In praising His worshipping slaves, He Most Glorified said, "Surely those who recite the Book of Allah, establish prayer, and donate from what We have provided for them – secretly and openly – [can] hope for an exchange

(1) *Al-'Ankabūt*, 45.

اللَّهمَّ اجعلنا ممَّنْ تلاهُ حقَّ تلاوتِه، وأدَّى حقوقَه وواجباتِه، وتدبَّرَ في آياتِهِ وكلماتِهِ.

آدابُ القراءةِ ومطالِبُها

اعلم - علَّمنا اللهُ تعالى وإيّاكَ - أنَّ الحكمَ على قولٍ أو فعلٍ بأنَّهُ عبادةٌ للهِ تعالى، أو قُربةٌ إلى اللهِ تعالى، أو حسنةٌ يُبتغَى ثوابُها عندَ اللهِ تعالى كلُّ ذلك يحتاجُ إلى دليلٍ من الشَّرعِ يُثبِتُ هذا الحكمَ، وإلّا فهو مردودٌ على قائلِهِ؛ لأنَّ وصفَ القولِ والفعلِ بأنّهُ عبادةٌ أو قربةٌ إلى اللهِ تعالى أو حسنةٌ أمرٌ توقيفيٌّ، أي: موقوفٌ على الورودِ في الشَّرعِ مع الإذنِ بذلك.

إذا علمتَ ذلك فاعلمْ أنَّ تلاوةَ القرآنِ الكريمِ هي عبادةٌ من أعظمِ العباداتِ، وقربةٌ تُزلِفُ إلى اللهِ تعالى من أقربِ القرباتِ، وحسنةٌ مِنْ أجمعِ الحسناتِ.

دليلُ ذلك:

أمّا أنّها عبادةٌ: فقد ذكرَها اللهُ تعالى في سياقِ العباداتِ أمراً وخبراً: قال تعالى: {اتْلُ مَا أُوحِيَ إِلَيْكَ مِنَ الْكِتَابِ وَأَقِمِ الصَّلَاةَ}[1] الآيةَ. وقال تعالى في ثنائه سبحانه على عبادِهِ العابدينَ: {إِنَّ الَّذِينَ يَتْلُونَ كِتَابَ اللَّهِ وَأَقَامُوا الصَّلَاةَ وَأَنفَقُوا مِمَّا رَزَقْنَاهُمْ سِرًّا وَعَلَانِيَةً يَرْجُونَ تِجَارَةً لَّن تَبُورَ}[2]. ولذلك جاءَ في الحديثِ كما تقدَّمَ عنه ﷺ: «أفضلُ عبادةِ أُمَّتي تلاوةُ القرآنِ»[3].

---

(١) العنكبوت: ٤٥.

(٢) فاطر: ٢٩.

(٣) أخرجه القضاعي في (مسند الشهاب) (١٢٨٤)، والبيهقي في (شعب الإيمان) (٢٠٢٢) باختلاف يسير.

that will never fail."[1]

This is why the hadith of the Prophet ﷺ that has already passed stated, "The best act of worship for my ummah is reciting the Qur'an."[2]

As for recitation of the Noble Qur'an being an act that draws one near to Allah Most High, Tirmidhī and Aḥmad in his *Musnad* have narrated on the authority of Abū Umāmah ﷺ that the Prophet ﷺ said, "Allah Most High does not listen attentively to a slave in anything better (or more) than two *rak ʿahs* of prayer, and righteousness is sprinkled over his head for as long as he is in prayer. The slave does not draw near to Allah Almighty and Exalted with anything similar to what has emanated from Him (i.e., the Noble Qur'an), because it has come from Him."[3] This is the wording of Tirmidhī and he said it is sound and rare (*gharīb*).

As for recitation being one of the most comprehensive good deeds, the hadith has already passed in which Prophet ﷺ said, "Whoever recites a letter of the Book of Allah receives a reward for it, and the reward is multiplied tenfold."[4]

Hence, when reciting the Noble Qur'an is an act of worship, a means of drawing near to Allah, and a comprehensive good deed, it will most definitely have a certain etiquette and requirements that the reciter is required to maintain. That is for their worship to reach completion, their drawing near to Allah to be effective, and their reward to be established. These proprieties are many, but we shall mention a number of more significant and familiar ones here.

---

(1) *Fāṭir*, 29.

(2) Al-Quḍāʿī in *Musnad al-Shihāb* (1284); Bayhaqī in *Shu ʿab al-Īmān* (2022).

(3) *Tirmidhī* (2911); *Aḥmad* (22306) with a slight difference.

(4) *Tirmidhī* (2910).

وأمّا أنَّ تلاوةَ القرآنِ الكريمِ قربةٌ إلى الله تعالى: فقد روى الترمذيُّ وأحمدُ في (المسنَدِ) عن أبي أُمامةَ رَضِيَ اللهُ عَنْهُ أنَّ النبيَّ صَلَّى اللهُ عَلَيْهِ وَآلِهِ وَسَلَّمَ قال: «ما أَذِنَ اللهُ تعالى لعبدٍ في شيءٍ أفضلَ من ركعتينِ أو أكثرَ من ركعتينِ، وإنَّ البِرَّ ليُذَرُّ فوقَ رأسِ العبدِ ما دامَ في صلاتِهِ، وما تقرَّبَ العبدُ إلى اللهِ عزَّ وجل بمثلِ ما خرج منه - أي: بدأَ منه - وهو القرآنُ الكريمِ؛ فإنّهُ منه بدأَ»[1]. وهذا لفظُ الترمذيِّ، وقال فيه: حسنٌ غريبٌ. وأمّا أنَّ تلاوةَ القرآنِ من أجمعِ الحسناتِ:

فقد تقدَّمَ في الحديث عنه صَلَّى اللهُ عَلَيْهِ وَآلِهِ وَسَلَّمَ أنه قال: «مَن قرأَ حرفاً من كتابِ اللهِ تعالى فله به حسنةٌ، والحسنةُ بعشرِ أمثالِها»[2]. الحديثَ.

فلمّا كانت تلاوةُ القرآن الكريم عبادةً وقربةً وحسنةً جامعةً فلا بُدَّ لها من آدابٍ ومطالبَ تُطلبُ مِنَ القارئِ؛ حتّى تَتِمَّ له عبادتُهُ، وتَصِحَّ له قربتُهُ، وتثبُتَ له حسنتُهُ، وهي كثيرةٌ نذكرُ منها جملةً مهمّةً شهيرةً.

---

(١) أخرجه الترمذي (٢٩١١)، وأحمد (٢٢٣٠٦) باختلاف يسير.

(٢) أخرجه الترمذي (٢٩١٠).

ONE: SINCERITY

The reciter should intend the pleasure of Allah Most High through their recitation, as is the requirement in all acts of worship. Allah Most High said, "They were only commanded to worship Allah [alone] with sincere devotion to Him in all uprightness, establish prayer, and pay alms-tax. That is the upright way."[1]

Bukhārī and Muslim narrated on the authority of ʿUmar ibn al-Khaṭṭāb ﷺ who said, "I heard the Messenger of Allah ﷺ saying, 'Actions are only according to intentions, and each person only receives what they intended.'"[2] Ibn ʿAbbās ﷺ said, "A person is only given according to their intention."

TWO: WUḌŪ'

It is desirable (*mustaḥabb*) for the reciter to be in the state of *wuḍū'*, because the Qur'an is the best form of remembrance and the Prophet ﷺ would like to remember Allah Most High in a state of purity as established in hadiths.

---

(1) *Al-Bayyinah*, 5.

(2) *Bukhārī* (1); *Muslim* (1907).

الأوَّل: الإخلاصُ:

فينبغي للقارئِ أن يقصِدَ بقراءتِهِ وجهَ اللهِ تعالى ورضاهُ، كما هو الشَّأنُ المطلوبُ في جميعِ العباداتِ، قال اللهُ تعالى: {وَمَا أُمِرُوا إِلَّا لِيَعْبُدُوا اللَّهَ مُخْلِصِينَ لَهُ الدِّينَ حُنَفَاءَ وَيُقِيمُوا الصَّلَاةَ وَيُؤْتُوا الزَّكَاةَ وَذَٰلِكَ دِينُ الْقَيِّمَةِ}[1]، أي: المِلَّةُ المستقيمةُ. وفي (الصَّحيحينِ) عن عمرَ بنِ الخطّابِ رَضِيَ اللهُ عَنْهُ قال: سمعتُ رسولَ الله صَلَّى اللهُ عَلَيْهِ وَآلِهِ وَسَلَّمَ يقول: «إنّما الأعمالُ بالنّياتِ، وإنّما لكلِّ امرئٍ ما نوى»[2]. الحديثَ. وقال ابنُ عباس رَضِيَ اللهُ عَنْهُمَا: (إنّما يُعطَى الرَّجلُ على قَدرِ نيّتِه).

الثاني: الوضوءُ:

يستحبُّ للقارئِ أن يكونَ متوضِّئاً؛ لأنَّ القرآنَ هو أفضلُ الأذكارِ، وقد كان النبيُّ صَلَّى اللهُ عَلَيْهِ وَسَلَّمَ

(١) البينة: ٥.

(٢) رواه البخاري (١)، ومسلم (١٩٠٧).

However, it is not disliked (*makrūh*) to recite without wuḍū'. It states in Bukhārī that when the Prophet ﷺ awoke from his sleep, he rubbed away the effects of sleep from his face using his hand. He then recited the last ten verses of *Sūrah Āl 'Imrān*, stood towards a hanging waterskin from which he performed *wuḍū'* thoroughly, and then stood to pray."[1]

THREE: SIWĀK

It is desirable for the reciter to use a *siwāk* (tooth-stick) to honour, purify, and freshen the mouth – the pathway to reciting the Qur'an.

Bazzār narrated with a good chain that 'Alī ﷺ commanded use of the *siwāk* and said that the Messenger of Allah ﷺ said, "When the slave uses a *siwāk* and then stands to pray, an Angel stands behind them to listen to their recitation. The Angel then comes close to them until it places its mouth over their mouth. Thus, nothing comes out of their mouth (i.e., the mouth of the reciter) except that it enters the Angel. So, purify your mouths for the Qur'an."[2] Ibn Mājah narrated on the authority of Ibn 'Abbās ﷺ as a *mawqūf* narration, "Indeed, your mouths are pathways for the Qur'an, so freshen them with the *siwāk*."[3]

Bayhaqī narrated on the authority of Samurah ﷺ, as a hadith attributed to the Prophet ﷺ, "Freshen your mouths with the *siwāk*, because they are the pathways of the Qur'an."[4]

FOUR: FACING THE QIBLAH

It is desirable for the reciter to face the *qiblah*, due to the narration on the authority of Ibn 'Abbās ﷺ that the Prophet ﷺ said, "The noblest

(1) *Bukhārī* (962).

(2) *Bazzār* (603)

(3) *Ibn Mājah* (291).

(4) Bayhaqī in *Shu'ab al-Īmān* (2119).

يُحِبُّ أن يذكرَ اللهَ تعالى على طهارةٍ، كما ثبتَ في الحديثِ، ولكنْ لا تُكرَهُ القراءةُ على غيرِ وضوءٍ، فقد جاء في البخاريِّ: «أنَّ النبيَّ ﷺ لمّا استيقظَ من منامِهِ فجعلَ يمسحُ النومَ عن وجههِ بيدِهِ، ثمَّ قرأَ العشرَ الآياتِ الخواتيمَ من سورةِ آلِ عمرانَ، ثمَّ قام إلى شَنٍّ معلَّقةٍ فتوضَّأَ منها فأحسنَ وضوءَه، ثمَّ قام يصلّي ﷺ»[1].

الثالث: السواكُ:

يستحبُّ للقارئِ أن يستاكَ؛ تعظيماً وتطهيراً وتطييباً للفمِ الذي هو طريقُ قراءةِ القرآن. روى البزّارُ بسندٍ جيّدٍ عن عليٍّ رضي اللهُ تعالى عنه أنّهُ أَمَرَ بالسِّواكِ، وقال: قال رسولُ الله ﷺ: «إنَّ العبدَ إذا تسوَّكَ ثمَّ قام يُصلِّي قام المَلَكُ خلفَهُ، فيستمِعُ لقراءتِهِ فيدنو منه حتّى يضعَ فاهُ على فيه، فما يخرجُ مِن فيه - أي: مِنْ فمِ القارئِ - شيءٌ إلّا صار في جوفِ المَلَكِ، فطهِّروا أفواهَكم للقرآنِ»[2]. وروى ابنُ ماجه عن ابنِ عبّاسٍ رضي الله عنهما موقوفاً: «إنَّ أفواهَكم طرقٌ للقرآنِ فطيِّبوها بالسّواكِ»[3]. وروى البيهقيُّ عن سَمُرةَ رضي الله عنه مرفوعاً: «طيِّبوا أفواهَكم بالسِّواكِ؛ فإنّها طُرُقُ القرآنِ»[4].

الرّابع: استقبالُ القِبلةِ:

يستحبُّ للقارئِ أنْ يستقبلَ القِبلةَ، لِما روي عن ابنِ عبّاسٍ رضي الله عنهما عن النبيِّ

---

(١) أخرجه البخاري (٩٩٢).

(٢) أخرجه البزار (٦٠٣).

(٣) أخرجه ابن ماجه (٢٩١).

(٤) أخرجه البيهقي في شعب الإيمان (٢١١٩).

gathering is the one which faces the *qiblah*."[1] Ṭabarānī narrated it.

Ṭabarānī and Ibn ʿAdī narrated on the authority of Ibn ʿUmar ﷺ that the Prophet ﷺ said, "The most honourable gathering is the one which faces the *qiblah*."[2]

The reciter should also sit with veneration, serenity, and dignity. If one recites whilst standing, lying down, in bed, or in any other state, it is permissible and one will be rewarded. However, the reward will be less. Allah Most High said, "Those who remember Allah whilst standing, sitting and lying on their sides."[3] And the Qur'an is the greatest form of divine remembrance. In the two *Ṣaḥīḥ* collections, Sayyidah ʿĀ'ishah ﷺ is reported to have said, "The Messenger of Allah ﷺ used to recite the Qur'an whilst his head was in my lap."[4] Abū Mūsā ﷺ said, "I recite the Qur'an in my prayer and I recite on my bed." Sayyidah ʿĀ'ishah ﷺ said, "I recite my litany of Qur'an whilst I am lying on my bed."

FIVE: PURITY AND CLEANLINESS OF THE PLACE

It states in *al-Itqān*, "It is *sunnah* to recite in a clean place, the best place being the masjid." Imam Nawawī said, "With respect to reciting on the path, the preferred opinion is that it is permissible without being disliked – provided the reciter is not distracted. If they are distracted, it is disliked, just as the Prophet ﷺ disliked for a drowsy person to recite lest they make a mistake. Abū Dāwūd narrated that Abū al-Dardā' would recite whilst on the path."

A person who is drowsy should not recite the Qur'an lest they make a mistake. Muslim narrated on the authority of Abū Hurayrah ﷺ that the Messenger of Allah ﷺ said, "When any of you stand to pray at night, but

(1) Ṭabarānī in *al-Awsaṭ* (2375).

(2) Ṭabarānī in *al-Awsaṭ*, vol. 8, p. 189; Ibn ʿAdī in *al-Kamil*, vol. 2, p. 376.

(3) *Āl ʿImrān*, 191.

(4) *Bukhārī* (7549).

ﷺ أنـه قال: «أشرفُ المجالسِ ما استُقبِلَ به القِبلةَ» [1]، رواهُ الطّبرانيُّ.

وروى الطّبرانيُّ وابنُ عَديّ عن ابنِ عمرَ رضي الله عنهما عن النبيّ ﷺ أنّهُ قال: «أكرمُ المجالسِ ما استُقبِلَ به القِبلةَ»[2]. وأنْ يجلسَ متخشِّعاً بسكينةٍ ووَقارٍ، فلو قرأَ قائماً، أو مضطجعاً، أو في فراشِهِ، أو على غيرِ ذلك من الأحوالِ جاز وله الأجرُ، ولكنْ دونَ الأوَّلِ، قال اللهُ تعالى: ﴿الَّذِينَ يَذْكُرُونَ اللَّهَ قِيَامًا وَقُعُودًا وَعَلَىٰ جُنُوبِهِمْ﴾[3] الآيةَ، والقرآنُ هو أفضلُ الأذكارِ الإلهيّةِ. وفي (الصّحيحين) عن السيدةِ عائشةَ رضي اللهُ عنها قالت: (كان رسولُ الله ﷺ يقرأُ القرآنَ ورأسُهُ في حِجري)[4]. وعن أبي موسى رضي الله عنه قال: (إنّي أقرأُ القرآنَ في صلاتي، وأقرأُ على فراشي). وعن عائشةَ السيدة رضي اللهُ عنها قالت: (إني لَأقرأُ حِزبي وأنا مضطجعةٌ على السّرير).

الخامس: طهارةُ المكانِ ونظافتُه:

قال في (الإتقان): تُسَنُّ القراءةُ في مكانٍ نظيفٍ، وأفضلُهُ المسجدُ. اهـ.

قال الإمامُ النوويُّ: وأمّا القراءةُ في الطَّريقِ فالمختارُ أنّها جائزةٌ غيرُ مكروهةٍ إذا لم يَلْتَهِ صاحبُها، فإنِ التهى عنها كُرِهَتْ كما كَرِهَ النبيُّ ﷺ القراءةَ للنّاعِسِ؛ مخافةَ الغلط.

وروى أبو داودَ عن أبي الدرداءِ رضي الله عنه أنّهُ كان يقرأُ في الطَّريق.

---

(١) أخرجه الطبراني في الأوسط (٢٣٧٥).

(٢) أخرجه الطبراني في (الأوسط) (٨/ ١٨٩)، وابن عدي في (الكامل) (٢/ ٣٧٦).

(٣) آل عمران: ١٩١.

(٤) أخرجه البخاري (٧٥٤٩).

the Qur'an is heavy on their tongue and they do not know what they are saying, they should go to sleep."[1]

SIX: PURITY FROM MAJOR IMPURITY (AL-ḤADATH AL-AKBAR)

Being pure from post-sexual impurity (*janābah*), menstruation, and postnatal bleeding are necessary to recite the Qur'an with the intention of recitation. Hence, it is unlawful for the person who is impure due to post-sexual impurity, menstruation, and postnatal bleeding to recite the Qur'an by way of recitation. It is permissible to read the Qur'an in one's minds without verbalizing it, and it is also permissible to look into the muṣḥaf without touching it. Tirmidhī, Ibn Mājah and Imam Aḥmad in his *Musnad* narrated on the authority of Ibn 'Umar ﷺ, as a hadith attributed to the Prophet ﷺ, "The person in post-sexual impurity or a menstruating woman cannot read anything of the Qur'an."[2] Imam Nawawī said, "There is a consensus of Muslims that it is permissible to say *tasbīḥ* (*Subḥān Allāh*), *tahlīl* (*Lā ilāha ill Allāh*), *taḥmīd* (*Alḥamdulillāh*), *takbīr* (*Allāhu Akbar*), blessings (*ṣalāt*) on the Prophet ﷺ, and other forms of remembrance for a person in post-sexual impurity and for a menstruating woman." As for when there is no intention of recitation, but rather the intention is remembrance or supplication, it is permissible and not unlawful for them. Remembrance is like a person in major impurity saying when mounting (a vehicle), "Glory be to the One Who has subjected these for us, for we could have never done so [on our own]"; or to say when afflicted, "Surely to Allah we belong and to Him we will [all return]", or to say, "Allah [alone] is sufficient [as an aid] for us and [He] is the best Protector", and similar verses without intending [to recite them as] the Qur'an. Supplication is like saying, "Our Lord, give us good in this world and good in the Hereafter, and save us from the punishment of Fire" and the likes thereof with the

(1) *Muslim* (787).

(2) *Tirmidhī* (131); *Ibn Mājah* (595).

ولا يقرأُ القرآنَ ناعِسٌ مخافةَ الغلَط:

روى مسلمٌ عن أبي هريرةَ رَضِيَ اللهُ عَنْهُ قال: قال رسولُ الله ﷺ: «إذا قام أحدُكُمْ من اللّيلِ فاستعجمَ القرآنُ على لسانِهِ فلم يَدْرِ ما يقولُ فليضْطجِع» [1].

السادسُ: الطّهارةُ من الحَدَثِ الأكبرِ:

الطّهارةُ من الجنابةِ والحَيضِ والنّفاسِ فرضٌ لقراءةِ القرآنِ بقصدِ القرآنِ؛ فيحرُمُ على الجُنُبِ والحائضِ والنّفساءِ قراءةُ القرآنِ مقصوداً، ويجوز لهم إجراءُ القرآنِ على قلوبِهم من غير تلفُّظٍ به، ويجوزُ لهم النَّظرُ في المصحفِ من غيرِ مسّهِ.

روى الترمذيُّ وابنُ ماجه والإمامُ أحمدُ في (مسنَدِه) عن ابنِ عمرَ رَضِيَ اللهُ عَنْهُمَا مرفوعاً: «لا يقرأُ الجُنُبُ ولا الحائضُ شيئاً من القرآنِ» [2]، كما في (الفتحِ الكبيرِ).

قال الإمامُ النوويُّ: وأجمعَ المسلمون على جوازِ التَّسبيحِ، والتَّهليلِ، والتَّحميدِ، والتَّكبيرِ، والصّلاةِ على النبيِّ ﷺ، وغيرِ ذلك من الأذكارِ للجُنُبِ والحائضِ. اهـ.

أمّا إذا لم يقصِدِ القرآنَ؛ بل قصدَ الذِّكرَ أو الدّعاءَ فهو جائزٌ ولا يحرُمُ عليهم.

فالذِّكرُ: كأنْ يقولَ الجُنُبُ أو الحائضُ عند الرُّكوبِ: «سبحان الذي سخر لنا هذا وما كنا له مقرنين وإنا إلى ربنا لمنقلبون»، وكقولِهِ عند المصيبةِ: «إنا لله وإنا إليه راجعون»، أو يقول: «حسبنا الله ونعم الوكيل»، ونحو ذلك دون أن يقصِدَ القرآنَ.

وأمّا الدعاءُ فكأن يقولَ: «ربنا آتنا في الدنيا حسنة وفي الآخرة حسنة وقنا عذاب النار»، وأمثال ذلك بقصدِ الدّعاءِ.

---

(١) أخرجه مسلم (٧٨٧).

(٢) أخرجه الترمذي (١٣١) وابن ماجه (٥٩٥).

intention of supplication. As for touching the muṣḥaf, it is unlawful for anyone in minor or major impurity, unless it is with something that is detached from their person and the muṣḥaf. The evidence for this is the narration of Imam Mālik in *al-Muwaṭṭa'* that the Messenger of Allah ﷺ wrote in his letter to ʿAmr ibn Ḥazm, "Only a pure person should touch the Qur'an."[1] The letter of ʿAmr received widespread acceptance. Yaʿqūb ibn Sufyān said, "I do not know of any letter more authentic than this letter, because the Companions of the Messenger of Allah ﷺ and the Followers (Tābiʿūn) would refer back to it and discard their own opinions." Ḥākim said, "ʿUmar ibn ʿAbd al-Azīz and Zuhrī attested to the authenticity of this letter." Ṭabarānī, Dāraquṭnī, and Ḥākim narrated on the authority of Ḥakīm ibn Ḥizām 🕭 that the Prophet ﷺ said, "Do not touch the Qur'an except that you are pure."[2] This is as stated in *al-Jāmiʿ al-Ṣaghīr*. Ṭabarānī narrated on the authority of Ibn ʿUmar 🕭, as a hadith attributed to the Prophet ﷺ, "Only a pure person should touch the Qur'an."[3] This is as stated in *al-Fatḥ al-Kabīr*. In the story of ʿUmar ibn al-Khaṭṭāb 🕭 converting to Islam, Dāraquṭnī narrated that his sister said to him before he accepted Islam, "You are impure and only the purified can touch this." There are a number of proofs from the hadiths but this is not the place to elaborate.

SEVEN: SEEKING REFUGE (TAʿAWWUDH) AND BASMALAH

It is *sunnah* to seek refuge before reciting, acting upon the saying of Allah Most High, "When you recite the Qur'an, seek refuge with Allah from Satan, the accursed."[4] The wording for seeking refuge according to most is: *Aʿūdhu billāhi min al-shayṭān al-rajīm* (I seek refuge with Allah from

(1) Mālik in *al-Muwaṭṭa'* (534).

(2) Ṭabarānī in *al-Awsaṭ* (3409).

(3) Ṭabarānī in *al-Kabīr* (13217).

(4) *Al-Naḥl*, 98.

وأما مسُّ المصحفِ: فيحرُمُ على المُحدِثِ حَدَثاً أصغرَ أو أكبرَ إلّا بشيءٍ منفصلٍ عنه وعن المصحفِ. والدّليلُ على ذلك ما رواهُ الإمامُ مالكٌ في (الموطّأ): أنَّ في الكتابِ الذي كتَبَهُ رسولُ اللهِ ﷺ لعمرِو بنِ حزمٍ: «أنْ لا يَمَسَّ القرآنَ إلّا طاهرٌ»[1]. الحديث. وكتابُ عمرٍو تلقّاهُ النّاسِ بالقَبول. وقال يعقوبُ بنُ سفيان: لا أعلمُ كتاباً أصحَّ من هذا الكتابِ، فإنَّ أصحابَ رسولِ الله ﷺ، والتّابعينَ يَرجعونَ إليه، ويَدَعونَ رأيَهم. وقال الحاكمُ: قد شهدَ عمرُ بنُ عبد العزيزِ، والزُّهريُّ لهذا الكتابِ بالصِّحةِ.

وروى الطبرانيُّ والدارقطنيُّ والحاكمُ عن حكيمِ بنِ حِزامٍ رَضِيَ اللهُ عَنْهُ أنَّ النبيَّ ﷺ قال له: «لا تمسَّ القرآنَ إلّا وأنتَ طاهرٌ»[2] كما في (الجامعِ الصَّغيرِ).

وروى الطبرانيُّ عن ابنِ عمرَ رَضِيَ اللهُ عَنْهُمَا مرفوعاً: «لا يمسُّ القرآنَ إلّا طاهرٌ»[3] كما في (الفتح الكبير). وروى الدارَقطنيُّ في قصّةِ إسلامِ عمرَ بنِ الخطّابِ أنَّ أختَه قالت له قبل أن يُسلِمَ: إنّكَ رجسٌ، ولا يمسُّهُ إلا المطهَّرونَ. وثَمّةَ عِدَّةٌ من الشّواهدِ الحديثيّةِ ليس هذا موضِعُ تفصيلِها.

السّابعُ: التعوُّذُ والبسملةُ:

يُسَنُّ للقارئِ أن يتعوَّذَ قبل القراءةِ؛ عملاً بقوله تعالى: ﴿فَإِذَا قَرَأْتَ الْقُرْآنَ فَاسْتَعِذْ بِاللَّهِ

---

(١) أخرجه مالك في (الموطأ) (٥٣٤).

(٢) أخرجه الطبراني في الأوسط (٣٤٠٩).

(٣) أخرجه الطبراني في الكبير (١٣٢١٧).

Satan, the accursed). It is also *sunnah* to seek refuge before reciting in the first *rak'ah* of prayer only. Likewise, it is *sunnah* to recite the *basmalah* (*Bismillāh al-Raḥmān al-Raḥīm*) at the beginning of every *sūrah* besides *Sūrah Barā'ah*.

The proof for reciting the *basmalah* before every *sūrah* is the narration of Bukhārī and others that Umm Salamah ﷺ was asked regarding the recitation of the Messenger of Allah ﷺ. She said, "He would recite each verse separately. 'In the name of Allah, the Most Compassionate, Most Merciful. All praise is for Allah, Lord of all worlds. The Most Compassionate, Most Merciful. Master of the Day of Judgement.'[1]"[2]

If one yawns whilst reciting, one should stop reciting. Mujāhid said, "When you yawn whilst you are reciting the Qur'an, stop reciting out of respect, until your yawning stops."

Bukhārī narrated that the Prophet ﷺ said, "When any of you yawn, they should place their hand on their mouth, because the devil enters with the yawn."[3]

EIGHT: CONTEMPLATING WHILST RECITING

One of the most important requirements is that during the course of the recitation, the reciter contemplates and tries to understand what they are reciting. This is because Allah Most High revealed the Book in order to reflect and be mindful. Allah Most High said, "This is a blessed Book which We have revealed to you [O Prophet] so that they may contemplate its verses, and people of reason may be mindful."[4] Reproaching and censuring those who fail to contemplate, He Most High said, "Do they not then reflect on the Qur'an? Or are there locks upon their hearts?"[5]

---

(1) *Al-Fātiḥah*, 1-4.

(2) *Abū Dāwūd* (4001).

(3) *Bukhārī* (3289).

(4) *Ṣād*, 29.

(5) *Muhammad*, 24.

مِنَ الشَّيْطَانِ الرَّجِيمِ}[1]، وصيغةُ التعوُّذِ عند الأكثرين هي: «أعوذُ باللهِ من الشيطانِ الرَّجيم»، ويُسَنُّ أيضاً التعوُّذُ قبلَ القراءةِ في أوَّلِ ركعةٍ من الصَّلاةِ فقط.

كما أنَّهُ يُسَنُّ للقارئِ الإتيانُ بالبسملةِ أوَّلَ كلِّ سورةٍ سوى سورةِ براءة.

والدَّليلُ على مشروعيّةِ البسملةِ أوَّلَ السّورةِ: ما رواهُ الإمامُ البخاريُّ وغيرُه عن أمِّ سلمةَ رضي اللهُ عنها أنها سُئِلَتْ عن قراءةِ رسولِ الله ﷺ؟ فقالت: كان يقطِّعُ قراءتَهُ آيةً آيةً. {بِسْمِ اللَّهِ الرَّحْمَٰنِ الرَّحِيمِ (١) الْحَمْدُ لِلَّهِ رَبِّ الْعَالَمِينَ (٢) الرَّحْمَٰنِ الرَّحِيمِ (٣) مَالِكِ يَوْمِ الدِّينِ}[2] [3]. وإذا تثاءبَ أثناءَ القراءةِ فينبغي له أن يُمسِكَ عن القراءةِ، قال مجاهدٌ: إذا تثاءبتَ وأنتَ تقرأُ القرآنَ فأمسِكْ عن القراءةِ؛ تعظيماً حتى يَذهبَ تثاؤُبُكَ. وفي البخاريِّ أنّه ﷺ قال: «إذا تثاءبَ أحدُكمْ فليضعْ يدَهُ على فيهِ - أي: فمِه - فإنَّ الشّيطانَ يدخلُ مع التثاؤب»[4].

الثامن: التدبُّر عند القراءةِ:

من أهمِّ المطالبِ أن يكونَ القارئُ في حالِ قراءتِهِ متدبّراً متفهّماً لِمَا يقرأ؛ لأنَّ اللهَ تعالى أنزلَ الكتابَ للتدبُّرِ والتذكُّرِ، قال اللهُ تعالى: {كِتَابٌ أَنزَلْنَاهُ إِلَيْكَ مُبَارَكٌ لِّيَدَّبَّرُوا آيَاتِهِ وَلِيَتَذَكَّرَ أُولُو الْأَلْبَابِ}[5]، وقال تعالى في الإنكارِ والتّوبيخِ لمن لم يتدبّرْ: {أَفَلَا

---

(١) النحل: ٩٨.

(٢) الفاتحة: ١-٤.

(٣) أخرجه أبو داود (٤٠٠١).

(٤) أخرجه البخاري (٣٢٨٩).

(٥) ص: ٢٩.

Sayyidunā ʿAlī ﷺ said, "There is no goodness in recitation without contemplation."

Ḥasan al-Baṣrī said, "The people before you (i.e., the Companions) considered this Qur'an as messages to them from their Lord. So, they would contemplate them by night and implement them by day."

Ḥāfiẓ al-Suyūṭī said, "The way to contemplate is to engage one's heart in pondering over the meaning of what they are saying, and thus understanding the meaning of every verse, pondering over the commands and prohibitions, and intending to accept it. If one had been negligent of it previously, they should apologize and seek forgiveness. If one comes across a verse of mercy, one should rejoice and ask Allah Most High for His grace. And when coming across a verse of punishment, one should be fearful and seek refuge; declare His transcendence and magnificence when coming across a verse of transcendence; and beseech and implore when coming across a verse of supplication."

Muslim narrated on the authority of Ḥudhayfah ﷺ who said, "I prayed with the Prophet ﷺ one night. He started to recite al-Baqarah and completed it. He then recited al-Nisā' and completed it, and then recited Āl ʿImrān and completed it, reciting slowly. When he would come across a verse containing *tasbīḥ*, he would say *tasbīḥ*; when he would come across a verse of supplication, he would supplicate; and when he would come across something from which to seek refuge, he would seek refuge."(1) Abū Dāwūd, Nasāʾī, and others narrated on the authority of Awf ibn Mālik ﷺ who said, "I stood with the Prophet ﷺ one night. He stood in prayer and recited *Sūrah al-Baqarah*. He did not come across any verse of mercy except that paused to supplicate, and he did not come across any verse of punishment except that he paused to seek refuge."(2)

When you recite the Qur'an, make yourself its addressee. So, when you come across a verse of promise or warning, or a command or prohibition,

(1) *Muslim* (772).

(2) *Abū Dāwūd* (873).

يَتَدَبَّرُونَ الْقُرْآنَ أَمْ عَلَىٰ قُلُوبٍ أَقْفَالُهَا﴾[1] الآيةَ.

قال سيّدُنا عليٌّ رَضِيَ اللهُ عَنْهُ: (لا خيرَ في قراءةٍ لا تدبُّرَ فيها).

وقال الحسنُ البصريُّ: إنَّ مَن كان قبلَكم - يعني: الصحابةَ رضي الله تعالى عنهم - رأَوا أنَّ هذا القرآنَ رسائلُ إليهم من ربِّهم، فكانوا يتدبَّرونها باللّيلِ وينفِّذونها في النّهارِ.

قال الحافظُ السُّيوطيُّ: وصفةُ التدبُّرِ أن يشغلَ - القارئُ - قلبَه بالتفكُّرِ في معنى ما يتلفَّظُ به، فيعرفَ معنى كلِّ آيةٍ، ويتأمَّلَ الأوامرَ والنّواهي، ويقصِدَ قَبولَ ذلك، فإن كان قصَّرَ عنه فيما مضى من عمرِهِ اعتذرَ واستغفرَ، وإنْ مرَّ بآيةِ رحمةٍ استبشرَ وسألَ اللهَ تعالى من فضلِهِ، وإذا مرَّ بآيةِ عذابٍ أشفقَ وتعوَّذَ، أو تنزيهٍ نزَّهَ وعظَّمَ، أو دعاءٍ تضرَّعَ وطلبَ.

أخرج مسلمٌ عن حُذيفةَ رَضِيَ اللهُ عَنْهُ قال: (صلَّيتُ مع النبيِّ صَلَّى اللهُ عَلَيْهِ وَآلِهِ وَسَلَّمَ ذاتَ ليلةٍ فافتتحَ البقرةَ فقرأَها، ثمَّ النِّساءَ فقرأَها، ثمَّ آلَ عمران فقرأَها، مترسِّلاً، وإذا مرَّ بآيةٍ فيها تسبيحٌ سبَّحَ، وإذا مرَّ بسؤالٍ سألَ، وإذا مرَّ بتعوُّذٍ تعوَّذَ)[2].

وروى أبو داودَ والنَّسائيُّ وغيرُهما عن عَوفِ بنِ مالكٍ رضي الله عنه قال: (قمتُ مع النبيِّ صلى الله عليه وسلم ليلةً فقام فقرأَ سورةَ البقرةِ، لا يمرُّ بآيةِ رحمةٍ إلّا وقفَ وسألَ، ولا يمرُّ بآيةِ عذابٍ إلا وقفَ وتعوَّذَ)[3]. اهـ.

وإذا قرأتَ القرآنَ فضعْ نفسَكَ موضِعَ المخاطَبِ، فإذا مررتَ بآيةِ الوعدِ والوعيدِ، أو الأمرِ والنّهيِ فانظُرْ في نفسِكَ مع مَن أنتَ تجدُها؟ مع المؤتمرين بها أمِ التّاركينَ لها؟

---

(١) محمد: ٢٤.

(٢) أخرجه مسلم (٧٧٢).

(٣) أخرجه أبو داود (٨٧٣).

look into yourself to see: with whom do you find yourself? Are you with those who comply or with those who neglect? Are you with those who desist or those who oppose? When you come across verses describing the believers and their characteristics, check yourself against them: are you amongst them? [If so,] praise Allah and seek an increase from Him. But if you are not amongst them, strive to be so and adopt their characteristics and attributes. And when you come across the description of the hypocrites, beware of being amongst them without realizing. When you come across His saying: "O believers", lend your ears and heart to what comes after it. If it is a command, fulfil it, and if it is a prohibition, desist from it. At His saying, "O believers", one of the Predecessors would say, "I am present, O my Lord, and at your command."

An example of this [introspection] is the saying of Allah Most High, "O believers! Protect yourselves and your families from a Fire whose fuel is people and stones."(1) So, contemplate your own situation and that of your family with respect to prayer, fasting, and what is necessary for them regarding purity, post-sexual impurity, menstruation, and postnatal bleeding. Look into their situation regarding this. If they are amongst those who know the relevant rulings and fulfil them as required, remind them more. But if they are negligent in this regard, you must command them, counsel them, and reprimand them. This is because you are responsible for them and will be asked regarding them. He Most High said, "Bid your family to pray and be diligent in observing it."(2) He ﷺ said, "Command your children to pray when they are seven, hit them for it when they are ten, and separate their beds."(3)

In explaining the meaning of: "Protect yourselves and your families from a Fire", ʿAlī ؓ said, "Teach yourselves and your families what is good, and teach them good manners." Similar to this is His saying, "O believers! Turn

(1) *Taḥrīm*, 6.

(2) *Ṭāhā*, 132.

(3) *Abū Dāwūd* (495).

ومع المنتهينَ أم مع المخالفينَ؟ وإذا مررتَ بالآياتِ التي فيها صفاتُ المؤمنينَ وأخلاقُهم فاعرِضْ نفسَك عليها، هل أنتَ منهم؟ فاحمَدِ اللهِ واستزِدْهُ، أم لستَ منهم فاسعَ لذلك وتخلَّقْ واتَّصفْ بصفاتِهم، وإذا مررتَ بصفاتِ المنافقينَ فاحذرْ أن تكونَ منهم وأنتَ لا تشعر، وإذا مررتَ بقولِهِ تعالى: {يَا أَيُّهَا الَّذِينَ آمَنُوا} فأرعِ سمعَكَ وقلبَكَ إلى ما بعدَها، فإن كان أمراً فأْتَمِرْ به، أو نهياً فانْتَهِ عمّا نهى.

وقد كان بعضُ السّلفِ يقولُ عند {يَا أَيُّهَا الَّذِينَ آمَنُوا}: لبَّيكَ ربي وسعدَيكَ. وذلك كقولِهِ تعالى: {يَا أَيُّهَا الَّذِينَ آمَنُوا قُوا أَنفُسَكُمْ وَأَهْلِيكُمْ نَارًا وَقُودُهَا النَّاسُ وَالْحِجَارَةُ}[1] الآيةَ.

فانظرْ في أمرِ نفسِكَ وأهلِكَ في صلاتِهم وصيامِهم، وما يجب عليهم في طهارتِهم وجَنابَتِهم وحيضِ النّساءِ ونِفاسِهنَّ، فتفقَّدْ أحوالَهنَّ في ذلك، فإنْ كنَّ ممّنْ يعلمُ أحكامَ ذلك ويؤدِّيها كما يجبُ فزِدْ في تذكيرهنَّ، وإنْ كُنَّ مقصِّراتٍ في ذلك فعليكَ بأمرهنَّ ووعظهنَّ وزجرهنَّ؛ لأنّكَ الرّاعي عليهنَّ، المسؤولُ عنهنَّ، قال تعالى: {وَأْمُرْ أَهْلَكَ بِالصَّلَاةِ وَاصْطَبِرْ عَلَيْهَا}[2] الآيةَ.

وقال ﷺ: «مُرُوا أولادَكُمْ بالصّلاةِ وهم أبناءُ سبعٍ، واضربوهم عليها وهم أبناءُ عشرٍ، وفرّقوا بينَهم في المضاجعِ»[3].

وقال عليٌّ كرّمَ اللهُ وجهَهُ في معنى قولِهِ تعالى: {قُوا أَنفُسَكُمْ وَأَهْلِيكُمْ نَارًا} الآية قال: علِّموا أنفسَكم وأهليكمُ الخيرَ وأدِّبوهم.

---

(١) التحريم: ٦.

(٢) طه: ١٣٢.

(٣) أخرجه أبو داود (٤٩٥).

to Allah in sincere repentance."[1] So, when you read this verse and similar verses, remember your evil deeds and repent to Allah from them. In this manner, move with the Noble Qur'an wherever it moves: Comply when it commands; desist when it prohibits; be fearful at places of fear; have hope at places of hope; seek forgiveness at verses of seeking forgiveness; take heed at verses of counsel; reflect at verses relating stories; reaffirm your belief and faith in verses of faith and creed; affirm in verses affirming [His attributes]; and declare His transcendence with verses of transcendence.

(1) *Taḥrīm*, 8.

وكذلك قولُه تعالى: {يَا أَيُّهَا الَّذِينَ آمَنُوا تُوبُوا إِلَى اللَّهِ تَوْبَةً نَّصُوحًا}[1] الآية.

فإذا قرأتَ هذه الآيةَ وأمثالَها فتذكَّرْ أفعالَكَ السيِّئةَ وتُبْ إلى اللهِ تعالى منها.

وهكذا تدورُ مع القرآنِ الكريمِ حيثُ دارَ، ائتماراً عند الأمرِ، وانتهاءً عند النّهي، وخوفاً عند الخوفِ، ورجاءً عند الرَّجاءِ، واستغفاراً عند آياتِ الاستغفار، واتّعاظاً عند آياتِ الوعظِ، واعتباراً عند آياتِ القَصصِ، واعتقاداً وإيماناً في آياتِ الإيمان والعقيدةِ، وإثباتاً في الإثباتِ، وتنزيهاً في التنزيه.

---

(١) التحريم: ٨.

THE COUNSEL OF AL-ṢIDDĪQ AL-AKBAR (THE GREAT TRUTHFUL ONE)

When al-Ṣiddīq al-Akbar ﷺ entrusted the radiant al-Fārūq (the one who distinguishes between truth and falsehood) with leadership, amongst the counsel he gave him was the following, "O 'Umar, I have appointed you my successor over the Companions of the Messenger of Allah ﷺ. O 'Umar, Allah Most High has rights by night which He does not accept by day, and rights by day which He does not accept by night. And He does not accept an additional action until the obligatory actions are performed. Have you not seen, O 'Umar, that the Scale of those whose Scale will be heavy on the Day of Judgement is only because they followed the truth and it was burdensome upon them? And a Scale in which only the truth will be placed tomorrow deserves to be heavy. Have you not seen, O 'Umar, that the Scale of those whose Scale will be light on the Day of Judgement is only because they followed falsehood and it was easy for them? And a Scale in which only falsehood will be placed deserves to be light. Have you not seen, O 'Umar, that hopeful verses only came down alongside stern verses and stern verses only came down alongside hopeful verses? That is so the believer is both hopeful and fearful. Neither should they have such hope that they desire from Allah that to which they are not entitled, nor should they have fear that lands them in destruction (i.e., by losing

وصيّةُ الصّدّيقِ الأكبرِ رضي الله تعالى عنه وعنّا به

ولمّا عَهِدَ الصِدّيقُ الأكبرُ رضي الله تعالى عنه بالخلافةِ إلى الفاروقِ الأنورِ عمرَ رَضِيَ اللهُ عَنْهُ كان فيما أوصاهُ أنْ قال له: (يا عمرُ إنّي قد استخلفتُكَ على أصحابِ رسولِ الله ﷺ، يا عمرُ إنَّ للهِ تعالى حقّاً في اللّيلِ ولا يقبلُهُ في النّهارِ، وحقّاً في النّهارِ ولا يقبلُهُ في اللّيلِ، وإنّه لا يقبلُ نافلةً حتى تُؤدّى الفريضةُ، ألم ترَ يا عمرُ أنّما ثَقُلَتْ موازينُ مَن ثَقُلَتْ موازينُهُ يومَ القيامةِ باتّباعِهِمُ الحقَّ، وثِقَلِهِ عليهم، وحقٌّ لميزانٍ لا يوضعُ فيه غداً إلّا حقّاً أن يكونَ ثقيلاً، ألم ترَ يا عمرُ أنّما خفَّتْ موازينُ مَن خفَّتْ موازينُهُ يومَ القيامةِ باتّباعِهِمُ الباطلَ، وخِفَّتِهِ عليهم، وحُقَّ لميزانٍ لا يوضعُ فيه غداً إلا باطلٌ أن يكون خفيفاً، ألم ترَ يا عمرُ أنّما أُنزِلَتْ آيةُ الرَّجاءِ مع آيةِ الشِدَّةِ، وآيةُ الشِّدَّةِ مع آيةِ الرَّجاءِ؛ ليكونَ المؤمنُ راغباً راهباً، لا يرغبَ رغبةً يتمنّى على اللهِ تعالى ما ليس له، ولا يرهبَ رهبةً يُلقي فيها بيديه - أي: بأن يقنطَ من رحمةِ اللهِ تعالى -، ألم ترَ يا عمرُ أنّما ذكرَ اللهُ تعالى أهلَ النّارِ بسوءِ أعمالِهم، فإذا ذكرتَهم قلتَ: إني لأرجو ألّا أكونَ منهم، وإنَّما ذكرَ أهلَ الجنّةِ بأحسنِ أعمالِهم؛ لأنّه تجاوز عمّا كان من سيّءٍ، فإذا ذكرتَها قلتَ: أينَ عملي من أعمالهم؟ فإن حفظتَ وصيّتي

hope of Allah's mercy). Have you not seen, O 'Umar, that Allah Most High only mentioned the people of Hellfire by their evil actions? So, when you mention them, you say, 'I hope not to be amongst them.' And He only mentioned the people of Paradise with the best of their actions, because He overlooked any evil they did. And so, when you mention them, you say, 'Where are my actions in comparison to theirs?' If you are mindful of my counsel, then nothing that is absent will be more beloved to you than death – which you cannot escape." He then passed away – may Allah be pleased with him.

SOME CONCISE WORDS REGARDING THE SAYING OF ALLAH MOST HIGH: "WE HAVE SURELY REVEALED TO YOU A BOOK, IN WHICH THERE IS YOUR MENTION. WILL YOU NOT THEN UNDERSTAND?" AND WHAT A MUSLIM'S STANCE TOWARDS THE QUR'AN SHOULD BE AND THE STORY OF AḤNAF IBN AL-QAYS IN THAT REGARD

Ḥāfiẓ Muhammad ibn Naṣr al-Marwazī mentioned in his monologue *Qiyām al-Layl* that Aḥnaf ibn al-Qays was sitting one day when the following verse appeared before him: "We have surely revealed to you a Book, in which there is your mention. Will you not then understand?"[1] He took note of this and said, "Bring me the muṣḥaf so I can look for my mention today and know who I am and whom I resemble." In other words, on realizing that the Qur'an has mentioned all the qualities of people, and detailed their attributes and ranks, he wanted to search for himself to see which group he is in. So, he opened the muṣḥaf and came across people who "used to sleep only little in the night, and pray for forgiveness before dawn. And in their wealth, there was a rightful share [fulfilled] for the beggar and the poor."[2] And he came across people who "abandon their

(1) *Al-Anbiyā'*, 10.

(2) *Al-Dhāriyāt*, 17-19.

فلا يكونُ غائبٌ أحبَّ إليك من المَوتِ، ولستَ بمعجِزِهِ - أي: لابُدَّ أن يدرِكَكَ، ثمّ توفِّيَ رَضِيَ اللَّهُ عَنْهُ).

كلماتٌ موجَزةٌ حولَ قولِ اللهِ تعالى: {لَقَدْ أَنزَلْنَا إِلَيْكُمْ كِتَابًا فِيهِ ذِكْرُكُمْ أَفَلَا تَعْقِلُونَ}[1] وماذا يجبُ على المؤمنِ أن يكونَ موقِفُهُ مع القرآنِ وفيه قصّةُ الأحنفِ بنِ قيسٍ

ذكر الحافظُ محمّدُ بنُ نصرٍ المروزيُّ في جزءِ (قيامِ اللّيلِ) للأحنفِ بنِ قَيسٍ أنه كان يوماً جالساً، فعرضَتْ له هذه الآيةُ: {لَقَدْ أَنزَلْنَا إِلَيْكُمْ كِتَابًا فِيهِ ذِكْرُكُمْ أَفَلَا تَعْقِلُونَ}[2] فانتبَهَ. فقال: عليّ بالمصحفِ؛ لألتمس ذِكري اليومَ، حتّى أعلمَ مَن أنا ومَن أُشْبِهُ، يعني: لمّا عَلِمَ أنَّ القرآنَ قد ذكرَ جميعَ صفاتِ البشرِ، وبيَّنَ صفاتِهم ومراتِبَهم أراد أن يبحثَ عن نفسِهِ في أيِّ الطبقاتِ هو؟ فنشرَ المصحفَ، فمرَّ بقومٍ {كَانُوا قَلِيلًا مِّنَ اللَّيْلِ مَا يَهْجَعُونَ (١٧) وَبِالْأَسْحَارِ هُمْ يَسْتَغْفِرُونَ (١٨) وَفِي أَمْوَالِهِمْ حَقٌّ لِّلسَّائِلِ وَالْمَحْرُومِ}[3]، ومرَّ بقومٍ {تَتَجَافَىٰ جُنُوبُهُمْ عَنِ الْمَضَاجِعِ يَدْعُونَ رَبَّهُمْ خَوْفًا وَطَمَعًا وَمِمَّا رَزَقْنَاهُمْ يُنفِقُونَ}[4]، ومرَّ بقومٍ {يَبِيتُونَ لِرَبِّهِمْ سُجَّدًا وَقِيَامًا}[5]، ومرَّ بقومٍ {يُنفِقُونَ

---

(١) الأنبياء: ١٠.

(٢) الأنبياء: ١٠.

(٣) الذاريات: ١٧- ١٩.

(٤) السجدة: ١٦.

(٥) الفرقان: ٦٤.

beds, invoking their Lord with hope and fear, and donate from what We have provided for them."[1] And he came across people who "who spend [a good portion of] the night, prostrating themselves and standing before their Lord."[2] And he came across people who "who donate in prosperity and adversity, control their anger, and pardon others. And Allah loves the good-doers."[3] And he came across people who "give preference over themselves even though they may be in need. And whoever is saved from the selfishness of their own souls, it is they who are [truly] successful."[4] And he came across people who "who avoid major sins and shameful deeds, and forgive when angered; who respond to their Lord, establish prayer, conduct their affairs by mutual consultation, and donate from what We have provided for them."[5] Aḥnaf ibn al-Qays paused and then said, "O Allah, I do not recognize myself here (i.e., he did not find these qualities in himself to include himself in that category)."

Then Aḥnaf ibn al-Qays took the other route. He thus came across people in the muṣḥaf who "whenever it was said to them [in the world], 'There is no god [worthy of worship] except Allah,' they acted arrogantly and argued, 'Should we really abandon our gods for a mad poet?'"[6] And he came across people regarding whom Allah Most High said, "When Allah alone is mentioned, the hearts of those who disbelieve in the Hereafter are filled with disgust. But as soon as those [gods] other than Him are mentioned, they are filled with joy."[7] And he came across people to whom it will be said, "'What has landed you in Hell?' They will reply, 'We were not of those who prayed nor did we feed the poor. We used to indulge [in falsehood] along with others and deny the Day of Judgement, until the

---

(1) *Al-Sajdah*, 16.

(2) *Al-Furqān*, 64.

(3) *Āl 'Imrān*, 134.

(4) *Al-Ḥashr*, 9.

(5) *Al-Shūrā*, 37-38.

(6) *Al-Ṣāffāt*, 35-36.

(7) *Al-Zumar*, 45.

فِي السَّرَّاءِ وَالضَّرَّاءِ وَالْكَاظِمِينَ الْغَيْظَ وَالْعَافِينَ عَنِ النَّاسِ ۗ وَاللَّهُ يُحِبُّ الْمُحْسِنِينَ}[1]، ومرَّ بقومٍ {يُؤْثِرُونَ عَلَىٰ أَنفُسِهِمْ وَلَوْ كَانَ بِهِمْ خَصَاصَةٌ ۚ وَمَن يُوقَ شُحَّ نَفْسِهِ فَأُولَٰئِكَ هُمُ الْمُفْلِحُونَ}[2]، ومرَّ بقومٍ {يَجْتَنِبُونَ كَبَائِرَ الْإِثْمِ وَالْفَوَاحِشَ وَإِذَا مَا غَضِبُوا هُمْ يَغْفِرُونَ (٣٧) وَالَّذِينَ اسْتَجَابُوا لِرَبِّهِمْ وَأَقَامُوا الصَّلَاةَ وَأَمْرُهُمْ شُورَىٰ بَيْنَهُمْ وَمِمَّا رَزَقْنَاهُمْ يُنفِقُونَ}[3]. فوقفَ الأحنفُ ثمَّ قال: اللَّهمَّ لستُ أعرِفُ نفسي هاهنا - يعني: لم يجدْ هذه الصّفاتِ في نفسِهِ حتَّى يَعُدَّ نفسَه من هذه الطبقة.

ثم أخذَ الأحنفُ السَّبيلَ الآخَرَ فمرَّ في المصحفِ بقومٍ {إِذَا قِيلَ لَهُمْ لَا إِلَٰهَ إِلَّا اللَّهُ يَسْتَكْبِرُونَ (٣٥) وَيَقُولُونَ أَئِنَّا لَتَارِكُو آلِهَتِنَا لِشَاعِرٍ مَّجْنُونٍ}[4]، ومرَّ بقومٍ قال اللهُ تعالى فيهم: {وَإِذَا ذُكِرَ اللَّهُ وَحْدَهُ اشْمَأَزَّتْ قُلُوبُ الَّذِينَ لَا يُؤْمِنُونَ بِالْآخِرَةِ ۖ وَإِذَا ذُكِرَ الَّذِينَ مِن دُونِهِ إِذَا هُمْ يَسْتَبْشِرُونَ}[5]، ومرَّ بقومٍ يقالُ لهم: {مَا سَلَكَكُمْ فِي سَقَرَ (٤٢) قَالُوا لَمْ نَكُ مِنَ الْمُصَلِّينَ (٤٣) وَلَمْ نَكُ نُطْعِمُ الْمِسْكِينَ (٤٤) وَكُنَّا نَخُوضُ مَعَ الْخَائِضِينَ (٤٥) وَكُنَّا نُكَذِّبُ بِيَوْمِ الدِّينِ (٤٦) حَتَّىٰ أَتَانَا الْيَقِينُ}[6]. فوقفَ الأحنفُ، ثمَّ قال: اللَّهمَّ إنِّي أبرأُ إليك من هؤلاء! فما زال الأحنفُ يقلِّبُ ورقَ المصحفِ، ويلتمسُ في أيِّ الطَّبقاتِ حتّى وقع على هذهِ الآية {وَآخَرُونَ اعْتَرَفُوا بِذُنُوبِهِمْ خَلَطُوا عَمَلًا صَالِحًا وَآخَرَ سَيِّئًا عَسَى

---

(١) آل عمران: ١٣٤.

(٢) الحشر: ٩.

(٣) الشورى: ٣٧-٣٨.

(٤) الصافات: ٣٥-٣٦.

(٥) الزمر: ٤٥.

(٦) المدثر: ٤٢-٤٧.

inevitable came to us.'"[1] Aḥnaf paused and said, "O Allah, I disassociate myself from these people before you." Aḥnaf then continued turning the pages of the muṣḥaf – looking for which category he is in – until he came across this verse, "Some others have confessed their wrongdoing: they have mixed goodness with evil. It is right to hope that Allah will turn to them in mercy. Surely Allah is All-Forgiving, Most Merciful."[2] Aḥnaf said, "I am from these people."

So look – O Muslim – where you find yourself in the Book of Allah Most High and in which category you are. And beware of being amongst those who fit the description of the hypocrites and the sinful – we seek refuge with Allah, the Greatest. Allah Most High said, "Surely in this is a reminder for whoever has a [mindful] heart and lends an attentive ear."[3]

O you who hearkens to the caller towards wretchedness,
Whereas the two announcers of death – grey hair and old age – have already called him.
If you do not listen to reminders, why then do you think
you have in your head, ears and eyes that perceive?
The deaf and blind are not but a person
Whom the two guides – the eyes and life itself – cannot show the way.
Neither time will remain nor this world nor the lofty sky
Nor the two radiant lights – the Sun and the Moon.
Surely from this world – even if they dislike to part with it
Its residents – both villagers and townsmen – will depart.

(1) *Al-Muddaththir*, 42-47.

(2) *Al-Tawbah*, 102.

(3) *Qāf*, 37.

اللَّهُ أَن يَتُوبَ عَلَيۡهِمۡۚ إِنَّ اللَّهَ غَفُورٞ رَّحِيمٌ}[1]. فقال الأحنفُ: أنا مِن هؤلاءِ.

فانظرْ أيُّها المسلمُ موضِعَ نفسِكَ من كتابِ اللهِ تعالى، وفي أيِّ الطَّبقاتِ أنتَ، واحذرْ أن تكونَ مِمّنْ تنطبقُ عليهمْ صفاتُ المنافقينَ أو الفاسقينَ، عياذاً باللهِ العظيمِ، قال تعالى: {إِنَّ فِي ذَٰلِكَ لَذِكۡرَىٰ لِمَن كَانَ لَهُۥ قَلۡبٌ أَوۡ أَلۡقَى السَّمۡعَ وَهُوَ شَهِيدٞ}[2].

يا مَن يَصيخُ إلى داعي الشَّقاءِ وقد ... نادى به النّاعيانِ الشَّيبُ والكِبَرُ

إذا كنتَ لا تسمعُ الذِّكرى ففيمَ ترى ... في رأسِكَ الواعيانِ السَّمعُ والبصرُ

ليسَ الأصَمُّ ولا الأعمى سوى رجلٍ ... لم يهدِهِ الهاديانِ العينُ والأثَرُ

لا الدَّهرُ يبقى ولا الدُّنيا ولا الفلكُ الأ ... على ولا النّيّرانُ الشَّمسُ والقمرُ

ليرحَلَنَّ عن الدُّنيا وإنْ كَرِها ... فراقَها الثّاوِيانِ البدوُ والحضرُ

(١) التوبة: ١٠٢.

(٢) ق: ٣٧.

THE STATIONS (MAQĀMĀT) OF THE QUR'AN RECITERS

It is reported in *al-Burhān* that one of the knowers (*ʿārifīn*) said people are on three stations (*maqāmāt*) with respect to reciting the Noble Qur'an.

The first is the one who observes the attributes of the Speaker in His Speech and familiarizes themselves with the meanings of His address. Thus, they look towards Him through His Speech, His discourse in His address, the enjoyment derived through secretly conversing with Him, and becoming acquainted with Him through His attributes. Every word imparts the meaning of a name, attribute, ruling, intention, or action (i.e., from the Names of Allah Most High, His attributes, His rulings, His intention, and His actions). This is because the Speech informs of the essence of the attributes and denotes the One whose attributes they are. This is the station of the knowers amongst the believers. They do not look towards themselves or their recitation, but rather they are confined to understanding from the Speaker, focused on pondering about Him, and totally engrossed in witnessing the Speaker. Imam Jaʿfar al-Ṣādiq ﵁ said, "Allah Most High manifested Himself to His creation through His Speech, but they do not see." The second is the one who witnesses with their heart, as though He Most High is addressing them and secretly conversing with them through His kindness, and winning them over through His bounties

مقاماتُ قُرّاءِ القرآنِ الكريم

نَقلَ في (البرهانِ) عن بعضِ العارفينَ رضي اللهُ تعالى عنهم أنه قال: النّاسُ في تلاوةِ القرآنِ الكريمِ على ثلاثةِ مقاماتٍ:

المقامِ الأوَّلِ: مَن يشهدُ أوصافَ المتكلّمِ في كلامِهِ، ومعرفةَ معاني خطابِهِ، فينظرُ إليه من كلامِهِ وتكلُّمِهِ في خطابه، وتملّيه بمناجاتِهِ، وتعرُّفه من صفاتِهِ، فإنَّ كلَّ كلمةٍ تُنبيءُ عن معنى اسمٍ، أو وصفٍ أو حكمٍ، أو إرادةٍ، أو فعلٍ؛ أي: من أسماءِ اللهِ تعالى، وأوصافِهِ، وأحكامِهِ، وإرادتِهِ، وأفعالِهِ؛ لأنَّ الكلامَ يُنبِئُ عن معاني الأوصافِ، ويدلُّ على الموصوفِ، وهذا مقام العارفينَ من المؤمنينَ؛ لأنّه لا ينظرُ إلى نفسِهِ ولا إلى قراءتِهِ؛ بل هو مقصورُ الفَهمِ عن المتكلِّمِ، موقوفُ الفكرِ عليه، مستغرِقٌ بمشاهدةِ المتكلِّمِ.

قال السّيّدُ الإمامُ جعفرُ الصّادقُ رضي اللهُ تعالى عنه: لقد تجلّى اللهُ تعالى لخلقِهِ بكلامِهِ، ولكن لا يبصرون.

الثاني: مَن يشهدُ بقلبِهِ كأنّهُ تعالى يخاطِبُهُ ويناجيه بألطافِهِ، ويتملَّقُهُ بإنعامِهِ وإحسانِهِ، فمقامُ هذا الحياءُ والتعظيمُ - لمقامِ اللهِ عَزَّوَجَلَّ - وحالُهُ الإصغاءُ، والفهمُ عن

and favours. The station of such a person is shyness and reverence (for the standing of Allah Almighty and Exalted). Their condition is to listen carefully and to understand from Allah Most High – this is for most of the Nearest (*Muqarrabūn*). The third is the one who sees that they are secretly conversing with their Lord Most Glorified. The station of such a reciter is that of imploring and flattering their Master. This station is reserved for the elite amongst the People of the Right (*Aṣḥāb al-Yamīn*).

Some of the knowers said that the Qur'an contains meadows, orchards, palaces, brides, silk brocade, and gardens. The *mīms* (i.e., *sūrahs* beginning with *Alif Lām Mīm*) are the meadows of the Qur'an, the *rās* are the orchards of the Qur'an, the *ḥās* are the palaces of the Qur'an, the *musabbiḥāt*[1] are the brides of the Qur'an, the *Ḥā Mīms* are the silk brocade of the Qur'an, and the *mufaṣṣalāt*[2] are its gardens. Thus, when the seeker enters the meadows, plucks fruits from the orchards, enters the palaces, sees the brides, wears the silk brocade, strolls in the gardens, and resides in the mansions of different levels, they become detached from everything else, halted by what they see, and they are preoccupied by the sights from all else. Bayhaqī narrated with his chain that the Prophet ﷺ said, "Recite the Qur'an with proper Arabic and search for its wonders."[3] Its wonders are its obligations and limits. Ibn Mas'ūd ؓ said, "Whoever wants the knowledge of the first and the last should thoroughly study the Qur'an, for it contains the knowledge of the first and the last."[4] Abū al-Dardā' ؓ said, "A person cannot truly understand until they consider numerous meanings for the Qur'an."[5] In others, they understand the meanings of the Qur'an from a number of perspectives.

---

(1) Translator's Note: Musabbiḥāt are those *sūrahs* that begin with *tasbīḥ*.

(2) Translator's Note: Details of these *sūrahs* are mentioned later in the book.

(3) Bayhaqī in *Shu'ab al-Īmān* (2293).

(4) Ibn al-Mubārak in *al-Zuhd* (814).

(5) Ibn Abī Shaybah in *al-Muṣannaf* (1793).

الله تعالى، وهذا لعمومِ المُقرَّبين.

الثالث: مَن يرى أنه يناجي ربَّه سبحانه، فمقامُ هذا القارئِ السؤالُ والتملُّقُ بمولاه، وحالُهُ الطَّلَبُ، وهذا المقامُ لخصوصِ أصحابِ اليمين.

وقال بعضُ العارفين: في القرآنِ ميادينُ وبساتينُ، ومقاصيرُ وعرائسُ، وديابيجُ ورياضٌ، فالميماتُ - أي: السُّوَرُ المُفتَتَحَةُ بـ: الم ميادينُ القرآنِ، والرّاءاتُ بساتينُ القرآنِ، والحاءاتُ مقاصيرُ القرآنِ، والمسبّحاتُ عرائسُ القرآنِ، والحواميمُ ديابيجُ القرآنِ، والمفصّلُ رياضُهُ، فإذا دخل المريدُ في الميادين، وقطفَ من البساتينِ، ودخلَ المقاصيرَ، وشهدَ العرائسَ، ولبس الديابيجَ، وتنزَّهُ في الرّياضِ، وسكنَ غُرُفاتِ المقاماتِ: اقتطعه عمّا سواه، وأوقفَهُ ما يراه، وشغلَهُ المشاهَدُ له عمّا عداه.

وروى البيهقيُّ بإسنادِهِ عنه ﷺ أنهّ قال: «أعرِبوا القرآنَ والتمِسوا غرائبَهُ»[1]، وغرائبُهُ: فرائضُهُ وحدودُهُ.

وقال ابنُ مسعودٍ رضي الله عنه: (مَن أراد علمَ الأوَّلين والآخرينَ فليثورَ - أي: فليبحثْ - القرآنَ، فإنَّ فيه علمَ الأوّلينَ والآخرينَ)[2].

وقال أبو الدرداءِ رضي الله عنه: (لا يفقَهُ الرَّجلُ حتّى يجعلَ للقرآنِ وجوهاً)[3]. أي: حتى يَفهَمَ معانيَ القرآنِ من عدّةِ أوجهٍ.

---

(١) أخرجه البيهقي في شعب الإيمان (٢٢٩٣).

(٢) رواه ابن المبارك في الزهد (٨١٤).

(٣) أخرجه ابن أبي شيبة في مصنفه (١٧٩٣).

THE PIOUS PREDECESSORS LIKED TO RECITE VERSES REPEATEDLY FOR THE SAKE OF CONTEMPLATION

Many of the Pious Predecessors would repeat a single verse many times to contemplate it. Each time they repeated it, new meanings would open up to them and various hues of light would manifest to them. They would attach themselves to this single verse out of hope, due to fear, to seek His mercy, or as a means of seeking intercession.

Imam Aḥmad narrated on the authority of Abū Dharr ﷺ who said, "The Messenger of Allah ﷺ stood to pray one night and recited a single verse until dawn. I said, 'O Messenger of Allah, you continued reciting this verse until dawn, bowing and prostrating upon it (i.e., reciting it in every *rak ʿah*). He ﷺ said, 'I asked my Lord Almighty and Exalted for Intercession for my ummah, so He granted me it. And it is – if Allah wills – for anyone who does not associate any partner with Allah.'"[1]

It is narrated that Tamīm al-Dārī ﷺ repeated the following verse until dawn: "Or do those who commit evil deeds [simply] think that We will make them equal – in their life and after their death – to those who believe and do good? How wrong is their judgement!"[2] ʿUbādah ibn Ḥamzah said, "I went to Asmā' ﷺ whilst she was reciting, 'So Allah has graced us and protected us from the torment of [Hell's] scorching heat.'[3] She paused at it, and began repeating it and supplicating." Imam Nawawī said this incident has also been narrated regarding Sayyidah ʿĀ'ishah ﷺ.

Ibn al-Mubārak narrated in his book *al-Zuhd* that Abū Rayḥānah ﷺ returned from an expedition. He ate supper, and then performed *wuḍū'* and went to his masjid. He recited a *sūrah* and continued reciting it until dawn. His wife said to him, "You went out on an expedition and were away, and then you came back. So, do we not have any share in you?" He said, "Of

---

(1) *Aḥmad* (21328).

(2) *Al-Jāthiyah*, 21.

(3) *Al-Ṭūr*, 27.

استحبابُ السَّلفِ الصّالحِ ترديدَ الآيةِ للتدبُّر

كان كثيرٌ من السَّلفِ الصَّالحِ مَن يردِّدُ الآيةَ الواحدةَ عدَّةَ مرّاتٍ؛ ليتدبَّرَ فيها، وكلّما أعادها انكشفَتْ له وجوهٌ من معانيها، وتجلَّتْ له ألوانٌ من أنوارِها، فهم يتعلَّقون بها رجاءً، أو يخشون منها خوفاً، أو يَسترحِمون بها ويَستَشْفِعون.

روى الإمامُ أحمدُ عن أبي ذرٍّ رَضِيَ اللهُ عَنْهُ أنه قال: قام رسولُ اللهِ صَلَّى اللهُ عَلَيْهِ وَآلِهِ وَسَلَّمَ ذاتَ ليلةٍ، فقرأَ بآيةٍ حتى أصبحَ، قلتُ: يا رسولَ الله، ما زلتَ تقرأُ هذه الآيةَ حتى أصبحتَ، تركعُ وتسجدُ بها؟ فقال صَلَّى اللهُ عَلَيْهِ وَآلِهِ وَسَلَّمَ: «إنّي سألتُ ربّي عزَّ وجلَّ الشَّفاعةَ لأمَّتي فأعطانيها، وهي إن شاءَ اللهُ لِمَن لا يُشرِكُ باللهِ شيئاً» [1].وعن تميم الداري رضي الله عنه أنه كرر هذه الآية {أَمْ حَسِبَ الَّذِينَ اجْتَرَحُوا السَّيِّئَاتِ أَن نَّجْعَلَهُمْ كَالَّذِينَ آمَنُوا وَعَمِلُوا الصَّالِحَاتِ} [2] الآية، حتى أصبح. وعن عبادةَ بنِ حمزةَ قال: دخلتُ على أسماءَ رضي الله تعالى عنها وهي تقرأُ {فَمَنَّ اللَّهُ عَلَيْنَا وَوَقَانَا عَذَابَ السَّمُومِ}[3] الآيةَ، قال: فوقفتُ عندَها فجعلَتْ تُعيدُها وتدعو. قال الإمامُ النوويُّ: رُويتْ هذه القصّةُ عن السيدة عائشةَ رضي الله عنها أيضاً.

وروى ابنُ المباركِ في كتابِهِ (الزُّهد) عن أبي ريحانةَ رضي الله تعالى عنه أنه قفلَ - رجع - من غزوةٍ له فتعشّى ثمَّ توضّأَ، وقام إلى مسجدِه، فقرأ سورةً، فلم يزلْ حتى أذّنَ للصُّبحِ، فقالتِ امرأتُهُ: غزوتَ فغِبتَ، ثمَّ قَدِمتَ، أفما كان

---

(١) أخرجه أحمد (٢١٣٢٨).

(٢) الجاثية: ٢١.

(٣) الطور: ٢٧.

course, by Allah. But if I had remembered you, you would have had a right over me." She asked, "So what preoccupied you?" He replied, "Pondering over the description Allah Most High has given of Paradise and its pleasures until I heard the call to prayer." Shaykh Ibrāhīm al-Khawwāṣ ﷺ said, "The cure of the heart is in five things: reciting the Qur'an with contemplation, keeping the stomach empty, standing to pray at night, beseeching [Allah] at dawn, and sitting with the righteous." Ibn Mas'ūd ﷺ kept repeating the saying of Allah Most High, "My Lord! Increase me in knowledge."[1] When Ḍaḥḥāk would recite the saying of Allah Most High, "They will have layers of fire above and below them. That is what Allah warns His servants with. So fear Me, O My servants!",[2] he would keep repeating it until dawn.

NINE: FEAR AND CRYING UPON RECITING THE QUR'AN

Allah Most High said, "And they fall down upon their faces weeping, and it increases them in humility."[3]

And Allah Most High said, "[It is] Allah [Who] has sent down the best message – a Book of perfect consistency and repeated lessons – which causes the skin [and hearts] of those who fear their Lord to tremble, then their skin and hearts soften at the mention of [the mercy of] Allah."[4]

Allah Most High has praised those who cry profusely when reciting the Qur'an. Allah Most High said, "Had We sent down this Qur'an upon a mountain, you would have certainly seen it humbled and torn apart in awe of Allah."[5] He Most Glorified has explained that if this Qur'an were to have been sent down upon solid, firm mountains, they would have humbled and torn apart in awe of Allah; so, what about the hearts if it were

---

(1) *Ṭāhā*, 114.

(2) *Al-Zumar*, 16.

(3) *Al-Isrā'*, 109.

(4) *Al-Zumar*, 23.

(5) *Al-Ḥashr*, 21.

لنا فيك نصيبٌ؟ قال: بلى واللهِ، ولو ذكرتُكِ لكان لكِ عليّ حقٌّ. قالتْ: فما الذي شغلَكَ؟ قال: التفكُّرُ فيما وصفَ اللهُ تعالى في جنَّتِهِ ولذَّاتِها، حتّى سمعتُ المؤذِّنَ.وقال الشَّيخُ إبراهيمُ الخَوّاصُ رضي الله تعالى عنه: دواءُ القلبِ خمسةُ أشياءَ: قراءةُ القرآنِ بالتدبُّرِ، وخَلاءُ البطنِ، وقيامُ اللّيل، والتضرُّعُ عند السَّحرِ، ومجالسةُ الصّالحين. وردَّدَ ابنُ مسعودٍ قولَه تعالى: {رَّبِّ زِدْنِي عِلْمًا}[1]. وكان الضَّحاكُ إذا تلا قولَهُ تعالى: {لَهُم مِّن فَوْقِهِمْ ظُلَلٌ مِّنَ النَّارِ وَمِن تَحْتِهِمْ ظُلَلٌ}[2] الآيةَ، كان يردِّدُها إلى السَّحر.

التاسع: الخشيةُ والبكاءُ لقراءةِ القرآنِ:

قال اللهُ تعالى: {وَيَخِرُّونَ لِلْأَذْقَانِ يَبْكُونَ وَيَزِيدُهُمْ خُشُوعًا}[3] الآية.

وقال اللهُ تعالى: {اللَّهُ نَزَّلَ أَحْسَنَ الْحَدِيثِ كِتَابًا مُّتَشَابِهًا مَّثَانِيَ تَقْشَعِرُّ مِنْهُ جُلُودُ الَّذِينَ يَخْشَوْنَ رَبَّهُمْ ثُمَّ تَلِينُ جُلُودُهُمْ وَقُلُوبُهُمْ إِلَىٰ ذِكْرِ اللَّهِ}[4].

فقد أثنى اللهُ تعالى على البكّائينَ عند قراءةِ القرآن. وقال اللهُ تعالى: {لَوْ أَنزَلْنَا هَٰذَا الْقُرْآنَ عَلَىٰ جَبَلٍ لَّرَأَيْتَهُ خَاشِعًا مُّتَصَدِّعًا مِّنْ خَشْيَةِ اللَّهِ}[5] الآيةَ.

فبيَّنَ سبحانه أنَّ هذا القرآنَ لو أُنزِلَ على الجبالِ الصُّمِّ القاسيةِ لَخَشَعَتْ وتصدَّعَتْ

---

(١) طه: ١١٤.

(٢) الزمر: ١٦.

(٣) الزمر: ١٦.

(٤) الزمر: ١٦.

(٥) الحشر: ٢١.

sent down on them? It is more becoming of the hearts that they humble, and it is surely detestable that the hearts be harder than a mountain.

In the two *Ṣaḥīḥ* collections, it is narrated that Ibn Mas'ūd ﵁ – after having recited to the Messenger of Allah ﷺ – said, "I turned around to see the eyes of the Messenger of Allah ﷺ flowing with tears."(1)

It is narrated on the authority of Sa'd ibn Abī Waqqāṣ ﵁ who said he heard the Messenger of Allah ﷺ say, "Indeed, this Qur'an was revealed with sorrow, so cry when you recite it. If you cannot cry, try to make yourself cry, and recite it melodiously. Whoever does not recite the Qur'an melodiously is not from us."(2) Ibn Mājah narrated it.

Imam Aḥmad narrated on the authority of Sayyidah 'Ā'ishah ﵂ who said, "When the Messenger of Allah ﷺ entered my house (i.e., during his final illness), he said, 'Instruct Abū Bakr to lead the people in prayer.' I said, 'O Messenger of Allah, Abu Bakr is a soft-hearted man; when he recites the Qur'an, he cannot hold back his tears. If you could instruct someone other than Abū Bakr.'"(3)

Ḥasan ﵀ said, "'Umar ibn al-Khaṭṭāb ﵁ would come across a verse in his litany at night and keep crying until he would faint. He would stay inside his house until he would be visited due to his illness."

Abū Rajā' said, "I saw that Ibn 'Abbās ﵄ had two lines like old laces under his eyes due to tears."

Abū Ṣāliḥ said, "Some people from Yemen came to Abū Bakr al-Ṣiddīq ﵁ and began reciting the Qur'an and crying. Abū Bakr al-Ṣiddīq ﵁ said, 'This is how we were (i.e. during the era of Allah's Messenger ﷺ).'"

Hishām said, "At times I would hear Muhammad ibn Sīrīn crying at night in his prayer." In other words, his neighbours could hear him crying inside his own house.

---

(1) *Bukhārī* (5050); *Muslim* (800).

(2) *Ibn Mājah* (1327).

(3) *Aḥmad* (25793).

من خشيةِ الله، فكيف إذا أُنزِلَ على القلوب؟! فهي أحقُّ بالخشيةِ وأجدَرُ، ومن القبيحِ أنْ يكونَ القلبُ أشدَّ قسوةً من الجبل.

وفي (الصَّحيحينِ) عن ابنِ مسعودٍ رَضِيَ اللَّهُ عَنْهُ، لمّا قرأَ على رسولِ الله ﷺ، قال ابنُ مسعودٍ: فالتفتُّ فإذا عَيْنَا رسولِ اللهِ تَذرِفان [١]. ورويَ عن سعدِ بنِ أبي وقّاصٍ رضي اللهُ عنه قال: سمعتُ رسولَ الله ﷺ يقول: «إنَّ هذا القرآنَ نزلَ بحزنٍ، فإذا قرأتموه فابكوا، فإنْ لم تبكوا فتباكَوا، وتغنَّوا به، فمَن لم يتغنَّ بالقرآنِ فليس منّا» [٢] رواه ابنُ ماجه. وروى الإمامُ أحمدُ عن السيدةِ عائشةَ رضي الله تعالى عنها قالت: لمّا دخلَ رسولُ الله ﷺ بيتي - أي: في مرضِ الوفاةِ - قال: «مُرُوا أبا بكرٍ فليُصَلِّ بالنّاس»، قالت السيدةُ عائشةُ رَضِيَ اللَّهُ عَنْهَا: فقلتُ: يا رسولَ اللهِ إنَّ أبا بكرٍ رجلٌ رقيقٌ، إذا قرأَ القرآنَ لا يَملِكُ دمعَهُ فلو أمرتَ غيرَ أبي بكرٍ [٣]. الحديثَ. وعن الحسنِ رضي الله تعالى عنه قال: كان عمرُ بنُ الخطّابِ رَضِيَ اللَّهُ عَنْهُ يمرُّ بالآيةِ من وِردِهِ بالليلِ فيبكي حتى يسقطَ، ويبقى في البيتِ حتى يُعادَ للمرضِ. وعن أبي رجاء قال: رأيتُ ابنَ عبّاسٍ رَضِيَ اللَّهُ عَنْهُمَا وتحتَ عينيه مثلُ الشِّراكِ البالي من الدُّموعِ. وعن أبي صالحٍ قال: قَدِمَ ناسٌ من أهل اليمنِ على أبي بكرٍ الصّديقِ رضي اللهُ تعالى عنه، فجعلوا يقرؤونَ القرآنَ ويبكون، فقال أبو بكرٍ رضي الله تعالى عنه: هكذا كُنّا، أي: على عهدِ رسولِ اللهِ ﷺ. وعن هشامٍ قال: ربَّما سمعتُ بكاءَ محمّدِ بنِ سيرينَ في اللّيلِ وهو في الصّلاةِ، أي: داخلَ بيتِه، يَسمَعُ صوتَ بكائِهِ الجيرانُ. وروى محمّدُ بنُ نصرٍ، والبيهقيُّ عن ابنِ عبّاسٍ رضي الله تعالى

---

(١) أخرجه البخاري (٥٠٥٠)، ومسلم (٨٠٠).

(٢) أخرجه ابن ماجه (١٣٣٧).

(٣) أخرجه أحمد في المسند (٢٥٧٩٣).

Muhammad ibn Naṣr and Bayhaqī narrated on the authority of Ibn ʿAbbās ﷺ as a hadith attributed to the Prophet ﷺ, "The person who recites the best is the one who, when they recite, you think they fear Allah."[1] A narration of Ṭabarānī states, "The person who recites the best is one who recites the Qur'an sorrowfully."[2]

It is narrated on the authority of Abū Hurayrah ﷺ that when the verses, "Do you find this Revelation astonishing, laughing [at it] and not weeping [in awe], while persisting in heedlessness?"[3] came down, the People of al-Ṣuffah cried until their tears flowed on their cheeks.[4] Bayhaqī narrated it.

Usayd ibn Ḥuḍayr ﷺ said, "If I were to stay in three states from all my states, I would be from the people of Paradise: when I recite the Qur'an, when I listen to it, and when I listen to the sermon of the Messenger of Allah ﷺ."

TEN: TARTĪL

It is a *sunnah* to recite the Qur'an with *tartīl* (i.e., to recite distinctly and with due measure). Allah Most High said, "And recite the Quran [properly] in a measured way."[5]

Umm Salamah ﷺ described the recitation of the Prophet ﷺ as being distinct and every letter being recited clearly.

Qatādah said that he asked Anas ﷺ regarding the recitation of the Prophet ﷺ. Anas ﷺ said, "He ﷺ used to stretch[6] properly." He then recited *Bismillāh al-Raḥmān al-Raḥīm* – stretching *Bismillāh*, stretching

(1) Bayhaqī in *Shu ʿab al-Īmān* (2293).

(2) *Ṭabarānī* (10852).

(3) *Al-Najm*, 59-60.

(4) Bayhaqī in *Shu ʿab al-Īmān* (798).

(5) *Al-Muzzammil*, 4.

(6) Translator's note: The Prophet ﷺ would ensure that the letters which need to be stretched are read clearly and not rushed or compressed. It does not mean he would overstretch letters beyond their fixed measure.

عنهما مرفوعاً: «أحسنُ النّاسِ قراءةً الذي إذا قرأَ رأيتَ أنّهُ يخشى اللّهَ»[1]، وفي روايةِ الطّبرانيِّ: «وأحسنُ النّاسِ قراءةً مَن قرأَ القرآنَ يتحزَّنُ بهِ»[2]. ورويَ عن أبي هريرةَ رضي الله تعالى عنه قال: لمّا نزلَتْ {أَفَمِنْ هَٰذَا الْحَدِيثِ تَعْجَبُونَ (٥٩) وَتَضْحَكُونَ وَلَا تَبْكُونَ..}[3] الآياتِ، بكى أصحابُ الصُّفّةِ حتى جرَتْ دموعُهُم على خدودِهم[4]. رواهُ البيهقيُّ. وقال أُسَيدُ بنُ حُضَيرٍ رضي الله تعالى عنه: لو أنّي أكونُ على أحوالٍ ثلاثةٍ من أحوالي لكنتُ من أهلِ الجنّةِ: حينَ أقرأُ القرآنَ، وحينَ أسمَعُهُ، وإذا سمعتُ خطبةَ رسولِ اللهِ ﷺ.

العاشرُ: التَّرتيلُ:

يُسَنُّ التَّرتيلُ في قراءةِ القرآنِ، قال اللهُ تعالى: {وَرَتِّلِ الْقُرْآنَ تَرْتِيلًا}[5]. وعن أمِّ سلَمةَ أنّها نعتَتْ قراءةَ النَّبيِّ ﷺ، فإذا هي تنعَتُ قراءتَهُ مفسَّرةً حرفاً حرفاً. وعن قَتادةَ سألتُ أنساً رضي الله عنه عن قراءةِ النبيِّ ﷺ فقال: كان ﷺ يمُدُّ مدّاً، ثمَّ قرأَ: بسم الله الرحمن الرحيم، يمُدُّ ببسمِ اللهِ، ويملأُ بالرَّحمنِ، ويمدُّ بالرَّحيمِ[6]. رواهُ البخاريُّ.

---

(١) أخرجه البيهقي في شعب الإيمان (١٩٥٨).

(٢) أخرجه الطبراني (١٠٨٥٢).

(٣) النجم: ٥٩- ٦٠.

(٤) أخرجه البيهقي في شعب الإيمان (٧٩٨).

(٥) المزمل: ٤.

(٦) أخرجه البخاري (٥٠٤٦).

al-Raḥmān, and stretching *al-Raḥīm*.[1] Bukhārī narrated it.

In the two *Ṣaḥīḥ* collections, it is narrated that a man said to Ibn Mas'ūd ﷺ, "I read all the *mufaṣṣal sūrahs* in one *rak'ah*." Ibn Mas'ūd ﷺ said, "Gabble like the gabble of poetry? Indeed, there are people who recite the Qur'an but it does not go beyond their collarbone. However, when it enters the heart and becomes embedded therein, it benefits."[2]

It states in *Sharḥ al-Muhadhdhab* that they (i.e., the scholars) are agreed on it being disliked to read excessively quickly. It is what is referred to as jabbering (*hadhramah*).

Ibn 'Abbās ﷺ is narrated to have said, "My reciting a *sūrah* with *tartīl* is more beloved to me than reciting the whole Qur'an."

ELEVEN: THE DESIRABILITY OF RESPONDING AFTER CERTAIN VERSES AND SŪRAHS WITH NARRATED PHRASES

It is desirable for the reciter to say phrases that have been narrated in the following manner:

Abū Hurayrah ﷺ said, "Whoever recites *Sūrah al-Tīn* and reads, 'Is Allah not the most just of all judges?'[3] should say, 'Yes, indeed, and I am amongst those who testify to this.'[4] And whoever recites *Sūrah al-Qiyāmah* and reaches the end, 'Is such [a Creator] not able to bring the dead back to life?'[5] should say, 'Yes, indeed.' And whoever recites al-Mursalāt and reaches, 'So what message after this [Qur'an] would they believe in?'[6] should say, 'We believe in Allah Most High.'"[7]

---

(1) *Bukhārī* (5046).

(2) *Bukhārī* (775); *Muslim* (822).

(3) *Al-Tīn*, 8.

(4) *Al-Tīn*, 8.

(5) *Al-Qiyāmah*, 40.

(6) *Al-Mursalāt*, 50.

(7) *Abū Dāwūd* (884).

وفي (الصَّحيحينِ) عن ابنِ مسعودٍ رَضِيَ اللهُ عَنْهُ أنَّ رجلاً قال له: إنِّي أقرأُ المفصَّلَ في ركعةٍ واحدةٍ! فقال: هذّاً كهذِّ الشِّعرِ؟ - وهو سرعةُ القراءةِ كما يُنشَدُ الشِّعرُ - إنَّ قوماً يقرؤونَ القرآنَ لا يجاوزُ تراقِيَهم، ولكنْ إذا وقعَ في القلبِ فرسَخَ فيه نفعَ [1].

قال في (شرحِ المهذَّبِ): واتَّفقوا على كراهةِ الإفراطِ في الإسراعِ - وهو المسمَّى: بالهذرمة -. وعن ابنِ عبّاسٍ رضي الله تعالى عنهما: (لَأَنْ أقرأَ سورةً أُرَتِّلَها أحبُّ إليَّ من أنْ أقرأَ القرآنَ كلَّهُ).

الحادي عشر: استحبابُ الإجابةِ بما ورد عند بعضِ الآياتِ والسُّوَرِ:

يستحبُّ للقارئِ أنْ يأتيَ بالواردِ على الوجهِ الآتي: عن أبي هريرةَ رضي الله تعالى عنه أنّه قال: (مَن قرأَ {وَالتِّينِ وَالزَّيْتُونِ}[2] فقال: {أَلَيْسَ اللَّهُ بِأَحْكَمِ الْحَاكِمِينَ}[3]، فليقُلْ: بلى، وأنا على ذلك من الشَّاهدين. ومَن قرأَ {لَا أُقْسِمُ بِيَوْمِ الْقِيَامَةِ}[4] فانتهى إلى آخرِها: {أَلَيْسَ ذَٰلِكَ بِقَادِرٍ عَلَىٰ أَن يُحْيِيَ الْمَوْتَىٰ}[5] فليقُلْ: بلى. ومَن قرأَ {وَالْمُرْسَلَاتِ}[6] فبلغ

---

(١) أخرجه البخاري (٧٧٥)، ومسلم (٨٢٢).

(٢) التين: ١.

(٣) التين: ٨.

(٤) القيامة: ١.

(٥) القيامة: ٤٠.

(٦) المرسلات: ١.

Imam Aḥmad narrated that the Prophet recited the verse, "Allah [Himself] is a Witness that there is no god [worthy of worship] except Him"(1) on the day of ʿArafah. After reciting it he said, "And I am also amongst those who testify on this, O my Lord."(2)

Ibn ʿAbbās narrated that when the Prophet used to recite, "Glorify the Name of your Lord, the Most High",(3) he would say, "Glorified is my Lord, the Most High."(4) Abū Dāwūd and Aḥmad narrated it.

Jābir narrated that the Messenger of Allah came out to his Companions and recited the entire *Sūrah al-Raḥmān* to them. They remained quiet, so he said, "I recited it to the jinn but they were better than you in responding. Every time I came to His saying, 'Then which of your Lord's favours will you [humans and jinn] both deny?'(5) they said, 'None of Your favours do we deny – O Lord – so for You is all praise.'"(6) Tirmidhī and Ḥākim narrated it.

Wā'il ibn Ḥujr narrated, "I heard the Prophet recite, '*Wa lā al-Ḍāllīn*' and then say, '*Āmīn*', stretching his voice therewith." Abū Dāwūd narrated it, and also Ṭabarānī with the wording, "He said, '*Āmīn*' thrice."(7) Bayhaqī narrated it with the wording, "O my Lord, forgive me. *Āmīn*."(8)

Abū ʿUbayd ibn Abī Maysarah reported that Jibrīl taught the Messenger of Allah to say *āmīn* at the end of al-Baqarah. He also reported that when Muʿādh ibn Jabal would complete *Sūrah al-Baqarah*, he would say *āmīn*.

Ibn Mardawayh, Daylamī, and Ibn Abī al-Dunyā narrated with an

---

(1) *Āl ʿImrān*, 18.

(2) *Aḥmad* (1421).

(3) *Al-Aʿlā*, 1.

(4) *Abū Dāwūd* (884).

(5) *Al-Raḥmān*, 13.

(6) *Tirmidhī* (3291).

(7) *Abū Dāwūd* (932); *Tirmidhī* (248).

(8) Tirmidhī mentioned it after hadith (248); *Aḥmad* (18843).

{فَبِأَيِّ حَدِيثٍ بَعْدَهُ يُؤْمِنُونَ}[1]، فليقُلْ: آمنَّا باللهِ تعالى) [2]. رواهُ أبو داودَ والترمذيُّ. وروى الإمامُ أحمدُ أنَّ النبيَّ ﷺ قرأَ {شَهِدَ اللَّهُ أَنَّهُ لا إِلَهَ إِلا هُوَ}[3] الآيةَ، يومَ عرفةَ ثمَّ قال بعد قراءتِها: «وأنا على ذلكَ من الشَّاهدينَ يا رب» [4]. وعن ابنِ عبّاسٍ رضي اللهُ عنهما أنَّ النبيَّ ﷺ كانَ إذا قرأَ {سَبِّحِ اسْمَ رَبِّكَ الْأَعْلَى}[5]، قال: «سبحانَ ربِّيَ الأعلى» [6]. رواهُ أبو داودَ وأحمدُ. وعن جابرٍ رضي الله عنه قال: خرجَ رسولُ الله ﷺ على الصّحابةِ، فقرأَ عليهم سورةَ الرَّحمنِ من أوَّلِها إلى آخِرِها، فسكتوا، فقال: «لقد قرأتُها على الجنِّ فكانوا أحسنَ مردوداً منكم، كنتُ كلَّما أتيتُ على قولِهِ: {فَبِأَيِّ آلَاءِ رَبِّكُمَا تُكَذِّبَانِ}[7] قالوا: لا بشيءٍ مِنْ نِعَمِكَ ربَّنا نُكذِّبُ، فَلَكَ الحمدُ» [8]. رواه الترمذيُّ والحاكمُ. وعن وائلِ بنِ حجرٍ رضي الله تعالى عنه قال: سمعتُ النبيَّ ﷺ قرأَ {وَلَا الضَّالِّينَ}، فقال: «آمين» يَمُدُّ بها صوتَه. رواهُ أبو داودَ والطَّبرانيُّ بلفظٍ قال: «آمين،

---

(١) المرسلات: ٥٠.

(٢) أخرجه أبو داود (٨٨٤).

(٣) آل عمران: ١٨.

(٤) أخرجه أحمد في المسند (١٤٢١).

(٥) الأعلى: ١.

(٦) أخرجه أبو داود (٨٨٤).

(٧) الرحمن: ١٣.

(٨) أخرجه الترمذي (٣٢٩١).

extremely weak chain that the Prophet ﷺ recited, "When My servants ask you [O Prophet] about Me: I am truly near. I respond to one's prayer when they call upon Me. So let them respond [with obedience] to Me and believe in Me, perhaps they will be guided [to the Right Way]."(1) He then said, "O Allah, You ordained supplication and guaranteed acceptance. O Allah, I am ever-present at Your service, O Allah. You have no partner, at Your service. Truly all praise, favour and sovereignty is Yours; You have no partner. I testify that You are Alone, One, the Sustainer. You never had offspring nor were You born. And there is none comparable to You. I testify that Your promise is true, meeting You is true, Paradise is true, Hellfire is true, and the Hour is certainly coming without a doubt, and You will surely resurrect those in the graves."(2)

It is narrated on the authority of 'Umar ibn al-Khaṭṭāb ؓ who said, "When Revelation would come down to the Messenger of Allah ﷺ, a sound like the buzzing of bees could be heard near his face. So we waited a little, then he faced the *qiblah*, lifted his hands, and said, 'O Allah, increase us and do not decrease us, honour us and do not humiliate us, grant us and do not deprive us, and prefer us and do not prefer [others] over us, and be pleased with us and please us.' Then he ﷺ said, 'Ten verses have been revealed to me; whoever establishes them will enter Paradise.' He then recited, 'Successful indeed are the believers; those who humble themselves in prayer'(3) until he completed all ten verses."(4)

Ibn Qāni' narrated on the authority of Ibn Abī Laylā that when the Prophet ﷺ would come across a verse in which there is mention of Hellfire, he would say, "Woe unto the people of Hellfire. I seek refuge with Allah from Hellfire."(5) It states in *al-Tibyān* that it is part of etiquette that when

(1) *Al-Baqarah*, 186.

(2) Bayhaqī in *al-Asmā' wa al-Ṣifāt*, vol. 1, pg. 161.

(3) *Al-Mu'minūn*, 1-2.

(4) *Tirmidhī* (3173); Nasā'ī in *al-Sunan al-Kubrā*; *Aḥmad* (223).

(5) *Abū Dāwūd* (881).

ثلاثَ مرّات»[1]. وأخرجهُ البيهقيُّ بلفظٍ قال: «ربِّ اغفرْ لي، آمين»[2]. وأخرجَ أبو عُبَيدٍ عن أبي مَيْسَرةَ أنَّ جبريلَ لقَّنَ رسولَ اللهِ ﷺ عند خاتمةِ البقرةِ «آمين». وأخرجَ عن معاذِ بنِ جبلٍ رضي الله عنه أنه كان إذا ختمَ سورةَ البقرةِ قال: «آمين». وأخرجَ ابنُ مَرْدَوَيْه والدَّيلميُّ وابنُ أبي الدُّنيا بسندٍ ضعيفٍ جدّاً عن النبيِّ صلى الله عليه وآله وسلم قرأ {وَإِذَا سَأَلَكَ عِبَادِي عَنِّي فَإِنِّي قَرِيبٌ أُجِيبُ}[3] الآيةَ، فقال: «اللَّهمَّ أمرتَ بالدُّعاءِ، وتكفَّلتَ بالإجابةِ، لبَّيكَ اللَّهمَّ لبَّيكَ، لا شريكَ لكَ لبَّيكَ إنَّ الحمدَ والنِّعمةَ لكَ والمُلكَ، لا شريكَ لكَ، أشهدُ أنَّكَ فردٌ أحدٌ صمدٌ، لم تلِدْ ولم تولَدْ، ولم يكن لك كفُواً أحدٌ. وأشهدُ أنَّ وعدَكَ حقٌّ، ولقاءَكَ حقٌّ، والجنَّة حقٌّ، والنَّارَ حقٌّ، والسّاعةَ آتيةٌ لا ريبَ فيها، وأنّكَ تبعثُ مَن في القبور»[4]. وعن عمرَ بنِ الخطّابِ رضي الله تعالى عنه قال: كان رسولُ اللهِ ﷺ إذا نزلَ عليه الوحيُ، يُسمَعُ عند وجهِهِ دَوِيٌّ كدَوِيِّ النَّحلِ، قال: فلبِثْنا ساعةً - أي: فنزلَ عليه الوحيُ يوماً - ثمَّ استقبلَ القِبلةَ ورفعَ يديه - أي: بعد انقضاءِ الوحي - وقال: «اللَّهمَّ زِدنا ولا تَنقُصنا، وأكرِمْنا ولا تُهِنّا، وأعطِنا ولا تحرِمْنا، وآثِرْنا ولا تُؤثِرْ علينا، وأَرضِنا وارضَ عنّا»، ثمَّ قال ﷺ: «أُنزِلَ عليَّ عشرُ آياتٍ مَن أقامَهنَّ - أي: حَفِظَهنَّ - دخلَ الجنّةَ، {قَدْ

(١) أخرجه أبو داود (٩٣٢)، والترمذي (٢٤٨).

(٢) أخرجه الترمذي معلقا بعد حديث (٢٤٨)، وأحمد (١٨٨٤٣).

(٣) البقرة: ١٨٦.

(٤) أخرجه البيهقي في (الأسماء والصفات) (١/١٦١).

one recites, "The Jews say, 'Ezra is the son of Allah'"; [1] "The Christians say, 'The Messiah is the son of Allah'";[2] "[Some among] the Jews said, 'Allah is tight-fisted'";[3] "They say, 'The Most Compassionate has offspring'"[4] and similar verses, one should lower their voice. Ibrāhīm al-Nakhaʿī ﷺ used to do this. Amongst these is what Ibn Abī Dāwūd narrated with a weak chain: that Shaʿbī was asked that when a person recites the verse, "Indeed, Allah showers His blessings upon the Prophet..."[5], should they invoke blessings on the Prophet ﷺ? He said, "Yes." O Allah, confer blessings on our master Muhammad and his family, and send peace.

THE DESIRABILITY OF BEAUTIFYING THE VOICE WHEN RECITING THE QUR'AN

Nawawī said in *al-Tibyān*, "The scholars amongst the predecessors and latter scholars – including the Companions, the Followers, and the scholars of various regions and the imams of the Muslims after them – are unanimous that it is desirable to beautify the voice when reciting the Qur'an. Their statements and actions are extremely well-known."

The hadiths regarding it being desirable are many. We shall mention a number of them.

Barā' ﷺ said, "I heard the Messenger of Allah ﷺ recite *Sūrah al-Tīn* in the *'ishā'* prayer. I have not heard anyone with a more beautiful voice." Bukhārī and Muslim narrated it."[6]

Abū Hurayrah ﷺ narrated that the Prophet ﷺ said, "Allah does not listen attentively to anything as much as to a Prophet with a beautiful

(1) *Al-Tawbah*, 30.

(2) *Al-Tawbah*, 30.

(3) *Al-Mā'idah*, 64.

(4) *Maryam*, 88.

(5) *Al-Aḥzāb*, 56.

(6) *Bukhārī* (7546); *Muslim* (464).

أَفۡلَحَ ٱلۡمُؤۡمِنُونَ (١) ٱلَّذِينَ هُمۡ فِي صَلَاتِهِمۡ خَاشِعُونَ}[١] حتّى ختمَ الآياتِ العشرة [٢]. رواهُ الترمذيُّ وأحمدُ. وروى ابنُ قانعٍ عن ابنِ أبي ليلى أنَّ النبيَّ ﷺ كان إذا مَرَّ بآيةٍ فيها ذِكرُ النارِ قال: «ويلٌ لأهلِ النّارِ، أعوذُ باللهِ من النّار»[٣]. قال في (التِّبيانِ): ومن الآداب: إذا قرأ قولَ الله عزَّ وجلَّ: {وَقَالَتِ ٱلۡيَهُودُ عُزَيۡرٌ ٱبۡنُ ٱللَّهِ}[٤]، {وَقَالَتِ ٱلنَّصَارَى ٱلۡمَسِيحُ ٱبۡنُ ٱللَّهِ}[٥]، {وَقَالَتِ ٱلۡيَهُودُ يَدُ ٱللَّهِ مَغۡلُولَةٌ}[٦]، {وَقَالُواْ ٱتَّخَذَ ٱلرَّحۡمَٰنُ وَلَدٗا}[٧] ونحوَ ذلك من الآياتِ: فينبغي أن يَخفِضَ بها صوتَهُ، كذا كان إبراهيمُ النَّخَعيُّ يفعَلُ رضي اللهُ تعالى عنه. ومنها: ما رواهُ ابنُ أبي داودَ بإسنادٍ ضعيفٍ عن الشَّعبيِّ أنّهُ قيل له: إذا قرأَ الإنسانُ {إِنَّ ٱللَّهَ وَمَلَٰٓئِكَتَهُۥ يُصَلُّونَ عَلَى ٱلنَّبِيِّ}[٨] الآيةَ، يُصلِّي على النبيِّ ﷺ؟ قال: نعم، اللهمَّ صلِّ على سيدنا محمد وعلى آله وسلم.

استحبابُ تحسينِ الصَّوتِ بالقرآنِ

قال النوويُّ في (التِّبيان): أجمع العلماءُ رَضِيَ اللهُ عَنهُم من السَّلفِ والخَلَفِ من الصّحابةِ،

(١) المؤمنون: ١-٢.

(٢) أخرجه الترمذي (٣١٧٣)، والنسائي في (السنن الكبرى) (١٤٣٩)، وأحمد (٢٢٣).

(٣) أخرجه أبو داود (٨٨١).

(٤) التوبة: ٣٠.

(٥) التوبة: ٣٠.

(٦) المائدة: ٦٤.

(٧) مريم: ٨٨.

(٨) الأحزاب: ٥٦.

voice, melodiously and audibly reciting the Qur'an."[1]

Faḍālah ibn ʿUbayd ﷺ narrated that the Prophet ﷺ said, "Allah listens more attentively to a person with a beautiful voice reciting the Qur'an than a person with a singing girl listens to her."[2] Aḥmad, Ibn Mājah, Ibn Ḥibbān, Ḥākim, and Bayhaqī narrated it.

Ibn Ḥibbān narrated on the authority of Abū Hurayrah ﷺ, as a hadith attributed to the Prophet ﷺ, "Allah does not listen more attentively to anything than He listens to the person who melodiously recites the Qur'an audibly."[3]

Barā' ibn ʿĀzib ﷺ narrated that the Messenger of Allah ﷺ said, "Beautify the Qur'an with your voices."[4] Abū Dāwūd, Nasā'ī, and Ibn Mājah narrated it.

It is narrated on the authority of Jābir ﷺ that the Messenger of Allah ﷺ said, "Amongst those with the best voice when reciting the Qur'an is the person who, when you hear them recite, you think they fear Allah."[5] Ibn Mājah narrated it.

ʿAbd al-Razzāq narrated in his *Jāmiʿ* and al-Ḍiyā' narrated on the authority of Anas ﷺ that the Prophet ﷺ said, "Everything has an adornment, and the adornment of the Qur'an is a beautiful voice."[6] This is as stated in *al-Fatḥ al-Kabīr*.

Ṭabarānī narrated on the authority of Ibn ʿAbbās ﷺ, as a hadith attributed to the Prophet ﷺ, "Beautify your voices in the Qur'an."[7] This is as stated in *al-Fatḥ al-Kabīr*.

Khaṭīb narrated on the authority of Maʿqil ibn Yasār ﷺ, as a hadith

---

(1) *Bukhārī* (6989); *Muslim* (1319).

(2) *Aḥmad* (23325); *Ibn Mājah* (1330).

(3) *Ibn Ḥibbān* (748).

(4) *Abū Dāwūd* (1291).

(5) Bayhaqī in *Shu ʿab al-Īmān* (1958).

(6) Al-Muttaqī al-Hindī in *Kanz al- ʿUmmāl* (2768).

(7) *Ṭabarānī* (12643).

والتّابعينَ، ومَن بعدَهم من علماءِ الأمصارِ أئمّةِ المسلمينَ على استحبابِ تحسينِ الصَّوتِ بالقرآنِ، وأقوالُهم وأفعالُهم مشهورةٌ نهايةَ الشُّهرةِ. اهـ. والأحاديثُ الواردةُ في استحبابِ ذلك كثيرةٌ، نذكرُ جملةً منها. عن البراءِ رضي الله تعالى عنه قال: (سمعتُ رسولَ الله صلى الله عليه وآله وسلم عنه قرأ في العشاءِ بالتّينِ والزَّيتونِ، فما سمعتُ أحداً أحسنَ صوتاً منه)[1]. رواه الشيخان. وعن أبي هريرة رضي الله تعالى عنه عن النبيِّ ﷺ قال: «ما أَذِنَ - أي: استمَعَ - اللهُ لشيءٍ كما أَذِنَ لنبيٍّ حَسَنِ الصَّوتِ يَتغنَّى بالقرآنِ، يجهرُ بهِ»[2]. رواه الشيخان. وعن فَضالَةَ بنِ عبيدٍ أَنَّ النبيَّ ﷺ قال: (للهُ أشدُّ أذَناً - أي: استماعاً - للرَّجلِ الحسنِ الصّوتِ بالقرآنِ مِن صاحبِ القَينةِ إلى قَينتِهِ»[3]. وهي: الأمَةُ التي تُغنّي لمولاها. رواه الإمامُ أحمدُ، وابنُ ماجه، وابنُ حِبّان، والحاكمُ، والبيهقيُّ. وروى ابنُ حِبّانَ عن أبي هريرةَ رضي الله تعالى عنه مرفوعاً: «ما أَذِنَ اللهُ لشيءٍ كأَذَنِهِ للّذي يتغنّى بالقرآنِ يَجهَرُ به»[4]. كما في (كنزِ العمّال). وعن البراءِ بنِ عازبٍ رضي الله تعالى عنه قال: قال رسول الله ﷺ: «زَيّنوا القرآنَ بأصواتِكم»[5]. رواهُ أبو داودَ، والنَّسائيُّ، وابنُ ماجه. ورويَ عن جابرٍ رضي الله تعالى عنه قال: قال رسولُ اللهِ ﷺ: «إنَّ من أحسنِ النّاسِ صوتاً بالقرآنِ الذي إذا سمعتُموهُ يقرأُ حَسِبتُموهُ يخشى اللهَ»[6]. رواهُ ابنُ

---

(١) أخرجه البخاري (٧٥٤٦)، ومسلم (٤٦٤).

(٢) أخرجه البخاري (٦٩٨٩) ومسلم (١٣١٩).

(٣) أخرجه أحمد في المسند (٢٣٣٢٥)، وابن ماجه (١٣٣٠).

(٤) أخرجه ابن حبان (٧٤٨).

(٥) أخرجه أبو داود (١٢٩١).

(٦) أخرجه البيهقي في شعب الإيمان (١٩٥٨).

attributed to the Prophet ﷺ, "Surely Allah does not listen attentively to anything from the inhabitants of Earth besides the prayer call of those who call to prayer and the beautiful voice when reciting the Qur'an."(1)

Abū Mūsā ؓ narrated that the Messenger of Allah ﷺ said to him, "You have been given one of the beautiful melodies (*mizmār*) of the family of Dāwūd."(2)

Barā' ibn ʿĀzib ؓ narrated that he heard the Messenger of Allah ﷺ say, "Beautify the Qur'an with your voices, because a beautiful voice increases the Qur'an in beauty."(3) Dārimī narrated it. Abū Lubābah ؓ narrated that he heard the Messenger of Allah say, "The person who does not recite the Qur'an melodiously is not from us."(4) Abū Dāwūd narrated it.

Ibn Abī Mulaykah was asked about a person who does not have a beautiful voice. He replied that he should beautify it as much as he can.

It states in *al-Tibyān*, "The scholars – may Allah have mercy on them – said it is desirable to beautify the voice when reciting the Qur'an and to adorn it, as long as it does not exceed the bounds of recitation by overstretching. If a person exceeds by adding or concealing a letter, it will be unlawful."

THE DESIRABILITY OF SEEKING GOOD RECITATIONS AND LISTENING TO THEM

Imam Nawawī said, "Know that many of the Predecessors would request people with good voices to recite whilst they listened. There is agreement on this being desirable – this is the habit of the elite worshippers and righteous slaves of Allah, and it is an established practice of the Messenger of Allah ﷺ.

(1) Al-Muttaqī al-Hindī in *Kanz al- 'Ummāl* (23209).

(2) *Bukhārī* (5048); *Muslim* (793).

(3) *Dārimī* (3501).

(4) *Abū Dāwūd* (1469)

ماجه. وروى عبدُ الرَّزاقِ في (جامِعِهِ) و(الضّياء) عن أنسٍ رَضِيَ اللهُ عَنْهُ عن النبيِّ صلى الله عليه وآله وسلم قال: «لكلِّ شيءٍ حِليَةٌ، وحِليَةُ القرآنِ الصَّوتُ الحَسَنُ» [1]. كما في (الفتحِ الكبيرِ). وروى الطبرانيُّ عن ابنِ عبّاسٍ رَضِيَ اللهُ عَنْهُمَا مرفوعاً: «أَحسِنوا الأصواتَ في القرآنِ» [2]. كما في (الفتح الكبيرِ). وروى الخطيبُ عن مَعقِلِ بنِ يَسارٍ رَضِيَ اللهُ عَنْهُ مرفوعاً: «إنَّ اللهَ تعالى لا يَأذَنُ – أي: لا يَستَمِعُ - لشيءٍ من أهلِ الأرضِ إلّا لأذانِ المُؤذِّنينَ، والصّوتِ الحسنِ بالقرآنِ» [3].

وعن أبي موسى رضي الله تعالى عنه قال: قال رسولُ اللهِ صلى الله عليه وآله وسلم لي: «لقد أُوتيتَ مزماراً من مزاميرِ آلِ داودَ» [4]. متفقٌ عليه. وعن البراءِ بنِ عازبٍ رضي الله تعالى عنه قال: سمعتُ رسولَ اللهِ صلى الله عليه وآله وسلم يقول: «حسّنوا القرآنَ بأصواتِكم؛ فإنَّ الصَّوتَ الحسنَ يزيدُ القرآنَ حُسناً» [5]. رواهُ الدارميُّ. وعن أبي لُبابةَ رضي الله تعالى عنه قال: سمعتُ رسولَ الله صلى الله عليه وآله وسلم يقول: «ليس منّا مَن لم يتغنَّ بالقرآنِ» [6]. رواه أبو داود. وقيل لابنِ أبي مُليكةَ: أرأيتَ إن لم يكن حَسَنَ الصَّوتِ؟ قال: يُحسِّنُهُ ما استطاع. قال في (التِّبيان): قال العلماءُ رَحِمَهُمُ اللهُ تَعَالَى: فيُستحَبُّ تحسينُ الصَّوتِ بالقراءةِ، وترتيبُها ما لم يَخرُجْ عن حَدِّ القراءةِ بالتمطيطِ، فإن أفرطَ حتّى زادَ حرفاً أو أخفاهُ فهو حرامٌ. اهـ.

---

(١) أخرجه المتقي الهندي في (كنز العمال) (٢٧٦٨).

(٢) أخرجه الطبراني (١٢٦٤٣).

(٣) أخرجه المتقي الهندي في (كنز العمال) (٣٢٠٠٩).

(٤) أخرجه البخاري (٥٠٤٨) واللفظ له، ومسلم (٧٩٣).

(٥) أخرجه الدارمي (٣٥٠١).

(٦) أخرجه أبو داود (١٤٦٩).

It is authentically established that ʿAbdullāh ibn Masʿūd ؓ said, 'The Messenger of Allah ﷺ said to me, "Recite the Qur'an to me." I said, "O Messenger of Allah, should I recite to you when it is upon you that it was sent down?" He said, "I like to hear it from someone other than myself." I thus recited *Sūrah al-Nisā'* to him until I reached the verse, "So how will it be when We bring a witness from every faith-community and bring you [O Prophet] as a witness against yours?"[1] He ﷺ said, "That is enough for now." I turned to see that his eyes were flowing with tears.'[2]

The Prophet ﷺ listened to the recitation of Ibn Masʿūd ؓ a number of times, and to Abū Mūsā al-Ashʿarī ؓ, Sālim the freed slave of Abū Ḥudhayfah ؓ, and others.

It is narrated in the *Musnad* and other works from Ibn Masʿūd ؓ that the Prophet ﷺ came with Abū Bakr and ʿUmar ؓ whilst ʿAbdullāh ibn Masʿūd ؓ was praying and had started *Sūrah al-Nisā'*. He recited it all in one go, so the Prophet ﷺ said, "Whoever likes to recite the Qur'an as fresh as it was revealed should recite like the recitation of Ibn Umm ʿAbd (i.e., Ibn Masʿūd ؓ)." Ibn Masʿūd ؓ then moved forward and supplicated, to which the Prophet ﷺ said, "Ask, for you shall be granted. Ask, for you shall be granted." Amongst his supplications, he said, "O Allah, I ask of You faith that does not waver, pleasure that does not cease, and the companionship of Your Prophet Muhammad ﷺ in the highest Garden of Paradise – the Garden of Eternity." ʿUmar ؓ went to ʿAbdullāh ibn Masʿūd ؓ to give him glad tidings that the Prophet ﷺ said, "Ask, for you shall be granted", only to find that Abū Bakr ؓ had already beaten him to him. He then said, "When did you do it? O Abū Bakr, you have always been one who rushes to do good."[3]

According to another narration, ʿUmar ؓ said, "Abū Bakr never raced

(1) *Al-Nisā'*, 40.

(2) *Bukhārī* (4582); *Muslim* (800).

(3) Nasā'ī in *al-Sunan al-Kubrā* (10705); *Aḥmad* (3662).

استحبابُ طلبِ القراءةِ الطيّبةِ والاستماعِ إليها

قال الإمامُ النوويُّ: اعلم أنَّ جماعاتٍ من السَّلفِ كانوا يطلبونَ من أصحابِ القراءةِ بالأصواتِ الحَسَنةِ أن يقرؤوا وهم يستمعونَ، وهذا متفقٌ على استحبابه، وهو عادةُ الأخيارِ المتعبّدينَ وعبادِ اللهِ الصَّالحين، وهو سُنَّةٌ ثابتةٌ عن رسول الله ﷺ. فقد صحّ عن عبدِ اللهِ بنِ مسعودٍ رضي الله تعالى عنه أنه قال: قال لي رسولُ اللهِ ﷺ: «اِقرَأْ عليَّ القرآنَ». فقلتُ: يا رسولَ اللهِ أقرأُ عليكَ وعليكَ أُنزِلَ؟ فقال: إنّي أحبُّ أن أسمعَ من غيري، فقرأتُ سورةَ النِّساءِ حتّى أتيتُ إلى هذه الآيةِ {فَكَيْفَ إِذَا جِئْنَا مِن كُلِّ أُمَّةٍ بِشَهِيدٍ وَجِئْنَا بِكَ عَلَىٰ هَٰؤُلَاءِ شَهِيدًا}[1] قال ﷺ: «حسبُكَ الآنَ»، فالتفتُّ فإذا عيناهُ تذرِفانِ ﷺ[2]. وقد استمعَ النبيُّ ﷺ إلى قراءةِ ابنِ مسعودٍ عِدَّةَ مرّاتٍ، وإلى أبي موسى الأشعريّ، وإلى سالمٍ مولى أبي حُذيفَةَ وغيرِهم.

ففي (المُسندِ) وغيرِهِ عن ابنِ مسعودٍ رضي الله تعالى عنه أنَّ النبيَّ صلى الله عليه آله وسلم أتاهُ بين أبي بكرٍ وعمرَ رضي الله تعالى عنهما، وعبدُ اللهِ بنُ مسعودٍ يصلّي فافتتحَ النّساءَ، فسَحَلَها - أي: قرأَها كلَّها متَّصِلةً - فقال النبي ﷺ: «مَن أحبَّ أن يقرأَ القرآنَ غضّاً كما أُنزِلَ فليقرأْهُ على قراءةِ ابنِ أمّ عبدٍ - يعني: ابنَ مسعودٍ رَضِيَ اللهُ عَنْهُ- ثم تقدَّمَ ابنُ مسعودٍ فسأل - أي: دعا اللهَ تعالى - فجعل النبيُّ ﷺ يقول: «سَلْ تُعطَه، سَلْ تُعطَه». فقال فيما سأل: اللّهمَّ إنّي أسألُكَ إيماناً لا يرتَدُّ، ونعيماً لا يَنفَدُ، ومرافقةَ نبيّكَ محمّدٍ ﷺ في أعلى الجنّةِ جنةِ الخُلدِ. فأتى عمرُ عبدَ اللهِ بنَ مسعودٍ رَضِيَ اللهُ عَنْهُ ليبُشِّرَهُ بقولِ

---

(١) النساء: ٤١.

(٢) أخرجه البخاري (٤٥٨٢)، ومسلم (٨٠٠).

me towards anything except that he beat me to it." They both then asked him (i.e., Ibn Mas'ūd) regarding his supplication. Ibn Mas'ūd said, "Amongst the supplication that I rarely leave is: O Allah, I ask of You faith that does not waver, pleasure that does not cease, and the companionship of Your Prophet Muhammad in the highest Garden of Paradise – the Garden of Eternity."

And I, 'Abdullāh, say: O Allah, I ask of You what 'Abdullāh ibn Mas'ūd asked of You, so grant me as You granted him his supplication. Surely You are the Hearer of supplications.

Sayyidah 'Ā'ishah narrated, "I once delayed in coming to the Messenger of Allah , to which he asked, 'O 'Ā'ishah, what kept you?' I said, 'O Messenger of Allah, there was a man in the masjid and I have never seen anyone recite better than him.' The Prophet then went to see and found that it was Sālim, the freed slave of Abū Ḥudhayfah . He then said, "All praise is for Allah Who has put people like you in my ummah."[(1)] Ibn Mājah, Aḥmad, and others narrated it.

Anas said, "Allah never sent any Prophet except that he had a beautiful face and a beautiful voice. And your Prophet had the most beautiful face and the most beautiful voice amongst them."[(2)] Tirmidhī narrated it.

The Prophet would seek out his Companions at night and listen to their recitation. Bukhārī and Muslim narrated on the authority of Abū Mūsā that the Messenger of Allah said, "I recognize the voices of the group of Ash'arīs when night falls, and I know their houses through hearing their voices reciting the Qur'an at night – even though I have not seen their houses when they are in them during the day."[(3)]

Abū Sa'īd al-Khudrī said, "The Messenger of Allah performed seclusion (*i'tikāf*) in the masjid and heard them reciting the Qur'an loudly.

---

(1) *Ibn Mājah* (1338).

(2) *Tirmidhī* (2728).

(3) *Bukhārī* (4232).

النبيّ ﷺ: «سَلْ تُعطَه»، فوجد أبا بكرٍ رَضِيَ اللهُ عَنْهُ قد سبقَه، فقال: أنّى فعلتَ!، لقد كنتَ يا أبا بكرٍ سبّاقاً للخيرِ[1].

وفي روايةٍ فقال عمرُ: ما بادرني أبو بكرٍ إلى شيءٍ إلّا سبقني إليه، فسألاه عن قولِه، أي: عمّا دعا فقال ابنُ مسعودٍ رَضِيَ اللهُ عَنْهُ: من دعائي الذي لا أكادُ أدَعُ، - أي: لا أكادُ أتركُهُ - اللّهمَّ إنّي أسألُكَ نعيماً لا يَبيدُ، وقُرَّةَ عينٍ لا تَنفَدُ، ومرافقةَ النبيِّ ﷺ في أعلى الجنَّةِ جنَّةِ الخُلدِ.

وأنا عبدُ اللهِ أقول: اللّهمَّ إنّي أسألُكَ ما سألكَ عبدُ اللهِ بنُ مسعودٍ، فأعطِني كما أعطيتَهُ سُؤلَهُ، إنّكَ سميعُ الدُّعاءِ. وعن السّيدةِ عائشةَ رضي الله تعالى عنها قالت: أبطأتُ على رسولِ اللهِ ﷺ فقال: ما حبَسَكِ يا عائشةُ؟ قالت: يا رسولَ اللهِ إنَّ في المسجدِ رجلاً ما رأيتُ أحداً أحسنَ قراءةً منه، قالت: فذهبَ النبيُّ ﷺ، فإذا هو سالمُ مولى أبي حذيفةَ رَضِيَ اللهُ عَنْهُ، فقال رسولُ اللهِ ﷺ: «الحمدُ للهِ الذي جعلَ في أمّتي مثلَكَ»[2]. رواهُ ابنُ ماجه، وأحمدُ، وغيرُهما. وقال أنسٌ رَضِيَ اللهُ عَنْهُ: (ما بعثَ اللهُ نبيّاً قطُّ إلّا حسَنَ الوجهِ، حسَنَ الصّوتِ، وكان نبيُّكُم ﷺ أحسنَهم وجهاً، وأحسنَهم صوتاً)[3]. رواه الترمذي. وكان النبيُّ ﷺ يتفقّدُ أصحابَهُ في اللّيلِ ويستمِعُ إلى قراءتِهم؛ فقد روى الشّيخانِ عن أبي موسى رضي الله تعالى عنه قال: قال رسولُ اللهِ ﷺ: «إنّي لأَعرِفُ أصواتَ رفقةِ الأشعريّينَ باللّيلِ حين يدخلُ اللّيلُ، وأعرفُ منازِلَهم من

---

(١) أخرجه النسائي في (السنن الكبرى) (١٠٧٠٥)، وأحمد (٣٦٦٢).

(٢) أخرجه ابن ماجه (١٣٣٨).

(٣) أخرجه الترمذي (٢٧٢٨).

He lifted his curtain and said, "Listen! All of you are conversing intimately with their Lord, so do not inconvenience one another and do not recite loudly over one another in prayer."[1] Abū Dāwūd, Tirmidhī and others narrated it.

Abū Qatadah ﷺ narrated that the Prophet ﷺ came out one night to find Abū Bakr ﷺ praying with a low voice. He then passed by 'Umar ibn al-Khaṭṭāb ﷺ who was praying with his voice raised. When they both came to the Prophet ﷺ, he ﷺ said, "O Abū Bakr, I passed by you when you were praying and your voice was low." Abū Bakr ﷺ said, "I made the One I was conversing with hear me." He ﷺ said, "Raise your voice slightly." He ﷺ said to 'Umar, "I passed by you when you were praying and your voice was raised." 'Umar ﷺ said, "O Messenger of Allah, I was waking up those who are drowsy and driving away the devil." He ﷺ said, "Lower your voice slightly."[2]

In another narration of Abū Dāwūd, the Prophet ﷺ said, "O Bilāl, I heard you reciting from this *sūrah* and that *sūrah* (i.e., from different *sūrahs*)." Bilāl ﷺ said, "It is good speech which Allah combines with each other." The Prophet ﷺ said, "All of you have done right."[3] Abū Dāwūd and Tirmidhī narrated it.

---

(1) *Abū Dāwūd* (1332) and this is his wording; *Aḥmad* (11896).

(2) *Abū Dāwūd* with a slight difference (1329); *Tirmidhī* (447).

(3) *Abū Dāwūd* (1330).

أصواتِهم بالقرآنِ في اللّيلِ، وإن كنتُ لم أرَ منازلَهم حين نزلوا بالنّهار»[1]. وعن أبي سعيدٍ الخدريّ رضي الله عنه قال: اعتكفَ رسولُ اللهِ صلى الله عليه وآله وسلم في المسجدِ، فسمِعَهم يجهرونَ بالقراءةِ، فكشفَ السِّترَ، وقال: «ألا إنَّ كلَّكم مناجٍ ربَّه فلا يؤذِيَنَّ بعضُكم بعضاً، ولا يرفعُ بعضُكم على بعضٍ في القراءةِ - أو قال -: في الصّلاةِ»[2]. رواهُ أبو داودَ والترمذيُّ وغيرُهما. وعن أبي قَتادةَ أنَّ النبيَّ صلى الله عليه وآله وسلم خرجَ ليلةً، فإذا هو بأبي بكرٍ رضي الله تعالى عنه يصلّي يَخفُضُ من صوتِه - أي: بالقراءة -، ومرَّ بعمرَ بنِ الخطّابِ رضي الله تعالى عنه وهو يصلّي رافعاً - صوتَه بالقراءةِ - فلمّا اجتمعا عند النبيِّ صلى الله عليه وآله وسلم، قال صلى الله عليه وآله وسلم: «يا أبا بكرٍ مررتُ وأنتَ تصلّي تخفضُ صوتَكَ»؟ فقال أبو بكرٍ رضي الله عنه: قد أسمعتُ مَن ناجَيتُ يا رسولَ الله، فقال صلى الله عليه وآله وسلم: «ارفعْ من صوتِكَ شيئاً» كما في روايةٍ.

وقال لعمرَ رضي الله عنه: «مررتُ بكَ وأنت تصلّي رافعاً صوتَك»؟ فقال عمرُ رضي الله عنه: يا رسولَ اللهِ أوقِظُ الوَسنانَ، وأطردُ الشَّيطانَ، فقال له صلى الله عليه وآله وسلم: «اخفِضْ شيئاً»[3].

وفي روايةٍ لأبي داودَ قال صلى الله عليه وآله وسلم: «وقد سَمِعتُكَ يا بلالُ وأنت تقرأُ من هذه السّورةِ ومن هذه السُّورةِ»؟ فقال بلالٌ رضي الله عنه: كلامٌ طيّبٌ يجمعُ اللهُ بعضَه إلى بعضٍ، فقال النبيُّ صلى الله عليه وآله وسلم: «كلُّكم قد أصابَ»[4]. رواه أبوداودَ والترمذيُّ.

---

(١) أخرجه البخاري (٤٢٣٢).

(٢) أخرجه أبو داود (١٣٣٢) واللفظ له، وأحمد (١١٨٩٦).

(٣) أخرجه أبو داود (١٣٢٩) باختلاف يسير، والترمذي (٤٤٧).

(٤) أخرجه أبو داود (١٣٣٠).

ILLUMINATING GATHERINGS WITH THE NOBLE QUR'AN

When the Companions of the Prophet ﷺ would gather, they would instruct a reciter to recite the Qur'an. Thus, they would initiate their gatherings with recitation of the Noble Qur'an, taking luminance from its lights, benefiting from its secrets and drawing from its blessings. He Most High said, "This is a blessed Book We have revealed. So follow it and be mindful [of Allah], so you may be shown mercy."(1)

Ḥākim narrated in *al-Mustadrak* from Abū Sa'īd ﷺ that when the Companions of Allah's Messenger ﷺ would gather, they would discuss knowledge and recite a *sūrah*.(2)

Dārimī and others narrated that 'Umar ibn al-Khaṭṭāb ﷺ would say to Abū Mūsā al-Ash'arī ﷺ, "Remind us of our Lord, O Abū Mūsā." He would then recite the Qur'an to him.(3)

'Umar ibn al-Khaṭṭāb ﷺ would at times instruct 'Uqbah ibn Āmir ﷺ to recite the Qur'an to him and his companions.

---

(1) *Al-An'ām*, 155.

(2) Ḥākim in *al-Mustadrak* (322).

(3) *Dārimī* (3493).

تنويرُ المجالسِ بالقرآنِ الكريمِ

كان أصحابُ النبيِّ ﷺ إذا اجتمعوا أَمَرُوا قارئاً يقرأُ القرآنَ، فيفتتحونَ مجالِسَهم بتلاوةِ القرآنِ الكريمِ، مستنيرينَ بأنوارِهِ، ومستفيضينَ من أسرارِهِ، ومتبرِّكينَ ببركاتِهِ. قال تعالى: {وَهَذَا كِتَابٌ أَنزَلْنَاهُ مُبَارَكٌ فَاتَّبِعُوهُ وَاتَّقُوا لَعَلَّكُمْ تُرْحَمُونَ}[1].

روى الحاكمُ في (المستدرَكِ) عن أبي سعيدٍ رضي الله عنه قال: كان أصحابُ رسولِ اللهِ صلى الله عليه وسلم إذا اجتمعوا تذاكَروا العِلمَ، وقرؤوا سورةً[2].

وروى الدارميُّ وغيرُهُ عن عمرَ بنِ الخطّابِ رضي الله عنه أنّهُ كان يقولُ لأبي موسى الأشعريِّ رضي الله عنه: (ذكِّرنا ربَّنا يا أبا موسى، فيقرأُ عندَهُ القرآنَ)[3]. وكان عمرُ بنُ الخطّابِ رضي الله عنه يأمرُ في بعضِ الأحيانِ عُقبةَ بنَ عامرٍ أن يقرأَ

---

(١) الأنعام: ١٥٥.

(٢) أخرجه الحاكم في المستدرك (٣٢٢).

(٣) أخرجه الدارمي (٣٤٩٣).

All of this proves the importance the Companions ﷺ gave to reciting the Noble Qur'an, how they venerated it, and their utmost eagerness to begin their gatherings and meetings with recitation of verses from the Reminder, rich in wisdom.

Abū Dāwūd narrated on the authority of Abū Sa'īd ﷺ who said, "I was sat amongst a group of poor Migrants (*Muhājirūn*), some of whom were hiding behind others due to nakedness, whilst a reciter was reciting [Qur'an] to us. The Messenger of Allah ﷺ came and stood over us. When the Messenger of Allah ﷺ stood there, the reciter went quiet. The Messenger of Allah ﷺ greeted with *salām* and then asked, 'What were you doing?' We said, 'We are listening to the Book of Allah Most High.' He said, 'All praise is for Allah Who has made amongst my ummah those with whom I have been commanded to persevere.' He then sat in between us, to make himself an equal amongst us. He then indicated with his hand (i.e., that they should gather around him), so they made a circle with their faces being visible to him. He said, 'Take glad tidings, O poor Migrants, of complete light on the Day of Judgement. You shall enter Paradise before other people by half a day, which is 500 years.'"(1)

Imam Nawawī ﷺ said, "In these places (i.e., gatherings), the reciter should recite what is appropriate and suited to the gathering. Moreover, his recitation should include verses of hope, fear, exhortation, being abstinent in this world, encouraging towards the Hereafter, preparing for it, restricting one's aspirations, and noble character traits."

THE MERIT OF LISTENING TO THE RECITATION OF THE NOBLE QUR'AN

Imam Aḥmad narrated in his *Musnad* from Abū Hurayrah ﷺ that the Messenger of Allah ﷺ said, "Whoever listens to a verse of the Book of Allah will have a multiplied reward recorded for them. And whoever

(1) *Abū Dāwūd* (3666) and this is his wording; *Aḥmad* (11934).

عليه وعلى أصحابِهِ القرآنَ. وفي هذا كلِّهِ دليلٌ على اهتمامِ الصَّحابةِ رَضِيَ اللهُ عَنْهُمْ بتلاوةِ القرآنِ الكريمِ، وتعظيمِهم له، وعلى حرصِهم الشَّديدِ أن تُفتحَ مجالسُهم واحتفالاتُهم، واجتماعاتُهم بتلاوةِ آيٍ من الذِّكرِ الحكيمِ. وروى أبو داودَ عن أبي سعيدٍ الخدريّ رَضِيَ اللهُ عَنْهُ قال: جلستُ في عصابةٍ - أي: جماعةٍ - من ضعفاءِ المهاجرين، وإنَّ بعضَهم لَيَستَتِرُ ببعضٍ من العُري، وقارئٌ يقرأُ علينا، إذ جاءَ رسولُ اللهِ صَلَّى اللهُ عَلَيْهِ وَآلِهِ وَسَلَّمَ فقامَ علينا، فلمّا قام رسولُ اللهِ صلى اللهُ عليهِ وآلهِ وسلم -أي: وقفَ مُشرِفاً علينا- سكتَ القارئُ، فسلَّمَ رسولُ اللهِ صَلَّى اللهُ عَلَيْهِ وَآلِهِ وَسَلَّمَ ثمَّ قال: «ما كنتُم تصنعونَ»؟ قلنا: نستمِعُ إلى كتابِ اللهِ تعالى، فقال: «الحمدُ للهِ الذي جعلَ من أمَّتي من أُمِرتُ أن أُصَبِّرَ نفسي معهم، فجلس وسطَنا ليعدلَ نفسَهُ فينا، ثمَّ قال صَلَّى اللهُ عَلَيْهِ وَآلِهِ وَسَلَّمَ بيدِه هكذا - أي: أشارَ إليهم أن يَلتفُّوا حولَه - فتحلَّقوا، وبرزَتْ وجوهُهُم له، فقال: «أبشِروا يا صعاليكَ المهاجرين - أي: يا فقراءَ المهاجرين - بالنّورِ التامِّ يومَ القيامةِ، تدخلونَ الجنّةَ قبل النّاسِ بنصفِ يومٍ، وذلك خمسمائةِ سنةٍ» [1]. قال الإمامُ النوويُّ رحمه اللهُ تعالى: وينبغي للقارئِ في هذه المواطِنِ - أي: في المجالِسِ - أن يقرأَ ما يليقُ بالمجلسِ ويناسِبُهُ، وأن تكونَ قراءتُه من آياتِ الرَّجاءِ والخَوفِ، والمواعظِ والتَّزهيدِ في الدُّنيا، والتَّرغيبِ في الآخرةِ، والتَّأهيبِ لها، وقِصَرِ الأملِ ومكارمِ الأخلاقِ. اهـ.

فضلُ الاستماعِ إلى تلاوةِ القرآنِ الكريمِ

روى الإمامُ أحمدُ في (مُسنَدِهِ) عن أبي هريرةَ رضي الله تعالى عنه أنَّ رسولَ اللهِ صَلَّى اللهُ عَلَيْهِ وَآلِهِ وَسَلَّمَ قال: «مَنِ استمَعَ إلى آيةٍ من كتابِ اللهِ كُتِبَتْ له حسنةٌ مضاعَفَةٌ، ومَن

(١) أخرجه أبو داود (٣٦٦٦) واللفظ له، وأحمد (١١٩٣٤).

recites it, it will be a light for them on the Day of Judgement."[1]

In *Musnad al-Firdaws*, it is narrated on the authority of Ibn ʿAbbās ﷺ, as a hadith attributed to the Prophet ﷺ, "The person supplication and the one saying *āmīn* share the reward, the reciter and the listener share the reward, and the scholar and the student share the reward."[2]

It has already passed in the hadith of Ibn Masʿūd ﷺ that the Prophet ﷺ instructed him to recite the Qur'an to him and said, "I like to hear it from someone other than myself."[3] The Prophet ﷺ listened to the recitation of Ibn Masʿūd ﷺ a number of times, and he listened to the recitation of Abū Mūsā al-Ashʿarī ﷺ, Sālim the freed slave of Abū Ḥudhayfah ﷺ, and others, as already mentioned.

THE ETIQUETTE AND REQUIREMENTS OF LISTENING TO THE NOBLE QUR'AN

Allah Most High said, "When the Qur'an is recited, listen to it attentively and be silent, so you may be shown mercy."[4] Allah Most Glorified and High has commanded listening to the reciter, and a command necessitates obligation (*wujūb*) – as long as there is nothing to divert it therefrom.

It states in *Radd al-Muḥtār*, "This is because the verse (i.e., the saying of Allah Most High: 'listen to it attentively') – albeit it is regarding prayer – however, consideration is given to the generality of the wording, not the specific cause. Furthermore, this is where there is no excuse. This is why al-Qunyah states that if a child is reciting in the house whilst the family are engaged in their work, they are excused for not listening if they started their work before the recitation. Otherwise (i.e., if they started their work after the recitation), they will not be excused for not listening. Likewise

(1) *Aḥmad* (8494).

(2) Al-Muttaqī al-Hindī in *Kanz al- 'Ummāl* (3194).

(3) *Bukhārī* (4582).

(4) *Al-A 'rāf*, 204.

تلاها كانتْ له نوراً يومَ القيامةِ»[1]. وفي (مسنَدِ الفردوسِ) عن ابنِ عبّاسٍ رضي الله عنهما مرفوعاً: «الدَّاعي والمؤمِّنُ شريكانِ في الأجرِ، والقارئُ والمستمِعُ في الأجرِ شريكانِ، والعالِمُ والمتعلِّمُ في الأجرِ شريكان»[2]. وقد تقدَّمَ في حديثِ ابنِ مسعودٍ رضي الله عنه أنَّ النبيَّ ﷺ أمَرَهُ أن يقرأَ عليه القرآنَ، وقال له: «إنّي أحبُّ أن أسمعَهُ من غيري»[3]. وقدِ استمعَ النبيُّ ﷺ إلى قراءةِ ابنِ مسعودٍ رضي الله عنه عِدَّةَ مرّاتٍ، واستمعَ إلى قراءةِ أبي موسى الأشعريِّ، وإلى سالمٍ مولى أبي حُذيفةَ، وغيرِهم رضوان الله عليهم أجمعين كما تقدَّم.

آدابُ ومطالبُ الاستماعِ لتلاوةِ القرآنِ الكريمِ

قال اللهُ تعالى: {وَإِذَا قُرِئَ الْقُرْآنُ فَاسْتَمِعُوا لَهُ وَأَنْصِتُوا لَعَلَّكُمْ تُرْحَمُونَ}[4].

فقد أمرَ اللهُ سبحانَهُ تعالى بالاستماعِ للقارئِ، والأمرُ يقتضي الوجوبَ ما لم يصرفْهُ عنه صارفٌ. قال في (ردِّ المحتارِ): لأنَّ الآيةَ يعني: قولَه تعالى: {فَاسْتَمِعُوا لَهُ} وإن كانتْ واردةً في الصّلاةِ، فالعبرةُ لعمومِ اللَّفظِ لا لخصوصِ السَّببِ، ثمَّ هذا حيثُ لا عذرَ، ولذا قال في (القُنية): صبيٌّ يقرأُ في البيتِ، وأهلُهُ مشغولون بالعملِ يُعذَرونَ في تركِ الاستماعِ إنِ افتتحوا العملَ قبل القراءة، وإلّا - أي: وإنِ افتتحوا العملَ بعدَ القراءةِ - لا يُعذَرونَ في تركِ الاستماعِ، وكذا قراءةُ الفقهِ عندَ قراءةِ القرآنِ.

---

(١) أخرجه أحمد (٨٤٩٤).

(٢) أخرجه المتقي الهندي في (كنز العمال) (٣١٩٤).

(٣) أخرجه البخاري (٤٥٨٢)، ومسلم (٨٠٠).

(٤) الأعراف: ٢٠٤.

is reading jurisprudence (*fiqh*) whilst the Qur'an is being recited. *Al-Fatḥ* states, citing from *al-Khulāṣah*, that if a person is writing jurisprudence whilst a person next to him is reciting the Qur'an, but he is unable to listen to the Qur'an, the sin will be on the reciter. Similar to this, if a person recites on the roof whilst people are sleeping, he will be sinful. This is because he is the cause for their turning away from listening to it or because he is troubling them by keeping them awake. Contemplate this. It states in *Sharḥ al-Munyah* that the default position is that listening to the Qur'an is a communal obligation (*farḍ kifāyah*), because it is to uphold its right by turning towards it attentively without breaching [its sanctity]. This is achieved by one person listening to it – similar to responding to greetings of *salām* where in consideration of the right of a [fellow] Muslim, one person suffices on behalf of all. However, it is necessary for the reciter to respect it, by not reciting it in the marketplace and where people are preoccupied. If someone recites in such places, they will be the ones breaching its sanctity and the sin will be upon them, not on the people who are busy. This is to remove undue difficulty. Ḥamawī reported from his teacher, the chief justice Yaḥyā – more commonly known as Munqārī Zādah – that he has a treatise in which he has established that listening to the Qur'an is an individual obligation (*farḍ ʿayn*)."

From this, the ruling of listening to the Noble Qur'an according to the Ḥanafīs is clear. As for the Shāfiʿīs, listening to the recitation is a *sunnah* according to them.

Amongst the requirements of listening to the reciter is to be silent, have veneration, and to cry. Allah Most High said, "When they listen to what has been revealed to the Messenger, you see their eyes overflowing with tears for recognizing the truth. They say, 'Our Lord! We believe, so count us among the witnesses.'"[1]

Zayd ibn Arqam ﷺ narrated that the Prophet ﷺ said, "Indeed, Allah Most High loves silence on three occasions: when the Qur'an is being

(1) *Al-Mā'idah*, 83.

وفي (الفتح) عن (الخُلاصة): رجلٌ يكتبُ الفقهَ وبجنبِهِ رجلٌ يقرأُ القرآنَ فلا يمكنُهُ استماعُ القرآنِ، فالإثمُ على القارئِ، وعلى هذا: لو قرأَ على السَّطحِ والنّاسُ نيامٌ يأثمُ. اهـ. أي: لأنّهُ يكونُ سبباً لإعراضِهِم عن استماعِهِ، أو لأنّه يؤذيهم بإيقاظِهم. تأمَّل.

وفي (شرحِ المُنيةِ): والأصلُ أنَّ الاستماعَ للقرآنِ فرضُ كفايةٍ؛ لأنّه لإقامةِ حقِّهِ، بأن يكون ملتفتاً إليه غيرَ مضيّعٍ، وذلك يحصلُ بإنصاتِ البعضِ، كما في ردِّ السَّلامِ، حين كان لرعايةِ حقِّ المسلِمِ كفى فيه البعضُ عن الكُلِّ، إلّا أنّهُ يجبُ على القارئِ احترامُهُ بأن لا يقرأَ في الأسواقِ، ومواضِعِ الاشتغالِ، فإذا قرأهُ فيها كان هو المضيّعَ لحُرمَتِهِ، فيكونُ الإثمُ عليه دونَ أهلِ الاشتغالِ؛ دفعاً للحرجِ.

ثمَّ قال في (ردِّ المُحتارِ): ونَقَلَ الحَمَويُّ عن أستاذِ قاضي القُضاةِ يحي الشَّهيرُ بمُنقاري زادَه: أنَّ له رسالةً حقَّقَ فيها أنَّ استماعَ القرآنِ فرضُ عينٍ. اهـ. (ردُّ المُحتار).

ومن هنا تبيَّنَ حكمُ استماعِ القرآنِ الكريمِ عند السَّادةِ الحنفيّةِ، وأمّا عند السَّادةِ الشافعيّةِ فالاستماعُ للقراءةِ سُنَّةٌ.

ومن مطالِبِ الاستماعِ للقارئِ: الإنصاتُ، والخشوعُ، والبكاءُ. قال اللهُ تعالى: {وَإِذَا سَمِعُوا مَا أُنزِلَ إِلَى الرَّسُولِ تَرَىٰ أَعْيُنَهُمْ تَفِيضُ مِنَ الدَّمْعِ مِمَّا عَرَفُوا مِنَ الْحَقِّ ۖ يَقُولُونَ رَبَّنَا آمَنَّا فَاكْتُبْنَا مَعَ الشَّاهِدِينَ}[1].

وعن زيدِ بنِ أرقمَ رَضِيَ اللهُ عَنْهُ عن النبيِّ صَلَّى اللهُ عَلَيْهِ وَآلِهِ وَسَلَّمَ قال: «إنَّ اللهَ تعالى يحبُّ الصَّمتَ - أي: السُّكوتَ - عند ثلاثٍ: عند تلاوةِ القرآنِ، وعند الزَّحفِ، وعند الجنازةِ»[2]. رواهُ الطبرانيُّ وأبو يَعلى، قال الحافظُ الهَيثميُّ: فيه رجلٌ لم يُسَمَّ. اهـ.

---

(١) المائدة: ٨٣.

(٢) أخرجه الطبراني في الكبير (٤٩٨٣).

recited, in the battlefield and in funerals."[1] Ṭabarānī and Abū Ya'lā narrated it. Ḥāfiẓ al-Haythamī said it contains an unnamed narrator.

The meaning of "in the battlefield" is when the ranks meet to fight during jihad in Allah's cause, because silence instils greater awe and fear. The meaning of "in funerals" is when walking with the funeral bier, and bathing and praying over it. Instead, one should frequently recite *Lā ilāha ill Allāh* silently, as mentioned in hadiths.

'Abd al-Razzāq narrated in his *Jāmi'* from Yaḥyā ibn Abī Kathīr as a *mursal* narration that the Prophet ﷺ said, "Surely Allah dislikes three things for you: futile talk during [recitation of] the Qur'an, raising one's voice in supplication, and placing the hands on the hips during prayer."[2]

Therefore, a Muslim should listen attentively to the Qur'an and remain silent, so that they may be shown mercy as a result. By listening attentively and remaining silent, one presents themselves to the mercy of Allah Most High. Whoever presents themselves to the mercy of Allah Most High will acquire their share thereof, but whoever turns away from it deprives themselves. He Most High said, "When the Qur'an is recited, listen to it attentively and be silent, so you may be shown mercy."[3]

So, take heed and contemplate this noble verse – when the Qur'an is recited, serenity and divine mercy descend, and the doors of the Heavens are opened.

Ṭabarānī narrated in *al-Awsaṭ* from Ibn 'Umar ﷺ that the Prophet ﷺ said, "The doors of the Heavens are opened for five things: recitation of the Qur'an; the meeting of the ranks (i.e., the Muslim ranks and enemy ranks); rainfall; the supplication of the oppressed; and the call to prayer."[4] This is as stated in *al-Fatḥ al-Kabīr* and its main text.

---

(1) Ṭabarānī in *al-Kabīr* (4983).

(2) 'Abd al-Razzāq in *al-Muṣannaf* (3343).

(3) *Al-A'rāf*, 204.

(4) *Ṭabarānī* (447).

والمرادُ بقولهِ ﷺ: «عند الزَّحفِ»: عند التقاءِ الصُّفوفِ للقتالِ جهاداً في سبيلِ اللهِ تعالى؛ فإنَّ الصَّمتَ أهيبُ وأرهبُ.

«وعند الجنازة»: المرادُ به عند المشيِ معها، والغَسلِ والصَّلاةِ عليها، وليكثر من قولِ لا إلهَ إلا اللهُ سرّاً، كما جاء في الحديث.

وروى عبدُ الرَّزَّاقِ في (جامعِهِ) عن يحيى بن أبي كثيرٍ مُرسَلاً عن النبيِّ ﷺ أنّهُ قال: «إنَّ اللهَ تعالى كَرِهَ لكم ثلاثاً: اللَّغوَ عندَ القرآنِ، ورفعَ الصَّوتِ في الدُّعاءِ، والتخصُّرَ في الصَّلاةِ» [1].

فينبغي للمسلمِ أن يستمعَ للقرآنِ، ويُنصِتَ لعلَّ اللهَ تعالى يرحمُهُ بذلك، لأنّهُ بالاستماعِ والإنصاتِ يكون قد تعرَّضَ لرحمةِ اللهِ تعالى، ومَن تعرَّضَ لرحمةِ اللهِ تعالى نالَهُ منها نصيبُهُ، ومَن أعرضَ عن ذلك فقد حَرَمَ نفسَهُ، قال تعالى: {وَإِذَا قُرِئَ الْقُرْآنُ فَاسْتَمِعُوا لَهُ وَأَنصِتُوا لَعَلَّكُمْ تُرْحَمُونَ} [2].

فاعتبِرْ وتدبَّرْ هذه الآيةَ الكريمةَ؛ فإنَّ القرآنَ إذا قُرِئَ تنزلَتِ السَّكينةُ، والرَّحمةُ الإلهيّةُ، وفُتِحَتْ أبوابُ السَّماءِ. روى الطَّبرانيُّ في (الأوسطِ) عن ابنِ عمرَ رضي الله عنهما عن النبيِّ ﷺ أنه قال: «تُفتَحُ أبوابُ السَّماءِ لخمسٍ: لقراءةِ القرآنِ، وللقاءِ الزَّحفَينِ - أي: الصَّفَّين صفِّ المسلمينَ وصفِّ الكافرين - ولنزولِ القطرِ، ولدعوةِ المظلومِ، وللأذانِ» [3]. كما في (الفتحِ الكبيرِ) وأصلِهِ.

---

(١) أخرجه عبد الرزاق في المصنف (٣٣٤٣).

(٢) الأعراف: ٢٠٤.

(٣) أخرجه الطبراني (٤٤٧).

THE MERIT OF LEARNING AND TEACHING THE NOBLE QUR'AN

Bukhārī narrated on the authority of ʿUthmān ibn ʿAffān ﷺ that the Messenger of Allah ﷺ said, "The best of you are those who learn the Qur'an and teach it."(1) In another narration, "Indeed, the most excellent of you are those who learn the Qur'an and teach it." Ibn Mājah narrated on the authority of Saʿd ﷺ that the Prophet ﷺ said, "The best of you are those who learn the Qur'an and teach others."(2) These hadiths are an answer to those who ask about the most excellent branch of knowledge, the most excellent student and the most excellent teacher. This is proven by the narration of Bayhaqī: "The most excellent of you are those who learn the Qur'an and teach it."(3) Tirmidhī, Nasāʾī, Ibn Mājah, and others narrated on the authority of Abū Hurayrah ﷺ that the Prophet ﷺ said, "Learn the Qur'an, recite it and sleep on it, because the example of the Qur'an for the one who learns it, recites it and stands with it (in prayer at night) is like a bag filled with musk whose fragrance spreads everywhere. And the likeness of the person who learns it and goes to sleep whilst it is inside him is like a bag of musk that is tied."(4)

Abū Dharr ﷺ narrated that the Messenger of Allah ﷺ said, "O Abū Dharr! For you to set out in the morning to learn a verse from the Book of Allah Most High is better for you than praying 100 *rakʿahs*, And to set out in the morning to learn a chapter of knowledge – regardless of whether it is practiced or not – is better for you than praying 1000 *rakʿahs*."(5) Imam Aḥmad narrated in his *Musnad* from ʿUqbah ibn Āmir ﷺ that the Prophet ﷺ said, "Learn the Book of Allah, keep revising it, and recite it

(1) *Bukhārī* (4739).

(2) *Ibn Mājah* (213).

(3) Bayhaqī in *Shuʿab al-Īmān* (1931).

(4) *Tirmidhī* (2876).

(5) *Ibn Mājah* (219).

فضلُ تعلُّمِ القرآنِ الكريمِ وتعليمِهِ

روى البخاريُّ عن عثمانَ بنِ عفَّانَ رَضِيَ اللهُ عَنْهُ قال: قال رسولُ الله صَلَّى اللهُ عَلَيْهِ وَآلِهِ وَسَلَّمَ: «خيرُكُمْ مَن تعلَّمَ القرآنَ وعلَّمَهُ» (١)، وفي روايةٍ: «إنَّ أفضلَكم مَن تعلَّمَ القرآنَ وعلَّمه».

وروى ابنُ ماجه عن سعدٍ رَضِيَ اللهُ عَنْهُ أنَّ النبيَّ صَلَّى اللهُ عَلَيْهِ وَآلِهِ وَسَلَّمَ قال: «خيارُكم مَن تعلَّمَ القرآنَ وعلَّمَهُ» (٢). وفي هذه الأحاديثِ جوابٌ لِمَن يسألُ عن أفضلِ علمٍ، وأفضل متعلِّمٍ، وأفضل معلِّمٍ. ويدلُّ على ذلك روايةُ البيهقيِّ: «إنَّ أفضلَكم مَن تعلَّمَ القرآنَ وعلَّمه» (٣).

وروى الترمذيُّ والنَّسائيُّ وابنُ ماجه وغيرُهم عن أبي هريرةَ رَضِيَ اللهُ عَنْهُ أنَّ النبيَّ صَلَّى اللهُ عَلَيْهِ وَآلِهِ وَسَلَّمَ قال: «تعلَّموا القرآنَ واقرؤوهُ وارقُدوا، فإنَّ مَثَلَ القرآنِ لِمَن تعلَّمَهُ فقرأَهُ، وقامَ به - أي: في اللّيلِ - كمَثَلِ جِرابٍ محشوٍّ مسكاً، يفوحُ ريحُهُ كلَّ مكانٍ، ومَثَلُ مَن تعلَّمَهُ فيرقدُ وهو في جوفِهِ كمَثَلِ جِرابٍ أُوكِئَ على مسكٍ» (٤). أي: مُلِئَ مسكاً، ورُبِطَ عليه.

وعن أبي ذرٍّ رَضِيَ اللهُ عَنْهُ قال: قال رسولُ اللهِ صَلَّى اللهُ عَلَيْهِ وَآلِهِ وَسَلَّمَ له: «يا أبا ذرٍّ لَأَنْ تغدوَ فتعلَّمَ - أي: تتعلَّمَ - آيةً من كتابِ اللهِ تعالى خيرٌ لك من أن تصلِّيَ مائةَ ركعةٍ، ولَأَنْ تغدوَ فتعلَّمَ باباً من العلمِ عُمِلَ به أو لم يُعمَلْ به خيرٌ لك من أنْ تصلِّيَ ألفَ ركعةٍ» (٥). وروى الإمامُ

---

(١) أخرجه البخاري (٤٧٣٩).

(٢) أخرجه ابن ماجه (٢١٣).

(٣) أخرجه البيهقي في شعب الإيمان (١٩٣١).

(٤) أخرجه الترمذي (٢٨٧٦).

(٥) أخرجه ابن ماجه (٢١٩).

melodiously. By the One in Whose Hand lies my soul, it escapes quicker than a camel escapes from its tether."[1] Thus, the Prophet ﷺ encouraged his ummah to learn the Qur'an, teach it, and to keep revising it lest they forget it, because it escapes quicker than a camel that is fastened with its tether.

THE ENCOURAGEMENT TO TEACH YOUNG CHILDREN HOW TO RECITE THE NOBLE QUR'AN

Ḥāfiẓ al-Suyūṭī said, "Teaching children the Qur'an is one of the foundations of Islam. They thus develop upon the natural disposition (*fiṭrah*), and the light of wisdom enters their heart before whims can take hold of them, and before they become darkened with the pollution of disobedience and misguidance. He ﷺ stipulated for the delegations of the Bedouins (after they would accept Islam) that they recite the Qur'an amongst themselves, teach them matters of the religion, and to appoint callers to prayer." The Prophet ﷺ explained the virtue of teaching one's child the Qur'an – this has come in many hadiths, some of which we shall mention. Buraydah narrated, "I was sitting with the Prophet ﷺ and heard him say, 'Learn al-Baqarah, because acquiring it is a blessing, neglecting it is a means of regret, and the sorcerers have no power against it.' He ﷺ then kept quiet for a moment and then said, 'Learn al-Baqarah and Āl 'Imrān, because they are the two radiant ones (*zahrāwān*) which will shade their reciters on the Day of Judgement, as though they are two clouds or two shades or two flights of birds. The Qur'an will meet its reciter on the Day of Judgement when the grave splits open, in the form of a pale man. It will say, 'Do you recognize me?' He will say, 'I do not recognize you.' It will then respond, 'I am your companion, the Qur'an, which kept you thirsty in the midday heat and kept you awake at night. Indeed, every tradesman is behind their trade (i.e., in pursuit of its profit),

(1) Aḥmad in *al-Musnad* (17030).

أحمدُ في (مسندِهِ) عن عُقبةَ بنِ عامرٍ رَضِيَ اللهُ عَنْهُ أنَّ النبيَّ عليه وآله وسلم قال: «تعلَّموا كتابَ اللهِ وتعاهدوه وتغنَّوا به، فوالَّذي نفسي بيده لهو أشَدُّ تفلُّتاً من المَخاضِ في العُقُلِ»[١].

فلقد حثَّ النبيُّ صلى الله عليه وآله وسلم أمَّته على تعلُّمِ القرآنِ، وتعليمِهِ، وتعاهدِهِ؛ خشيةَ النّسيانِ، فإنّهُ أشدُّ تفلُّتاً من الإبِلِ المخاضِ المربوطةِ بعُقُلِها، أي: أزِمَّتها.

الحثُّ على تعليمِ الأولادِ الصِّغار قراءةَ القرآنِ الكريمِ

قال الحافظُ السيوطيُّ رَحِمَهُ اللهُ تعالى: تعليمُ الصّبيانِ القرآنَ أصلٌ من أصولِ الإسلامِ فيَنشؤونَ على الفِطرةِ، ويسبقُ إلى قلوبِهم أنوارُ الحكمةِ قبلَ تمكُّنِ الأهواءِ منها، وسوادِها بأكدارِ المعصيةِ والضَّلالِ.

قال رَحِمَهُ اللهُ تعالى: وكان صلى الله عليه وآله وسلم يشترطُ على وفودِ الأعرابِ - بعد إسلامهم - قراءةَ القرآنِ بينَهم، وتعليمَهم أمرَ الدِّين، وإقامةَ المؤذِّنين. اهـ.

وقد بيَّنَ النبيُّ صلى الله عليه وآله وسلم فضلَ الذي يُعلِّمُ ولدَهُ القرآنَ، جاء ذلكَ في كثيرٍ من الأحاديثِ نذكرُ أطرافَها:

عن بُرَيدةَ رَضِيَ اللهُ عَنْهُ قال: كنت جالساً عند النبيِّ صلى الله عليه وآله وسلم، فسمعتُه يقولُ: «تعلَّموا البقرةَ؛ فإنَّ أخْذَها بركةٌ، وتركَها حسرةٌ، ولا يستطيعُها البَطَلَةُ - أي: السَّحرةُ - ثمَّ سكتَ صلى الله عليه وآله وسلم ساعةً، ثمَّ قال: «تعلَّموا البقرةَ، وآلَ عمرانَ؛ فإنَّهما الزَّهراوانِ، يُظِلّانِ صاحبَهما يومَ القيامةِ كأنَّهما غَمامتانِ، أو غيايتانِ أو فِرقانِ من طيرٍ صوافٍّ، وإنَّ القرآنَ يَلقى صاحبَه يومَ القيامةِ حين ينشَقُّ عنه قبرُهُ كالرَّجلِ الشَّاحبِ، فيقولُ - أي: القرآنُ لصاحبِه -: هل تعرِفُني؟ فيقول: ما أعرِفُك، فيقول:

---

(١) أخرجه أحمد في المسند (١٧٠٣٠).

and today you are behind the trade with the greatest profit.' He will then be given kingdom in his right hand, eternity in his left hand, and the crown of dignity will be placed on his head. His parents will be clothes in a suit of clothes with which the whole world cannot compare in value. They will ask, 'Why have we been clothed with this?' It will be said to them, 'Because of your child learning the Qur'an.'"[1]

A narration of Ṭabarānī states, "'Through your child learning the Qur'an.' It will then be said (to the reciter), 'Read and rise through the levels and mansions of Paradise. He will continue rising as long as he is reciting – be it fast recitation or slow recitation."[2] Ḥāfiẓ al-Haythamī said that Aḥmad narrated it, and its narrators are narrators of the *Ṣaḥīḥ* collections. Ibn Mājah narrated part of it.

It is narrated on the authority of Abū Hurayrah ﵁ from the Messenger of Allah ﷺ, "No man teaches their child the Qur'an in this world except that the father will be crowned on the Day of Judgement with a crown of Paradise, whereby the people of Paradise will recognize him. This is because he taught his child the Qur'an in this world."[3] Ṭabarānī narrated it, albeit it has some weakness in it.

Ḥākim narrated, and declared authentic according to the criteria of Muslim, on the authority of Buraydah ﵁ that the Messenger of Allah ﷺ said, "Whoever reads the Qur'an, learns it, and acts upon it, their parents will be given a crown of light whose light will be like that of the Sun. And their parents will be clothed in a suit with which the whole world cannot compare in value. They will ask, 'Why have we been clothed with this?' It will be said to them, 'Because of your child learning the Qur'an.'"[4]

Anas ﵁ narrated that the Messenger of Allah ﷺ said, "Whoever teaches their child the Qur'an looking in (i.e., into the muṣḥaf) will have their past

(1) *Aḥmad* (22950); *Dārimī* (3391).

(2) Ṭabarānī in *al-Mu'jam al-Awsaṭ* (5764).

(3) Ṭabarānī in *al-Mu'jam al-Awsaṭ* (96).

(4) *Ḥākim* (2029).

أنا صاحبُكَ القرآنُ الذي أظمأتُكَ في الهواجِرِ، وأسهرتُ ليلَكَ، وإنَّ كلَّ تاجرٍ وراءَ تجارتِهِ - أي: يطلبُ ربحَها - وإنَّكَ اليومَ من وراءِ كلِّ تجارةٍ أعظمُ ربحاً، فيُعطى - أي: صاحبُ القرآنِ - المُلكَ بيمينِهِ والخُلدَ بشِمالِهِ، ويوضَعُ على رأسِهِ تاجُ الوَقارِ، ويُكسى والداهُ حُلَّتينِ لا تقومُ لهما - أي: لا تقدَّرُ بهما - الدُّنيا، فيقولانِ: بمَ كُسينا هذا؟ فيُقالُ: بأخذِ ولدِكما القرآنَ»[1].

وفي روايةِ الطبرانيِّ: «بتَعلُّمِ ولدِكما القرآنَ، ثمَّ يُقالُ - أي: للقارئِ -: اقرأْ، واصعَدْ في دَرَجِ الجنَّةِ وغُرَفِها، فهو في صعودٍ ما دام يقرأُ، هذّاً كان أو ترتيلاً»[2]. قال الحافظُ الهيثميُّ: رواهُ أحمدُ، ورجالُهُ رجالُ الصَّحيحِ، وروى ابنُ ماجه طرفاً منه.

وعن أبي هريرةَ رَضِيَ اللهُ عَنْهُ يبلُغُ به النبيَّ صَلَّى اللهُ عَلَيْهِ وَآلِهِ وَسَلَّمَ قال: «ما مِن رجلٍ يعلِّمُ ولدَهُ القرآنَ في الدُّنيا إلا تُوِّجَ أبوه يومَ القيامةِ بتاجٍ في الجنّةِ يَعرِفُهُ به أهلُ الجنّةِ، بتعليمِ ولدِهِ القرآنَ في الدُّنيا»[3]. رواه الطبرانيُّ على ضعفٍ فيه. وروى الحاكمُ - وقال: صحيحٌ على شرطِ مسلمٍ - عن بُريدةَ رَضِيَ اللهُ عَنْهُ قال: قال رسول الله صَلَّى اللهُ عَلَيْهِ وَآلِهِ وَسَلَّمَ: «مَن قرأَ القرآنَ وتعلَّمهُ وعَمِلَ به أُلبِسَ والداهُ يومَ القيامةِ تاجاً من نورٍ ضوؤهُ مثلُ ضوءِ الشَّمسِ، ويُكسى والداه حُلَّتَينِ لا تقومُ لهما الدُّنيا، فيقولان: بِمَ كُسينا هذا؟ فيُقالُ: بأخذِ ولدِكما القرآنَ»[4].

وعن أنسٍ رَضِيَ اللهُ عَنْهُ قال: قال رسولُ الله صَلَّى اللهُ عَلَيْهِ وَآلِهِ وَسَلَّمَ: «مَن علَّمَ ابنَهُ القرآنَ نظراً - أي: في المصحفِ - غُفِرَ له ما تقدَّمَ مِن ذنبِهِ وما تأخَّرَ، ومن علَّمَهُ إيّاهُ ظاهراً - أي: عن ظهرِ

---

(١) أخرجه أحمد (٢٢٩٥٠)، والدارمي (٣٣٩١).

(٢) أخرجه الطبراني في الأوسط (٥٧٦٤).

(٣) أخرجه الطبراني في الأوسط (٩٦).

(٤) أخرجه الحاكم (٢٠٢٩).

and future sins forgiven. Whoever teaches it to their child from memory, Allah Most High will raise them on the Day of Judgement like the full moon on the fourteenth night and their child will be told to recite. For every verse he recites, Allah will elevate the father by one rank until he reaches the end of the Qur'an he has to memory."[1]

The Leader of the Believers (Amīr al-Mu'minīn) ʿAlī ﷺ narrated that the Prophet ﷺ said, "Train your children upon three qualities: love for your Prophet; love for his household; and recitation of the Qur'an. The bearers of the Qur'an will be under the shade of Allah on the Day of Judgement – on the day there shall be no shade besides His – along with His Prophets and close slaves."[2]

Therefore, a child's guardian should begin teaching them the Qur'an from a young age. This is so that they focus on believing Allah Most High to be their Lord and that this is His Speech. In this way, the spirit of the Qur'an will permeate their hearts, and its light will illuminate their intellect, thoughts, faculties, and senses. Furthermore, it is so they learn the beliefs of the Qur'an from a young age and are nurtured on love for the Qur'an, attachment to it, intense love for it, fulfilling its commands, desisting from its prohibitions, adopting its characteristics, and treading its path. Moreover, learning something at a young age makes it more grounded in the memory, more lasting in the mind, more settled in the heart, and it leaves a greater impression on the soul.

THE IMPORTANCE GIVEN BY THE PROPHET ﷺ TO TEACHING THE NOBLE QUR'AN AND DISSEMINATING IT

Imam Aḥmad narrated on the authority of Abū ʿAbd al-Raḥmān al-Sulamī ﷺ who said, "It was related to me by the Companion of the Prophet ﷺ

(1) Ṭabarānī in *al-Awsaṭ* (1935).

(2) Abū Naṣr ʿAbd al-Karīm al-Shīrāzī in his *Fawā'id*; Daylamī; and Ibn al-Najjār – as cited by Suyūṭī in *al-Jāmiʿ al-Ṣaghīr* (311).

قلبٍ - بعثَهُ اللهُ تعالى يومَ القيامةِ على صورةِ القمرِ ليلةَ البدرِ، ويُقالُ لابنِهِ: اقرأْ، فكلّما قرأَ آيةً رفعَ اللهُ عزَّ وجل الأبَ بها درجةً، حتى ينتهيَ إلى آخرِ ما معهُ من القرآنِ»[1].

وعن أميرِ المؤمنينَ عليّ كرَّمَ اللهُ تعالى وجهَهُ عن النبيّ ﷺ قال: «أدِّبوا أولادَكم على ثلاثِ خصالٍ: حبِّ نبيّكم، وحبِّ أهلِ بيتِهِ، وقراءةِ القرآنِ؛ فإنَّ حمَلَةَ القرآنِ في ظلِّ اللهِ يومَ القيامةِ يومَ لا ظِلَّ إلا ظِلُّه مع أنبيائِهِ وأصفيائِه»[2]. فينبغي لوليّ الصَّغيرِ والصغيرةِ أن يبدأَ بتعليمِهما القرآنَ مُنذُ الصِّغرِ؛ وذلك لأجلِ أن يَتوَجَّها إلى اعتقادِ أنَّ اللهَ تعالى هو ربُّهم، وأنَّ هذا كلامُهُ تعالى، ولأجلِ أن تسريَ روحُ القرآنِ في قلوبِهم، ويُشرِقَ نورُهُ في عقولِهم، وأفكارِهم، ومدارِكِهم، وحواسِّهم، ولأجلِ أن يتلقَّنا عقائدَ القرآنِ مُنذُ الصِّغَرِ، وأنْ يَنْشَأا ويَشِبّا على محبّةِ القرآنِ، والتعلُّقِ والتعشُّقِ به، والائتمارِ بأوامرِهِ والانتهاءِ عن مناهيه، والتخلُّقِ بأخلاقِهِ، والسَّيرِ على منهاجِهِ، ولأنَّ التعلُّمَ في حالِ الصِّغَرِ هو أرسخُ في الحافظةِ، وأبقى في الذّاكرةِ، وأوقعُ في القلبِ، وأشدُّ انطباعاً في النَّفْسِ.

عنايةُ النبيِّ صلى الله عليه وآله وسلم بتعليمِ القرآنِ الكريمِ ونشرِهِ

روى الإمامُ أحمدُ عن أبي عبدِ الرّحمنِ السُّلَميّ قال: حدَّثنا مَن كان يُقرِئُنا من أصحابِ النّبيِّ ﷺ: أنّهم كانوا يَقتَرِئونَ مِن رسولِ اللهِ ﷺ عشرَ آياتٍ، فلا يأخذون في العشرِ

(١) أخرجه الطبراني في الأوسط (١٩٣٥).

(٢) أخرجه أبو نصر عبدالكريم الشيرازي في (فوائده) والديلمي وابن النجار كما في (الجامع الصغير) للسيوطي (٣١١).

who used to teach us the Qur'an that they would learn ten verses from the Messenger of Allah ﷺ, and not move onto the next ten until they had learnt the knowledge and action contained in these ten. They said that we learnt knowledge and action [together]."[1]

Muhammad ibn Naṣr narrated that Ibn Masʿūd ﷺ said, "When we would learn ten verses of the Qur'an from the Prophet ﷺ, we would not learn the following ten verses until we had learnt the action that has come down in these verses."

This is proof that they would pay particular attention to understanding the meanings of the Qur'an and applying it practically. The Prophet ﷺ sent Muṣʿab ibn ʿUmayr ﷺ to the radiant city of Medina in the second pledge of ʿAqabah, to teach the Helpers (Anṣār) the Qur'an and help them understand of the religion. He stayed with Asʿad ibn Zurārah ﷺ and was called the teacher (*muqri'*) and reciter (*qārī*). The Messenger of Allah ﷺ sent Muʿādh ibn Jabal ﷺ as a judge to Yemen to teach people the Qur'an and teachings of Islam, and to judge between them. The Prophet ﷺ appointed ʿAmr ibn Ḥazm al-Khazrajī al-Najjārī ﷺ over Najran, to help people understand the religion, teach them the Qur'an, and take charity from them – as mentioned in *al-Istīʿāb*.

The portico (*ṣuffah*) of the Prophet's Masjid was a madrasah for Qur'anic recitation, where the poor Companions without any family would take refuge. They would study the Qur'an amongst themselves and learn it, whereafter they would travel to distant lands and teach it to people.

Many of the Companions had dedicated themselves to teaching the Qur'an in Medina under the instruction of the Prophet ﷺ, until Medina was filled with reciters.

Muʿādh ibn Jabal and Ibn ʿAbbās ﷺ paid particular attention to teaching the Qur'an and disseminating its sciences to countless people in the honoured city of Mecca.

---

(1) Aḥmad in *al-Musnad* (23482).

الأُخرى حتى يعلَموا ما في هذه العشرِ من العلمِ والعمل، قالوا: فعَلِمْنا العلمَ والعملَ [1].

وروى محمَّدُ بنُ نصرٍ عن ابنِ مسعودٍ رضي الله تعالى عنه قال: كنَّا إذا تعلَّمْنا من النبيِّ ﷺ عشراً من القرآنِ لم نتعلَّمِ العشرَ التي بعدَها حتى نعلمَ ما نَزَلَ في هذه مِنَ العملِ. وهذا دليلٌ على أنَّهم كانوا يهتَّمونَ بفهمِ معاني القرآنِ وتحقيقِهِ عملاً.

وقد بعثَ النبيُّ ﷺ مصعبَ بنَ عُميرٍ رَضِيَ اللَّهُ عَنْهُ في بيعةِ العَقَبةِ الثّانيةِ إلى المدينةِ المنوَّرةِ؛ لِيعَلِّمَ الأنصارَ القرآنَ، ويُفقِّهَهُم في الدّين، فنزلَ على أسعدَ بنِ زُرارة وكان يسمّى المقرئَ والقارئَ.

وبعثَ رسولُ الله ﷺ معاذَ بنَ جبلٍ رَضِيَ اللَّهُ عَنْهُ قاضياً إلى اليمنِ؛ ليعلِّمَ النَّاسَ القرآنَ وشرائعَ الإسلامِ، ويقضيَ بينَهم.

واستعملَ النبيُّ ﷺ عمرَو بنَ حزمٍ الخزرجيَّ النجاريَّ على نجران؛ ليُفقِّهَهُم في الدّينِ، ويعلِّمَهُمُ القرآنَ، ويأخذَ الصَّدقاتِ منهم. كما ذكرَ ذلك في (الاستيعاب).

وكانتْ صُفَّةُ المسجدِ النّبويّ مدرسةً للقراءةِ، يأوي إليها فقراءُ الصّحابةِ رَضِيَ اللَّهُ عَنْهُمْ أجمعينَ ممَّنْ لا أهلَ لهم يتدارسونَ القرآنَ ويتعلَّمونه، ثمَّ يذهبونَ في نواحي البلادِ فيعلِّمُونَهُ النَّاسَ.

وقد كان جماعةٌ من الصَّحابةِ نصَبوا أنفسَهم للإقراءِ في المدينةِ، بأمرِ النبيِّ ﷺ حتّى امتلأتِ المدينةُ بالقُرّاءِ. وكان لمعاذِ بنِ جبلٍ رَضِيَ اللَّهُ عَنْهُ ثمَّ ابنِ عبّاسٍ رَضِيَ اللَّهُ عَنْهُمَا عنايةٌ بتعليمِ القرآنِ، ونشرِ علومِهِ لأُناسٍ كثيرين، لا يُحصيهِمُ العَدُّ في مكَّةَ المكَّرمةِ.

وكان ابنُ مسعودٍ رَضِيَ اللَّهُ عَنْهُ يَجلِسُ في مسجدِ الكوفةِ، فيعلِّمُ النّاسَ القراءةَ حتى بلغَ عددُ الثِّقاتِ الذين أخَذوا عنه القراءةَ مباشرةً أو بواسطةٍ ما يقرُبُ من نحوِ أربعةِ آلافِ

---

(١) أخرجه أحمد في المسند (٢٣٤٨٢).

Ibn Mas'ūd ﷺ would sit in the masjid of Kufa to teach people recitation to the extent that the number of reliable people who studied recitation under him – be it directly or indirectly – is close to 4000 reciters.

Abū Mūsā al-Ash'arī ﷺ had dedicated himself to teach the Qur'an in the masjid of Basra. Abū Rajā' says, "He would seat us in circles and teach us the Qur'an." Abū al-Dardā' ﷺ would teach people the Qur'an in the masjid of Damascus daily from sunrise until afternoon. He would split students into groups of ten and appoint a monitor over each group to teach them the Qur'an. He would overlook all of them and they would refer to him if they made a mistake in anything. This is as stated in *Tārīkh Ibn 'Asākir*.

The imam and teacher, Ibn 'Āmir, had 400 monitors in Damascus who would teach the Qur'an under his supervision. May Allah reward them well.

A MUSLIM ADOPTING A LITANY OF RECITATION FROM THE NOBLE QUR'AN

A Muslim should adopt a litany of recitation from the Noble Qur'an every day and night, reciting with contemplation, *tartīl*, presence of mind, veneration, and respect. One must strictly beware of neglecting recitation and turning away from it, lest one is affected by the warning in His saying, "The Messenger has cried, 'O my Lord! My people have indeed received this Qur'an with neglect.'"(1)

That is through some people neglecting belief in the Qur'an; some neglecting acting upon it, its rulings, and commands; and some neglecting its recitation.

The proof for it being a *sunnah* practice to adopt a litany of Qur'an in which one recites a number of parts – according to one's ability and enthusiasm, without any tediousness or fatigue – is the narration of Abū

(1) *Al-Furqān*, 30.

قارئٍ.

وأبو موسى الأشعريُّ رَضِيَٱللَّهُعَنْهُ نصَبَ نفسَهُ لتعليمِ القرآنِ في مسجدِ البَصرةِ، قال أبو رجاء: فكان يُقعِدُنا حِلَقاً حِلَقاً، يُقرِئُنا القرآنَ.

وكان أبو الدَّرداءِ رَضِيَٱللَّهُعَنْهُ يُعلِّمُ القرآنَ كلَّ يومٍ في جامعِ دمشقَ من طلوعِ الشَّمسِ إلى الظُّهرِ، ويُقسِّمُ المتعلِّمينَ عشرةً عشرةً، ويُعَيِّنُ لكلِّ عشرةٍ عريفاً يُعلِّمُهُمُ القرآنَ، وهو يُشرِفُ على الجميعِ، ويَرجِعونَ إليه إذا غَلِطوا في شيءٍ. كما ورد ذلك في (تاريخِ ابنِ عساكر). وكان الإمامُ المقرئُ ابنُ عامرٍ في دمشقَ له أربعمائةِ عريفٍ، يقومون بتعليمِ القرآنِ تحتَ إشرافِهِ. جزاهمُ اللهُ تعالى خيراً.

اتِّخاذُ المسلمِ ورداً من تلاوةِ القرآنِ الكريم

ينبغي للمسلمِ أن يتَّخِذَ لنفسِهِ ورداً من تلاوةِ القرآنِ الكريمِ كلَّ يومٍ وليلةٍ مع التَّدَبُّرِ والترتيلِ والحضورِ والخشوعِ والأدبِ، ولْيحذَرْ كلَّ الحذرِ من هجرِ التّلاوةِ والإعراضِ عنها؛ مخافةَ أنْ ينالَهُ وعيدٌ من قولِهِ تعالى: {وَقَالَ الرَّسُولُ يَا رَبِّ إِنَّ قَوْمِي اتَّخَذُوا هَٰذَا الْقُرْآنَ مَهْجُورًا} (1).

وذلك أنَّ بعضَ النّاسِ مَن هجرَ الإيمانَ بالقرآنِ، ومنهم مَن هجرَ العملَ به، وبأحكامِهِ وأوامرِهِ، ومنهم مَن هجرَ تلاوتَهُ.

ودليلُ سُنّيةِ اتّخاذِ وِردٍ من القرآنِ يقرأُ فيه أجزاء حسبَ سِعَتِه ونشاطِهِ دونَ مللٍ ولا كسلٍ، دليلُ ذلكَ ما رواهُ أبوداودَ عن ابنِ الهادِ قال: سألَني نافعُ بنُ جُبيرِ بنِ مُطعِمٍ، فقال لي: في كم تقرأُ القرآنَ؟ فقلتُ: ما أُحزِّبُهُ، فقال لي نافعٌ: لا تقل ما أُحزِّبُهُ؛

(1) الفرقان: ٣٠.

Dāwūd from Ibn al-Hād who said, "Nāfi' ibn Jubayr ibn Muṭ'im asked me, 'In how many days do you recite the [whole] Qur'an?' I said, 'I do not recite it in parts.' Nāfi' said to me, 'Do not say you do not make it into parts, because the Messenger of Allah ﷺ said, 'I recited a part (*juz'*) of the Qur'an.' I think he mentioned this on the authority of Mughīrah ibn Shu'bah ﷺ."[1]

Imam Aḥmad and Abū Dāwūd narrated on the authority of Aws ibn Ḥudhayfah ﷺ who said, "We came to the Messenger of Allah ﷺ in the delegation of Thaqīf. The Messenger of Allah ﷺ would come to us every night after *'ishā'* prayer and talk to us. One night, he came later than the time he would usually come to us. We said, 'O Messenger of Allah, you came to us late tonight.' He said, 'I suddenly remembered my litany of the Qur'an and I disliked to come until I had completed it.' I asked the Companions of Allah's Messenger ﷺ how they used to split the Qur'an into portions. They said into three, five, seven, nine, eleven, thirteen, and the portion of *al-mufaṣṣal*."[2]

The meaning is three *sūrahs*, from the beginning of *Sūrah al-Baqarah* until the end of *Sūrah al-Nisā'*; five *sūrahs*, from the beginning of *Sūrah al-Mā'idah* until the end of *Sūrah al-Tawbah*; seven *sūrahs*, from the beginning of *Sūrah Yūnus* until the end of *Sūrah al-Naḥl*; nine *sūrahs*, from the beginning of *Sūrah al-Isrā'* until the end of *Sūrah al-Furqān*; eleven *sūrahs*, from the beginning of *Sūrah al-Shu'arā'* until the end of *Sūrah Yāsīn*; and thirteen *sūrahs*, from the beginning of *Sūrah al-Ṣāffāt* until the end of *Sūrah al-Ḥujurāt*. The *mufaṣṣal* refers to the last seventh part which consists of three types: lengthy (*ṭiwāl*), medium (*awsāṭ*) and short (*qiṣār*), as detailed in books of jurisprudence.

The Prophet ﷺ said to 'Abdullāh ibn 'Amr ﷺ, "Recite the Qur'an in a month." 'Abdullāh ﷺ said, "I can do better than that." He ﷺ said, "Then recite it in every ten days." 'Abdullāh ﷺ said, "I can do better than that."

---

(1) *Abū Dāwūd* (1392).

(2) *Abū Dāwūd* (1393) and this is his wording; *Ibn Mājah* (1345); *Aḥmad* (19021).

فإنَّ رسولَ اللهِ ﷺ قال: «قرأتُ جزءاً من القرآن» [1]. قال: حسبتُ أنّه ذَكَرهُ عن المغيرةِ بنِ شعبةَ رضي الله عنه.

وروى الإمامُ أحمدُ وأبو داودَ عن أوسِ بنِ حُذيفةَ رضي الله عنه قال: قَدِمنا على رسولِ اللهِ ﷺ في وفدِ ثَقيفٍ، قال: وكان رسولُ اللهِ ﷺ يأتينا كلَّ ليلةٍ بعد العشاءِ يُحَدِّثُنا، قال: فلمّا كانتْ ليلةً أبطأَ عن الوقتِ الذي كان يأتينا فيه، فقلنا: يا رسولَ اللهِ لقد أبطأتَ عنّا الليلةَ؟ فقال: «إنه طرأَ عليَّ حزبٌ من القرآنِ، فكرهتُ أن أجيءَ حتّى أُتِمَّهُ»، قال أَوسٌ: فسألتُ أصحابَ رسولِ الله عليه الصلاة والسلام كيف يُحزِّبونَ القرآنَ؟ فقالوا: ثلاثٌ، وخمسٌ، وسبعٌ، وتسعٌ، وإحدى عشرةَ، وثلاثَ عشرةَ، وحزبُ المفصَّلِ [2].

والمرادُ: ثلاثُ سورٍ: هي من أوَّلِ سورةِ البقرةِ إلى آخرِ النِّساءِ، وخمسُ سورٍ: من أوَّلِ سورةِ المائدةِ إلى آخرِ سورةِ التَّوبةِ، وسبعُ سورٍ: من أوَّلِ سورةِ يونسَ إلى آخرِ سورةِ النَّحلِ، وتسعُ سورٍ: من أوَّلِ سورةِ الإسراءِ إلى نهايةِ سورةِ الفرقانِ، وإحدى عشرةَ سورةً: هي من أوَّلِ سورةِ الشُّعراءِ حتّى آخرَ سورةِ ياسين، وثلاثَ عشرةَ سورةً: من أوَّلِ سورةِ الصّافاتِ إلى آخرِ سورةِ الحُجُراتِ.

والمفصّلُ: عبارةٌ عن السُّبُعِ الأخيرِ، وهو على ثلاثةِ أقسامٍ: طوالٍ وأوساطٍ وقصارٍ، كما هو مفصَّلٌ في كتبِ الفقهِ.

وقد قال النبيُّ ﷺ لعبدِ اللهِ بنِ عمرٍو رضي الله عنهما: «اقرأ القرآنَ في كلِّ شهرٍ»، قال عبدُ اللهِ: فإنّي أُطيقُ أفضلَ من ذلك، قال ﷺ: «فاقرأهُ في كلِّ عشرٍ» قال عبدُ اللهِ: فإنّي أطيقُ أفضلَ من ذلك، فقال له ﷺ: «فاقرأهُ في كلِّ سبعِ ليالٍ، ولا تزِدْ على ذلك»

---

(١) أخرجه أبو داود (١٣٩٢).

(٢) أخرجه أبو داود (١٣٩٣) واللفظ له، وابن ماجه (١٣٤٥)، وأحمد (١٩٠٢١).

He ﷺ said, "Then recite it in every seven nights and do not do more than that."(1)

This prohibition was not to deem unlawful (*taḥrīm*), but rather as guidance (*irshād*) and to facilitate for him (*is'ād*), as the narration of Hushaym states that the Prophet ﷺ said to 'Abdullāh ibn 'Amr ﷺ, "Recite it in every three days."

THE HABITS OF THE PREDECESSORS IN COMPLETING THE NOBLE QUR'AN

Imam Nawawī ﷺ said, "The Pious Predecessors had varying habits with respect to the time in which they would complete [the Qur'an]. It is narrated that some of the Predecessors would complete it once every two months; some once a month; some once every ten nights; some once every eight nights; most of them once every seven nights; some once every six nights; some once every five nights; some once every four nights; some once every three nights; some once every two nights; some once every day and night; some twice every day and night; some three times; and some eight times – four times by night and four times by day.

Amongst those who would complete it once every day and night were Sayyidunā 'Uthmān ﷺ, Tamīm al-Dārī ﷺ, Sa'īd ibn Jubayr, Imam Shāfi'ī, and others."

'Abdullāh ibn 'Amr ﷺ narrated that a man brought a son of his to the Prophet ﷺ and said, "O Messenger of Allah, this son of mine recites the muṣḥaf all day and sleeps at night." The Messenger of Allah ﷺ said, "Your grievance against your son is because he spends the day in remembrance and sleeps soundly?"(2) Aḥmad narrated it with a sound chain.

Amongst those who would complete it three times daily are Sulaym ibn 'Itr, the judge of Egypt during the caliphate of Mu'āwiyah ﷺ. It is reported

(1) *Bukhārī* (1978); *Muslim* (1159).

(2) *Aḥmad* (6614).

[1]. وهذا النَّهيُ ليس للتحريمِ؛ وإنّما هو للإرشادِ والإسعادِ. فقد جاء في روايةِ هشيمٍ أنَّ النبيَّ ﷺ قال لعبدِ الله بنِ عمرٍو: «اقرأْهُ في كلِّ ثلاثٍ».

عاداتُ السَّلفِ الصَّالحِ في ختمِ القرآنِ الكريمِ

قال الإمامُ النوويُّ: كان السَّلفُ الصَّالحُ رضي الله تعالى عنهم لهم عاداتٌ مختلفةٌ في قدرِ ما يَختمونَ فيه، فرويَ عن بعضِ السَّلفِ أنَّهم كانوا يَختِمونَ في كلِّ شهرينِ ختمةً واحدةً، وعن بعضِهم في كلِّ شهرٍ ختمةً، وعن بعضِهم في كلِّ عشرِ ليالٍ ختمةً، وعن بعضِهم في كلِّ ثماني ليالٍ، وعن الأكثرينَ في كلِّ سبعِ ليالٍ، وعن بعضِهم في كلِّ ستٍّ، وعن بعضِهم في كلِّ خمسٍ، وعن بعضِهم في كلِّ أربعٍ، وعن كثيرينَ في كلِّ ثلاثٍ، وعن بعضِهم في كلِّ ليلتين، وختَمَ بعضُهم في كلِّ يومٍ وليلةٍ ختمةً، ومنهم مَن كان يختِمُ في كلِّ يومٍ وليلةٍ ختمتينِ، ومنهم مَن كان يختِمُ ثلاثاً، وختَم بعضُهم ثمانيَ ختَماتٍ: أربعاً بالليلِ، وأربعاً بالنَّهارِ. فمِنَ الذين يختمونَ ختمةً كلَّ يومٍ وليلةٍ: سيِّدُنا عثمانُ رضي الله تعالى عنه، وتميمٌ الداريُّ، وسعيدُ بنُ جُبَيرٍ، والإمامُ الشافعيُّ، وغيرُهم. وعن عبدِ اللهِ بنِ عمرٍو رضي الله عنهما: أنَّ رجلاً أتى النبيَّ ﷺ بابنٍ له فقال: يا رسولَ اللهِ إنَّ ابني هذا يقرأُ المصحفَ بالنَّهارِ ويبيتُ باللَّيلِ! فقال رسولُ اللهِ ﷺ: «أمَا تَنقِمُ أنَّ ابنَكَ يَظَلُّ ذاكراً، ويَبيتُ سالماً» [2]. رواهُ أحمدُ بسندٍ حسنٍ. ومِنَ الذين كانوا يختمونَ كلَّ يومٍ وليلةٍ ثلاثَ ختَماتٍ: سُليمُ بنُ عترٍ قاضي مصرَ في خلافةِ معاويةَ رضي الله عنهم. ورويَ أنّهُ كان يختِمُ في اللّيلةِ أربعَ ختَماتٍ، وكان ابنُ الكاتبِ يختمُ في النَّهارِ أربعَ ختَماتٍ،

---

(١) أخرجه البخاري (١٩٧٨)، ومسلم (١١٥٩).

(٢) أخرجه أحمد (٦٦١٤).

that he would complete it four times every night. Ibn al-Kātib would complete it four times by day and four times by night. Imam Nawawī says, "This is the most that has reached us regarding a single day and night."

The illustrious master, Aḥmad Dawraqī, narrated with his chain that Manṣūr ibn Dhādhān, one of the devout worshippers amongst the Followers, used to complete the Qur'an between the *ẓuhr* and *ʿaṣr* prayers, and he would also complete it between the *maghrib* and *ʿishā'* prayers in Ramadan. They would delay the *ʿishā'* prayer in Ramadan until a quarter of the night had passed. This is also narrated in *al-Ḥilyah*.

Abū Dāwūd narrated with his authentic chain that Mujāhid would complete the Qur'an between the *maghrib* and *ʿishā'* prayers. ʿAlī al-Azdī would complete it between the *maghrib* and *ʿishā'* prayers daily in Ramadan. Ibrāhīm ibn Saʿd said that his father would squat and fasten his knees together (*ḥabwah*), and he would not unfasten himself until he had completed the Qur'an.

As for those who complete the Qur'an in one *rakʿah*, they are too many to count. Amongst the earlier of them are ʿUthmān ibn ʿAffān, Tamīm al-Dārī, and Saʿīd ibn Jubayr ﷺ.

Ḥāfiẓ Muhammad ibn Naṣr al-Marwazī reported that Thābit al-Bunānī would recite the Qur'an once daily and he would fast all year. Ḥumayd al-Ṭawīl said, "Thābit al-Bunānī did not leave any pillar in the masjid except that he completed the Qur'an by it in prayer. He never travelled for any need except that the first thing he said was *Subḥān Allāh wa al-ḥamdu lillāh wa Lā ilāha ill Allāh wa Allāhu Akbar*. Thereafter, he would express his need."

Abū Ḥamzah would complete the Qur'an every day and night, and pray between the *ẓuhr* and *ʿaṣr* prayers and the *maghrib* and *ʿishā'* prayers. He would also fast all year.

Ṣāliḥ ibn Kaysān left for Hajj, and at times, he would complete the Qur'an twice in one night whilst on his saddle.

It has come in *Tadhkirat al-Ḥuffāẓ* that the Qur'an teacher, Abū Bakr ibn ʿAyyāsh, did not lie down (i.e., to sleep) for 40 years. When the time of death came to him, his daughter started to cry. He said to her, "Look

وفي اللّيلِ أربعَ خَتَمَاتٍ. قال الإمامُ النوويُّ: وهذا أكثرُ ما بلَغَنا في اليومِ واللّيلةِ.

وروى السيّدُ الجليلُ أحمدُ الدورقيُّ بإسنادِهِ عن منصورِ بنِ زاذان من عبّادِ التّابعينَ أنّهُ كان يختمُ القرآنَ فيما بين الظُّهرِ والعصرِ، ويختمهُ أيضاً بين المَغرِبِ والعِشاءِ في رمضانَ، وكانوا يُؤَخِّرونَ العِشاءَ في رمضانَ إلى أن يمضيَ رُبُعُ اللّيلِ. رواهُ أيضاً في (الحلية). وروى أبو داودَ بإسنادِهِ الصّحيحِ أنَّ مجاهداً كان يختمُ القرآنَ فيما بين المَغربِ والعشاءِ، وكان عليٌّ الأزديُّ يختمُ فيما بين المَغربِ والعِشاءِ كلَّ ليلةٍ من رمضانَ، وعن إبراهيمَ بنِ سعدٍ: كان أبي يحتبي فما يحُلُّ حبَوتَهُ حتى يختمَ القرآنَ.

وأما الذين يختمون في ركعةٍ فلا يُحصَونَ؛ لكثرتِهم، فمِنَ المتقدِّمينَ: عثمانُ بنُ عفّانَ، وتميمٌ الداريُّ، وسعيدُ بنُ جُبَيرٍ رضي اللهُ تعالى عنهم. ونقل الحافظُ محمّدُ بنُ نصرٍ المروزيُّ أنَّ ثابتاً البُنانيَّ كان يقرأُ القرآنَ في كلِّ يومٍ وليلةٍ، ويصومُ الدَّهرَ. وقال حُمَيدٌ الطَّويلُ: ما تركَ ثابتٌ البُنانيُّ في المسجدِ ساريةً - أي: عموداً - إلّا وقد ختمَ عندَها القرآنَ في صلاةٍ، وما سار في حاجةٍ إلّا كان أوّلَ ما يقول: سبحان اللهِ، والحمدُ لله، ولا إله إلا اللهُ، واللهُ أكبر، ثمَّ يتكلَّمُ بحاجته. وكان أبو حمزةَ يختمُ القرآنَ كلَّ يومٍ وليلةٍ، ويصلّي ما بين الظّهرِ والعصرِ والمغربِ والعشاءِ، وكان يصومُ الدَّهرَ. وخرجَ صالحُ بنُ كيسان إلى الحجّ فربَّما ختم القرآنَ مرَّتينِ في ليلةٍ واحدةٍ بين طرفي رَحْلِهِ.

وجاء في (تذكرةِ الحُفّاظِ): أنَّ أبا بكرِ بنِ عيّاشٍ المقرئَ لم يضعْ جَنبَه - أي: للنّومِ على الأرضِ - أربعينَ سنةً، ولمّا حضَرَتْهُ الوفاةُ بكت أختُهُ، فقال لها: انظري إلى تلكَ الزَّاويةِ، ختمتُ فيها ثمانيَ عشرةَ ألفِ ختمةٍ. أي: وهذا سِوى ما ختَمَهُ في سائرِ الأماكن.

وقال عبدُ اللهِ بنُ أحمدَ بنِ حنبلٍ: كان أبي يقرأُ في كلِّ أسبوعٍ خَتمَتين: إحداهُما في اللّيلِ والأُخرى في النّهار.

قال القاضي أبو يَعلى: وقد ختمَ إمامُنا أحمدُ بنُ حنبلٍ القرآنَ في ليلةٍ واحدةٍ بمكّةَ

towards that corner. I have completed the Qur'an 10,000 times there." This was besides the completions he made in other places.

ʿAbdullāh ibn Aḥmad ibn Ḥanbal said, "My father used to complete the Qur'an twice a week: one by night and the other by day." Qāḍī Abū Yaʿlā said, "Our Imam, Aḥmad ibn Ḥanbal, completed the Qur'an in a single night in Mecca in his prayer."

If we were to study the attention given to the Noble Qur'an by the Predecessors of this ummah and how they recited it abundantly, the topic could not be encompassed in writing.

THE DESIRABILITY OF BEING REGULAR IN A LITANY OF QUR'ANIC RECITATION IN THE MIDDLE OF THE NIGHT

Allah Most High said, "There are some among the People of the Book who are upright, who recite Allah's Revelations throughout the night, prostrating [in prayer]."[1]

A Muslim should have a litany from the Noble Qur'an which they recite at night, and it is better that this be recited in prayer at night.

Imam Nawawī said, "Know that the virtue of the night prayer and reciting therein is achieved with a little and large amount [of recitation]. However, the more one recites the better, unless it covers the whole night – it is disliked to do this consistently – and unless it causes one harm. The proof that this virtue is achieved even with a little amount is the hadith of ʿAbdullāh ibn ʿAmr ﷺ that the Messenger of Allah ﷺ said, "Whoever stands with ten verses will not be written amongst the heedless. Whoever stands with 100 verses is written amongst the obedient. Whoever stands with 1000 verses is written amongst the extremely rich (in reward)."[2] Abū Dāwūd narrated it.

Tamīm al-Dārī ﷺ narrated that the Prophet ﷺ said, "Whoever recites

(1) *Āl 'Imrān*, 113.

(2) *Abū Dāwūd* (1398).

مصلّياً به.

ولو أنّنا تتبَّعْنا ما كان عليه سلفُ الأمَّةِ منَ الاهتمامِ بالقرآنِ الكريمِ، والاستكثارِ منه لعَجِزَ القلمُ عن استقصاءِ ذلك.

استحبابُ المواظبةِ على وردٍ من القرآنِ في جوفِ اللّيلِ

قال اللهُ تعالى: {مِّنْ أَهْلِ الْكِتَابِ أُمَّةٌ قَائِمَةٌ يَتْلُونَ آيَاتِ اللَّهِ آنَاءَ اللَّيْلِ وَهُمْ يَسْجُدُونَ}[1].

ينبغي للمؤمنِ أن يكونَ له وِردٌ من القرآنِ الكريمِ يقومُ به في اللّيلِ، والأفضلُ أن يقومَ به في صلاتِهِ من اللّيلِ.

قال الإمامُ النوويُّ: واعلم أنَّ فضيلةَ قيامِ اللّيلِ، والقراءةِ فيه تحصلُ بالقليلِ والكثيرِ، وكلَّما كَثُرَ كان أفضل، إلّا أن يستوعبَ اللَّيلَ كلَّه؛ فإنَهُ يُكرَهُ الدَّوامُ عليه، وإلّا أن يَضُرَّ بنفسِهِ، وممّا يدلُّ على حصولِهِ بالقليلِ حديثُ عبدِ اللهِ بنِ عمرٍو رضي الله تعالى عنهما قال: قال رسولُ الله ﷺ: «مَن قام بعشرِ آياتٍ لم يُكتَبْ من الغافلينَ، ومَن قام بمائةِ آيةٍ كُتِبَ من القانتينَ، ومَن قام بألفِ آيةٍ كُتِبَ من المُقنطِرين»[2]. رواهُ أبو داودَ.

وعن تميمٍ الداريِّ عن النبيِّ ﷺ: «مَن قرأَ عشرَ آياتٍ في ليلةٍ كُتِبَ له قنطارٌ، والقنطارُ خيرٌ من الدُّنيا وما فيها، فإذا كان يومُ القيامةِ يقول ربُّك عزَّ وجل: اقرأْ وارقَ بكلِّ آيةٍ درجةً، حتّى ينتهيَ إلى آخرِ آيةٍ معه، يقولُ اللهُ عزَّ وجل للعبد: اقبِضْ، فيقولُ

(١) آل عمران: ١١٣.

(٢) أخرجه أبو داود (١٣٩٨).

ten verses at night has a heap (*qinṭār*) written for them, and a heap is better than the whole world and whatever it contains. On the Day of Judgement, your Lord Almighty and Exalted will say, 'Recite and rise one rank for every verse.' This will continue until they reach the last verse they have with them. Allah Almighty and Exalted will say to the slave, 'Take.' The slave will say, indicating with their hand, 'O my Lord, You know best.' He will say, '[Take] eternity with this hand and bliss in this hand.'"[1] Ṭabarānī narrated it with a good chain, as stated in al-Mundhirī's *al-Targhīb*.

Ibn 'Umar ﵄ narrated that the Messenger of Allah ﷺ said, "There is no envy except in two things: a man whom Allah has granted this Book (and in another narration: whom Allah has taught the Qur'an) and he stands to recite it throughout the night and day, and a man whom Allah has granted wealth and he gives it in charity throughout the night and day."[2] Bukhārī and Muslim narrated it.

The houses of the Pious Predecessors would resonate with the sound of the Noble Qur'an being recited – by their elders and youngsters, and men and women – throughout the year in general, and in particular during the days and nights of Ramadan.

Abū al-Aḥwaṣ said, "A man amongst the Companions would come to the camp at night and hear from them a buzzing like that of bees. So, what makes these people feel safe from what those feared?"

Umm Hāni' ﵂ said, "I used to hear the Prophet ﷺ reciting at night whilst I was on the roof of my house." Abū al-Zinād said, "I used to leave in the early morning towards the Prophet's Masjid and would not pass by any house except that there was someone reciting inside it. When as youngsters we would want to go out for something, we would say, 'Your [meeting] time is when the reciters stand [in prayer].'"

Aḥmad ibn Abi al-Ḥawārī said, "I recite the Qur'an and ponder over it one verse at a time. My mind is stunned and I am astonished at how those

(1) Ṭabarānī in *al-Kabīr* (1253).

(2) *Bukhārī* (865); *Muslim* (442).

العبدُ بيده: يا ربِّ أنتَ أعلمُ، يقول: بهذهِ اليدِ الخُلد، وبهذه اليدِ النَّعيم»[1]. رواهُ الطبرانيُّ بإسنادٍ حسنٍ كما في (ترغيبِ المُنذريّ).

وعن ابنِ عمرَ رضي الله تعالى عنهما قال: قال رسولُ اللهِ ﷺ: «لا حسدَ إلّا في اثنتينِ - أي: لا يُغبَطُ العبدُ إلّا في خَصلتينِ - رجلٌ آتاهُ اللهُ هذا الكتابَ - وفي روايةٍ: علّمَهُ اللهُ القرآنَ - فقامَ به آناءَ اللّيلِ وآناءَ النّهارِ، ورجلٌ أعطاهُ اللهُ مالاً فتصدَّقَ به آناءَ اللّيلِ وآناءَ النّهارِ»[2]. رواهُ البخاريُّ ومسلمٌ.

وكانت بيوتُ السَّلفِ الصَّالحِ تدوي بقراءةِ القرآنِ الكريمِ من كبيرِهم وصغيرِهم، ورجالِهم ونسائِهم في سائرِ السَّنَةِ عامّةً، وفي شهرِ رمضانَ خاصّةً ليلَ نهارٍ.

قال أبو الأحوصِ: إنّهُ كان الرَّجُلُ من الصّحابةِ رضي الله عنهم لَيطرقُ الفُسطاطَ ليلاً فيَسمعُ لهم دَوِيّاً كدَويِّ النَّحلِ، فما بالُ هؤلاءِ يأمنونَ، ما كان أولئكَ يخافون؟

وقالت أمُّ هانئٍ: كنتُ أسمعُ قراءةَ النبيِّ ﷺ من اللّيلِ، وأنا على عريشِ أهلي.

وقال أبو الزّنادِ: كنتُ أخرجُ من السَّحَرِ إلى مسجدِ النّبيِّ ﷺ فلا أمرُّ ببيتٍ إلّا وفيه قارئٌ، وكنّا ونحنُ فِتيانٌ نريد أن نخرجَ لحاجةٍ، فنقولُ: موعدُكم قيامُ القُرّاءِ.

وقال أحمدُ بنُ أبي الحواريِّ: إنّي لَأقرأُ القرآنَ، وأنظرُ فيه آيةً آيةً، فيتحيَّرُ عقلي، وأعجَبُ من حفّاظِ القرآنِ كيف يَهنيهُمُ النَّومُ، أو يَسَعُهُمْ أن يشتغلوا بشيءٍ من الدُّنيا وهم يتلونَ كلامَ اللهِ تعالى؟ أمَا إنّهم لو فَهِموا ما يقرؤونَ، وعرَفوا حقَّهُ، وتلذَّذوا به، واستحلَوا المناجاةَ به لذهبَ عنهمُ النَّومُ بما قد رُزِقوا.

وأنشدَ ذو النُّونِ المِصريُّ رضي الله عنه:

---

(١) أخرجه الطبراني في الكبير (١٣٥٣).

(٢) أخرجه البخاري (٨٦٥)، ومسلم (٤٤٢).

who have memorized the Qur'an can sleep so merrily or engage with anything of the world when they recite the Speech of Allah Most High. If they understood what they are reciting, recognized its rights, derived pleasure from it, and experienced the sweetness of secretly conversing therewith, their sleep would disappear for what they have been granted."

Dhū al-Nūn al-Miṣrī ﷺ read the following verses of poetry:

The Qur'an, with its promises and warnings
stopped the eyes from sleeping, thus their nights are sleepless.
They understood the Speech of the Sovereign, All-Majestic,
thus their necks humbly submit and bow before Him.

THE RULING OF A PERSON WHO OVERSLEEPS AND MISSES THEIR LITANY

ʿUmar ﷺ narrated that the Messenger of Allah ﷺ said, "Whoever oversleeps and misses their night litany or part of it, and recites it between the *fajr* and *ẓuhr* prayers, it will be recorded for them as though they had read it at night."[1] Muslim narrated it.

ONE SHOULD RECITE THE QUR'AN ABUNDANTLY IN THE MONTH OF RAMADAN

Allah Most High said, "Ramadan is the month in which the Qur'an was revealed as a guide for humanity with clear proofs of guidance and the standard [to distinguish between right and wrong]."[2]

Allah Most High brought down this Qur'an all at once to the closest Heavens in the House of Honour (Bayt al-ʿIzzah), and then it began to be gradually sent down to the Prophet ﷺ in the month of Ramadan – the leader and the best of all months. This bringing down (*inzāl*) [to the closest

---

(1) *Muslim* (747).

(2) *Al-Baqarah*, 185.

منعَ القُرانُ بوعدِهِ ووعيدِهِ مُقَلَ العيونِ فليلها لا تَهجَعُ
فِهموا عن المَلِكِ الجليلِ كلامَهُ فهماً تَذِلُّ له الرِّقابُ وتخضَعُ

حُكمُ مَن نام عن وِردِهِ

عن عمرَ رضي اللهُ تعالى عنه قال: قال رسولُ الله ﷺ: «مَن نام عن حِزبِهِ مِنَ اللّيلِ، أو عن شيءٍ منه فقرَأَهُ ما بين صلاةِ الفجرِ وصلاةِ الظُّهرِ كُتِبَ له كأنَّما قرأَهُ من اللّيلِ» [1]. رواهُ مسلمٌ.

ينبغي الإكثارُ من تلاوةِ القرآنِ في شهرِ رمضانَ

قال اللهُ تعالى: {شَهْرُ رَمَضَانَ الَّذِي أُنزِلَ فِيهِ الْقُرْآنُ هُدًى لِّلنَّاسِ وَبَيِّنَاتٍ مِّنَ الْهُدَىٰ وَالْفُرْقَانِ}[2] الآيةَ.

أنزل اللهُ تعالى هذا القرآنَ جملةً إلى السَّماءِ الدُّنيا في بيتِ العِزَّةِ، وبدأ تنزيلُهُ تدريجاً على النبيِّ ﷺ في شهرِ رمضانَ الذي هو سيّدُ الشُّهورِ وأفضلُها، وكان هذا الإنزالُ وهذا التنزيلُ في أفضلِ ليلةٍ من الشَّهرِ، وهي ليلةُ القدرِ ذاتُ المقدارِ والفضلِ كما وصفَها سبحانه بقولِه: {لَيْلَةُ الْقَدْرِ خَيْرٌ مِّنْ أَلْفِ شَهْرٍ}[3]، يعني: أنَّ العملَ الصَّالحَ فيها خيرٌ من ألفِ شهرٍ، ووافقَتْها أيضاً معاً ليلةُ التَّقديرِ والفضلِ كما وصفَها سبحانه بقوله: {حم (١)

---

(١) أخرجه مسلم (٧٤٧).

(٢) البقرة: ١٨٥.

(٣) القدر: ٣.

Heavens] and sending down (*tanzīl*) [to the Prophet ﷺ] was on the best night of the month, namely the Night of Glory (Laylah al-Qadr) – a night of great rank and virtue. It is as He Most Glorified has described, "The Night of Glory is better than a thousand months."(1) In other words, righteous actions therein are better than a thousand months. It also concurs with the night of decree and virtue, as He Most Glorified describes it, "*Ḥā Mīm*. By the clear Book. Indeed, We sent it down on a blessed night, for We always warn [against evil]. On that night every matter of wisdom is ordained by a command from Us, for We have always sent [Messengers]."(2) Thus, what a magnificent and noble night it is. It states in a hadith that the divine Books were sent down in the month of Ramadan. However, the Qur'an was distinguished by being sent down in the best night of the month.

Imam Aḥmad narrated with a good chain from Wāthilah ibn al-Asqaʿ ﷺ that the Messenger of Allah ﷺ said, "The scrolls of Ibrāhīm ﷺ were sent down on the first night of Ramadan, the Torah was sent down on the sixth of Ramadan, the Evangel was sent down on the thirteenth of Ramadan, and the Criterion (i.e., the Qur'an) was revealed on the twenty-fourth of Ramadan." Bayhaqī has also narrated it in *al-Shuʿab*. Using this hadith, many of the Companions and Followers substantiated that the Night of Glory is the twenty-fourth. That is certainly the case at times, but it also circulates in the last ten nights. Thus, the month of Ramadan is a receptacle for the coming down of the Noble Qur'an, and this receptacle has gathered those Qur'anic secrets and lights which no other month has gathered. This is because the secrets of the Qur'anic Revelations and the lights of the godly manifestations (*tajalliyāt*) have their proven effects that are coloured by their moments and vessels, and their receptacles of time and place. Hence, it is befitting that a believer increase their recitation of the Qur'an in the month of Ramadan, in the hope that they will be coloured with these lights and dive into the ocean of these secrets.

---

(1) *Al-Qadr*, 3.

(2) *Al-Dukhān*, 1-5.

وَالْكِتَابِ الْمُبِينِ (٢) إِنَّا أَنزَلْنَاهُ فِي لَيْلَةٍ مُّبَارَكَةٍ إِنَّا كُنَّا مُنذِرِينَ (٣) فِيهَا يُفْرَقُ كُلُّ أَمْرٍ حَكِيمٍ (٤) أَمْرًا مِّنْ عِندِنَا إِنَّا كُنَّا مُرْسِلِينَ}[1] الآياتِ. فما أعظمَها من ليلةٍ، وما أشرفَها.

وقد ورد في الحديثِ: أنَّ الكتبَ الإلهيّةَ أُنزِلَتْ في شهرِ رمضانَ، ولكنَّ القرآنَ خُصَّ بنزولِهِ في أفضلِ ليلةٍ منه.

روى الإمامُ أحمدُ بسندٍ حسنٍ عن واثلةَ بنِ الأَسقعِ رضي الله تعالى عنه: أنَّ رسولَ الله ﷺ قال: «أُنزِلَتْ صُحُفُ إبراهيمَ عليه السَّلامُ في أوَّلِ ليلةٍ من رمضانَ، وأُنزِلَتِ التّوراةُ لستٍّ مَضَينَ من رمضانَ، والإنجيلُ لثلاثَ عشرةَ خَلَتْ من رمضانَ، وأُنزِلَ الفرقانُ لأربعٍ وعشرينَ خَلَتْ من رمضانَ»[2]. ورواهُ البيهقيُّ أيضاً في (الشُّعب).

وقد استَدلَّ بهذا الحديثِ كثيرٌ من الصحابةِ والتابعينَ على أنَّ ليلةَ القدرِ هي ليلةُ أربعٍ وعشرينَ، نعم قد تكونُ كذلك، وقد تنتقلُ في العشرِ الأخيرِ.

فشهرُ رمضانَ هو ظرفُ تنزُّلاتِ القرآنِ الكريمِ، وجَمَعَ هذا الظَّرفُ مِنَ الأسرارِ والأنوارِ القرآنيّةِ ما لا يجمَعُهُ أيُّ شهرٍ سواهُ؛ ذلك لأنَّ أسرارَ التنزيلاتِ القرآنيّةِ، وأنوارَ التجليّاتِ الرَّبانيّةِ لها آثارُها الثابتةُ المُنصَبِغةُ في أوانِها وأوانيها، وظروفُها الزّمانيّةِ والمكانيّةِ، فجديرٌ بالمؤمن أن يُكثِرَ في شهرِ رمضانَ من تلاوةِ القرآنِ لعلَّهُ ينصبغُ بتلك الأنوارِ، وينغمسُ في بحرِ تلك الأسرار.

جاء في (الصَّحيحين) عن ابنِ عبّاسٍ رضي الله تعالى عنهما قال: (كان رسولُ اللهِ ﷺ أجودَ النَّاسِ، وكان أجودَ ما يكونُ في رمضانَ حين يلقاهُ جبريلُ عليه السلام، وكان – أي: جبريلُ عليه السلام - يلقاهُ في كلِّ ليلةٍ من رمضانَ، فيدارِسُهُ القرآنَ، فلَرسولُ

---

(١) الدخان: ١-٥.

(٢) أخرجه أحمد (١٦٩٨٤).

It has come in the two *Ṣaḥīḥ* collections from Ibn ʿAbbās ﷺ who said, "The Messenger of Allah ﷺ was the most generous of people, and he was most generous in Ramadan when Jibrīl ﷺ would meet him. He would meet him every night during Ramadan and revise the Qur'an with him. And the Messenger of Allah ﷺ would be more generous in goodness than a blowing wind."[1] He ﷺ would lengthen his recitation when standing to pray in Ramadan more than in other months. This is as narrated by Imam Aḥmad on the authority of Ḥudhayfah ﷺ who said, "I came to the Prophet ﷺ one night during Ramadan. He stood to pray, and once he had said the *takbir*, he said, 'Allah is the greatest - the Owner of dominion, might, grandeur and immensity.' He then recited al-Baqarah, followed by Āl ʿImrān, and then al-Nisā'. He did not come across any verse of fear except that he paused at it."[2] ʿUmar ﷺ instructed Ubayy ibn Kaʿb ﷺ and Tamīm al-Dārī ﷺ to lead people in prayer in Ramadan. Each of them reciting would recite 200 verses per *rak'ah* and the people would not head back from the Ramadan prayer (i.e., *tarāwīḥ*) except at the end of the night for the pre-dawn meal.Amongst the Pious Predecessors some would complete the Qur'an once every three nights, some every seven nights, and some every ten nights. ʿAllāmah Ibn Ḥajar al-Haytamī said, "Shāfiʿī ﷺ would complete 60 recitations in Ramadan out of prayer. The same is reported from Abū Ḥanīfah. When Ramadan would enter, Zuhrī would say, 'Now there is only recitation of the Qur'an and giving food.' When Ramadan would enter, Imam Mālik would stop reading hadiths and sitting with people of knowledge, and instead focus on reciting the Qur'an from the muṣḥaf. Nawawī would leave all acts of worship (i.e., his habitual additional acts of worship) and focus on reciting the Qur'an."

Thus, whoever spends Ramadan between standing in night prayer and fasting during the day will be granted their reward in full without

(1) *Bukhārī* (4997).

(2) *Aḥmad* (23447).

اللهِ ﷺ أجودُ بالخيرِ من الرّيحِ المُرسَلةِ)[1].

وكان ﷺ يطيلُ القراءةَ في قيامِ رمضانَ ليلاً أكثرَ من غيرِهِ، كما روى الإمامُ أحمدُ عن حذيفةَ رضي الله عنه أنه قال: أتيتُ النبيَّ ﷺ في ليلةٍ من رمضانَ، فقام يصلّي فلمّا كبّرَ، قال: «اللهُ أكبرُ، ذو المَلكوتِ والجبروتِ، والكبرياءِ والعَظَمة، ثمَّ قرأَ البقرةَ، ثمَّ آلَ عمران، ثمَّ النِّساءَ، لا يمُرُّ بآيةِ تخويفٍ إلّا وقفَ عندَها»[2]. الحديثَ. وأمرَ عمرُ رضي الله تعالى عنه أُبَيَّ بنَ كعبٍ وتميماً الداريَّ رضي الله عنهما أن يقوما بالنّاسِ في رمضانَ، فكان القارئُ منهما يقرأُ بالمئتينِ في الرَّكعةِ الواحدةِ، وما كانوا ينصرفونَ من قيامِ رمضانَ - أي: صلاةِ التَّراويحِ - إلّا آخرَ اللَّيلِ؛ لإدراكِ السّحور. وقدكان من السَّلفِ الصَّالحِ مَن يختم في صلاةِ التراويحِ في كلِّ ثلاثِ ليالٍ ختمةً، ومنهم من يختم فيها كلَّ سبعٍ، ومنهم كلَّ عشرٍ.

قال العلّامةُ ابنُ حجرٍ الهيتميُّ: وكان للشافعيِّ رضي الله عنه في رمضانَ ستّونَ ختمةً يقرؤها في غيرِ الصّلاةِ، وعن أبي حنيفةَ رضي الله تعالى عنه مثل ذلك أيضاً، وكان الزُّهريُّ إذا دخل رمضانُ قال: إنّما هو تلاوةُ القرآنِ وإطعامُ الطَّعامِ.

وكان الإمامُ مالكٌ رضي الله تعالى عنه إذا دخل رمضانُ يُمسِكُ عن قراءةِ الحديثِ، ومجالسةِ أهلِ العلمِ، ويُقبِلُ على تلاوةِ القرآنِ في المصحفِ. وكان النَّوويُّ يتركُ جميعَ العبادةِ - أي: نوافلَهُ المعتادَةَ له - ويُقبِلُ على تلاوةِ القرآنِ. اهـ. فمَن كان في رمضانَ بين قيامِ الليلِ وصومِ النَّهارِ وُفِّيَ أجرَه بغيرِ حسابٍ، ونال شفاعةَ الصّيامِ والقرآنِ، كما ورد في (المُسنَدِ) وغيرِهِ عنه ﷺ قال: «الصّيامُ والقرآنُ يشفعانِ للعبدِ يومَ القيامةِ،

---

(١) أخرجه البخاري (٤٩٩٧).

(٢) أخرجه أحمد (٢٣٤٤٧).

measure, and will attain the intercession of the fast and the Qur'an. This is as narrated in the *Musnad* and other works from the Prophet ﷺ who said, "The fast and the Qur'an shall intercede for the slave on the Day of Judgement. The fast will say, 'O Lord, I stopped him from food and sensual desires, so accept my intercession for him.' The Qur'an will say, 'I stopped him from sleeping at night, so accept my intercession for him.' Hence, their intercession will be accepted."(1) A group of the Pious Predecessors considered it good to recite *Sūrah al-Fatḥ* on the first night of Ramadan, in seeking to open the doors of goodness and bring down blessings and mercy. Ḥāfiẓ al-Silafī narrated with his chain from Mas'ūdī who said, "It has reached me that whoever recites 'Indeed, We have granted you a clear triumph [O Prophet]' in additional prayers on the first night of Ramadan will be protected during that year."

THE DESIRABILITY OF RECITING LOUDLY IN THE MIDDLE OF THE NIGHT AS LONG AS IT DOES NOT TROUBLE OTHERS

Abū Umāmah ﷺ narrated that he heard the Messenger of Allah ﷺ say, "Allah Most High does not listen attentively to anything as much as He listens attentively to a slave reciting the Qur'an in the middle of the night."(2) Tirmidhī narrated it. The meaning is that Allah Most High listens with particular attention to recitation at night. Tirmidhī narrated on the authority of Ibn Mas'ūd ﷺ that the Prophet ﷺ said, "Three people are loved by Allah Almighty and Exalted: a man who stands at night reciting the Book of Allah; a man who gives charity with the right hand whilst concealing it from the left hand; and a man who went out in battle, and after his companions were defeated, faced the enemy [alone]."(3)

---

(1) *Aḥmad* (6626).

(2) *Tirmidhī* (2911)

(3) *Tirmidhī* (2567).

يقول الصّيامُ: أيْ ربِّ منعتُهُ الطَّعامَ والشَّهواتِ بالنهارِ فشفِّعني فيه، ويقولُ القرآنُ: منعتُهُ النَّومَ باللّيلِ فشفِّعني فيه، فيُشَفَّعانِ فيه» [1].

وقد استحسَنَ جماعةٌ من السَّلفِ الصَّالحِ تلاوةَ سورةِ الفتحِ {إِنَّا فَتَحْنَا لَكَ} في أوَّلِ ليلةٍ من رمضانَ؛ استفتاحاً لأبوابِ الخيرِ، واستنزالاً للبركةِ والرَّحمةِ. وروى الحافظُ السّلفيُّ بإسنادِهِ عن المسعوديّ أنه قال: بلَغَني أنَّ مَن قرأَ أوَّلَ ليلةٍ من رمضانَ {إِنَّا فَتَحْنَا لَكَ فَتْحًا مُّبِينًا}[2] في التطوع - أي: صلاةِ النافلة - حُفِظَ ذلك العام.

استحبابُ القراءةِ في جوفِ اللّيلِ جهرةً ما لم يُؤذِ غيرَه

عن أبي أُمامةَ رضي الله تعالى عنه قال: سمعتُ رسولَ الله ﷺ يقول: «ما أَذنَ اللهُ تعالى - أي: ما استمَعَ - لشيءٍ ما أَذنَ لعبدٍ يقرأُ القرآنَ في جوفِ اللَّيلِ» [3]. الحديث. رواه الترمذيُّ. والمرادُ: أنَّ اللهَ تعالى يستمعُ لقراءةِ اللَّيلِ استماعاً خاصّاً.

وروى الترمذيُّ عن ابنِ مسعودٍ رضي الله تعالى عنه أنَّ النبيَّ ﷺ قال: «ثلاثةٌ يحبُّهُمُ اللهُ عزَّ وجلَّ: رجلٌ قام من اللَّيلِ يتلو كتابَ الله، ورجلٌ تصدَّقَ صدقةً بيمينِهِ يُخفِيها عن شمالِهِ، ورجلٌ كان في سَرِيّةٍ فانهزَمَ أصحابُهُ فاستقبلَ العدوَّ» [4].

---

(١) أخرجه أحمد في مسنده (٦٦٢٦).

(٢) الفتح: ١.

(٣) أخرجه الترمذي (٢٩١١).

(٤) أخرجه الترمذي (٢٥٦٧).

THE ETIQUETTE OF COMPLETING THE NOBLE QUR'AN

The imams amongst the reciters and the scholars of the multiple readings (*qirā'āt*) have mentioned a number of points of etiquette that are required when completing the Noble Qur'an. Amongst them are the following:

Takbīr: This is as explained by the imam of the reciters, Shaykh Ibn al-Jazarī ﷺ, in *Taqrīb al-Nashr*, "In reality, this is the *sunnah* of *takbīr* when completing the great Qur'an at all times, but it has spread, become widespread, and is successively reported from them (i.e., the imams of the *qirā'āt*). The people received it from them with widespread acceptance until it became a practice in all lands. They also have *marfū'* and *mawqūf* hadiths that are narrated in this regard."

He then narrated with his chain from Aḥmad ibn Abī Bazzah (i.e., al-Bazzī) who said he heard 'Ikrimah ibn Sulayman say, "I recited to Ismā'īl ibn 'Abdillāh of Qusṭanṭīn. When I reached, 'By the morning sunlight (i.e., *Sūrah al-Ḍuḥā*)', he said, 'Say *takbīr* until you complete [the Qur'an], because I recited to 'Abdullāh ibn Abī Kathīr and when I reached, "By the morning sunlight", he said to me, "Say *takbīr* until you complete."' He (i.e., 'Abdullāh ibn Abī Kathīr) informed him that he had recited to Mujāhid who instructed him the same. Mujāhid informed him that Ibn 'Abbās ﷺ instructed him the same. Ibn 'Abbās ﷺ informed him (i.e., Mujāhid) that

آدابُ ختمِ القرآنِ الكريم

ذكر أئمّةُ القُرّاءِ، والعلماءُ بالقراءاتِ آداباً متعدّدةً مطلوبةً عند ختمِ القرآنِ الكريمِ. فمن ذلك: التكبيرُ: كما بيّنَ ذلك إمامُ القرّاءِ الشّيخُ ابنُ الجزريّ رحمه الله تعالى في (تقريبِ النّشر)، وهو في الأصلِ سُنّةُ التّكبيرِ عند ختمِ القرآنِ العظيم عامّةً، وشاع ذلك عنهم - أي: عن أئمّةِ القراءاتِ - واستفاض وتواتر، وتلقّاهُ النّاسُ عنهم بالقَبول حتى صار العملُ عليه في سائرِ الأمصار، ولهم في ذلك أحاديثُ وردَتْ مرفوعةً وموقوفةً.

ثمّ روى بإسنادِهِ عن أحمدَ بنِ أبي بزّةَ - يعني: البزّيّ - قال: سمعتُ عكرمةَ بنَ سليمانَ يقول: قرأتُ على إسماعيلَ بنِ عبدِ اللهِ بنِ قُسطَنطين، فلمّا بلغتُ {والضُّحَى} قال لي: كبّرْ حتى تختمَ، فإنّي قرأتُ على عبدِ اللهِ بنِ كثيرٍ، فلما بلغتُ {والضُّحَى} قال: كبّرْ حتى تختمَ، وأخبره أنه قرأَ على مجاهدٍ فأمرَهُ بذلك، وأخبرَهُ مجاهدٌ أنَّ ابنَ عبّاسٍ رضي الله عنهما أمرَهُ بذلك، وأخبرَهُ ابنُ عبّاسٍ رضي الله عنهما أنَّ أُبَيَّ بنَ كعبٍ رضي الله عنه أمرَهُ بذلك، وأخبرَهُ أُبَيٌّ أنَّ النبيَّ صلى الله عليه آله وسلم أمرَهُ بذلك.

ثمّ قال رحمه الله تعالى: رواهُ الحاكمُ في (مستدركِهِ الصّحيحِ) عن أبي يحيى محمّدِ بنِ عبدِ اللهِ

he recited to Ubayy ibn Kaʿb ﷺ who instructed him the same. Ubayy ﷺ informed him (i.e., Ibn ʿAbbās ﷺ) that the Prophet ﷺ instructed him the same.'"

Ibn al-Jazarī ﷺ then said, "Ḥākim narrated it in his *Mustadrak al-Ṣaḥīḥ* from Abū Yaḥyā Muhammad ibn ʿAbdillāh ibn Yazīd – the Imam in Mecca – from Muhammad ibn ʿAlī ibn Zayd al-Ṣā'igh al-Bazzī. He said, 'This is a hadith whose chain is authentic, and Bukhārī and Muslim did not report it.' I (i.e., Imam Ibn al-Jazarī ﷺ) say that nobody has narrated the hadith of *takbīr* as a hadith attributed to the Prophet ﷺ besides Bazzī. The rest of the people have narrated it as *mawqūf* until Ibn ʿAbbās ﷺ, Mujāhid, and others. It is reported that Imam Shāfiʿī said, 'If you leave the *takbīr*, you will be abandoning one of the *sunnah*s of your Prophet ﷺ.' Our shaykh Ḥāfiẓ Ibn Kathīr ﷺ said, 'This necessitates that he considered this hadith to be authentic.'" Ibn al-Jazarī ﷺ then explained that the wording of *takbīr* is *Allāhu Akbar*. The addition of *tahlīl* is reported from a group of them, and that is for you to say: *Lā ilāha ill Allah wa Allāhu Akbar*. The addition of *taḥmīd* is also reported from other reciters, due to it being narrated from ʿAlī ﷺ who said, "When you recite the Qur'an and reach the *qiṣār al-mufaṣṣal*, say *taḥmīd* and *takbīr*." All of this is said before the *basmalah*, as he has stated in *Taqrīb al-Nashr*. Hence, the sequence to this will be: *Lā ilāha ill Allah wa Allāhu Akbar wa Lillāh al-ḥamd. Bismillāh al-Raḥmān al-Raḥīm.*

The place to recite *takbīr* is from the end of *Sūrah al-Ḍuḥā* until the end of *Sūrah al-Nās*. It is also said it is from the beginning of *Sūrah al-Ḍuḥā* until the end of *Sūrah al-Nās*.

Likewise, it is *sunnah* for the reciter to read *Sūrah al-Fātiḥah* and the beginning of *Sūrah al-Baqarah* until "And it is they who will be successful"(1) upon completion. This is due to the hadith of Tirmidhī and others which has come previously, wherein the Prophet ﷺ was asked which action

(1) *Al-Baqarah*, 5.

بنِ يزيد الإمامِ بمكَّةَ، عن محمدِ بنِ عليِّ بنِ زيدٍ الصائغِ عن البزِّيِّ قال: هذا حديثٌ صحيحُ الإسنادِ، ولم يخرِّجْهُ البخاريُّ ومسلمٌ. قلتُ - القائل: هو الإمامُ ابنُ الجزريِّ رحمه الله تعالى -: لم يَرفَعْ أحدٌ حديثَ التَّكبيرِ إلا البزِّيُّ، وسائرُ النّاسِ - رَوَوهُ موقوفاً على ابنِ عبّاسٍ رَضِيَ اللهُ عَنْهُمَا ومجاهدٍ وغيرِهما. قال رَحِمَهُ اللهُ تَعَالَى: ورويَ عن الإمامِ الشافعيِّ رَحِمَهُ اللهُ تَعَالَى أنه قال: إنْ تركتَ التَّكبيرَ فقد تركتَ سنَّةً من سُنَنِ نبيِّكَ عَلَيْهِ الصَّلَاةُ وَالسَّلَامُ.

قال شيخُنا الحافظُ ابنُ كثيرٍ رَحِمَهُ اللهُ تَعَالَى: وهذا يقتضي تصحيحَهُ لهذا الحديثِ. اهـ.

ثمَّ بيَّنَ الشَّيخُ ابنُ الجزريِّ رَحِمَهُ اللهُ تَعَالَى أنَّ لفظَ التكبيرِ هو «اللهُ أكبر»، ونُقِلَ عن جماعةٍ زيادةُ التهليلِ قبلَه وذلك بأن تقول: «لا إلهَ إلا اللهُ واللهُ أكبر».

ونُقلَ أيضاً عن آخرينَ من القُرّاءِ زيادةُ التَّحميدِ، لِما رويَ عن عليٍّ رضي الله تعالى عنه أنه قال: إذا قرأتَ القرآنَ فبلغتَ قِصارَ المفصَّلِ فاحمَدِ اللهَ وكبِّرْ.

وجميعُ ذلك قبلَ البسملةِ، كما نصَّ على ذلك في (تقريب النشر)، فيكون ترتيبُ ذلك: «لا إلهَ إلا اللهُ، واللهُ أكبر، وللهِ الحمدُ، بسم الله الرحمن الرحيم».

ومحلُّ التكبيرِ من آخرِ سورةِ {والضحى} إلى آخرِ سورةِ (النّاسِ)، وقيل: من أوَّلِ سورةِ {والضحى} إلى أوّلِ سورةِ (النَّاسِ).

كما أنه يُسَنُّ للقارئِ إذا ختمَ أن يقرأَ الفاتحةَ وأوَّلَ سورةِ البقرةِ إلى {هُمُ الْمُفْلِحُونَ}[1]؛ وذلك لِما تقدَّمَ في الحديثِ الذي رواه الترمذيُّ وغيرُهُ: أنَّ النبيَّ صَلَّى اللهُ عَلَيْهِ وَآلِهِ وَسَلَّمَ سُئِلَ: أيُّ الأعمالِ أحبُّ إلى الله تعالى؟ فقال صَلَّى اللهُ عَلَيْهِ وَآلِهِ وَسَلَّمَ: «الحالُّ المُرتحِلُ»، ثمَّ بيَّنَ ذلك بقولِهِ: «الذي يَضرِبُ من أوَّلِ القرآنِ إلى آخِرِه، كلَّما حَلَّ ارتحلَ»[2].

---

(١) البقرة: ٥.

(٢) أخرجه الترمذي (٢٩٤٨).

was most beloved to Allah. He ﷺ replied, "The one who dismounts then proceeds." He ﷺ explained this further by saying, "The one who reads from the beginning of the Qur'an until the end; whenever he dismounts, he proceeds."(1)

IT IS PART OF THE ETIQUETTE OF COMPLETING THE NOBLE QUR'AN TO DO SO AT THE BEGINNING OF THE DAY OR NIGHT

It states in *al-Itqān*, "It is best (for the reciter) to complete at the beginning of the day or the beginning of the night. This is due to the narration of Dārimī with a sound chain from Sa'd ibn Abī Waqqāṣ ؓ who said, 'When the completion of the Qur'an coincides with the beginning of the night, the Angels pray for them until the morning. And if it coincides with the beginning of the day, the Angels pray for them until the evening.'(2) It states in *al-Iḥyā'*, 'The completion at the beginning of the day will be in the two [*sunnah*] *rak'ahs* of fajr and at the beginning of the day in the two *sunnah rak'ahs* of *maghrib*.' In other words, this is regarding the completion which one recites in their prayers. Ibn al-Mubārak ؒ said, 'It is desirable to complete at the beginning of the night in winter and at the beginning of the day in summer.' What he intended by that was for the prayers of the Angels to extend for the during of the night and day. It states in the book *al-Ri'āyah* that Mujāhid said, 'Whoever completes the Qur'an during the day, 70000 Angels are appointed to pray for them until the evening. And whoever completes the Qur'an at night, 70000 Angels are appointed to pray for them until the morning.'"

Daylamī narrated in *al-Firdaws* from 'Amr ibn Shu'ayb from his father from his grandfather, as a hadith attributed to the Prophet ﷺ, "When the slave completes the Qur'an, 70000 Angels pray for him upon its completi-

(1) *Tirmidhī* (2948).

(2) Abū Nu'aym in *al-Ḥilyah*.

ومن آدابِ خَتمِ القرآنِ الكريمِ أن يكونَ أوَّلَ النَّهارِ، أو أوَّلَ اللَّيلِ:

قال في (الإتقان): الأفضلُ - للقارئِ - أن يختِمَ أوَّلَ النَّهارِ أو أوَّلَ اللَّيلِ؛ لِما رواه الدارميُّ بسندٍ حسنٍ عن سعدِ بنِ أبي وقّاصٍ رَضِيَ اللَّهُ عَنْهُ أنه قال: إذا وافقَ ختمُ القرآنِ أوَّلَ اللَّيلِ صلَّتْ عليه الملائكةُ حتى يُصبِحَ، وإنْ وافقَ ختمُهُ أوَّلَ النَّهارِ صلَّتْ عليه الملائكةُ حتى يُمسِيَ[1].

قال في (الإحياء): ويكونُ الختمُ أوَّلَ النَّهارِ في ركعتي الفجرِ، وأوَّلَ اللَّيلِ في ركعتي سُنَّةِ المَغربِ. اهـ. يعني: هذا في الخَتمةِ التي يقرؤها في صَلَواتِه.

وقال ابنُ المباركِ رَحِمَهُ اللَّهُ تَعَالَىٰ: يُستحَبُّ الختمُ في الشِّتاءِ أوَّلَ اللَّيلِ، وفي الصَّيفِ أوَّلَ النَّهار. اهـ. ويعني بذلك: امتداد صلواتِ الملائكةِ بامتداد اللّيلِ والنَّهارِ.

وفي كتاب (الرعاية) قال مجاهدٌ: مَن ختم القرآنَ نهاراً وُكِّلَ به سبعونَ ألف مَلَكٍ يُصلّونَ عليه حتى يمسيَ، ومَن ختَمَ القرآنَ ليلاً وُكِّلَ به سبعونَ ألف مَلَكٍ يُصلُّونَ عليه حتى يصبِحَ. اهـ.

وروى الديلميُّ في (الفردوس) عن عمرِو بنِ شُعَيبٍ عن أبيه عن جَدِّه مرفوعاً: «إذا ختمَ العبدُ القرآنَ صلى عليه عند خَتمِهِ ستّونَ ألف مَلَكٍ»[2].

ويُستحَبُّ صيامُ يومِ الخَتمِ إلّا أن يصادِفَ يوماً نهى الشَّرعُ عن صيامِه، فقد روى ابنُ أبي داودَ بإسناده الصَّحيحِ عن جماعةٍ من التَّابعينَ أنَّهم كانوا يُصبِحونَ في يوم خَتمِهم صياماً.

---

(١) أخرجه أبو نعيم في (حلية الأولياء) (٣٠/٥).

(٢) ذكره السيوطي في (الجامع الصغير) (٥٦٨).

on."[1] It is also desirable to fast on the day of completion, unless it coincides with a day which is forbidden to fast according to the sacred law. Ibn Abī Dāwūd has narrated with his authentic chain regarding a group of followers that they would fast on the day of their completion.

THE DESIRABILITY OF ATTENDING THE GATHERING OF THE COMPLETION OF THE QUR'AN AND ITS IMMENSE VIRTUE

Imam Nawawī said, "It is highly desirable to attend the gathering of the completion of the Qur'an. It is established in the two *Ṣaḥīḥ* collections that the Messenger of Allah ﷺ would instruct women in their menses to also go out on Eid, so that they can participate in the goodness and the supplications of the Muslims.[2] Dārimī and Ibn Abi Dāwūd narrated with their chains that Ibn ʿAbbās would appoint a person to observe someone reciting the Qur'an, and when they wanted to complete it, he would inform Ibn ʿAbbās so he can also participate."

Ṭabarānī narrated with a chain of reliable narrators, that when Anas would complete the Qur'an, he would gather his family members and supplicate.[3]

Ḥakam ibn ʿUtaybah said, "Mujāhid and ʿAbdah ibn Abī Lubābah called for me and said, 'We called for you because we want to complete the Qur'an, and supplications upon the completion of the Qur'an are accepted.' It used to be said that mercy descends upon the completion of the Qur'an.' Mujāhid said that they used to gather upon completing the Qur'an and say that mercy is descending."

---

(1) Suyūṭī in *al-Jāmiʿ al-Ṣaghīr* (568).

(2) *Bukhārī* (351); *Muslim* (890).

(3) Haythamī in *Majmaʿ al-Zawāʾid*, vol. 7, p. 172.

استحبابُ حضورِ مجلسِ ختمِ القرآنِ، وفضله الكبير

قال الإمامُ النوويُّ رَحِمَهُ اللَّهُ تَعَالَى: ويُستَحبُّ حضورُ مجلسِ ختمِ القرآنِ استحباباً متأكِّداً؛ فقد ثبت في (الصّحيحينِ) أنَّ رسولَ الله ﷺ أَمَرَ الحُيَّضَ بالخروجِ يومَ العيدِ؛ ليَشهدْنَ الخيرَ ودعوةَ المسلمين[1].

وروى الدارميُّ وابنُ أبي داودَ بإسنادِهما عن ابنِ عبّاسٍ رَضِيَ اللَّهُ عَنْهُمَا أنّهُ كان يجعلُ رجلاً يُراقِبُ رجلاً يقرأُ القرآنَ، فإذا أراد أن يختمَ أعلمَ ابنَ عبّاسٍ رَضِيَ اللَّهُ عَنْهُمَا فيشهدُ ذلك. اهـ. وأخرج الطبرانيُّ بإسنادِ الثِّقاتِ عن أنسٍ رَضِيَ اللَّهُ عَنْهُ: أنّهُ كان إذا ختمَ القرآنَ جمعَ أهلَه، ودعا[2].

وعن الحَكَمِ بنِ عُتيبةَ قال: أرسلَ إليَّ مجاهدٌ، وعبدةُ بنُ أبي لُبابةَ، فقالا: إنّا أرسلنا إليك؛ لأنّا أردْنا أن نختمَ القرآنَ، والدعاءُ يُستجابُ عند ختمِ القرآنِ، وإنّه كان يُقالُ: إنَّ الرَّحمةَ تنزلُ عندَ خاتمةِ القرآنِ.

وقال مجاهدٌ: كانوا يجتمعونَ عند ختمِ القرآنِ، يقولون: تنزلُ الرَّحمةُ.

---

(١) أخرجه البخاري (٣٥١)، ومسلم (٨٩٠).

(٢) ذكره الهيثمي في (مجمع الزوائد) (٧/ ١٧٢).

THE DESIRABILITY OF SUPPLICATING UPON COMPLETION DUE TO IT BEING ACCEPTED

Imam Nawawī ﷺ said, "It is highly desirable to supplicate after the completion. Dārimī narrated with his chain that Ḥumayd al-A'raj said, 'Whoever recites the Qur'an and then supplicates, 4000 Angels say *āmīn* upon their supplication.'[1] One should supplicate imploringly, supplicate for important matters and supplicate much for the well-being of the Muslims." Ṭabarānī narrated on the authority of 'Irbāḍ ibn Sāriyah ﷺ that the Prophet ﷺ said, "Whoever prays the obligatory prayer has an accepted supplication, and whoever completes the Qur'an has an accepted supplication."[2]

Khaṭīb narrated on the authority of Anas ﷺ, as a hadith attributed to the Prophet ﷺ, "The reciter of the Qur'an has an accepted supplication upon its completion, and such a tree in Paradise that if a crow were to fly from its roots, it would not reach its branches before turning old."[3]

Ibn Mardawayh narrated on the authority of Anas ﷺ, as a hadith attributed to the Prophet ﷺ, "The reciter of the Qur'an has an accepted

(1) *Dārimī* (3481).

(2) Haythamī in *Majma' al-Zawā'id*, vol. 7, p. 172.

(3) Al-Muttaqī al-Hindī in *Kanz al- 'Ummāl* (2280).

استحبابُ الدُّعاءِ عند الختمِ؛ لأنّهُ مُجابٌ

قال الإمامُ النوويُّ رَحِمَهُ ٱللَّهُ: ويُستحَبُّ الدُّعاءُ عقبَ الخَتمِ استحباباً متأكِّداً.

روى الدارميُّ بإسناده عن حُميدٍ الأعرجِ قال: (مَن قرأَ القرآنَ ثمَّ دعا أمَّن على دعائِهِ أربعةُ آلافِ مَلَكٍ)(١).

قال: وينبغي أن يُلِحَّ في الدُّعاء، وأن يدعوَ بالأمورِ المُهمّةِ، وأنْ يكثرَ من ذلك في صلاحِ المسلمين. اهـ. وروى الطبرانيُّ عن العِرباضِ بنِ ساريةَ رَضِيَ ٱللَّهُ عَنْهُ أن النبي صَلَّى ٱللَّهُ عَلَيْهِ وَسَلَّمَ قال: «مَن صلّى صلاة فريضة فله دعوةٌ مستجابةٌ، ومَن ختمَ القرآنَ فله دعوةٌ مستجابةٌ»(٢).

وروى الخطيبُ عن أنسٍ رَضِيَ ٱللَّهُ عَنْهُ مرفوعاً: «إنَّ لصاحبِ القرآنِ عند خَتمِهِ دعوةً مستجابةً، وشجرةً في الجنّةِ لو أنَّ غُراباً طار من أصلِها لم يَنْتهِ إلى فَرعِها حتَّى يُدرِكَهُ

---

(١) أخرجه الدارمي (٣٤٨١).

(٢) ذكره الهيثمي في (مجمع الزوائد) (٨ / ١٧٢).

supplication. If he wishes he can make it in this life, and if he wishes he can defer it to the Hereafter."[1]

In Bayhaqī's *Shu 'ab al-Īmān*, it is narrated on the authority of Anas ﷺ, as a hadith of the Prophet ﷺ, "Whoever recites the Qur'an, praises the Lord, invokes blessings on the Prophet ﷺ, and seeks forgiveness from their Lord has sought goodness from its source."[2]

It states in *al-Itqān* after relating this hadith, "It is a *sunnah* after completing one recitation to start another thereafter, due to the hadith of Tirmidhī in which he ﷺ was asked which action was most beloved to Allah. He ﷺ replied, 'The one who dismounts then proceeds.' He asked, 'What is the one who dismounts then proceeds?' He ﷺ replied, 'The one who reads from the beginning of the Qur'an until the end; whenever he dismounts, he proceeds.[3] Dārimī has reported with a sound chain from Ibn 'Abbās from Ubayy ibn Ka'b ﷺ that when the Prophet ﷺ would recite *Sūrah al-Nās* (i.e., when completing the Qur'an), he would start from *Sūrah al-Fātiḥah*, then recite from al-Baqarah until 'And it is they who will be successful.'[4] Thereafter, he would make the supplication for completion and then stand to leave."

Daylamī narrated in *al-Firdaws* from Abū Umāmah ﷺ, as a hadith attributed to the Prophet ﷺ, "When any of you complete [the Qur'an], they should say, 'O Allah, grant me comfort in my loneliness in my grave.'"[5]

One of the supplications reported from the Prophet ﷺ is, "O Allah, have mercy upon me through the Qur'an, and make it for me a leader, light, guidance, and mercy. O Allah, remind me of what I have forgotten thereof and teach me of it that which I do not know. Grant me its recitation in the hours of the night and at the ends of the day, and make it a proof for me,

---

(1) Suyūṭī in *al-Jāmi ' al-Ṣaghīr* (2402).

(2) Bayhaqī in *Shu 'ab al-Īmān* (2084).

(3) *Tirmidhī* (2948).

(4) *Al-Baqarah*, 5.

(5) *Daylamī* (99).

الهَرَم»[1]. وروى ابنُ مَرْدَوَيْه عن أنسٍ رَضِيَ اللهُ عَنْهُ مرفوعاً: «إنَّ لقارئِ القرآنِ دعوةً مستجابةً، فإنْ شاءَ صاحبُها تعجَّلَها في الدُّنيا، وإن شاءَ أخَّرها إلى الآخرةِ» [2].

وفي «شُعَبِ البيهقيِّ» من حديثِ أنسٍ رَضِيَ اللهُ عَنْهُ مرفوعاً: «مَن قرأَ القرآنَ، وحَمِدَ الرَّبَّ، وصلَّى على النبيِّ صَلَّى اللهُ عَلَيْهِ وَآلِهِ وَسَلَّمَ، واستغفرَ ربَّهُ فقد طلبَ الخيرَ من مكانِهِ»[3].

قال في (الإتقان) بعدَما أورد هذا الحديثَ: ويُسَنُّ إذا فرغَ من الخَتمةِ أن يَشْرَعَ في خَتمةٍ أُخرى عَقِبَ الخَتمِ - الأوَّلِ -؛ لحديثِ الترمذيِّ لمّا سُئِلَ: أيُّ الأعمالِ أحبُّ إلى اللهِ تعالى؟ قال صَلَّى اللهُ عَلَيْهِ وَآلِهِ وَسَلَّمَ: «أحَبُّ الأعمالِ إلى اللهِ تعالى الحالُّ المُرتحِلُ، قيل: وما الحالُّ المرتحلُ؟ قال: الذي يضربُ من أوَّلِ القرآنِ إلى آخرِهِ، كلَّما حلَّ ارتحلَ»[4].

وأخرج الدارميُّ بسندٍ حسنٍ عن ابنِ عبّاسٍ عن أُبَيِّ بنِ كعبٍ رَضِيَ اللهُ عَنْهُمْ: أنَّ النبيَّ صَلَّى اللهُ عَلَيْهِ وَآلِهِ وَسَلَّمَ كان إذا قرأَ {قُلْ أَعُوذُ بِرَبِّ النَّاسِ}، أي: ختمَ القرآنَ افتتحَ منَ {الحَمْدُ}، ثمَّ قرأَ من البقرةِ إلى {وَأُولَٰئِكَ هُمُ الْمُفْلِحُونَ}[5] ثمَّ دعا بدعاءِ الختمةِ، ثمَّ قام. اهـ. من (الإتقان).

وروى الديلميُّ في (الفردوس) عن أبي أُمامةَ رَضِيَ اللهُ عَنْهُ مرفوعاً: «إذا خَتَمَ أحدُكُم فليقُلْ: اللَّهمَّ آنِسْ وَحشَتي في قبري»[6].

---

(1) أخرجه المتقي الهندي في (كنز العمال) (٢٢٨٠).

(2) ذكره السيوطي في (الجامع الصغير) (٢٤٠٢).

(3) أخرجه البيهقي في (شعب الإيمان) (٢٠٨٤).

(4) أخرجه الترمذي (٢٩٤٨).

(5) البقرة: ٥.

(6) أخرجه الديلمي (٩٩).

O Lord of all worlds."

It is also reported from the narration of Aḥmad, Bazzār, Abū Yaʿlā, Ibn Ḥibbān, Ḥākim, and others, on the authority of Ibn Masʿūd ﷺ that the Messenger of Allah ﷺ said, "No one experiences any worry or grief and then says, 'O Allah, I am Your slave, the son of Your male slave and the son of Your female slave, in Your grasp. My forelock is in Your hand, I am subject to Your decree, and Your decision on me is just. I ask You by every name of Yours, by which You have named Yourself, or which You have revealed in Your Book, or which You have taught any one of Your Creation, or which You have kept to Yourself in the knowledge of the Unseen with You, that You make the Qur'an the light of my breast, the springtime of my heart, the removal of my sorrow, and the departure of my worry and sorry,' except that Allah Almighty and Exalted will remove their worry and replace it with happiness."(1)

It is also good to read the supplication narrated by Tirmidhī from Sayyidunā ʿAlī ﷺ, which he learnt from the Messenger of Allah ﷺ, "O Allah, have mercy on me by making me leave sins forever as long as you keep me alive, have mercy on me by saving me from burdening myself with that which does not concern me, and provide me insight into what will make You pleased with me.

O Allah – Originator of the Heavens and the Earth, Lord of Majesty and Honour, and Might that cannot be intended – I ask you, O Allah, O Most Compassionate, by Your glory and the light of Your Countenance, to make memorization of Your Book firmly stick to my heart as You have taught me, and grant me the ability to recite it in the manner that will make You pleased with me.

O Allah – Originator of the Heavens and the Earth, Lord of Majesty and Honour, and Might that cannot be intended – I ask you, O Allah, O Most Compassionate, by Your glory and the light of Your Countenance, to illuminate my sight with Your Book; make my tongue flow therewith;

---

(1) *Aḥmad* (3712) and this is his wording; *Ibn Ḥibbān* (972).

ومن الأدعيةِ الواردةِ عنه ﷺ: «اللَّهمَّ ارحمْني بالقرآنِ، واجعلْهُ لي إماماً ونوراً وهدىً ورحمةً، اللَّهمَّ ذكِّرْني منه ما نُسِّيتُ وعلِّمني منه ما جَهِلتُ، وارزقني تلاوتَه آناءَ اللَّيلِ وأطرافَ النَّهار، واجعله لي حُجَّةً يا ربَّ العالمين».

ومن الواردِ عنه ﷺ ما رواه أحمدُ والبزَّارُ وأبو يَعلى وابنُ حِبّانَ والحاكمُ وغيرُهم عن ابنِ مسعودٍ رَضِيَ اللَّهُ عَنْهُ أنَّ رسولَ الله ﷺ قال: «ما أصابَ أحداً قطُّ همٌّ ولا حزنٌ، فقال: اللَّهمَّ إنِّي عبدُكَ، وابنُ عبدِك، وابنُ أَمَتِك ناصيتي بيدِك، ماضٍ فيَّ علمُك، عدلٌ فيَّ قضاؤكَ، أسألُكَ بكلِّ اسمٍ هو لك، سمَّيتَ به نفسَكَ،

أو أنزلتَهُ في كتابِكَ، أو علَّمْتَهُ أحداً من خلقِكَ، أو استأثرتَ به في علمِ الغَيبِ عندَكَ أنْ تجعلَ القرآنَ العظيمَ ربيعَ قلبي، ونورَ صدري، وجَلاءَ حُزني وذهابَ همِّي، إلّا أذهبَ اللهُ عزَّ وجل همَّهُ، وأبدلَهُ مكانَهُ فرحاً»[1] الحديثَ.

ويحسُنُ الدُّعاءُ بما رواه الترمذيُّ عن سيدِنا عليٍّ رَضِيَ اللَّهُ عَنْهُ في الدُّعاءِ الذي تعلَّمه من رسول الله ﷺ: «اللَّهمَّ ارحمْني بتركِ المعاصي أبداً ما أبقيْتَني، وارحمْني أن أتكلَّفَ ما لا يَعنيني، وارزقني حُسنَ النَّظرِ فيما يُرضيكَ عني، اللَّهمَّ بديعَ السَّمواتِ والأرضِ، ذا الجلالِ والإكرامِ، والعزَّةِ التي لا تُرام، أسألُكَ يا اللهُ يا رحمنُ بجلالكَ، ونورِ وجهِكَ أنْ تُلزِمَ قلبي حفظَ كتابِكَ كما علَّمتَني، وارزقني أن أتلوَهُ على النَّحوِ الذي يُرضيكَ عني، اللَّهمَّ بديعَ السَّمواتِ والأرضِ، ذا الجلالِ والإكرامِ، والعزَّةِ التي لا تُرام، أسألُكَ يا اللهُ يا رحمنُ بجلالكَ، ونورِ وجهِكَ الكريمِ أن تنوِّرَ بكتابك بصري، وأنْ تُطلِقَ به لساني، وأن تُفرِّجَ به عن قلبي، وأن تشرحَ به صدري، وأن تغسلَ به بدني؛ فإنَّه لا يُعينُني على الحقِّ

---

(١) أخرجه أحمد (٣٧١٢) واللفظ له، وابن حبان (٩٧٢).

remove [sorrow] from my heart thereby; to expand my chest therewith; and to wash my body therewith. Nobody can help me upon the truth besides You, nobody can grant it besides You, and there is no might or power except with Allah, Most High, the Greatest."[1]

THE RULINGS OF THE PROSTRATION OF RECITATION (SAJDAH AL-TILĀWAH)

Allah Most High said, "Do you find this Revelation astonishing, laughing [at it] and not weeping [in awe], while persisting in heedlessness? Instead, prostrate to Allah and worship [Him alone]!"[2] He Most High said, "So what is the matter with them that they do not believe, and when the Qur'an is recited to them, they do not bow down [in submission]?"[3]

Abū Hurayrah ﵁ narrated that the Messenger of Allah ﷺ said, "When the son of Adam recites a [verse of] prostration and then prostrates, the devil retreats whilst crying and says, 'Woe unto him! The son of Adam was ordered to prostrate and thus prostrated, so for him is Paradise. But I was ordered to prostrate and refused, so for me is the Fire."[4] Muslim narrated it.

The scholars differ regarding the ruling of the prostration of recitation: the Ḥanafīs opine it is necessary (*wājib*) and they substantiate this through the above two verses. Allah commanded prostration upon reciting the Qur'an in the first verse, and in the second verse He censured those who do not prostrate when the Qur'an is recited to them. This contains proof of its necessity.

The Shāfiʿīs opine that it is a *sunnah*. Imam Nawawī said, "Our stance is that it is a *sunnah* and not necessary. This is what the majority of scholars say." He then said that they substantiate this with what is in the two *Ṣaḥīḥ*

(1) *Tirmidhī* (3570).

(2) *Al-Najm*, 59-62.

(3) *Al-Inshiqāq*, 20-21.

(4) *Muslim* (81).

غيرُك، ولا يُؤتيهِ إلَّا أنتَ، ولا حولَ ولا قوَّةَ إلا باللهِ العليِّ العظيمِ»[1]. آمين.

أحكامُ سجدةِ التّلاوةِ

قال اللهُ تعالى: {أَفَمِنْ هَٰذَا الْحَدِيثِ تَعْجَبُونَ (٥٩) وَتَضْحَكُونَ وَلَا تَبْكُونَ (٦٠) وَأَنتُمْ سَامِدُونَ (٦١) فَاسْجُدُوا لِلَّهِ وَاعْبُدُوا} [2].

وقال تعالى: {فَمَا لَهُمْ لَا يُؤْمِنُونَ (٢٠) وَإِذَا قُرِئَ عَلَيْهِمُ الْقُرْآنُ لَا يَسْجُدُونَ}[3].

وعن أبي هريرةَ رَضِيَ اللهُ عَنْهُ قال: قال رسولُ الله صَلَّى اللهُ عَلَيْهِ وَسَلَّمَ: «إذا قرأَ ابنُ آدمَ السَّجدةَ فسجد اعتزلَ الشَّيطانُ يبكي، يقول: يا ويلَهُ- وفي روايةٍ: يا ويلي - أُمِرَ ابنُ آدمَ بالسُّجودِ فسجَدَ، فلهُ الجنَّةُ، وأُمِرتُ بالسُّجودِ فأبَيتُ فلِيَ النَّارُ»[4]. رواهُ مسلمٌ.

وقد اختلَفَ الأئمّةُ في حكمِ سجدةِ التّلاوةِ: فذهبتِ الحنفيّةُ إلى أنّها واجبةٌ، واحتجُّوا على ذلك بالآيتينِ السّابقتينِ؛ حيثُ إنَّ اللهَ أمرَ بالسُّجودِ عند قراءةِ القرآنِ في الآيةِ الأُولى، وذمَّ في الآيةِ الثّانيةِ وأنكرَ على الذين لا يسجدونَ إذا قُرِئَ عليهم، وفي ذلكَ دليلُ الوجوبِ. وذهبَتِ الأئمّةُ الشّافعيةُ إلى أنّها سنَّةٌ. قال الإمامُ النوويُّ: مذهبُنا أنَّهُ- أي: سجودُ التّلاوةِ - سنّةٌ وليس بواجبٍ، وبهذا قال جمهورُ العلماء. ثمّ قال: واحتجُّوا على ذلك بما في (الصَّحيحَينِ) عن زيدِ بنِ ثابتٍ رَضِيَ اللهُ عَنْهُ أنَّهُ قال: قرأتُ

---

(١) أخرجه الترمذي (٣٥٧٠).

(٢) النجم: ٥٩-٦٢.

(٣) الانشقاق: ٢٠-٢١.

(٤) أخرجه مسلم (٨١).

collections from Zayd ibn Thabit ﵁ who said, "I recited *Sūrah al-Najm* to the Messenger of Allah ﷺ but he did not prostrate in it."(1) And also through the hadith of the Bedouin reported in the two *Ṣaḥīḥ* collections where the Prophet ﷺ said to him, "Five prayers during the day and night." The Bedouin asked, "Is there anything else that is binding on me?" He said, "No, unless you do so voluntarily."(2) They also substantiate it by the fact ʿUmar ibn al-Khaṭṭāb ﵁ recited *Sūrah al-Naḥl* on the pulpit on Friday. When the prostration came, he stepped down and prostrated, and the people also prostrated. When he recited it again the following Friday and he came to the prostration, he said, "O people! We have come across a prostration: whoever prostrates has done the right thing, but whoever does not prostrate has no sin upon them." ʿUmar ﵁ did not prostrate. In one narration, ʿUmar ﵁ said, "Indeed, Allah has not made the prostration obligatory – unless we want to [we can prostrate]."(3) Bukhārī narrated it.

THE METHOD OF THE PROSTRATION OF RECITATION

According to the Ḥanafīs, it is one prostration between two *sunnah takbīrs* and two desirable standings – without raising the hands, *tashahhud*, and *salām*. One will say the *takbīr* whilst standing, proceed to the prostration, say *takbīr* again and stand up. The conditions for prayer such as purity, facing the *qiblah*, and so forth, are also stipulated for it – besides the consecrating *takbīr* and specifically intending it to be for such-and-such verse; it is sufficient to intend it for the recitation. The details of this are in works of jurisprudence. As for the Shāfiʿīs, it is a *sunnah* according to them, as mentioned previously. Its conditions are intention, the consecrating *takbīr*, and saying *salām* after the sitting. Hence, it is a prostration in between a consecrating *takbīr* with intention and *salām* after sitting.

---

(1) *Bukhārī* (1073); *Muslim* (577).

(2) *Bukhārī* (46); *Muslim* (11).

(3) *Bukhārī* (1077).

على رسولِ الله ﷺ {وَالنَّجمِ} فلم يسجدْ فيها[1]. وبما في (الصَّحيحَينِ) من حديثِ الأعرابيِّ لمّا قال له النبيُّ ﷺ: «خمسُ صلواتٍ في اليومِ واللَّيلةِ، فقال الأعرابيُّ: هل عليَّ غيرُها؟ قال: «لا، إلّا أن تطَّوَّعَ»[2]. واحتجُّوا أيضاً بأنَّ عمرَ بنَ الخطّابِ رضي الله عنه قرأَ يومَ الجُمُعَةِ على المنبرِ سورةَ النحل، حتى إذا جاء السجدةَ نزل فسجدَ، وسجدَ النَّاسُ، حتى إذا كانتِ الجُمُعَةُ القابلةُ قرأها، حتى إذا جاء السجدةَ قال: يا أيُّها النّاسُ إنّما نمرُّ بالسُّجودِ؛ فمَنْ سجدَ فقد أصابَ، ومَن لم يسجدْ فلا إثمَ عليه، ولم يسجدْ عمرُ رضي الله عنه. وفي روايةٍ: قال عمرُ رضي الله عنه: إنَّ اللهَ لم يفرضِ السُّجودَ إلَّا أن نشاءَ[3]. رواه البخاري.

وأما كيفيَّةُ سجدةِ التِّلاوةِ:

فعند الحنفيّةِ هي: سجدةٌ بين تكبيرتينِ مَسنونتَينِ، وقيامين مُستحبَّينِ، بلا رفعِ يدٍ، وبلا تشهُّدٍ، وسلامٍ، فيكبِّرُ قائماً، ثم يهوي إلى السُّجود، ثم يكبِّرُ، وينهضُ قائماً، ويشترَطُ لها ما يُشترَطُ للصَّلاةِ من الطَّهارةِ واستقبالِ القبلةِ، ونحوِ ذلك ما عدا التَّحريمةَ، ونيَّةَ التعيينِ عن آيةِ كذا؛ بل يكفي كونُها عنِ التِّلاوةِ، وتفصيلُ ذلك في كتبِ الفقهِ.

وأما عند الشّافعيّةِ فهي سنَّةٌ كما تقدَّمَ، ويُشترَطُ لها: النّيّةُ، وتكبيرةُ الإحرامِ، وسلامٌ بعد الجلوس، فهي سجدةٌ بين تكبيرةِ إحرامٍ مع النّيّةِ، وبينَ سلامٍ بعد الجلوس.

---

(١) أخرجه البخاري (١٠٧٣) واللفظ له، ومسلم (٥٧٧).

(٢) أخرجه البخاري (٤٦)، ومسلم (١١).

(٣) أخرجه البخاري (١٠٧٧).

THE REMEMBRANCES FOR THE PROSTRATION OF RECITATION

If it the prostration of recitation is in an obligatory prayer, one will say thrice: "Glory be to my Lord, the Most High." If it is in an additional prayer or outside of prayer, one can say the supplications that have been narrated beyond the [standard] *tasbīḥ*s. This is such as saying: "O Allah, to You have I prostrated, and in You I believe, and to You I submit. My face has prostrated to the One Who created and shaped it, and formed my hearing and sight. Blessed is Allah, the Best of Creators." One can also say: "Most Glorious and Most Holy, Lord of the Angels and the Spirit." And, "O Allah, write reward for me with You thereby, remove from me my sins because of it, make it a treasure for me with You, and accept it from me as You accepted it from your slave Dāwūd, upon him be peace."

THE DIVINE COUNSEL AND THE PROPHETIC COUNSEL TO FOLLOW THE BOOK AND SUNNAH AND FIRMLY ABIDE BY THEM

Allah Most High said, "This is a blessed Book We have revealed. So follow it and be mindful [of Allah], so you may be shown mercy."(1)

The meaning is: if you are hopeful of Allah's mercy in your worldly life and the Hereafter – mercy that is comprehensive to all types of fortune, goodness, and happiness – you must firmly abide by the commands of this great Book and refrain from its prohibitions. Through this, you will attain happiness, wellness, salvation, and success.

He Most High said, "As for those who firmly abide by the Book and establish prayer – surely We never discount the reward of the reformers."(2) Thus, those who firmly abide by the Book are righteous and reformers. A person cannot be a reformer unless they are righteous, and one cannot be

(1) *Al-An'ām*, 155.

(2) *Al-A'rāf*, 170.

وأمّا أذكارُ سجدةِ التِّلاوةِ:

فإن كانتْ في صلاةٍ مفروضةٍ قال: سبحانَ ربّيَ الأعلى «ثلاثاً»، وإن كانت في صلاةٍ نافلةٍ، أو في غيرِ الصَّلاةِ فله أن يأتيَ فوقَ التَّسبيحاتِ بما وَرَدَ، كأن يقولَ: «اللّهمَّ لك سجدتُ، وبك آمنتُ، سجد وجهي للذي خَلَقَهُ، وصوَّرَهُ، وشقَّ سمعَهُ وبصرَهُ بحولِهِ وقوَّتِهِ، تباركَ اللهُ أحسنُ الخالقين، ويقول: «سبُّوحٌ قدُّوسٌ ربُّ الملائكةِ والرُّوحِ»، ويقول: «اللّهمَّ اكتُبْ لي بها عندك أجراً، واجعلها لي عندك ذُخراً، وضَعْ عني بها وِزراً، واقبلها منّي كما قَبِلتَها من عبدِكَ داودَ ﷺ».

الوصايا الإلهيّةُ ثمَّ النّبويّةُ
باتّباعِ الكتابِ والسُّنّةِ والتمسُّكِ بهما

قال اللهُ تعالى: {وَهَذَا كِتَابٌ أَنْزَلْنَاهُ مُبَارَكٌ فَاتَّبِعُوهُ وَاتَّقُوا لَعَلَّكُمْ تُرْحَمُونَ}[1].

والمعنى: إنْ كنتُم ترجون رحمةَ اللهِ تعالى في دنياكم وآخرتِكم، تلك الرَّحمةَ الجامعةَ لأنواعِ السَّعاداتِ والخيراتِ والمسرَّاتِ فعليكم باتّباع أوامرِ هذا الكتابِ العظيمِ، واتّقاءِ مناهيه، فبذلك تنالون السَّعادةَ والصَّلاحَ، والنَّجاحَ والفلاحَ.

وقال تعالى: {وَالَّذِينَ يُمَسِّكُونَ بِالْكِتَابِ وَأَقَامُوا الصَّلَاةَ إِنَّا لَا نُضِيعُ أَجْرَ الْمُصْلِحِينَ}[2]. فالمتمسّكون بكتابِ اللهِ تعالى هم الصّالحونَ والمصلِحون؛ فلا يكونُ الإنسانُ مُصلِحاً إلّا إذا كان صالحاً، ولا يكون صالحاً إلّا أن يكون مُتَّبِعاً متمسّكاً

(١) الأنعام: ١٥٥.

(٢) الأعراف: ١٧٠.

righteous unless they follow and firmly abide by the Book of Allah Most High. May Allah Most High make us amongst them.

Allah Most High said, "Whatever the Messenger gives you, take it. And whatever he forbids you from, leave it."[1]

On all the occasions in which the Prophet ﷺ was bidding farewell, he exhorted to firmly abiding by the Book of Allah Most High, taking guidance from its light, firmly abiding by his *Sunnah*, and treading his path.

Imam Muslim and Aḥmad narrated on the authority of Zayd ibn Arqam ؓ who said, "The Messenger of Allah ﷺ stood one day to address us at a watering place called Khumm (between Mecca and Medina). He praised Allah, extolled Him, advised, and reminded, and then said, 'Listen, O people! I am only a man, and the time is close when my Lord's messenger will come and I shall respond (i.e., his demise). I am leaving two weighty things amongst you. The first is the Book of Allah, which contains guidance and light. So, take the Book of Allah and firmly abide by it.' The Prophet ﷺ exhorted to the Book of Allah and encouraged people regarding it. He then said, 'The members of my family. I remind you to fear Allah with respect to my family members. I remind you to fear Allah with respect to my family members.'" A person asked Zayd ibn Arqam ؓ, "Who are his family members? Are they not his wives?" Zayd ؓ said, "His wives are from his family members. However, his family members are those who were prohibited from taking charity after him." He asked, "Who are they?" He said, "They are the family of ʿAlī, the family of ʿAqīl, the family of Jaʿfar, and the family of ʿAbbās." The man asked, "Have all of them been prohibited from charity?" Zayd ؓ said, "Yes."[2]

In another narration of Muslim, the Prophet ﷺ said, "The Book of Allah, which contains guidance and light. Whoever firmly abides by it and

(1) *Al-Ḥashr*, 7.

(2) *Muslim* (2408).

بكتابِ اللهِ تعالى. جعلَنَا اللهُ تعالى منهم. وقال الله تعالى: {وَمَا آتَاكُمُ الرَّسُولُ فَخُذُوهُ وَمَا نَهَاكُمْ عَنْهُ فَانتَهُوا ۚ وَاتَّقُوا اللَّهَ ۖ إِنَّ اللَّهَ شَدِيدُ الْعِقَابِ}[1].

وقد أوصى النبيُّ ﷺ في مواقفِ وداعِهِ كلِّها بالتمسُّكِ بكتاب اللهِ تعالى، والاهتداءِ بنورِهِ، وبالتمسُّكِ بسنَّتِهِ ﷺ، والسَّيرِ على منهاجِها.

فقد روى الإمامُ مسلمٌ وأحمدُ عن زيدِ بنِ أرقمَ رضي الله تعالى عنه أنه قال: قام رسولُ اللهِ ﷺ يوماً فينا خطيباً، بماءٍ يُدعى خُمّاً - أي: مكانٍ يُسمَّى خُمّاً بينَ مكَّةَ والمدينةَ - فحَمِدَ اللهَ تعالى وأثنى عليه، ووعظَ وذكَّرَ، ثمَّ قال: «أما بعدُ: ألَا أيُّها النّاسُ فإنّما أنا بشرٌ يُوشِكُ أن يأتيَ رسولُ ربِّي فأُجيبَ - يريدُ بذلك وفاتَهُ عليه الصلاة والسلام - وأنا تاركٌ فيكم ثَقَلَينِ، أوَّلهما: كتابُ اللهِ، فيه الهدى والنّورُ، فخذوا بكتابِ اللهِ واستمسِكوا به، فحثَّ النبيُّ ﷺ على كتابِ اللهِ، ورغَّبَ فيه, ثمَّ قال: «وأهلَ بيتي، أُذكِّرُكُمُ اللهَ في أهلِ بيتي، أُذكِّرُكُمُ اللهَ في أهلِ بيتي»، فقال رجلٌ لزيدِ بنِ أرقمَ: ومَن أهلُ بيتِهِ يا زيدُ، أَليسَ نساؤه ﷺ؟ فقال زيدٌ: نساؤُهُ من أهلِ بيتِهِ، ولكنَّ أهلَ بيتِهِ مَن حُرِمَ الصَّدقةَ بعدَه. قال: ومَن هم؟ قال: هم آلُ عليٍّ وآلُ عقيلٍ وآلُ جعفر وآلُ عبَّاسٍ، قال: كلُّ هؤلاءِ حُرِمَ الصَّدقةَ؟ قال زيدٌ: نعم[2].

وفي روايةٍ لمسلمٍ: أنَّ النبيَّ ﷺ قال: «كتابُ اللهِ فيه الهدى والنّورُ، مَنِ استمسكَ به وأخَذَ به كان على الهدى، ومَن أخطأه ضَلَّ»[3].

وعن عبدِ اللهِ بنِ عمرٍو رضي الله عنهما أنّهُ قال: خرجَ علينا رسولُ الله ﷺ يوماً

---

(١) الحشر: ٧.

(٢) أخرجه مسلم (٢٤٠٨).

(٣) أخرجه مسلم (٢٤٠٨).

adheres to it is on guidance, and whoever misses it is astray."[1]

ʿAbdullāh ibn ʿAmr ﵁ narrated, "The Messenger of Allah ﷺ came out to us once, as though he was bidding farewell. He said, 'I am Muhammad, the Unlettered Prophet. I am Muhammad, the Unlettered Prophet. I am Muhammad, the Unlettered Prophet – there is no Prophet after me. I have been granted the opening, concluding, and concise words. I have been told how many keepers of Hellfire and how many bearers of the Throne there are. I have been pardoned, and my ummah and I have been granted well-being. Therefore, listen and obey for as long as I am amongst you. When I am taken, then adhere to the Book of Allah Most High; consider what it has made lawful as lawful, and what it has made unlawful as unlawful."[2] Aḥmad and others narrated it.

Ṭabarānī narrated on the authority of Ibn ʿAbbās ﵁ that the Prophet ﷺ said, "Whoever follows the Book of Allah, He guides them out of misguidance and saves them from strict reckoning on the Day of Judgement."[3]

Therefore, it is necessary for the intelligent to firmly abide by the Book of Allah Most High, and to seek help in this regard by supplicating Allah Most High to enable them and assist them in that. The Messenger of Allah ﷺ taught his ummah to supplicate for this, as narrated by Ṭabarānī in *al-Awsaṭ* that the Prophet ﷺ said to ʿAlī ﵁, "Say, 'O Allah, open the ears of my heart to Your remembrance, and grant me obedience to You, obedience to Your Messenger, and acting upon Your Book.'"[4]

Ṭabarānī narrated in *al-Kabīr* and Ibn Ḥibbān also narrated on the authority of Abū Shurayḥ ﵁ who said, "The Messenger of Allah ﷺ came out to us and said, 'Rejoice and give glad tidings. Do you not testify that there is no deity besides Allah and that I am the Messenger of Allah?' They

(1) *Muslim* (2408).

(2) *Aḥmad* (6606).

(3) Ibn Abī Shaybah in *al-Muṣannaf* (30453).

(4) Ṭabarānī in al-*Mu ʿjam al-Awsaṭ* (1308)

كالمودِّعِ فقال: «أنا محمدٌ النبيُّ الأمّيُّ، أنا محمّدٌ النبيُّ الأمّيُّ، أنا محمدٌ النبيُّ الأُميُّ، ولا نبيَّ بعدي، أوتيتُ فواتحَ الكَلِمِ وخواتيمَهُ وجوامِعَه، وعُلِّمْتُ كم خَزَنةُ النّارِ، وحمَلةُ العرشِ وتُجوِّزَ بي، وعوفيتُ وعوفيَتْ أمّتي، فاسمعوا وأطيعوا ما دمتُ فيكم، فإذا ذُهِبَ بي فعليكم بكتابِ اللهِ تعالى أَحِلُّوا حلالَه، وحَرِّموا حرامَه»[1]. رواه أحمدُ وغيرُه.

وروى الطبرانيُّ عن ابنِ عبّاسٍ رَضِيَ اللَّهُ عَنْهُمَا عن النبيِّ عليه ﷺ أنه قال: «مَنِ اتَّبعَ كتابَ اللهِ هداهُ من الضّلالةِ، ووقاهُ سوءَ الحسابِ يومَ القيامة»[2].

فالواجبُ على العاقلِ أن يتمسَّكَ بكتابِ اللهِ تعالى، وأن يستعينَ على ذلك بالدُّعاءِ بأنْ يُوفِّقَهُ اللهُ تعالى لذلك، ويُعينَهُ على ذلك.

وقد علَّمَ رسولُ اللهِ ﷺ أُمّتَهُ أن يدعوا بذلك، كما روى الطبرانيُّ في «الأوسطِ» عن عليٍّ رضي الله تعالى عنه أنَّ النبيَّ ﷺ قال له: «قل: اللّهمَّ افتَحْ مسامِعَ قلبي لذِكرِكَ، وارزقْني طاعتَكَ، وطاعةَ رسولِكِ، والعملَ بكتابِكَ»[3].

وروى الطبرانيُّ في (الكبيرِ) وابنُ حِبّانَ عن أبي شُريحٍ رَضِيَ اللَّهُ عَنْهُ قال: خرجَ علينا رسولُ الله ﷺ، فقال: «أَبشِروا وبشِّروا، أليسَ تشهدونَ أنْ لا إلهَ إلّا اللهُ وأنّي رسولُ اللهِ؟ فقالوا: بلى، فقال ﷺ: «إنَّ هذا القرآنَ طَرَفُهُ بيدِ اللهِ، وطَرَفُهُ بأيديكم، فتمسَّكوا به؛ فإنّكم لن تضلّوا، ولن تهلِكوا بعدَه أبداً»[4].

ورواه ابنُ أبي شَيبةَ بلفظِ: «إنَّ هذا القرآنَ سببٌ - أي: حبلٌ - طَرَفُهُ بيدِ اللهِ،

---

(١) أخرجه أحمد (٦٦٠٦).

(٢) أخرجه ابن أبي شيبة في المصنف (٣٠٤٥٣).

(٣) أخرجه الطبراني في الأوسط (١٣٠٨).

(٤) أخرجه الطبراني في الكبير (٢٦٨١).

said, 'Yes, of course.' He ﷺ said, 'Indeed, one end of this Qur'an is in Allah's Hand and its other end is in your hands. So, firmly abide by it, for you will never go astray or perish thereafter.'"[(1)]

Ibn Abī Shaybah narrated it with the wording: "Indeed, this Qur'an is a rope whose one end is in Allah's Hand and whose other end is in your hands. So, firmly abide by it, for you will never go astray or perish thereafter."[(2)]

Ibn ʿAsākir narrated on the authority of Abū Masʿūd ﷺ, as a hadith attributed to the Prophet ﷺ, "Worship Allah and do not associate any partner with Him. Move with the Qur'an wherever it moves (i.e., firmly abide by it and leave your own whims wherever you may be). Accept the truth from whomever brings it – be they young or old, and even if they are despised. And return falsehood back to whomever brings it – be they young or old, and even if they are beloved and related."[(3)]

The Prophet ﷺ also explained that this Noble Qur'an contains guidance and light, and that whoever seeks guidance elsewhere will be led astray by Allah Most High. Whatever opposes the Noble Qur'an is misguidance, corruption, and evil for its proponent and whoever acts upon it.

Imam Tirmidhī narrated on the authority of ʿAlī ﷺ who said, "I heard the Messenger of Allah ﷺ say, 'Know that there will soon be tribulation.' I asked, 'What is the way out from it, O Messenger of Allah?' He said, 'The Book of Allah Most High. It contains news of what happened before you; information of what is to come after you; and judgement for your mutual matters. It is a decisive Word; it is not a joke. Whoever amongst the oppressors leaves it will be crushed by Allah Most High, and whoever seeks guidance elsewhere will be led astray by Allah Most High. It is Allah's firm rope; it is the Reminder, full of wisdom; and it is the Straight Path. It is that which whims cannot distort, tongues do not find difficult, the scholars can

(1) Ṭabarānī in *al-Muʿjam al-Kabīr* (2681).

(2) *Ibn Ḥibbān* (122).

(3) Ibn ʿAsākir in *Tarīkh Dimashq*, vol. 36, p. 269.

وطَرَفُهُ بأيديكم، فتمسَّكوا به؛ فإنَّكم لن تضلُّوا، ولن تهلِكوا بعدَه أبداً»[1].

وروى ابنُ عساكرَ عن أبي مسعودٍ مرفوعاً: «اعبُدِ اللهَ ولا تشركْ به شيئاً، وزُلْ مع القرآنِ حيثُ زالَ - أي: كن متمسِّكاً به، تاركاً هوى نفسِكَ حيثُ كنتَ - واقبَلِ الحقَّ ممَّنْ جاء به من صغيرٍ أو كبيرٍ وإن كان - الذي جاء به - بغيضاً، وأدِّ الباطلَ على مَن جاء به من صغيرٍ أو كبيرٍ وإنْ كان حبيباً قريباً»[2].

وقد بيَّنَ النبيُّ ﷺ أنَّ هذا القرآنَ الكريمَ فيه الهدى والنّورُ، وأنَّ مَنِ ابتغى الهدى في غيرِهِ أضلَّهُ اللهُ تعالى، فكلُّ ما خالف القرآنَ الكريم فهو ضلالٌ وفسادٌ وشرٌّ على صاحبِهِ وعلى مَن عَمِلَ به.

روى الإمامُ الترمذيُّ عن عليٍّ كرَّمَ اللهُ تعالى وجهَه قال: سمعتُ رسولَ الله ﷺ يقول: «أمَا إنَّها ستكونُ فتنةٌ»، قلتُ: فما المَخرَجُ منها يا رسول الله؟ قال: «كتابُ اللهِ تعالى، فيه نبأُ ما قبلَكم، وخبرُ ما بعدَكم، وحكمُ ما بينَكم، هو الفَصلُ ليس بالهَزلِ، مَن تركَهُ مِن جبّارٍ قصمه اللهُ تعالى، ومَنِ ابتغى الهدى في غيرِهِ أضلَّهُ اللهُ تعالى، وهو حبلُ اللهِ المَتينِ، وهو الذِّكرُ الحكيمُ، وهو الصِّراطُ المستقيمُ، وهو الذي لا تزيغُ به الأهواءُ، ولا تلتبسُ به الألسنةُ، ولا تشبعُ منه العلماءُ، ولا يَخلَقُ على كثرةِ الرَّدِّ، ولا تنقضي عجائبُهُ، وهو الذي لم تنتهِ الجنُّ إذ سمعَتْهُ حتّى قالوا: {إِنَّا سَمِعْنَا قُرْآنًا عَجَبًا (١) يَهْدِي إِلَى الرُّشْدِ فَآمَنَّا بِهِ}[3]، مَن قال به صَدَقَ، ومَن عَمِلَ به أُجِرَ، ومَن حكمَ به عَدَلَ، ومَن دعا

---

(١) أخرجه ابن حبان (١٢٢).

(٢) أخرجه ابن عساكر في (تاريخ دمشق) (٣٦/٢٦٩).

(٣) الجن: ١-٢.

never get enough of, does not become tedious due to constant repetition, and whose wonders never cease. It is that which, when the jinn heard, they could not resist but to say, "Indeed, we have heard a wondrous recitation. It leads to Right Guidance, so we believed in it."[1] Whoever speaks it speaks the truth, whoever acts upon it is rewarded, whoever judges by it is fair, and whoever calls towards it has been guided to the Straight Path.'"[2]

Moreover, just as the Prophet ﷺ ordered his ummah to firmly abide by the Book of Allah Most High, he ordered them to firmly abide by his *Sunnah*. And just as he warned his ummah of not acting upon the Book of Allah, he warned them of not acting upon what has come from him ﷺ.

Ḥākim narrated, and declared authentic, on the authority of Ibn ʿAbbās that the Messenger of Allah ﷺ delivered a sermon during the Farewell Hajj (Hajjah al-Widāʿ) and said, "Indeed, the devil has lost hope of being worshipped in your land. However, he is pleased to be obeyed in other things - your actions which you consider to be trivial - so beware. I have left amongst you that with which - provided you hold onto firmly - you will never go astray: the Book of Allah Most High and the *Sunnah* of His Prophet."[3] This is as cited in Mundhiri's *al-Targhīb*.

It is narrated on the authority of Abū Saʿīd al-Khudrī that the Messenger of Allah ﷺ said, "Whoever eats pure things, practices the *Sunnah*, and people are safe from his harm shall enter Paradise." They said, "O Messenger of Allah, this is very prevalent in your ummah today." He ﷺ said, "And it will be likewise in the generations after me."[4]

Ḥāfiẓ al-Mundhirī said, "It was narrated by Ibn Abī al-Dunyā, and Ḥākim (and the wording is his) who said its chain is authentic."

ʿĀ'ishah narrated that the Prophet ﷺ said, "There are six whom I have cursed and whom Allah has cursed - and every Prophet's supplication is

---

(1) *Al-Jinn*, 1-2.

(2) *Tirmidhī* (2850).

(3) Ḥākim in *al-Mustadrak* (324).

(4) *Tirmidhī* (2520).

إليه هُدِيَ إلى صراطٍ مستقيم»[1].

وكما أمرَ النبيُّ عليه الصلاة والسّلامُ أُمَّتَهُ بالتمسُّكِ بكتابِ الله تعالى، أمَرَهم بالتمسُّكِ بسُنَّتِهِ ﷺ، وكما حذَّر أُمَّتَهُ من تركِ العمل بكتاب اللهِ تعالى حذَّرَهُم من تركِ العملِ بما جاء عنه ﷺ.

روى الحاكمُ وقال: صحيحُ الإسنادِ عن ابنِ عبّاسٍ رَضِيَ اللَّهُ عَنْهُمَا أنَّ رسولَ اللهِ ﷺ: خطبَ النَّاسَ في حِجَّةِ الوداعِ، فقال ﷺ: «إنَّ الشَّيطانَ قد أَيِسَ أن يُعبَدَ بأرضِكم، ولكنْ رَضِيَ أن يُطاع فيما سوى ذلك ممّا تُحاقِرونَ من أعمالِكم فاحذَروا، إنّي قد تركتُ فيكم ما إنِ اعتصمتُمْ به فلن تضِلّوا أبداً، كتابَ اللهِ تعالى، وسنَّةَ نبيِّهِ»[2]. الحديثَ كما في (ترغيبِ المنذريّ).

وعن أبي سعيدٍ الخدريّ رَضِيَ اللَّهُ عَنْهُ قال: قال رسولُ اللهِ ﷺ: «مَن أكل طيّباً وعَمِلَ في سُنّةٍ، وأَمِنَ النّاسُ بوائِقَه - أي: أذاهُ وشرَّهُ - دخلَ الجنَّةَ»، قالوا: يا رسولَ اللهِ إنَّ هذا في أمّتِكَ اليومَ كثيرٌ، قال ﷺ: «وسيكونُ في قرونٍ بعدي»[3]. قال الحافظُ المنذريُّ: رواه ابنُ أبي الدُّنيا، والحاكمُ - واللَّفظُ له - وقال: صحيحُ الإسناد. اهـ.

وعن عائشةَ رَضِيَ اللَّهُ عَنْهَا أنَّ رسولَ الله ﷺ قال: «ستّةٌ لعنْتُهُمْ ولعنَهُمُ اللهُ وكلُّ نبيٍّ مُجاب: الزّائدُ في كتابِ اللهِ عزَّ وجل، والمكذِّبُ بقدَرِ اللهِ، والمتسلِّطُ على أُمَّتي بالجبروتِ؛ لِيُذِلَّ مَن أعزَّ اللهُ، ويُعِزَّ من أذلَّ اللهُ، والمستحِلُّ حرمةَ اللهِ تعالى،

---

(١) أخرجه الترمذي (٢٨٥٠).

(٢) أخرجه الحاكم في المستدرك (٣٢٤).

(٣) أخرجه الترمذي (٢٥٢٠).

accepted: the one who adds to the Book of Allah Almighty and Exalted; the one who denies Allah's predestination (*qadar*); the one who takes control over my ummah by force, to disgrace those whom Allah has honoured and to honour those whom Allah has disgraced; the one who violates Allah's sacred things; the one who violates what Allah has made sacred of my family; and the one who abandons the *Sunnah*."(1)

Mundhirī said, "Ṭabarānī narrated it in *al-Kabīr*, Ibn Ḥibbān in his *Ṣaḥīḥ*, and Ḥākim, who said its chain is authentic and I know of no defect for it."

WHOMSOEVER THE QUR'AN REACHES IS AS THOUGH THEY HAVE SEEN THE MESSENGER OF ALLAH ﷺ AND HEARD FROM HIM

Ibn Mardawayh, Abū Nuʿaym, and Khaṭīb reported on the authority of Ibn ʿAbbās ؓ that the Prophet ﷺ said, "Whomsoever the Qur'an reaches, it is as though I have spoken it to him." He then recited, "And this Qur'an has been revealed to me so that, with it, I may warn you and whoever it reaches."(2)

Regarding the saying of Allah Most High: "And this Qur'an has been revealed to me so that, with it, I may warn you and whoever it reaches",(3) Muhammad ibn Kaʿb al-Quraẓī said, "Whomsoever the Qur'an has reached, it is as though they have seen the Prophet ﷺ."

In another narration, he said, "Whomsoever the Qur'an reaches – such that they understand and comprehend it –they are like the person who saw the Messenger of Allah ﷺ and spoke to him."(4) In other words, they have no argument for their turning away and their deficiency. Ibn Abī Shaybah, Ibn Jarīr, Ibn al-Mundhir and others narrated it.

(1) *Tirmidhī* (2154).

(2) Al-Anʿām, 19; *Tārīkh Baghdād*, vol. 2, p. 49.

(3) *Al-Anʿām*, 19.

(4) Suyūṭī in *al-Durr al-Manthūr*, vol. 3, p. 257.

والمستحِلُّ مِن عِترتي ما حرَّمَ اللهُ تعالى، والتّاركُ السُّنَّةَ»[1].

قال المنذريُّ: رواه الطبرانيُّ في (الكبير)، وابنُ حِبّان في صحيحه، والحاكمُ، وقال: صحيحُ الإسنادِ، ولا أعرِفُ له علّةً. اه.

مَن بَلَغَهُ القرآنُ فكأنّما رأى رسولَ اللهِ صلى الله عليه وسلم وسمع منه

أخرج ابنُ مَرْدَوَيْه وأبو نُعيم والخطيبُ عن ابنِ عبّاسٍ رَضِيَ اللهُ عَنْهُمَا أنَّ النبيَّ صَلَّى اللهُ عَلَيْهِ وَآلِهِ وَسَلَّمَ قال: «مَن بَلَغَهُ القرآنُ فكأنّما شافهتُهُ به - أي: كلَّمتُهُ - ثمَّ قرأ {وَأُوحِيَ إِلَيَّ هَٰذَا الْقُرْآنُ لِأُنذِرَكُم بِهِ وَمَن بَلَغَ}[2]»[3].

وعن محمّدِ بنِ كعبٍ القرظيّ في قوله تعالى: {وَأُوحِيَ إِلَيَّ هَٰذَا الْقُرْآنُ لِأُنذِرَكُم بِهِ وَمَن بَلَغَ}[4] قال: مَن بلَغَهُ القرآنُ فكأنّما رأى النبيّ صلى الله عليه وآله وسلم.

وفي روايةٍ عنه أنه قال: مَن بلَغَهُ القرآنُ حتّى يفهمَهُ ويعقِلَهُ كان كمَن عايَنَ رسولَ الله صلى الله عليه وآله وسلم، وكلّمه[5]. أي: فلا حجّةَ له في إعراضِهِ وتقصيرِهِ. رواه ابنُ أبي شيبةَ وابنُ جَريرٍ وابنُ المنذرِ وغيرُهم.

---

(١) أخرجه الترمذي (٢١٥٤).

(٢) الأنعام: ١٩.

(٣) أخرجه الخطيب البغدادي في تاريخ بغداد (٢/٤٩).

(٤) الأنعام: ١٩.

(٥) ذكره السيوطي في (الدر المنثور) (٣/٢٥٧).

WARNING MUSLIMS AGAINST NOT ACTING UPON THE NOBLE QUR'AN

Allah Most High sent down His Noble Book to be followed and implemented, not to be neglected or treated carelessly. Thus, it is necessary upon every accountable (*mukallaf*) person to have believe in the beliefs of this Qur'an, comply with its commands, and refrain from its prohibitions.

Allah Most High said, "This is a blessed Book We have revealed. So follow it and be mindful [of Allah], so you may be shown mercy."(1) In other words, fulfil its commands and refrain from its prohibitions.

WARNING AGAINST DISCONNECTING THE SUNNAH FROM THE QUR'AN AND CLAIMING THERE IS NO NEED FOR IT

Allah Most High said, "Whatever the Messenger gives you, take it. And whatever he forbids you from, leave it."(2)

Therefore, whoever does not act upon the *Sunnah* is not acting upon the Qur'an, as the explicit wording of this verse states. Moreover, Allah Most High has paired the Qur'an and the *Sunnah* together due to their being mutually indispensable. He Most High said, "Allah has revealed to you the Book and wisdom."(3) The meaning of wisdom here is the *Sunnah* of Prophet Muhammad ﷺ, consisting of his sayings, actions, and confirmations. It has come down through Revelation from Allah Most High and it is an explanation of Allah's Book.

He Most High said, "Remember Allah's favours upon you as well as the Book and wisdom (i.e., the *Sunnah*) He has sent down."(4) And He Most High said, "[Always] remember what is recited in your homes of Allah's

(1) *Al-An'ām*, 155.

(2) *Al-Ḥashr*, 7.

(3) *Al-Nisā'*, 113.

(4) *Al-Baqarah*, 231.

تحذيرُ المسلمِ من تركِ العملِ بالقرآنِ الكريم

إن اللهَ تعالى أنزل كتابَهُ الكريمَ للاتّباعِ والعملِ، لا للهجرِ والكسلِ، فحقٌّ على كلِّ مكلَّفٍ الاعتقادُ بعقائدِ هذا القرآنِ، والائتمارُ بأوامرِهِ، والانتهاءُ عن مناهيه.

قال اللهُ تعالى: {وَهَذَا كِتَابٌ أَنْزَلْنَاهُ مُبَارَكٌ فَاتَّبِعُوهُ وَاتَّقُوا لَعَلَّكُمْ تُرْحَمُونَ}[1]. أي: فاتَّبِعوا أوامرَهُ، واتَّقوا مناهيه.

التحذيرُ من فصلِ السُّنّةِ عن القرآنِ ومِن دَعوى الاستغناءِ به عن السُّنّةِ

قال اللهُ تعالى: {وَمَا آتَاكُمُ الرَّسُولُ فَخُذُوهُ وَمَا نَهَاكُمْ عَنْهُ فَانتَهُوا}[2] الآيةَ.

فمَن لم يعمَلْ بالسُّنَّةِ لم يعملْ بالقرآنِ كما هو نصُّ الآيةِ، وقد قرنَ اللهُ تعالى بين الكتابِ والسُّنَّةِ؛ لتلازُمِهما، فقال تعالى: {وَأَنزَلَ اللَّهُ عَلَيْكَ الْكِتَابَ وَالْحِكْمَةَ}[3]، والمراد بالحكمةِ هنا: السُّنّةُ النبويّةُ المحمديّةُ المشتملةُ على أقوالِهِ وأفعالِهِ وتقريراتِهِ ﷺ، فهي نازلةٌ بالوحي من اللهِ تعالى، وهي بيانٌ لكتابِ الله تعالى.

وقال تعالى: {وَاذْكُرُوا نِعْمَتَ اللَّهِ عَلَيْكُمْ وَمَا أَنزَلَ عَلَيْكُم مِّنَ الْكِتَابِ وَالْحِكْمَةِ}[4] أي: السُّنّةَ.

---

(١) الأنعام: ١٥٥.

(٢) الحشر: ٧.

(٣) النساء: ١١٣.

(٤) الجن: ٢١٣.

Revelations and [prophetic] wisdom (i.e., the *Sunnah*)."[1]

Allah Most High also commanded the Prophet ﷺ to teach his ummah the Book and wisdom. He Most High said, "He is the One Who raised for the illiterate [people] a messenger from among themselves - reciting to them His Revelations, purifying them, and teaching them the Book and wisdom, for indeed they had previously been clearly astray."[2]

Furthermore, the Prophet ﷺ informed of the misguided person who will claim to suffice upon the Book of Allah Most High to understand what is lawful and unlawful, without referring to the hadiths of the Messenger of Allah ﷺ. In fact, this person will reject and turn away from hadiths. The Prophet ﷺ warned against the misguiding of such people.

Tirmidhī and Abū Dāwūd narrated on the authority of Miqdām ibn Ma'dī Karib ؓ that the Messenger of Allah ﷺ said, "Perhaps there will be a man to whom a hadith of mine reaches whilst he is reclining on his couch, and he will say, 'Between us and you is the Book of Allah. Whatever we find to be lawful in there we consider lawful, and whatever we find to be unlawful in there we consider unlawful.' Indeed, what the Messenger of Allah ﷺ has deemed unlawful is just the same as what Allah made unlawful."[3] This is the narration of Tirmidhī.

The narration of Abū Dāwūd states that the Messenger of Allah ﷺ said, "Listen! I have been given this Book and the likes thereof with it. Listen! There will soon be a man, having eaten to his fill and on his couch, saying, 'Stick to this Qur'an. So, whatever you find to be lawful therein, take it as lawful. And whatever you find to be unlawful therein, take it as unlawful.' Listen! Neither domesticated donkeys are lawful for you, nor predatory animals with fangs, nor the found property of a *mu 'āhid*[4] unless its owner

(1) *Al-Aḥzāb*, 34.

(2) *Al-Jumu 'ah*, 2.

(3) *Tirmidhī* (2664).

(4) Translator's Note: A *mu 'āhid* is a non-Muslim who enters into a pact ensuring their protection and security whilst they reside in Muslim lands.

وقال تعالى: {وَاذْكُرْنَ مَا يُتْلَىٰ فِي بُيُوتِكُنَّ مِنْ آيَاتِ اللَّهِ وَالْحِكْمَةِ}[1] أي: السُّنّة.

وقد أمر اللهُ تعالى النبيَّ صلى الله عليه آله وسلم أن يعلِّمَ أُمَّتهُ الكتابَ والحكمةَ قال تعالى: {هُوَ الَّذِي بَعَثَ فِي الْأُمِّيِّينَ رَسُولاً مِّنْهُمْ يَتْلُو عَلَيْهِمْ آيَاتِهِ وَيُزَكِّيهِمْ وَيُعَلِّمُهُمُ الْكِتَابَ وَالْحِكْمَةَ وَإِن كَانُوا مِن قَبْلُ لَفِي ضَلَالٍ مُّبِينٍ}[2]. وقد أخبرَ النبيُّ ﷺ عن الرَّجلِ الضّالِّ، الذي يزعمُ أنّه يكتفي في معرفةِ الحلالِ والحرامِ بكتابِ اللهِ تعالى، من غيرِ أن يرجعَ إلى أحاديثِ رسولِ اللهِ ﷺ؛ بل يردُّها ويُعرِضُ عنها، وحذَّرَ ﷺ من تضليلِه. فقد روى الترمذيُّ وأبو داودَ عن المقدامِ بن مَعدِي كرِبٍ رضي الله عنه قال: قال رسولُ اللهِ صلى الله عليه وآله وسلم: «ألَا هل عسى رجلٌ يبلُغهُ الحديثُ عنّي وهو متّكِئٌ على أريكتِهِ، فيقولُ: بينَنا وبينَكم كتابُ اللهِ، فما وجَدْنا فيه حلالًا استحلَلْناهُ، وما وجَدنا فيه حراماً حرَّمناهُ، وإنَّ ما حرَّمَ رسولُ اللهِ الله ﷺ كما حرَّمَ اللهُ»[3]. هذه رواية الترمذيّ.

وروايةُ أبي داودَ قال: قال رسولُ الله ﷺ: «ألَا إنّي أُوتيتُ هذا الكتابَ ومثلَهُ معَه، ألَا يوشِكُ رجلٌ شبعانُ على أريكتِهِ، يقول: عليكُم بهذا القرآنِ فما وجَدتُم فيه من حلالٍ فأحِلُّوه، وما وجدتُم فيه من حرامٍ فحرِّموه، ألَا لا يَحِلُّ لكم الحمارُ الأهليُّ، ولا كلُّ ذي نابٍ من السِّباعِ، ولا لُقَطَةُ مُعاهدٍ إلا أن يستغنيَ عنها صاحبُها، ومَن نزل بقومٍ فعليهم أن يُقروهُ، فإن لم يُقروه فله أن يَعقِبَهم بمثلِ قِراه»[4].

---

(١) الأحزاب: ٣٤.

(٢) الجمعة: ٢.

(٣) أخرجه الترمذي (٢٦٦٤).

(٤) أخرجه أبو داود (٤٦٠٤).

does not care for it. Whoever lodges with a people, then it is their duty to provide hospitality to them. But if they do not provide it to them, they are entitled to take from them their rightful hospitality as reimbursement."[1]

Allāmah al-Khaṭṭābi said in the commentary of this hadith, "His saying 'I have been given this Book and the likes thereof with it' has two possible interpretations.

The first is that it means he was granted hidden Revelation that is unrecited just as he was granted apparent Revelation that is recited. The second is that he was granted the Book as Revelation, and was granted the likes thereof as explanation. In other words, he was given permission to clarify the Book; thus, he could specify, generalize, add [explanation] to it, and legislate that which is not in the Book. Thus, in terms of the necessity to follow and accept it, it is like the apparent, recited text of the Qur'an."

Abū Rāfi' ؓ narrated that the Messenger of Allah ﷺ said, "Let it not come to my knowledge that a matter I have ordained or prohibited comes to a man amongst you who is reclining on his couch, and he then says, 'We do not know what this is. We have the Book of Allah and this is not in there.' It does not behove the Messenger of Allah ﷺ to say that which opposes the Qur'an when it is through the Qur'an that Allah has guided him."[2] Abū Dāwūd and Tirmidhī narrated it.

WARNING THE MUSLIM AGAINST NEGLECTING THE QUR'ANIC COMMANDS

'Abd al-Raḥmān ibn Shibl ؓ narrated that the Prophet ﷺ said, "Recite the Qur'an and act upon it. Do not be neglectful of it, do not exceed the limits regarding it, do not eat through it, and do not amass wealth through it."[3] Aḥmad narrated it in the *Musnad*, and it states in *al-Fatḥ* that its chain

(1) *Abū Dāwūd* (4604).

(2) *Abū Dāwūd* (4605).

(3) *Aḥmad* (15110).

قال العلّامةُ الخطّابيُّ في شرحِ هذا الحديث: قولُه ﷺ: «أُوتيتُ هذا الكتابَ ومثلَه» يحتملُ وجهينِ من التأويلِ:

أحدَهما: أنَّ معناهُ أنّه أُوتيَ من الوحيِ الباطنِ غيرِ المَتلوِّ مثلَما أُعطيَ من الظّاهرِ المَتلوِّ.

والثاني: أنّهُ ﷺ أُوتيَ الكتابَ وحياً، وأُوتيَ من البيانِ مثلَهُ، أي: أُذِنَ له أن يُبيِّنَ ما في الكتابِ فيَعُمُّ ويَخُصُّ، ويَزيدُ عليه، ويُشَرِّعُ ما ليس في الكتابِ، فيكونُ في وجوبِ العملِ به ولزومِ قَبولِهِ كالظّاهرِ المتلوِّ من القرآنِ. اهـ.

وعن أبي رافعٍ رَضِيَ اللَّهُ عَنْهُ أنَّ رسولَ اللهِ ﷺ قال: «لا أَعرِفَنَّ الرَّجلَ منكم يأتيهِ الأمرُ من أمري، إمّا أَمرتُ به أو نهيتُ عنه وهو مُتَّكِئٌ على أريكتِهِ، فيقولُ: ما ندري ما هذا، عندَنا كتابُ اللهِ وليسَ هذا فيه، وما لرسولِ اللهِ ﷺ أن يقولَ ما يُخالِفُ القرآنَ، وبالقرآنِ هداهُ اللهُ»(١).

أخرجهُ الترمذيُّ وأبو داودَ.

تحذيرُ المسلمِ من تركِ الأوامرِ القرآنيّةِ

عن عبد الرَّحمنِ بنِ شبلٍ رَضِيَ اللَّهُ عَنْهُ عن النبيِّ ﷺ قال: «اقرَؤُوا القرآنَ واعملوا به، ولا تَجفوا عنه، ولا تغلوا فيه، ولا تأكُلوا به، ولا تَستكثِروا به»(٢). رواه أحمدُ في المسندِ، وقال في (الفتح): سندُهُ قويٌّ.

وفي المسنَدِ أيضاً عن حذيفةَ رَضِيَ اللَّهُ عَنْهُ قال: قال رسولُ الله ﷺ: «يا حذَيفةُ تعلَّمْ

---

(١) أخرجه أبو داود (٤٦٠٥).

(٢) أخرجه أحمد (١٥١١٠).

is strong. Another hadith in the *Musnad* on the authority of Ḥudhayfah ﷺ states that the Messenger of Allah ﷺ said, "O Ḥudhayfah, learn the Book of Allah and follow what it contains." He said this three times.(1)

WARNING THE MUSLIM AGAINST CONSIDERING UNLAWFUL MATTERS OF THE QUR'AN AS LAWFUL

It is narrated that the Prophet ﷺ said, "That person has not believed in the Qur'an who considers its unlawful things as lawful."(2) 'Allāmah al-Ṭībī said, "Whoever considers lawful what Allah Most High has made unlawful has categorically committed disbelief. However, he mentioned the Qur'an in particular, due to its magnificence and greatness. This is the meaning of the statement of Anas ibn Mālik ﷺ, 'How many a person recites the Qur'an whilst the Qur'an curses them.'"

AMONGST THE WORST OF PEOPLE ARE THOSE WHO RECITE THE QUR'AN BUT DO NOT REPENT

Nasā'ī narrated on the authority of Abū Sa'īd ﷺ that the Messenger of Allah ﷺ delivered a sermon to the people on his way to Tabuk with his back against a date tree. He said, "Shall I not inform you of the best of people and the worst of people? The best of people is a person who strives in the path of Allah on horseback, camelback, or by foot, until death comes to him. And the worst of people is a sinful audacious person who recites the Book of Allah but does not repent."(3) In other words, he does not desist or refrain from the loathsome things prohibited by the Qur'an. Aḥmad narrated it, as did Ḥākim who authenticated it.

Ṭabarānī narrated on the authority of 'Abdullāh ibn Mas'ūd ﷺ that the

(1) *Aḥmad* (23282).

(2) *Tirmidhī* (2861).

(3) *Nasā'ī* (3106); *Aḥmad* (11319).

كتابَ اللهِ، واتَّبِع ما فيه»[1] قال ذلك ثلاثَ مرّاتٍ.

تحذيرُ المسلمِ أن يستَحِلَّ محارمَ القرآنِ

رويَ عن النبيِّ ﷺ أنّه قال: «ما آمنَ بالقرآنِ مَنِ استَحَلَّ مَحارِمَه»[2]. رواه الترمذيُّ عن صُهَيبٍ رضي الله عنه.

قال العلاّمةُ الطّيبيُّ: مَنِ استَحَلَّ ما حرَّمَ اللهُ تعالى فقد كَفَر مطلقاً، فخَصَّ القرآنَ؛ لعظمتِهِ وجلالتِهِ، وهذا معنى قولِ أنسِ بنِ مالكٍ رضي الله عنه: (رُبَّ تالٍ للقرآنِ والقرآنُ يلعنُهُ).

إنَّ مِن شرِّ النّاسِ مَن يقرأُ القرآنَ ولا يَرعَوي

روى النَّسائيُّ عن أبي سعيدٍ رضي الله عنه أنَّ رسولَ الله ﷺ خطبَ النَّاسَ عامَ تَبُوكٍ، وهو مُسنِدٌ ظهرَهُ إلى نخلةٍ، فقال: «ألَا أُخبِرُكم بخيرِ النّاسِ وشرِّ النّاس؟ إنَّ مِن خيرِ النّاسِ رجلاً عَمِلَ في سبيلِ اللهِ على ظهرِ فرسِهِ، أو على ظهرِ بعيرِهِ، أو على قَدَمَيهِ، حتّى يأتيَهُ الموتُ، وإنَّ مِن شرِّ النّاسِ رجلاً فاجراً جريئاً قرأَ كتابَ اللهِ ولا يرعوي»[3] - أي: لا ينكَفُّ ولا يَنزجِرُ - عن القُبحِ الذي نهى عنه القرآنُ. ورواه أحمدُ، والحاكمُ وصحَّحهُ. وروى الطبرانيُّ عن عبدِ اللهِ بنِ مسعودٍ رضي الله عنه أنَّ النبيَّ صلى الله عليه وآله

---

(١) أخرجه أحمد (٢٣٢٨٢).

(٢) أخرجه الترمذي (٢٨٦١).

(٣) أخرجه النسائي (٣١٠٦)، وأحمد (١١٣١٩) واللفظ له.

Prophet ﷺ said, "Recite the Qur'an for as long as it deters you. And if it does deter you, you have not truly recited it."(1) Abū Nu'aym and Daylamī narrated it, as cited in *al-Jāmi' al-Ṣaghīr* and the commentary of *al-Iḥyā'*.

The meaning is: as long as you recite the Qur'an, fulfilling its commands, and desisting from its prohibitions and reprimands, you are an accomplished reciter. In this manner, the Noble Qur'an will be a proof for you before the Lord of Honour. But if you are not like that, your condition itself is a warning and you are in a dangerous position.

Ṭabarānī narrated in *al-Kabīr* from Ibn 'Amr ﷺ that the Messenger of Allah ﷺ said, "How many a bearer of jurisprudence are there who are not jurists themselves. Whoever does not benefit from his knowledge will be harmed by his ignorance. Recite the Qur'an for as long as it stops you. If it does not stop you, then you have not truly recited it."(2) This is as cited in al-Mundhirī's *al-Targhīb*.

WHOEVER DOES NOT ACT UPON THE NOBLE QUR'AN, THEIR PUNISHMENT WILL BEGIN IN THE REALM OF BARZAKH (I.E., THE GRAVE) UNTIL THE RESURRECTION AND BEYOND

Bukhārī narrated on the authority of Samurah ibn Jundub ﷺ that the Messenger of Allah ﷺ would frequently ask his Companions if any of them had seen a dream. Then whoever Allah wished for would relate their dream to him. One morning, he ﷺ said, "Two people came to me last night (i.e., Jibrīl ﷺ and Mīkā'īl n) and woke me up. They said to me, 'Come,' so I went with them."(3) In one narration, "They took me by my hand and took me out towards the Blessed Land."(4) In a narration of Aḥmad, "[They

---

(1) Ṭabarānī in *al-Mu'jam al-Kabīr* (14543).

(2) Ṭabarānī in *Musnad al-Shāmiyyīn* (1345).

(3) *Bukhārī* (7047).

(4) *Bukhārī* (2085).

وسلم قال: «اِقرَأِ القرآنَ ما نهاكَ، فإنْ لم ينهَكَ فلستَ تقرَؤُهُ» (١). وكذا رواهُ أبو نُعيمٍ والدَّيلميُّ، كما في (الجامع الصغير) و(شرح الإحياء). والمعنى: أنَّكَ ما دُمتَ تقرأُ القرآنَ، مُؤتمِراً بأمرِهِ ومُنتهِياً بنهيِهِ وزَجرِهِ، فأنتَ القارئُ الكاملُ، وبذلك يكون القرآنُ الكريمُ حُجّةً لك بين يدي ربِّ العِزّة، وإن لم تكنْ كذلك فحالُكَ نذيرٌ، وموقفُكَ خطيرٌ.

وقد رواه الطبرانيُّ في (الكبير) عن ابنِ عمرٍو رَضِيَ اللهُ عَنهُما قال: قال رسولُ اللهِ صَلَّى اللهُ عَلَيهِ وَآلِهِ وَسَلَّمَ: «رُبَّ حاملٍ فقيرٍ غيرِ فقيهٍ، ومَن لم ينفَعْهُ عِلمُهُ ضرَّهُ جهلُه، اقرأِ القرآنَ ما نهاكَ؛ فإنْ لم ينهَكَ فلستَ تقرؤُهُ» (٢). كما في (ترغيب المنذري).

مَن لم يعملْ بما في القرآنِ الكريمِ
يبدأُ عذابُهُ في عالمِ البرزخِ - أي: القبرِ إلى ما وراءَهُ مِن الحشرِ

روى البخاريُّ عن سَمُرَةَ بنِ جُندبٍ رَضِيَ اللهُ عَنهُ قال: كان رسولُ اللهِ صَلَّى اللهُ عَلَيهِ وَآلِهِ وَسَلَّمَ يُكثِرُ أن يقولَ لأصحابِهِ: «هل رأى أحدٌ منكُم رؤيا»؟ فيقُصُّ عليه مَن شاء اللهُ أن يَقُصَّ، وإنّهُ صلى الله عليه وآله وسلم قال ذاتَ غداةٍ: «إنّهُ أتاني اللّيلةَ آتِيانِ - وهما: جبريلُ وميكائيلُ كما ورد في آخرِ الحديثِ - وإنّهما ابتَعثاني، فقالا لي: انطلِقْ، وإنّي انطلقْتُ معَهما» (٣).

وفي روايةٍ: «فأخَذا بيدي فأخرَجاني إلى الأرضِ المقدَّسةِ» (٤).

---

(١) أخرجه الطبراني في الكبير (١٤٥٤٣).

(٢) أخرجه الطبراني في الشاميين (١٣٤٥).

(٣) أخرجه البخاري (٧٠٤٧).

(٤) أخرجه البخاري (٢٠٨٥).

took me] to an open land or flat land. We came upon a man who was lying down and another man was standing over him holding a boulder. He dropped the boulder on his head and crushed it. The boulder rolled away, so he went to retrieve it. No sooner did he return that his head returned back to its former state. He then turned to him again and did to him as he did the first time." The Prophet ﷺ said, "I said, '*Subḥān Allāh*. Who are these two?'" The two Angels responded to him thereafter and said to the Prophet ﷺ, "As for the man you came upon whose head was being crushed with a stone, it was a person who acquired the Qur'an but then refused it (i.e., to practice on it) and sleeps through the obligatory prayer."(1)

In a narration of Bukhārī in the Chapter of Funerals, the two Angels said, "As for the person whose head you saw being crushed, it was a person whom Allah taught the Qur'an, but he slept heedless of it by night and did not act upon it by day. He will be dealt with in this manner until the Day of Judgement."(2) The hadith is thus in the Chapter of Funerals and the Chapter of Interpretation in *Ṣaḥīḥ al-Bukhārī*.

THE QUR'AN DISPUTING WITH THE PERSON WHO DOES NOT ACT UPON IT AND DEFENDING THE PERSON WHO ACTS UPON IT

'Abdullāh ibn 'Amr ؓ narrated that the Prophet ﷺ said, "A person will be brought on the Day of Judgement and the Qur'an will be presented before him. This person would neglect its obligations, trespass its bounds, disobey it, and perpetrate what it deemed sinful. The Qur'an will say, 'O my Lord, You made him bear my verses, but what an evil bearer of mine he was. He neglected my obligations, trespassed my bounds, disobeyed me, and perpetrated what I deemed sinful.' It will then continue presenting proofs against him until it is told, 'Do as you wish with him.' It will thus

(1) *Aḥmad* (20094).

(2) *Bukhārī* (1386).

وفي روايةِ أحمدَ: «إلى أرضٍ فضاءٍ أو أرضٍ مستويةٍ، وإنّا أتَينا على رجلٍ مضطَجعٍ، وإذا آخرُ قائمٌ عليه بصخرةٍ، وإذا هو يَهوي بالصَّخرةِ لرأسِهِ، فيَثلغُ - أي: يشْدَخ رأسهُ - فيتهَدْهَدُ الحجرُ - أي: يتدحرجُ - هاهنا، فيتبَعُ الحجرَ فيأخُذُهُ، فلا يرجعُ إليه حتى يصِحَّ رأسُهُ كما كان، ثمَّ يعودُ عليه، فيفعلُ به مثلَ ما فعلَ المرَّةَ الأُولى»، قال ﷺ: «فقلتُ لهما سبحانَ اللهِ ما هذان»؟ ثمَّ أجابَهُ الملَكانِ بعد ذلك، فقالا للنبيِّ ﷺ: «أمَّا الرَّجلُ الذي أَتيتَ عليه يثلَغُ رأسَهُ بالحجرِ؛ فإنّهُ الرَّجلُ يأخذُ القرآنَ فيرفضُهُ - أي: لا يتقبَّلُ العملَ به - وينامُ عن الصّلاةِ المكتوبةِ» [1].

وفي روايةٍ للبخاريِّ في «كتابِ الجَنائزِ»: قالا: «وأمَّا الذي رأيتَ يُشدَخُ رأسُهُ فرجلٌ علَّمَهُ اللهُ القرآنَ، فنام عنه باللَّيلِ، ولم يعملْ فيه بالنَّهارِ، يُفعَلُ به - أي: يُعذَّبُ بذلك - إلى يومِ القيامةِ» [2]. الحديثَ، كما في (كتابِ الجنائزِ والتعبيرِ من البخاريِّ).

مخاصمةُ القرآنِ لِمَن لم يعملْ به وانتصارُهُ للعاملِ بهِ

عن عبدِ اللهِ بنِ عمرٍو رَضِيَ اللهُ عَنْهُمَا عن النبيِّ ﷺ قال: «يُؤتى برجلٍ يومَ القيامةِ، ويُمثَّلُ له القرآنُ قد كان يُضيِّعُ فرائضَه، ويتعدَّى حدودَه، ويخالِفُ طاعتَه، ويركَبُ معاصيه، فيقولُ: أيْ ربِّ حَمَّلتَهُ آياتي فبئسَ حاملي، تعدَّى حدودي، وضيَّعَ فرائضي، وتركَ طاعتي، ورَكِبَ معصيتي، فما يزالُ يقذفُ عليه بالحُجَجِ حتى يُقالَ له: فشأنُكَ به، فيأخذُ بيدِهِ فما يفارقُهُ حتّى يُكِبَّهُ على مِنخَرِهِ - أي: على وجهِهِ - في النّارِ، ويُؤتى بالرَّجلِ قد كان يحفظُ حدودَ القرآنِ، ويعملُ بفرائضِهِ، ويعملُ بطاعتِهِ، ويجتنبُ معصيَتَهُ،

---

(١) أخرجه أحمد (٢٠٠٩٤).

(٢) أخرجه البخاري (١٣٨٦).

take him by the hand and not part with him until it casts him face forward into the Fire. Another man will be brought who would safeguard the limits of the Qur'an, act upon its obligations, act in obedience to it, and refrain from disobeying it. The Qur'an will argue on his behalf, saying, 'O my Lord, You made the best of bearers bear my verses. He was mindful of my limits, acted upon my obligations, obeyed me, and refrained from disobeying me.' It will then continue presenting proofs for him until it is told, 'Do as you wish with him.' It will then remain with him until it clothes him with a garment of silk, places the crown of kingdom on him, and makes him drink from the cup of kingdom."(1)

It states in *Majma ʿ al-Zawāʾid*, "Bazzār narrated it. It contains Ibn Isḥāq who is reliable but a mudallis.(2) The rest of its narrators are reliable." Ibn Abī Shaybah and Ibn Ḍurays, as stated in Muntakhab al-Kanz.

THE QUR'AN WILL BE A PROOF WITH ALLAH MOST HIGH

Abū Mālik al-Ashʿarī ﷺ narrated that the Messenger of Allah ﷺ said, "Purity is half of faith. *Al-ḥamdu lillāh* fills the Scales. *Subḥān Allāh wa al-ḥamdu lillāh* fills the expanse between the Heavens and the Earth. Prayer is a light, charity is a proof, and patience is luminance. The Qur'an is either a proof for you or against you. Every person sets off in the morning selling his soul, either setting it free or destroying it."(3) Muslim narrated it.

ʿAbd al-Raḥmān ibn ʿAwf ﷺ narrated that the Prophet ﷺ said, "Three things will be under the Throne on the Day of Judgement: the Qur'an – which will have an outer and inner – and will be the slaves' disputant; trust; and kinship which proclaim, 'Whoever joins me, may Allah Most High

(1) Ibn Abī Shaybah in *al-Muṣannaf* (30667); Bazzār, as stated in Haythamī's *Majma ʿ al-Zawāʾid*, vol. 7, p. 163.

(2) Translator's Note: A mudallis is a narrator who often omits or changes the name of their teacher in the chain of a hadith.

(3) *Muslim* (223).

فيصيرُ خصماً دونَه، فيقول: أيْ ربِّ حمّلتَ آياتي خيرَ حاملٍ: اتّقى حدودي، وعملَ بفرائضي، واتّبعَ طاعتي، واجتنبَ معصيَتي، فلا يزالُ يقذفُ له بالحُجَجِ حتّى يُقالَ له: فشأنُكَ به، فيأخُذُ بيدِهِ، فما يزالُ حتى يكسُوَهُ حُلّةَ الإستبرقِ، ويضعَ عليه تاجَ المُلكِ، ويسقيَه بكأسِ المُلكِ» [1].

قال في (مجمع الزوائد): رواهُ البزّارُ، وفيه ابنُ إسحاقَ، وهو ثقةٌ ولكنّهُ مدلِّسٌ، وبقيّةُ رجالِهِ ثقاتٌ. اهـ. ورواه ابنُ أبي شَيبةَ، وابن الضُّريس كما في (منتخب الكنز).

القرآنُ هو الحُجّةُ عند اللهِ تعالى

عن أبي مالكٍ الأشعريّ رَضِيَ اللهُ عَنْهُ قال: قال رسولُ اللهِ ﷺ: «الطُّهورُ شَطرُ الإيمانِ، والحمدُ للهِ تملأُ الميزانَ، وسبحانَ اللهِ والحمدُ للهِ تملآنِ أو تملأُ ما بينَ السّماءِ والأرضِ، والصّلاةُ نورٌ، والصَّدقةُ برهانٌ، والصَّبرُ ضياءٌ، والقرآنُ حُجّةٌ لك أو عليكَ، كلُّ النّاسِ يغدو فبائعٌ نفسَهُ فمعتِقُها أو موبِقُها» [2]. رواهُ مسلمٌ.

وعن عبدِ الرَّحمنِ بنِ عَوفٍ رَضِيَ اللهُ عَنْهُ عن النبيِّ ﷺ قال: «ثلاثةٌ تحتَ العرشِ يومَ القيامة: القرآنُ له ظهرٌ وبطنٌ يُحاجُّ العبادَ، والأمانةُ، والرَّحمُ تُنادي: ألَا مَن وصَلَني وصلَهُ اللهُ تعالى، ومَن قطَعَني قطَعَهُ اللهُ» [3]. رواهُ البغَويُّ في (شرحِ السُّنّةِ)، ورواهُ الحكيمُ الترمذيُّ، ومحمّدُ بنُ نصرٍ.

فإذا كان يومُ القيامةِ وقف القرآنُ موقفَ الاحتجاجِ، فإمّا أن يحتجَّ للعبدِ؛ وذلك

---

(١) أخرجه ابن أبي شيبة في (المصنف) (٣٠٦٦٧)، والبزار كما في (مجمع الزوائد) للهيثمي (١٦٣/٧).

(٢) رواه مسلم (٢٢٣).

(٣) أخرجه البزار (١٠٥٢).

join them. And whoever cuts me off, may Allah cut them off.'"[1] Baghawī narrated it in *Sharḥ al-Sunnah*, and Ḥakīm al-Tirmidhī and Muhammad ibn Naṣr also narrated it.

When the Day of Judgement comes, the Qur'an will assume the role of presenting evidence. It will either present evidence for the slave if they acted upon it, or it will present evidence against the slave if they opposed what the Qur'an brought.

Abū Mūsā al-Ashʿarī ﵁ said, "Indeed, this Qur'an will be a reward for you or it will be a burden against you. So, follow the Qur'an and do not make the Qur'an follow you. Whoever follows the Qur'an will be taken by it to the gardens of Paradise. But whoever makes the Qur'an follow them (by not acting on it), it will hurl them by the neck and cast them into the Fire."[2]

It is narrated that ʿAlī ﵁ said, "The Qur'an is better than everything besides Allah Most High. Thus, whoever respects it has respected Allah Most High, and whoever does not respect it has slighted the right of Allah Most High. The Qur'an is an intercessor whose intercession is accepted and a truthful witness. For whomsoever the Qur›an intercedes, its intercession will be accepted. And for whomsoever the Qur'an testifies, its testimony will be accepted. Whoever puts the Qur'an in front of them, it will lead them to Paradise. Whoever puts the Qur'an behind them, it will drag them to Hellfire."[3]

---

(1) *Bazzār* (1052).

(2) *Ibn Abī Shaybah* (34175).

(3) *Ibn Ḥibbān* (124).

إن كان عَمِلَ به، وإمّا أن يحتجَّ على العبدِ؛ وذلك إنْ كان خالَفَ ما جاء به القرآنُ.

قال أبو موسى الأشعريُّ رَضِيَ اللهُ عَنْهُ: (إنَّ هذا القرآنَ كائنٌ لكم أجراً، وكائنٌ عليكم وِزراً، فاتَّبِعوا القرآنَ ولا يتَّبِعَنَّكم القرآنُ؛ فإنّهُ مَن اتّبَعَ القرآنَ - أي: عَمِلَ به - هبطَ به على رياضِ الجنّةِ، ومَنِ اتَّبَعَهُ القرآنُ بأن لم يعملْ به زجَّ في قفاهُ، فقذفَهُ في النّارِ) [1].

وعن عليّ كرَّمَ اللهُ تعالى وجهَهُ أنّه قال: (إنَّ القرآنَ أفضلُ من كلِّ شيءٍ دونَ اللهِ تعالى، فمَن وقَّرَ القرآنَ فقد وقَّرَ اللهَ، ومَن لم يوقِّرِ القرآنَ فقد استخفَّ بحقِّ اللهِ، والقرآنُ شافعٌ مشفَّعٌ، وماحِلٌ مصدَّقٌ، فمَن شفعَ له القرآنُ شفِّعَ، ومَن مَحَلَ به القرآنُ صُدِّقَ، ومَن جعل القرآنَ أمامَهُ قادَهُ إلى الجنّةِ، ومَن جعلَهُ خَلفَهُ ساقَهُ إلى النّارِ) [2]. الأثر كما تقدَّم.

---

(١) أخرجه ابن أبي شيبة (٣٤١٧٥).

(٢) أخرجه ابن حبان (١٢٤). الماحل: الشاهد.

The specialities of certain sūrahs and verses and the encouragement to recite them

خصائصُ بعضِ السُّوَرِ والآياتِ والتّرغيبُ في قراءتِها

SŪRAH AL-FĀTIḤAH
IT IS THE GREATEST SŪRAH IN THE NOBLE QUR'AN

Bukhārī narrated on the authority of Abū Sa'īd ibn al-Mu'allā ﷺ who said, "I was praying in the masjid and the Messenger of Allah ﷺ called me, but I did not respond to him. I then came to him and said, 'O Messenger of Allah, I was praying.' He said, 'Does Allah not say, "Respond to Allah and His Messenger when he calls you to that which gives you life?"(1)' He then said, 'Shall I teach you a *sūrah* which is the greatest *sūrah* in the Qur'an?' He then said, 'All praise is for Allah, Lord of the worlds. It is the seven oft-repeated verses and the great Qur'an that I have been granted.'"(2)

SŪRAH AL-FĀTIḤAH IS THE MOST VIRTUOUS PART

It is narrated on the authority of Anas ﷺ that the Prophet ﷺ said, "The most virtuous part of the Qur'an is 'All praise is for Allah, Lord of the worlds.'(3)"(4)

(1) *Al-Anfāl*, 24.

(2) *Bukhārī* (4474).

(3) *Al-Fātiḥah*, 1.

(4) *Ibn Ḥibbān* (774); *Ḥākim* (2056).

سورةُ الفاتحةِ هي أعظمُ سورةٍ في القرآنِ الكريمِ

روى البخاريُّ عن أبي سعيدِ بنِ المُعَلَّى رضي اللهُ تعالى عنه قال: كنتُ أُصلّي في المسجدِ، فدعاني رسولُ اللهِ ﷺ فلم أُجِبْه، ثُمَّ أَتَيْتُهُ فقلتُ: يا رسولَ اللهِ إنّي كنتُ أُصلّي، فقال: «أَلَمْ يَقُلِ اللهُ تعالى: {اسْتَجِيبُوا لِلَّهِ وَلِلرَّسُولِ إِذَا دَعَاكُمْ لِمَا يُحْيِيكُمْ}[1]»، ثمَّ قال لي: «لأُعلّمنَكَ سورةً هي أعظمُ سورةٍ في القرآنِ»، فقال صلى اللهُ عليه وآلهِ وسلَّمَ: «{الْحَمْدُ لِلَّهِ رَبِّ الْعَالَمِينَ} هي السَّبعُ المثاني، والقرآنُ العظيمُ الذي أُوتيتُهُ»[2].

سورةُ الفاتحةِ هي أفضلُ القرآنِ الكريمِ

عن أنسٍ عن النبيِّ ﷺ قال: «أفضلُ القرآنِ {الْحَمْدُ لِلَّهِ رَبِّ الْعَالَمِينَ}»[3].

---

(١) الأنفال: ٢٤.

(٢) أخرجه البخاري (٤٤٧٤).

(٣) أخرجه ابن حبان (٧٧٤)، والحاكم (٢٠٥٦).

SŪRAH AL-FĀTIḤAH IS THE ESSENCE OF THE NOBLE QUR'AN

Tirmidhī narrated on the authority of Abū Hurayrah ﷺ that the Messenger of Allah ﷺ came out to Ubayy ibn Kaʿb ﷺ and called him whilst he was praying. He turned around but did not reply. Ubayy ﷺ shortened his prayer and then went to the Messenger of Allah ﷺ and said, "Peace be upon you, O Messenger of Allah." The Messenger of Allah ﷺ said, "Peace be upon you also. What stopped you from replying when I called you, O Ubayy?" He said, "O Messenger of Allah, I was in prayer." He ﷺ said, "Did you not find, 'Respond to Allah and His Messenger when he calls you to that which gives you life' amongst that which has been revealed to me?" Ubayy ﷺ said, "Yes. I will not do it again – if Allah wills." He said, "Do you want me to teach you a *sūrah* the like of which has not been revealed in the Torah, Evangel, Psalms, and even in the Criterion (i.e., the Qur'an)?" He said, "Yes, O Messenger of Allah." He then recited the Essence of the Qur'an (Umm al-Qur'an). He ﷺ said, "By the One in Whose Hand lies my soul, the likes thereof has not been revealed in the Torah, Evangel, Psalms, and even in the Qur'an. It is the seven oft-repeated verses and the great Qur'an I have been granted."(1) *Sūrah al-Fātiḥah* is called the Essence of the Qur'an because the essence (*umm*) of a thing is its origin and source. This is why Mecca is called the Mother of all cities (Umm al-Qurā), because it is the origin. The first part of the Earth created by Allah Most High is this piece, after which the rest of the earth was spread out from underneath it.

Moreover, all cities return to it in their prayer and their pilgrimage. It was here that the Messenger of Allah ﷺ was sent to the entirety of mankind from the east to the west. In a similar manner, all of the objectives of the Qur'an and its core meanings return summarily to *Sūrah al-Fātiḥah*, due to it comprising divine issues (*ilāhiyyāt*), prophetic issues (*nubuwwāt*), religious laws, the states of the beginning (*mabdaʾ*) and afterlife (*ma ʿād*),

(1) *Tirmidhī* (2875).

سورةُ الفاتحةِ أمُّ القرآنِ الكريمِ

روى الترمذيُّ عن أبي هريرةَ رَضِيَ اللهُ عَنْهُ أنَّ رسولَ اللهِ صلى اللهُ عليه وسلَّمَ خرج على أُبَيِّ بنِ كعبٍ، فقال صَلَّى اللهُ عَلَيْهِ وَآلِهِ وَسَلَّمَ: «يا أُبَيُّ»، وهو - أي: أُبَيٌّ - يُصلِّي، فالتفتَ فلم يُجبْهُ، وصلّى أُبَيٌّ فخفَّفَ، ثمَّ انصرفَ إلى رسولِ اللهِ صَلَّى اللهُ عَلَيْهِ وَآلِهِ وَسَلَّمَ، فقال: السّلامُ عليكَ يا رسولَ اللهِ، فقال رسولُ اللهِ صَلَّى اللهُ عَلَيْهِ وَآلِهِ وَسَلَّمَ: «وعليكَ السَّلامُ، ما منعكَ يا أُبَيُّ أن تُجيبَني إذ دَعوتُكَ»، فقال: يا رسولَ اللهِ إنّي كنتُ في الصّلاةِ، قال: «أفلمْ تجدْ فيما أُوحيَ إليّ أنِ {اسْتَجِيبُوا لِلَّهِ وَلِلرَّسُولِ إِذَا دَعَاكُمْ لِمَا يُحْيِيكُمْ} (١)»؟، قال أُبَيٌّ: بلى ولا أعودُ إن شاء اللهُ، قال: «تُحبُّ أنْ أعلِّمَكَ سورةً لم يَنزلْ في التّوراةِ، ولا في الإنجيلِ، ولا في الزّبورِ، ولا في الفُرقانِ مثلُها»؟ قال: نعم يا رسولَ اللهِ، فقال رسولُ اللهِ صلى اللهُ عليه وآلِهِ وسلَّمَ: «كيف تقرأُ في الصّلاةِ؟»، فقرأَ أمَّ القرآنِ، فقال صَلَّى اللهُ عَلَيْهِ وَآلِهِ وَسَلَّمَ: «والذي نفسي بيدِهِ ما أُنزلَتْ في التّوراةِ، ولا في الإنجيلِ، ولا في الزّبورِ، ولا في القرآنِ مثلُها، وإنّها سبعٌ من المثاني، والقرآنُ العظيمُ الذي أعطيتُه» (٢).

فسورةُ الفاتحةِ تُسمّى أُمَّ القرآنِ؛ وذلك لأنَّ أمَّ الشيءِ أصلُهُ ومرجِعُهُ، ولذلك سُمّيَتْ مكّةُ أُمَّ القُرى؛ لأنَّها الأصلُ؛ فإنَّ أوّلَ ما خلق اللهُ تعالى من الأرض تلك البقعةَ، ثم دُحيَتِ الأرضُ من تحتِها، وإليها ترجعُ سائرُ القُرى في صلاتِها وحجِّها، وفيها بُعثَ رسولُ اللهِ صَلَّى اللهُ عَلَيْهِ وَآلِهِ وَسَلَّمَ إلى النّاسِ كافّةً في مشارقِ الأرضِ ومغاربِها، وكذلك سورةُ الفاتحةِ ترجعُ إليها سائرُ مقاصدِ القرآنِ ومجامعِ علومِهِ إجمالاً؛ لِما تضمّنَتْهُ من الإلهيّاتِ،

---

(١) الأنفال: ٢٤.

(٢) أخرجه الترمذي (٢٨٧٥).

and so forth – as explained by the expert scholars. Sayyidunā ʿAlī ﷺ said, "If I wanted, I could load 70 camels with the exegesis of *Sūrah al-Fātiḥah*."[1]

SŪRAH AL-FĀTIḤAH IS CALLED THE CHAPTER OF SECRETLY CONVERSING (SŪRAH AL-MUNĀJĀH)

Abū Hurayrah ﷺ narrated that he heard the Messenger of Allah ﷺ say, "Allah Most High said, 'I have divided the prayer between Myself and My slave into two parts, and My slave will have what He requests. When he says, 'All praise is for Allah, Lord of all worlds', Allah Most High says, 'My slave has praised Me.' When he says, 'The Most Compassionate, Most Merciful', Allah Most High says, 'My slave has extolled Me.' When he says, 'Master of the Day of Judgement', Allah Most High says, 'My slave has exalted Me (and on one occasion, he said: My slave has consigned to Me.' When he says, 'You [alone] we worship and You [alone] we ask for help', He says, 'This is between Me and My slave, and My slave will have what he requests.' When he says, 'Guide us along the Straight Path, the Path of those You have blessed – not of those You are displeased with, or those who are astray', Allah says, 'This is for My slave, and My slave will have what he requests.'"[2] Muslim narrated it. In a narration of Bayhaqī, "When he says (at the beginning of *Sūrah al-Fātiḥah*), 'In the name of Allah, the Most Compassionate, Most Merciful', Allah Most High says, 'My slave has remembered Me.'"[3]

IT IS CALLED THE CURER (AL-SHĀFIYAH) AND THE INCANTATION (AL-RUQYAH)

Abū Saʿīd ﷺ narrated, "We were on a journey and dismounted somewhere when a girl came and said, 'The leader of this tribe has been bitten. Does any one of you treat through incantations (*ruqyah*)?' A man whom we did

(1) *Qūt al-Qulūb*, vol. 1, p. 50.

(2) *Muslim* (395).

(3) Bayhaqī in *al-Sunan al-Kubrā*.

والنُّبوّاتِ، والشَّرائعِ، وأحوالِ المَبدَأِ والمعادِ، ونحوِ ذلك كما بيَّنهُ المحقِّقونَ. قال سيِّدُنا عليٌّ كرَّمَ اللهُ وجهَهُ: (لو شئتُ لأَوقَرتُ سبعينَ بعيراً من تفسيرِ فاتحةِ الكتابِ) (١).

سورةُ الفاتحةِ تُسمَّى سورةَ المناجاةِ

عن أبي هريرةَ رَضِيَ اللهُ عَنْهُ قال: سمعتُ رسولَ اللهِ صَلَّى اللهُ عَلَيْهِ وَسَلَّمَ يقول: «قال اللهُ تعالى: قسمتُ الصَّلاةَ بيني وبينَ عبدي نصفَينِ، ولعبدي ما سألَ، فإذا قالَ: {الْحَمْدُ لِلَّهِ رَبِّ الْعَالَمِينَ}، قال اللهُ تعالى: حَمِدَني عبدي، وإذا قال: {الرَّحْمَٰنِ الرَّحِيمِ}، قال اللهُ تعالى: أثنى عليَّ عبدي، فإذا قال: {مَالِكِ يَوْمِ الدِّينِ}، قال اللهُ تعالى: مجَّدَني عبدي، وقال مرَّةً: فوَّضَ إليَّ عبدي، فإذا قال: {إِيَّاكَ نَعْبُدُ وَإِيَّاكَ نَسْتَعِينُ} قال: هذا بيني وبينَ عبدي، ولعبدي ما سَأَلَ، فإذا قال: {اهْدِنَا الصِّرَاطَ الْمُسْتَقِيمَ صِرَاطَ الَّذِينَ أَنْعَمْتَ عَلَيْهِمْ غَيْرِ الْمَغْضُوبِ عَلَيْهِمْ وَلَا الضَّالِّينَ} قال اللهُ: هذا لعبدي ولعبدي ما سألَ» (٢). رواهُ مسلمٌ. وفي روايةٍ للبيهقيِّ: «فإذا قال: {بِسْمِ اللَّهِ الرَّحْمَٰنِ الرَّحِيمِ} يعني: في أوَّلِ الفاتحةِ ، قال اللهُ تعالى: ذكَرَني عبدي» (٣).

وتُسمَّى الشَّافيةَ والرُّقيةَ

عن أبي سعيدٍ رَضِيَ اللهُ عَنْهُ قال: كنّا في مسيرٍ لنا فنزَلنا، فجاءت جاريةٌ، فقالت: إن سيِّدَ الحيِّ سَليمٌ – أي: لديغٌ - فهل منكم راقٍ؟ فقام معها رجلٌ ما كُنّا نأبِنَهُ برقيةٍ، فرَقاهُ –

---

(١) ينظر (قوت القلوب) (١/٥٠).

(٢) أخرجه مسلم (٣٩٥).

(٣) أخرجه البيهقي في السنن الكبرى (٢٣٦٨).

not know to treat through incantations went with her and treated him (i.e., read *Sūrah al-Fātiḥah* over him). He was thus cured, instructed that 30 goats be given to him, and he also gave us milk to drink. When he (i.e., Abū Sa'īd) returned, we said to him, 'Did you know from before how to treat with incantations properly?' He said, 'I did not treat him except with Umm al-Kitāb (i.e., Sūrah al-Fātiḥah).' We said, 'Do not relate anything (regarding the goats) until we ask the Messenger of Allah ﷺ.' When we arrived in Medina, we mentioned it to the Prophet ﷺ and he said, 'How did he know it is an incantation? Distribute the goats amongst yourselves and give me a share also.'"[1] This is proof for the permissibility of using incantations comprising the Qur'an, and also proof for those who say it is permissible to take remuneration upon reciting.

IT IS CALLED THE CURE (AL-SHIFĀ')

Dārimī narrated on the authority of Abū Sa'īd ؓ that the Prophet ﷺ said, "The Opener of the Book is a cure for every poison."[2]

IT IS CALLED THE OPENER OF THE BOOK (FĀTIḤAH AL-KITĀB)

Muslim narrated on the authority of Ibn 'Abbās ؓ who said, "Whilst Jibrīl ؑ was sitting with the Prophet ﷺ, he (i.e., the Prophet ﷺ) heard a sound from above and looked up towards the sky. He (i.e., Jibrīl) said, 'This is a door in the Heavens which has opened today and has never opened before.' Then an Angel came down from it and Jibrīl said, 'This is an Angel who has come down to Earth and he has never come down except today.' He greeted with *salām* and said, 'Rejoice over two lights which you have been given and which no Prophet has ever been given before you: the

---

(1) *Bukhārī* (2276).

(2) Dārimī in his *Sunan* (3370).

أي: فقرأَ عليه سورةَ الفاتحةِ - فَبَرِئَ، فأَمَرَ له بثلاثين شاةً، وسقانا لَبَناً، فلمّا رجعَ - أبوسعيدٍ - قلنا له: أكنتَ تُحسِنُ الرُّقيةَ؟ قال: لا، ما رَقَيتُ إلا بأمّ الكتابِ - أي: سورةِ الفاتحة - قلنا: لا تُحدِثوا شيئاً - في الشِّياهِ - حتّى نسألَ رسولَ اللهِ ﷺ، فلمّا قَدِمنا المدينةَ ذكرناهُ للنبيِّ ﷺ، فقال: «وما يُدريهِ أنّها رقيةٌ؟ اقسِموا الشِّياهَ واضربوا لي بسهمٍ» [1]. رواهُ البخاريُّ. وفي هذا دليلُ مشروعيّةِ الرُّقيةِ بالقرآنِ، ودليلُ مَن قال: بجوازِ أخذِ الأُجرَةِ على القراءةِ.

وتُسمّى الشِّفاءَ

روى الدارميُّ عن أبي سعيدٍ عن النبيِّ ﷺ قال: «فاتحةُ الكتابِ شفاءٌ مِن كلِّ سُمٍّ» [2].

وتسمّى فاتحةَ الكتابِ

روى مسلمٌ عن ابنِ عبّاسٍ رضي الله عنهما قال: (بينما جبريلُ عليه السّلامُ قاعدٌ عند النبيِّ صلى الله عليه وآله وسلم إذ سمعَ نقيضاً - أي: صوتاً - من فوقِهِ، فرفع رأسَهُ إلى السّماءِ، فقال - أي: جبريلُ -: هذا بابٌ من السّماءِ فُتِحَ اليومَ لم يُفتَحْ قطُّ إلا اليوم، فنزلَ منه مَلَكٌ، فقال جبريلُ: هذا مَلَكٌ نزل إلى الأرضِ لم ينزِلْ قطُّ إلا اليومَ، فسلَّمَ وقال: أبشِرْ بنورَينِ أُوتيتَهما لم يُؤتَهما نبيٌّ قبلَكَ: فاتحةِ الكتابِ، وخواتيمِ سورةِ البقرةِ، لم تَقرأْ بحرفٍ منهما

---

(١) أخرجه البخاري (٢٢٧٦).

(٢) أخرجه الدارمي في سننه (٣٣٧٠).

Opener of the Book (*Fātiḥah al-Kitāb*) and the last verses of *Sūrah al-Baqarah*. You will not recite a single letter of them except that you will be granted it.'"[1]

It is also called the Sufficer (al-Kāfiyah) as it suffices from others besides it, and it is called the Treasure (al-Kanz), as well as many other names.

IT IS THE MOST VIRTUOUS SŪRAH IN THE NOBLE QUR'AN

Ibn Ḥibbān narrated in his *Ṣaḥīḥ*, and Ḥākim – who said it is authentic according to the criteria of Muslim – on the authority of Anas ﷺ who said, "The Prophet ﷺ was on a journey when he dismounted and a man dismounted next to him. The Prophet ﷺ turned to him and said, 'Shall I not inform you of the most virtuous part of the Qur'an?' He said, 'Yes, of course.' He recited, 'All praise is for Allah, Lord of the worlds.'"[2] This is as cited in al-Mundhirī's *al-Targhīb*.

THE VIRTUES OF SŪRAH AL-BAQARAH IN GENERAL AND THE SPECIFIC VIRTUES OF CERTAIN VERSES SŪRAH AL-BAQARAH IS THE PEAK OF THE QUR'AN

It is narrated on the authority of Ma'qil ibn Yasār ﷺ that the Messenger of Allah ﷺ said, "*Al-Baqarah* is the peak of the Qur'an and its pinnacle. With every verse, 80000 Angels came down. *Āyah al-Kursī*[3] (the Verse of the Throne) was extracted from a treasure under the Throne and then joined with *Sūrah al-Baqarah*. *Yā Sīn* is the heart of the Qur'an. No person reads it seeking Allah and the abode of the Hereafter except that they will be forgiven. Recite it over your deceased."[4] Aḥmad narrated it.

---

(1) *Muslim* (806).

(2) *Ibn Ḥibbān* (774).

(3) *Al-Baqarah*, 255.

(4) *Aḥmad* (20300).

إلا أُعطيتَه»[1]. وتسمّى الكافيةَ؛ لأنّها تكفي عن غيرِها، وتسمّى: الكنز. ولها أسماءُ كثيرةٌ.

وهي أفضلُ سورةٍ في القرآنِ الكريمِ

فقد روى ابنُ حِبّانَ في (صحيحِهِ)، والحاكمُ وقال: صحيحٌ على شرطِ مسلمٍ عن أنسٍ رضي الله عنه قال: (كان النبيُّ صلى الله عليه وسلم في مَسيرٍ، فنزلَ ونزلَ رجلٌ إلى جانِبِه، قال: فالتفتَ النبيُّ صلى الله عليه وسلم فقال: «ألا أخبِرُكَ بأفضلِ القرآنِ»؟، قال: بلى، فتَلا {الْحَمْدُ لِلَّهِ رَبِّ الْعَالَمِينَ})[2] كما في (ترغيب المنذري).

ما وردَ في فضلِ سورةِ البقرةِ عامّةً وبعضِ آياتٍ منها خاصّةً

سورةُ البقرةِ سنامُ القرآنِ: عن مَعقِلِ بنِ يَسارٍ أنَّ رسولَ اللهِ ﷺ قال: «البقرةُ سنامُ القرآنِ وذِروتُه، نزلَ مع كلِّ آيةٍ منها ثمانون مَلَكاً، واستُخرِجَتْ: {اللَّهُ لَا إِلَٰهَ إِلَّا هُوَ الْحَيُّ الْقَيُّومُ}[3] آيةُ الكرسيِّ مِن كنزٍ تحتَ العرشِ، فوُصِلَتْ بسورةِ البقرةِ، و{يس} قلبُ القرآنِ لا يقرؤُها رجلٌ يريدُ اللهَ والدّارَ الآخرةَ إلّا غُفِرَ له، اقرَؤُوها على مَوتاكُم»[4]. رواهُ الإمامُ أحمدُ.

---

(١) أخرجه مسلم (٨٠٦).

(٢) أخرجه ابن حبان (٧٧٤).

(٣) البقرة: ٢٥٥.

(٤) أخرجه أحمد (٢٠٣٠٠).

SŪRAH AL-BAQARAH IS A FORTRESS AGAINST THE DEVILS

Muslim narrated on the authority of Abū Hurayrah ﷺ that the Messenger of Allah ﷺ said, "Do not make your houses into graveyards (i.e., illuminate them with prayer and the Qur'an), because the devils do not enter the house in which *Sūrah al-Baqarah* is recited."[1]

It is narrated on the authority of Sahl ibn Sad ﷺ that the Messenger of Allah ﷺ said, "Indeed, everything has a peak, and the peak of the Qur'an is al-Baqarah. Whoever recites it in their house at night, the devil will not enter it for three nights. And whoever recites it in their house during the day, the devil will not enter it for three days."[2] Ṭabarānī narrated it and Ibn Ḥibbān in his *Ṣaḥīḥ*.

SŪRAH AL-BAQARAH IS THE BATTLE CRY OF THE FIGHTERS AND THE CAMP OF THOSE WHO DO ACTIONS

It is narrated in the Prophetic biographies that when the Prophet ﷺ noticed some of his Companions were lagging behind on the occasion of Ḥunayn, he called them saying, "O people of the tree (i.e., O people who pledged the Allegiance of Pleasure with him upon death)." ʿAbbās ﷺ called out, "O people of *Sūrah al-Baqarah*." This was to incite them and spark determination within them, because Allah Most High said in *Sūrah al-Baqarah*, "How many times has a small force vanquished a mighty army by the Will of Allah! And Allah is [Always] with the steadfast."[3] They then started heading towards the Messenger of Allah ﷺ from every direction. Similarly, in the Battle of Yamāmah against Musaylimah al-Kadhdhāb,

---

(1) *Muslim* (780)

(2) *Ibn Ḥibbān* (780); Ṭabarānī in *al-Muʿjam al-Kabīr* (5864).

(3) *Al-Baqarah*, 249.

سورةُ البقرةِ حصنٌ من الشّياطينِ:

روى مسلمٌ عن أبي هريرةَ أنَّ رسولَ الله ﷺ قال: «لا تجعلوا بيوتَكم قبوراً - أي: نوِّروها بالصّلاةِ والقرآنِ - فإنَّ البيتَ الذي تُقرَأُ فيه سورةُ البقرةِ لا يدخُلُهُ الشّيطانُ»[1]. وعن سهلِ بنِ سعدٍ رضي الله عنه أنَّ رسولَ الله ﷺ قال: «إنَّ لكلِّ شيءٍ سَناماً، وإنَّ سَنامَ القرآنِ البقرةُ، وإنَّ مَن قرَأَها في بيتِهِ ليلاً لم يدخلْهُ الشَّيطانُ ثلاثَ ليالٍ، ومَن قرَأَها في بيتِهِ نهاراً لم يدخلْهُ شيطانٌ ثلاثةَ أيامٍ»[2]. رواه الطّبرانيُّ، وابنُ حِبّانَ في (صحيحِه).

سورةُ البقرةِ شِعارُ المجاهدين، وفُسطاطُ العاملين:

جاء في السِّيَرِ: أنَّ النبيَّ صلى الله عليه وسلم لمّا رأى يومَ حُنَينٍ في بعضِ أصحابِهِ تأخُّراً أمَرَ العبّاسَ رضي الله عنه فناداهم: يا أصحابَ الشَّجرةِ - يعني: أهلَ بيعةِ الرِّضوانِ الذين بايعوه فيها على المَوت. وجعل العبّاسُ رضي الله عنه يُنادي: يا أصحابَ سورةِ البقرةِ؛ لينشِّطَهم ويبعثَ فيهِمُ الهمّةَ؛ لأنَّ اللهَ تعالى يقول في سورة البقرة: {كَم مِّن فِئَةٍ قَلِيلَةٍ غَلَبَتْ فِئَةً كَثِيرَةً بِإِذْنِ اللَّهِ وَاللَّهُ مَعَ الصَّابِرِينَ}[3]. فجعلوا يُقبِلونَ على رسولِ اللهِ ﷺ مِن كلِّ صَوبٍ وجهةٍ، وكذلك يومَ اليمامةِ في الحربِ مع مسيلمةَ الكذّابِ، جَعَلَ المهاجرينَ والأنصارَ يتنادَون: يا أصحابَ سورةِ البقرةِ، حتّى فتحَ اللهُ

---

(١) أخرجه مسلم (٧٨٠).

(٢) أخرجه ابن حبان (٧٨٠)، والطبراني في المعجم الكبير (٥٨٦٤).

(٣) البقرة: ٢٤٩.

the Migrants and the Helpers began calling out "O people of *Sūrah al-Baqarah*" until Allah Most High granted them victory and assisted them.

Khālid ibn Maʿdān used to call *Sūrah al-Baqarah* the camp (*fusṭāṭ*) of the Qur'an, due to its magnificence, and its comprising beliefs, rulings, transactions, character, and manners.

Ibn ʿUmar ﷺ spent eight years studying it, contemplating it, and applying it practically, until he completed it all. He then slaughtered a camel out of gratitude to Allah.

TEN VERSES OF SŪRAH AL-BAQARAH ARE A PROTECTION FROM EVERY DISLIKED THING

Dārimī narrated on the authority of Ibn Masʿūd ﷺ who said, "Whoever recites ten verses from *Sūrah al-Baqarah* at night, no devil will enter that house on that night: four verses from the beginning; Āyah al-Kursī; the two verses after it; and three verses at its end. Neither will any devil approach them or their family on that night nor anything they dislike. They are not recited upon a person suffering a seizure except that they will recover."[1]

ĀYAH AL-KURSĪ IS THE LEADER OF THE QUR'AN

Tirmidhī narrated on the authority of Abū Hurayrah ﷺ that the Messenger of Allah ﷺ said, "Everything has a peak, and the peak of the Qur'an is *Sūrah al-Baqarah*. It contains a verse which is the leader of the Qur'an's verses: Āyah al-Kursī."[2]

ĀYAH AL-KURSĪ IS THE GREATEST VERSE IN THE BOOK OF ALLAH MOST HIGH

It is narrated on the authority of Ubayy ibn Kaʿb ﷺ that the Prophet ﷺ

(1) *Dārimī* (3249).

(2) *Tirmidhī* (2878).

تعالى عليهم ونصَرَهم. وكان خالدُ بنُ مَعدانَ يُسمّي سورةَ البقرةِ فُسطاطَ القرآنِ؛ وذلك لِعَظَمتِها، وحَمْلِها للعقائدِ، والأحكامِ، والمعاملاتِ، والأخلاقِ، والآدابِ. وقد أقام ابنُ عمرَ رَضِيَ اللهُ عَنْهُمَا ثمانيَ سنينَ يتعلَّمُها ويتدبَّرُها، ويُحقِّقُ العملَ بها حتّى ختمَ ذلك كلَّه، فنحرَ بدنةً؛ شكراً لله.

عشرُ آياتٍ من سورةِ البقرةِ أمانٌ مِن كلِّ مكروهٍ

روى الدارميُّ عن ابنِ مسعودٍ رَضِيَ اللهُ عَنْهُ أنّهُ قال: (مَن قرأَ عشرَ آياتٍ من سورةِ البقرةِ في ليلةٍ لم يدخلْ ذلك البيتَ شيطانٌ تلكَ اللّيلةِ، أربعُ آياتٍ من أوَّلِها، وآيةُ الكرسيِّ، وآيتانِ بعدَها، وثلاثُ آياتٍ من آخِرِها، لم يقرَبْهُ ولا أهلَهُ يومئذٍ شيطانٌ، ولا شيءٌ يكرَهُهُ، ولا تُقرأُ على مصروعٍ إلّا أفاقَ)[1].

آيةُ الكرسيِّ هي سيّدةُ آيِ القرآنِ

روى الترمذيُّ عن أبي هريرةَ رَضِيَ اللهُ عَنْهُ قال: قال رسولُ اللهِ صَلَّى اللهُ عَلَيْهِ وَآلِهِ وَسَلَّمَ: «لكلِّ شيءٍ سَنامٌ، وإنَّ سنامَ القرآنِ سورةُ البقرةِ، وفيها آيةٌ هي سيّدةُ آيِ القرآنِ: آيةُ الكرسيِّ»[2].

آيةُ الكرسيِّ أعظمُ آيةٍ في كتابِ اللهِ تعالى

عن أُبَيِّ بنِ كعبٍ رَضِيَ اللهُ عَنْهُ أنَّ النبيَّ صَلَّى اللهُ عَلَيْهِ وَآلِهِ وَسَلَّمَ سأله: أيُّ آيةٍ في كتابِ اللهِ أعظمُ؟ قال:

---

(١) أخرجه الدارمي (٣٢٤٩).

(٢) أخرجه الترمذي (٢٨٧٨).

asked him, "Which verse in the Book of Allah is the greatest?" He said, "Allah and His Messenger know best." The Prophet ﷺ repeated this a number of times. Ubayy ؓ then said, "Āyah al-Kursī." He ﷺ said, "May knowledge be blessed for you, O Abū al-Mundhir. By the One in Whose Hand lies my soul, it has a tongue and two lips, and it exalts the Sovereign by the feet of the Throne."[(1)] Imam Aḥmad narrated it.

Ibn Masʿūd ؓ said, "The greatest verse in the Qur'an is Āyah al-Kursī. The verse with greatest mention of justice in the Qur'an is: 'Indeed, Allah commands justice, grace, as well as courtesy to close relatives.'[(2)] The most frightening verse in the Qur'an is: 'So whoever does an atom's weight of good will see it. And whoever does an atom's weight of evil will see it.'[(3)] And the verse which gives most hope is: 'Say, [O Prophet, that Allah says,] 'O My servants who have exceeded the limits against their souls! Do not lose hope in Allah's mercy.''[(4)]"

ĀYAH AL-KURSĪ COMPRISES THE GREATEST NAME (AL-ISM AL-AʿẒAM)

It is narrated on the authority of Asmā' bint Yazīd ؓ that regarding these two verses: "Allah! There is no god [worthy of worship] except Him, the Ever-Living, All-Sustaining"[(5)] and "*Alif Lām Mīm*. Allah! There is no god [worthy of worship] except Him, the Ever-Living, All-Sustaining"[(6)], she heard the Messenger of Allah ﷺ say, "Indeed, Allah's Greatest Name (al-Ism al-Aʿẓam) is in them."[(7)]

(1) *Aḥmad (20588).*

(2) *Al-Naḥl*, 90.

(3) *Al-Zilzāl*, 7-8.

(4) *Al-Zumar*, 53.

(5) *Al-Baqarah*, 255.

(6) *Āl 'Imrān*, 1-2.

(7) *Tirmidhī* (3478).

اللهُ ورسولُهُ أعلمُ، فردَّها مراراً، ثمَّ قال أُبَيٌّ: آيةُ الكرسيِّ، فقال ﷺ: «لِيَهنِكَ العلمُ أبا المنذرِ، والذي نفسي بيده إنَّ لها لساناً وشفَتَينِ تُقدِّسُ المَلِكَ عند ساقِ العرشِ»(١). رواه الإمامُ أحمدُ.

وقال ابنُ مسعودٍ رَضِيَ اللهُ عَنْهُ: أعظمُ آيةٍ في القرآنِ آيةُ الكرسيِّ، وأعدلُ آيةٍ في القرآنِ {إِنَّ اللَّهَ يَأْمُرُ بِالْعَدْلِ وَالْإِحْسَانِ} (٢) إلى آخِرها، وأخوفُ آيةٍ في القرآنِ {فَمَن يَعْمَلْ مِثْقَالَ ذَرَّةٍ خَيْرًا يَرَهُ (٧) وَمَن يَعْمَلْ مِثْقَالَ ذَرَّةٍ شَرًّا يَرَهُ} (٣)، وأرجى آيةٍ {قُلْ يَا عِبَادِيَ الَّذِينَ أَسْرَفُوا عَلَىٰ أَنفُسِهِمْ لَا تَقْنَطُوا مِن رَّحْمَةِ اللَّهِ} (٤).

آيةُ الكرسيِّ مُشتَمِلَةٌ على الاسمِ الأعظمِ

عن أسماءَ بنتِ يزيدَ رَضِيَ اللهُ عَنْهَا قالت: سمعتُ رسولَ اللهِ صلى اللهُ عليه وآلِهِ وسلَّمَ يقول في هاتينِ الآيتينِ: {اللَّهُ لَا إِلَٰهَ إِلَّا هُوَ الْحَيُّ الْقَيُّومُ}(٥) و {الم، اللَّهُ لَا إِلَٰهَ إِلَّا هُوَ الْحَيُّ الْقَيُّومُ}(٦) «إنَّ فيهما اسمَ اللهِ الأعظمِ»(٧). رواه الترمذيُّ.

---

(١) أخرجه أحمد (٢٠٥٨٨).

(٢) النحل: ٩٠.

(٣) الزلزلة: ٧-٨.

(٤) الزمر: ٥٣.

(٥) البقرة: ٢٥٥.

(٦) آل عمران: ١-٢.

(٧) أخرجه الترمذي (٣٤٧٨).

ĀYAH AL-KURSĪ IS A FORTIFIED FORTRESS

Bukhārī narrated on the authority of Abū Hurayrah ؓ who said, "The Messenger of Allāh ﷺ entrusted me to safeguard the *zakāh* of Ramadan. Someone came to me and began taking handfuls of food. I caught him and said, 'I am going to take you to the Messenger of Allah ﷺ.' He said, 'Leave me, because I am a needy person and I have a family to support. I am desperately in need.' So I pitied him and let him go. The next morning, the Prophet ﷺ said to me, 'O Abū Hurayrah, what happened to your captive last night?' I said, 'O Messenger of Allah, he complained of great need and having a family, so I pitied him and let him go.' He ﷺ said, 'He lied to you and he is going to return.' So, I knew he would return – because the Prophet ﷺ said so – and I waited for him. He came and took handfuls of food, so I caught him and said, 'I am going to take you to the Messenger of Allah ﷺ.' He said, 'Leave me, because I am a needy person and I have a family to support. I will not do it again.' So, I pitied him and let him go. The next morning, the Messenger of Allah said to me, 'O Abū Hurayrah, what happened to your captive last night?' I said, 'O Messenger of Allah, he complained of great need and having a family, so I pitied him and let him go.' He ﷺ said, 'He lied to you and he is going to return.' So I waited for him a third time, and so he came and took handfuls of food. I caught him and said, 'I am going to take you to the Messenger of Allah ﷺ. This is the last of three occasions. You claim you are not going to come back but then you return.' He said, 'Let me go and I will teach you some words through which Allah will benefit you.' I asked, 'What are they?' He said, 'When you retire to your bed, read Āyah al-Kursī, because you will have a protector from Allah constantly over you and the devil will not be able to approach you until morning.' I then let him go. The next morning, the Messenger of Allah ﷺ said to me, 'What happened to your captive last night?' I said, 'O Messenger of Allah, he said he will teach me some words through which Allah will benefit me, so I let him go.' He asked, 'What are they?' I said, 'He said to me, "When you retire to your bed, read Āyah al-Kursī until the end, for you will have a protector from Allah constantly over you and

آيةُ الكرسيِّ حصنٌ حصينٌ

روى البخاريُّ عن أبي هريرةَ رَضِيَ اللَّهُ عَنْهُ قال: وكَّلني رسولُ اللهِ صَلَّى اللَّهُ عَلَيْهِ وَآلِهِ وَسَلَّمَ بحفظِ زكاةِ رمضانَ، فأتاني آتٍ فجعلَ يحثو - أي: يتناولُ - من الطّعامِ، فأخَذتُهُ، وقلتُ: لَأرفعنَّكَ إلى رسولِ اللهِ صَلَّى اللَّهُ عَلَيْهِ وَآلِهِ وَسَلَّمَ، فقال: دَعني - اتركني - فإنّي محتاجٌ وعليَّ عِيالٌ، ولي حاجةٌ شديدةٌ، قال: فخلَّيتُ عنه فأصبحتُ، فقال النبيُّ صَلَّى اللَّهُ عَلَيْهِ وَآلِهِ وَسَلَّمَ: يا أبا هريرةَ ما فعلَ أسيرُكَ البارحةَ»؟ قلتُ: يا رسولَ اللهِ شكى حاجةً شديدةً وعيالاً، فرَحِمتُهُ وخلّيتُ سبيلَه، فقال صلى اللهُ عليه وآلِهِ وسلَّمَ: «أمَا إنّهُ قد كذبَكَ وسيعودُ»، قال أبو هريرةَ: فعرَفْتُ أنّهُ سيعودُ؛ لقولِ النبيِّ صَلَّى اللَّهُ عَلَيْهِ وَآلِهِ وَسَلَّمَ: «إنّهُ سيعود»، فرصدتُهُ - فرقبتُهُ - فجاءَ يحثو الطَّعامَ فأخذتُهُ، فقلتُ: لأرفعنَّكَ إلى رسولِ اللهِ صلى اللهُ عليه وآلِهِ وسلَّمَ؟ فقال: دعني فإنّي محتاجٌ وعليَّ عيالٌ، لا أعودُ، فرَحِمتُهُ فخلّيتُ سبيلَهُ، فأصبحتُ، فقال لي رسولُ اللهِ صَلَّى اللَّهُ عَلَيْهِ وَآلِهِ وَسَلَّمَ: «يا أبا هريرةَ ما فعلَ أسيرُكَ البارحةَ»؟ قلتُ: يا رسولَ اللهِ شكا حاجةً وعيالاً، فرحمتُهُ فخلّيتُ سبيلَه، قال: «أمَا إنّهُ قد كذَبَكَ وسيعودُ»، قال أبو هريرةَ رَضِيَ اللَّهُ عَنْهُ: فرصدتُهُ الثّالثةَ، فجاء يحثو من الطّعامِ فأخذتُهُ، فقلتُ: لأرفعنَّكَ إلى رسولِ اللهِ صَلَّى اللَّهُ عَلَيْهِ وَآلِهِ وَسَلَّمَ، وهذا آخرُ ثلاثِ مرّاتٍ تزعُمُ أنّكَ لا تعودُ ثمّ تعودُ، فقال: دَعني أعلِّمْكَ كلماتٍ ينفعُكَ اللهُ بها، قلتُ: وما هي؟ قال: إذا أَويتَ إلى فراشِكَ فاقرأْ آيةَ الكرسيِّ؛ فإنّكَ لن يزالَ عليك من اللهِ حافظٌ، ولا يقربُكَ الشَّيطانُ حتى تصبحَ، قال أبو هريرةَ: فخليتُ سبيلَه فأصبحتُ، فقال لي رسولُ اللهِ صَلَّى اللَّهُ عَلَيْهِ وَآلِهِ وَسَلَّمَ: «ما فعلَ أسيرُكَ البارحةَ»؟، فقلتُ: يا رسولَ اللهِ زَعَمَ أنّهُ يعلِّمُني كلماتٍ ينفعُني اللهُ بها، فخلّيتُ سبيلَه، فقال: «ما هي»؟ فقال أبو هريرةَ رضي اللهُ عنه: قال: إذا أويتَ إلى فراشِكَ فاقرأْ آيةَ الكرسيِّ حتى تختمَ الآيةَ، فلن يزالَ عليك من اللهِ حافظٌ، ولا يقربُكَ شيطانٌ حتّى تصبحَ، وكانوا - أي: الصحابة - أحرصَ شيءٍ

the devil will not be able to approach you until morning.'" They (i.e., the Companions) were extremely eager for good things. The Prophet ﷺ asked, 'Do you know who you have been speaking to for three nights, O Abū Hurayrah?' I said, 'No.' He said, 'That was the devil.'"(1) In other words, he appeared in the form of a person in need of food.

RECITING ĀYAH AL-KURSĪ AFTER THE PRAYERS IS ONE OF THE GREATEST GOOD DEEDS

It is narrated on the authority of Abū Umāmah ﷺ that the Prophet ﷺ said, "Whoever recites Āyah al-Kursī after the obligatory prayer, nothing is stopping them from entering Paradise besides death."(2) Ibn Mardawayh narrated it.

Ḥāfiẓ Ibn Kathīr said, "Nasā'ī narrated it in *'Amal al-Yawm wa al-Laylah* from Ḥasan ibn Bishr. Ibn Ḥibbān reported it in his *Ṣaḥīḥ* from the hadith of Muhammad ibn Ḥumayd al-Ḥimṣī - one of the narrators of Bukhārī. Thus, it is a chain according to the criteria of Bukhārī." One of the secrets of Āyah al-Kursī is that which many of the scholars of the recitations mention, namely that Allah Most High has been mentioned in it 16 times - either as an apparent noun or pronoun. Some have even taken it up to 20, considering the hidden pronouns in: the Ever-Living, All-Sustaining, the Most High, and the Greatest. Whoever contemplates it will realize this.

THE FINAL VERSES OF SŪRAH AL-BAQARAH ARE FROM A TREASURE UNDER THE THRONE

It is narrated on the authority of Abū Dharr ﷺ that the Messenger of Allah ﷺ said, "I was granted the last verses of *Sūrah al-Baqarah* from a treasure under the Throne. No Prophet before me was granted them."(3) Imam

---

(1) *Bukhārī* (2311).

(2) Nasā'ī in *al-Sunan al-Kubrā* (9928)

(3) *Aḥmad* (23299).

على الخيرِ، فقال النبيُّ ﷺ: «أَمَا إِنّهُ صَدَقَكَ وهو كذوبٌ، تعلَمُ مَن تخاطِبُ مُنذُ ثلاثِ ليالٍ يا أبا هريرةَ»؟ قلت: لا، قال: «ذاك شيطانٌ»[1] أي: تمثَّلَ بصورةِ إنسانٍ محتاجٍ إلى طعامٍ.

تلاوةُ آيةِ الكرسيِّ عَقِبَ الصّلواتِ من أكبَرِ الحسناتِ

عن أبي أُمامةَ عن النبيِّ ﷺ أنّهُ قال: «مَن قرأَ دُبُرَ - وراءَ - كلِّ صلاةٍ مكتوبةٍ - مفروضةٍ - آيةَ الكرسيِّ لم يمنعْهُ من دخولِ الجنّةِ إلا أن يموتَ»[2]. رواه ابنُ مردوَيهِ. قال الحافظُ ابنُ كثيرٍ: ورواهُ النَّسائيُّ في عملِ (اليومِ واللّيلةِ) عن الحسنِ بنِ بشرٍ، وأخرجَهُ ابنُ حِبّانَ في (صحيحِهِ) من حديثِ محمّدِ بنِ حُميدٍ الحمصيِّ، وهو من رجالِ البخاريِّ، فهو إسنادٌ على شرطِ البخاريِّ. اهـ. ومن أسرارِ آيةِ الكرسيِّ ما ذكَرَهُ كثيرٌ من العلماءِ بالقراءاتِ رَضِيَ اللهُ عَنهُم أنّها ذُكِرَ اللهُ تعالى في ستّةَ عشرَ موضعاً منها ما بين اسمٍ ظاهرٍ ومُضمَرٍ، وأوصلَها بعضُهم إلى عشرينَ، باعتبارِ الضَّمائرِ المستَتِرَةِ في اسمِ «الحيِّ، القيومِ، العليِّ، العظيمِ» ويَعلَمُ ذلك مَن تأمَّلَه.

خواتيمُ سورةِ البقرةِ مِن كنزٍ تحتَ العرشِ

عن أبي ذرٍّ رَضِيَ اللهُ عَنهُ قال: قال رسولُ الله ﷺ: «أُعطيتُ خواتيمَ سورةِ البقرةِ من

---

(١) أخرجه البخاري (٢٣١١).

(٢) أخرجه النسائي في (السنن الكبرى) (٩٩٢٨).

Aḥmad narrated it. Sayyidunā ʿAlī ﷺ said, "I do not see how anyone who has understood Islam can sleep until they have read Āyah al-Kursī and the last verses of *Sūrah al-Baqarah*, because they are from a treasure your Prophet ﷺ has been granted from under the Throne." Bukhārī narrated on the authority of Ibn Masʿūd ﷺ that the Messenger of Allah ﷺ said, "Whoever recites the last two verses of *Sūrah al-Baqarah* at night, they shall be sufficient for them."(1) In other words, they are sufficient in place of other words of seeking refuge, or they are sufficient against evil, calamities, and disliked things. It is narrated on the authority of Nuʿmān ibn Bashīr ﷺ that the Prophet ﷺ said, "Indeed, Allah wrote a record 2000 years before He created the Heavens and the Earth. He sent down therein two verses with which He concluded *Sūrah al-Baqarah*. They are not recited in any house for three nights for the devil to then approach it."(2)

THE CONCLUSION OF SŪRAH AL-BAQARAH IS A SUPPLICATION ALLAH MOST HIGH HAS TAUGHT HIS SLAVES AND HE HAS GUARANTEED HE WILL ACCEPT IT

Muslim narrated on the authority of Abū Hurayrah ﷺ in a lengthy hadith in which he said, "Allah Most High revealed, 'Our Lord! Do not punish us if we forget or make a mistake.' Allah Most High said, 'Yes.' 'Our Lord! Do not place a burden on us like the one you placed on those before us.' Allah Most High said, 'Yes.' 'Our Lord! Do not burden us with what we cannot bear.' Allah Most High said, 'Yes.' 'Pardon us, forgive us, and have mercy on us. You are our [only] Guardian. So grant us victory over the disbelieving people.' Allah Most High said, 'Yes.'" In another narration, "Allah Most High said, 'Yes, I have done it.'"(3)

---

(1) *Bukhārī* (4008).

(2) *Tirmidhī* (2882).

(3) *Muslim* (126).

كنزٍ تحتَ العرشِ لم يُعطَهُنَّ نبيٌّ قبلي»[1]. رواه الإمامُ أحمدُ. وقال سيّدُنا عليٌّ رَضِيَ اللهُ عَنْهُ: (لا أرى أحداً عقلَ الإسلامَ ينام حتى يقرأَ آيةَ الكرسيّ وخواتيمَ سورةِ البقرةِ؛ فإنَّها من كنزٍ أُعطِيَهُ نبيُّكم صَلَّى اللهُ عَلَيْهِ وَآلِهِ وَسَلَّمَ من تحتِ العرشِ). وروى البخاريُّ عن ابنِ مسعودٍ رَضِيَ اللهُ عَنْهُ قال: قال رسولُ الله صَلَّى اللهُ عَلَيْهِ وَآلِهِ وَسَلَّمَ: «مَن قرأَ بالآيتينِ من آخرِ سورةِ البقرةِ في ليلةٍ كَفَتاهُ»[2] أي: عن غيرِهما من التّعاويذِ، أو من الشُّرورِ، والآفاتِ، والمكارِهِ. وعن النُّعمانِ بنِ بَشيرٍ رضي الله عنه عن النبيّ صَلَّى اللهُ عَلَيْهِ وَآلِهِ وَسَلَّمَ قال: «إنَّ اللهَ كتبَ كتاباً قبلَ أنْ يخلقَ السّمواتِ والأرضَ بألفي عامٍ، أنزلَ فيه آيتينِ ختمَ بهما سورةَ البقرةِ، ولا يُقرأُ بهنَّ في دارٍ ثلاثَ ليالٍ فيقربُها شيطانٌ»[3]. رواه الترمذيُّ.

آخرُ سورةِ البقرةِ دعاءٌ لقّنهُ اللهُ تعالى عبادَهُ وضَمِنَ لهمُ الإجابةَ

روى مسلمٌ عن أبي هريرةَ رَضِيَ اللهُ عَنْهُ في حديثٍ طويلٍ قال فيه: فأنزلَ اللهُ تعالى: {رَبَّنَا لَا تُؤَاخِذْنَا إِن نَّسِينَا أَوْ أَخْطَأْنَا} قال اللهُ تعالى: «نعم». {رَبَّنَا وَلَا تَحْمِلْ عَلَيْنَا إِصْرًا كَمَا حَمَلْتَهُ عَلَى الَّذِينَ مِن قَبْلِنَا} قال الله تعالى: «نعم».{رَبَّنَا وَلَا تُحَمِّلْنَا مَا لَا طَاقَةَ لَنَا بِهِ} قال الله تعالى: «نعم». {وَاعْفُ عَنَّا وَاغْفِرْ لَنَا وَارْحَمْنَا أَنتَ مَوْلَانَا فَانصُرْنَا عَلَى الْقَوْمِ الْكَافِرِينَ} قال الله تعالى: «نعم». وفي حديثٍ آخَرَ: قال الله تعالى: «قد فعلتُ»[4].

---

(١) أخرجه أحمد (٢٣٢٩٩).

(٢) أخرجه البخاري (٤٠٠٨).

(٣) أخرجه الترمذي (٢٨٨٢).

(٤) أخرجه مسلم (١٢٦).

Ḥākim and Bayhaqī narrated that the Prophet ﷺ said, "Indeed, Allah concluded *Sūrah al-Baqarah* with two verses He granted me from His treasure underneath the Throne. So learn it, and teach it to your women and children, for it is a prayer, recital, and supplication."[1]

THE VIRTUES MENTIONED FOR SŪRAH AL-BAQARAH AND SŪRAH ĀL 'IMRĀN

It is narrated on the authority of Abū Umāmah ؓ who said he heard the Messenger of Allah ﷺ say, "Recite the Qur'an, as it will come as an intercessor for its reciters on the Day of Judgement. Recite the two radiant ones –al-Baqarah and Āl 'Imrān – because they will come on the Day of Judgement as though they are two clouds or two shades or two flights of birds, arguing on behalf of their reciter. Recite al-Baqarah, because acquiring it is a blessing, neglecting it is a means of regret, and the sorcerers have no power against it."[2] It is narrated in the two *Ṣaḥīḥ* collections on the authority of Ibn 'Abbās ؓ who says he spent the night with his aunt Maymūnah ؓ – the wife of the Prophet ﷺ. He said, "I slept along the width of the bed whilst the Messenger of Allah ﷺ and his wife slept along the length of it. The Messenger of Allah ﷺ slept until half the night had passed, or a little before or after it. He then woke up from his sleep and began to rub the effects of sleep away from his face using his hand."[3] In the narration of Ibn Mardawayh: "He lifted his head to the sky and said, 'Glorified be the King, Most Holy' three times. He then recited the last ten verses of Āl 'Imrān, and thereafter he stood towards a hanging waterskin and thoroughly performed *wuḍū'* from it. He then stood to pray, so I also stood and did as he did. I then went and stood next to him. The Messenger of Allah ﷺ placed his right hand on my head and held my right ear and

(1) Qāsim ibn al-Sallām in *Faḍā'il al-Qur'an* (352).

(2) *Muslim* (804).

(3) *Bukhārī* (4572).

وروى الحاكمُ والبيهقيُّ عن النبيِّ ﷺ أنّهُ قال: «إنَّ اللهَ ختمَ سورةَ البقرةِ بآيتينِ أَعطانيهما من كنزِهِ الذي تحتَ العرشِ، فتعلَّمُوهما، وعلِّمُوهما نساءَكم وأبناءَكم؛ فإنَّهما صلاةٌ وقرآنٌ ودعاءٌ»[1].

ما وردَ في فضل سورتي البقرةِ وآلِ عمران

عن أبي أُمامةَ رَضِيَ اللهُ عَنْهُ قال: سمعتُ رسولَ الله ﷺ يقول: «اقرَؤُوا القرآنَ فإنّهُ يأتي يومَ القيامةِ شفيعاً لأصحابِهِ، اقرَؤُوا الزَّهراوَينِ - المُنيرتَينِ - البقرةَ وآلَ عِمران؛ فإنَّهما يأتيانِ يومَ القيامةِ كأنَّهما غَمامتانِ، أو كأنَّهما غيايَتانِ، أو كأنَّهما فِرقانٌ من طيرٍ صوافٍّ تُحاجّانِ عن صاحبِهما، اقرَؤُوا البقرةَ؛ فإنَّ أَخْذَها بركةٌ، وتركَها حسرةٌ، ولا تستَطيعُها البَطَلَةُ»[2]. رواه مسلم. وفي (الصَّحيحينِ) عن ابنِ عبّاسٍ رَضِيَ اللهُ عَنْهُمَا أنّهُ باتَ عند ميمونةَ زوجِ النبيِّ عَلَيْهِ الصَّلَاةُ وَالسَّلَامُ - وهي خالتُه - قال: (اضطجَعْتُ في عَرضِ الوِسادةِ، واضطجعَ رسولُ اللهِ ﷺ وأهلُه في طولِها، فنامَ رسولُ الله ﷺ حتّى إذا انتصفَ اللّيلُ، أو قبلَهُ بقليلٍ أو بعدَه بقليلٍ استيقَظَ رسولُ اللهِ ﷺ من منامِهِ، فجعلَ يمسحُ النَّومَ عن وجهِهِ بيدِه[3]. وفي روايةِ ابنِ مردوَيهِ: فرفعَ رأسَهُ إلى السَّماءِ فقال: «سبحانَ المَلِكِ القدُّوسِ» ثلاثَ مرّاتٍ، ثمَّ قرأَ العشرَ الخواتِمَ من سورةِ آلِ عِمران، ثمَّ قام إلى شَنٍّ مُعلَّقَةٍ، فتوضَّأَ منها، فأحسنَ وضوءَهُ، ثمَّ قام يصلّي - قيامَ الليل - فقمتُ فصنعتُ مثلَ ما صنع، ثمَّ ذهبتُ وقمتُ إلى جَنبِهِ، فوضعَ رسولُ اللهِ صلى الله عليه وآله وسلم

---

(١) أخرجه ذكره القاسم بن سلام في (فضائل القرآن) (٣٥٢).

(٢) أخرجه مسلم (٨٠٤).

(٣) أخرجه البخاري (٤٥٧٢).

twisted it. He then prayed two *rak ʿahs*, then another two *rak ʿahs*, then another two *rak ʿahs*, then another two *rak ʿahs*, then another two *rak ʿahs*, then another two *rak ʿahs*, and then he prayed the *witr* prayer. He then lay down until the caller to prayer came to him. He stood to perform two light *rak ʿahs*, whereafter he went out and prayed the morning prayer."

It is narrated in the hadith of Ibn Mardawayh that when the verse: "Indeed, in the creation of the Heavens and the Earth and the alternation of the day and night there are signs for people of reason"(1) was revealed to him, he ﷺ said, "Woe unto the one who recites it but does not reflect on it."(2) This is because it encourages one to reflect, take lessons, contemplate, and be reminded. Abū al-Shaykh and others narrated that the Prophet ﷺ once went out to his Companions and said, "Do not reflect over Allah, but rather reflect over what He has created."(3) The reason behind prohibiting them from reflecting over the Essence of Allah Most High is because they cannot encompass Him in their knowledge or attain full knowledge and understanding of Him. "No vision can encompass Him, but He encompasses all vision. For He is the Most Subtle, All-Aware."(4)

THE VERSE "ALLAH [HIMSELF] IS A WITNESS THAT THERE IS NO GOD [WORTHY OF WORSHIP] EXCEPT HIM" IS THE GREATEST TESTIMONY IN THE BOOK OF ALLAH MOST HIGH

Imam Aḥmad narrated that the Prophet ﷺ recited this verse on the day of ʿArafah and said after reciting it, "And I am also amongst those who testify, O my Lord."(5)

---

(1) *Āl ʿImrān*, 190.

(2) *Ibn Ḥibbān* (260).

(3) Abū al-Shaykh in *al-ʿAẓamah*; Bayhaqī in *al-Asmāʾ wa al-Ṣifāt* (271); Abū Nuʿaym in *al-Ḥilyah* from the hadith of ʿAbdullāh ibn Salām, vol. 6, p. 66.

(4) *Al-Anʿām*, 107.

(5) *Aḥmad* (1421).

يدَهُ اليُمنى على رأسِي وأخذ بأُذني اليمنى ففتلَها، فصلَّى رَكعتين، ثمَّ ركعتينِ، ثمَّ ركعتينِ، ثمَّ ركعتينِ، ثمَّ ركعتينِ، ثمَّ ركعتينِ، ثمَّ أوترَ، ثمَّ اضطجعَ حتّى جاءَهُ المؤذِّنُ، فقام فصلَّى ركعتينِ خفيفتينِ، ثمَّ خرجَ النبيُّ صلى الله عليه وآله وسلم فصلَّى الصُّبحَ. وفي الحديثِ الذي رواهُ ابنُ مَرْدَوَيْه: لمّا نزلَتْ عليه آيةُ {إِنَّ فِي خَلْقِ السَّمَاوَاتِ وَالْأَرْضِ وَاخْتِلَافِ اللَّيْلِ وَالنَّهَارِ لَآيَاتٍ لِّأُولِي الْأَلْبَابِ} (١) قال: «ويلٌ لِمَن قرَأَها ولم يتفكَّرْ فيها»(٢)؛ وذلك لأنَّ فيها الحثَّ على التفكُّرِ والاعتبارِ، والتدبُّرِ والادِّكارِ. كما روى أبو الشَّيخِ وغيرُهُ أنَّ النبيَّ ﷺ خرجَ يوماً إلى أصحابِهِ وهم يتفكَّرونَ فقال: «لا تتفكَّروا في اللهِ تعالى، ولكن تفكَّروا فيما خَلقَ» (٣)؛ وإنَّما نهاهُمْ عن التفكُّرِ في ذاتِ اللهِ تعالى؛ لأنَّهم لا يُحيطونَ به علماً، ولا يُدرِكونه خِبرةً وفهماً {لَّا تُدْرِكُهُ الْأَبْصَارُ وَهُوَ يُدْرِكُ الْأَبْصَارَ وَهُوَ اللَّطِيفُ الْخَبِيرُ}(٤).

آيةُ {شهد الله أنه لا إله إلا هو}
هي أعظمُ شهادةٍ في كتابِ اللهِ تعالى

روى الإمامُ أحمدُ أنَّ النبيَّ صلى اللهُ عليه وآلهِ وسلَّمَ قرأَ هذه الآيةَ يومَ عرفةَ، ثمَّ قال

---

(١) آل عمران: ١٩٠.

(٢) أخرجه ابن حبان (٢٦٠).

(٣) أخرجه أبو الشيخ في العظمة, والبيهقي في الأسماء والصفات (٢٧١), ورواه من حديث عبد الله بن سلام أبو نعيم في الحلية (٦/ ٦٦).

(٤) الأنعام: ١٠٣.

It is narrated that after he performed the *ẓuhr* prayers in Medina, two priests from the Levant came to him. When they saw Medina, one of them said to the other, "How similar this city is to the city of the Prophet who will appear in the end days." When they then came to the Messenger of Allah ﷺ, they recognized him through his description. They asked him, "Are you Muhammad?"

He said, "Yes." They asked, "Are you Aḥmad?" He said, "Yes." They said, "We are going to ask you about a certain testimony. If you can tell us about it, we will bring faith in you and believe in you." He said, "Ask me." They said, "Tell us about the greatest testimony in the Qur'an."

Allah then revealed this verse, and they thus embraced Islam.

Hence, this is the greatest testimony in Allah's Books, and they recognized him due to his description mentioned in the Torah and the Evangel.

THE VERSE "SAY, [O PROPHET,] "O ALLAH! LORD OVER ALL AUTHORITIES!"

Ṭabarānī narrated with his chain that the Prophet ﷺ said, "The Greatest Name of Allah through which He accepts when He is supplicated is in this verse: 'Say: [O Prophet,] O Allah! Lord over all authorities! You give authority to whoever You please and remove it from who You please.' [1]"[2]

Ibn Abī al-Dunyā narrated on the authority of Muʿādh رضي الله عنه who said, "I complained to the Prophet of Allah ﷺ of a debt I owed. He said, 'O Muʿādh, do you want your debt to be fulfilled?' I said, 'Yes.' He told me to say, 'Say, [O Prophet,] "O Allah! Lord over all authorities! You give authority to whoever You please and remove it from who You please; You honour whoever You please and disgrace who You please – all good is in Your Hands. Surely You [alone] are Most Capable of everything."[3] O Most

(1) *Āl ʿImrān*, 26.

(2) Ṭabarānī in *al-Muʿjam al-Awsaṭ* (514).

(3) *Āl ʿImrān*, 26.

بعدَ قراءتِها: «وأنا على ذلك من الشّاهدينَ يا ربّ»[1]. ورويَ أنّهُ ﷺ بعدما ظهر في المدينةِ، قَدِمَ عليه حبرانِ من أحبارِ الشّامِ، فلمّا أبصَرا المدينةَ قال أحدُهما لصاحبِهِ: ما أشبَهَ هذه المدينةَ بمدينةِ النبيّ الذي يخرجُ في آخرِ الزّمان ﷺ، فلمّا دخلا على رسولِ اللهِ صلى اللهُ عليه وآلهِ وسلّمَ عرَفَاه بالصّفةِ، فقالا له: أنتَ محمّدٌ - صلى اللهُ عليه وآلهِ وسلّمَ -؟ قال: «نَعَم» قالا: أنتَ أحمدُ - صلى اللهُ عليه وآلهِ وسلّمَ -؟ قال: «نعم» قالا: إنّا نسألُكَ عن شهادةٍ؛ فإنْ أنتَ أخبرتَنا بها آمنّا بكَ وصدّقناكَ. فقال لهما: «سَلاني»، فقالا له: أخبِرنا عن أعظمِ شهادةٍ في كتابِ اللهِ تعالى؟ فأنزلَ اللهُ تعالى هذه الآيةَ، فأسلَمَا. فهي أعظمُ شهادةٍ في كتبِ الله تعالى، وإنّما عرَفَاه عليه الصلاة والسلام بموجَبِ الصّفاتِ المذكورةِ في التّوراةِ والإنجيلِ.

آيةُ (قل اللهم مالك الملك)

روى الطّبرانيُّ بإسنادِهِ أنّ النبيّ ﷺ قال: «اسمُ اللهِ الأعظمُ الذي إذا دُعِيَ به أجابَ في هذه الآيةَ: {قُلِ اللَّهُمَّ مَالِكَ الْمُلْكِ تُؤْتِي الْمُلْكَ مَن تَشَاءُ وَتَنزِعُ الْمُلْكَ مِمَّن تَشَاءُ}[2]» [3] الآيةَ. وروى ابنُ أبي الدُّنيا عن معاذٍ رضي اللهُ عنه قال: شكوتُ إلى النبيّ صلى اللهعليهوآلهوسلم دَيناً كان عليّ، فقال: «يامعاذُأتحبُّ أنْ يُقضَى دَينُكَ»؟ قلت: نعم، قال: «{قُلِ اللَّهُمَّ مَالِكَ الْمُلْكِ تُؤْتِي الْمُلْكَ مَن تَشَاءُ وَتَنزِعُ الْمُلْكَ مِمَّن تَشَاءُ وَتُعِزُّ مَن تَشَاءُ وَتُذِلُّ

(١) أخرجه أحمد (١٤٢١).

(٢) آل عمران: ٢٦.

(٣) أخرجه الطبراني في الأوسط (٥١٤).

Compassionate in this world and the Hereafter, and O Most Merciful in both of them. You grant of them to whomsoever You want, and You deprive of them whomsoever You want. Fulfil my debt for me.' He ﷺ said, 'If you owed the whole earth fill of gold, it would be repaid on your behalf.'"[1] Ṭabarānī has narrated the same hadith with a good chain.

THE VERSE "BUT IF THEY TURN AWAY, THEN SAY, [O PROPHET,] 'ALLAH IS SUFFICIENT FOR ME. THERE IS NO GOD [WORTHY OF WORSHIP] EXCEPT HIM. IN HIM I PUT MY TRUST. AND HE IS THE LORD OF THE MIGHTY THRONE.'"[2]

Abū Dāwūd narrated on the authority of Abū al-Dardā' ؓ who said, "Whoever says seven times in the morning and evening 'Allah is sufficient for me. There is no god [worthy of worship] except Him. In Him I put my trust. And He is the Lord of the Mighty Throne', Allah will suffice them for all their concerns in this world and the Hereafter."[3] Ibn al-Sunnī narrated it as a hadith attributed to the Prophet ﷺ.

SŪRAH AL-ISRĀ'

Sayyidah 'Ā'ishah ؓ narrated that the Messenger of Allah ﷺ used to recite *Sūrah Banī Isrā'īl* (i.e., *Sūrah al-Isrā'*) and *Sūrah al-Zumar* every night.[4] Tirmidhī, Nasā'ī, and others narrated it.

(1) Ṭabarānī in *Musnad al-Shāmiyyīn* (2398).

(2) *Al-Tawbah*, 129.

(3) Ibn al-Sunnī in *'Amal al-Yawm wa al-Laylah* (132); Ibn 'Asākir, vol. 36, p. 196.

(4) *Tirmidhī* (3405)

مَن تَشَاءُ بِيَدِكَ الْخَيْرُ إِنَّكَ عَلَىٰ كُلِّ شَيْءٍ قَدِيرٌ}[1] رحمنَ الدُّنيا والآخرةِ ورحيمَهما، تُعطي منهما ما تشاءُ، وتمنعُ منهما ما تشاءُ، اقضِ عنّي دَيني»، قال صلى اللهُ عليه وآلِهِ وسلَّمَ: «فلو كان عليكَ ملءُ الأرضِ ذهباً أُدِّيَ عنكَ »[2]. وروى الطَّبرانيُّ نحوَ هذا الحديثِ بالسَّندِ الجيّدِ.

آيةُ {فَإِنْ تَوَلَّوا فَقُلْ حَسْبِيَ اللَّهُ لَا إِلَٰهَ إِلَّا هُوَ عَلَيْهِ تَوَكَّلْتُ وَهُوَ رَبُّ الْعَرْشِ الْعَظِيمِ}

روى أبو داودَ عن أبي الدَّرداءِ رَضِيَ اللهُ عَنْهُ أنّهُ قال: (مَن قال حينَ يُصبِحُ وحينَ يُمسِي: {حَسْبِيَ اللَّهُ لَا إِلَٰهَ إِلَّا هُوَ عَلَيْهِ تَوَكَّلْتُ وَهُوَ رَبُّ الْعَرْشِ الْعَظِيمِ}[3] - سبعَ مرّاتٍ - كفاهُ اللهُ ما أهمَّهُ من الدُّنيا والآخرةِ)[4]. ورواه ابن السُّنّيِّ مرفوعاً.

سورةُ الإسراءِ

عن السّيدةِ عائشةَ رَضِيَ اللهُ عَنْها قالت: (كان رسولُ الله صَلَّى اللهُ عَلَيْهِ وَآلِهِ وَسَلَّمَ يقرأُ كلَّ ليلةٍ: بني إسرائيلَ والزُّمَر - أي: سورةَ الاسراءِ، وسورةَ الزُّمُر -)[5]. رواه الترمذيُّ والنَّسائيُّ وغيرُهما.

---

(١) آل عمران: ٢٦.

(٢) أخرجه الطبراني في مسند الشاميين (٢٣٩٨).

(٣) التوبة: ١٢٩.

(٤) أخرجه ابن السني في (عمل اليوم والليلة) (١٣٢)، وابن عساكر (٣٦/ ١٩٦).

(٥) أخرجه الترمذي (٣٤٠٥).

THE LAST VERSE OF SŪRAH AL-ISRĀ'

Imam Aḥmad narrated with his chain that the Prophet ﷺ said that the verse of honour is: "And say, 'All praise is for Allah, Who has never had [any] offspring; nor does He have a partner in [governing] the kingdom; nor is He pathetic, needing a protector. And revere Him immensely.'"[1]

Ibn Abī al-Dunyā and Bayhaqī in *al-Asmā' wa al-Ṣifāt* narrated with their chains that the Prophet ﷺ said, "I have never been distressed by any matter except that Jibrīl ﷺ has come to me and said, 'O Muhammad, say, "I have placed my trust in the Ever-Living Who never dies. All praise is for Allah, Who has never had [any] offspring; nor does He have a partner in [governing] the kingdom; nor is He pathetic, needing a protector. And revere Him immensely."[2]'"[3]

Abū Ya'lā and Ibn al-Sunnī narrated on the authority of Abū Hurayrah ﷺ who said, "The Messenger of Allah ﷺ and I went out and came across a man in a shabby state. He said, 'O So-and-so, what has led you to this illness and hardship I see? Shall I not teach you some words that will take away your illness and hardship? Say, "I have placed my trust in the Ever-Living Who never dies. 'All praise is for Allah, Who has never had [any] offspring (until the end of the verse).'" The Messenger of Allah ﷺ then came to him again (after some time) and his condition had become good. He ﷺ asked, 'What is this?' He replied, 'I continued reading the words you taught me, O Messenger of Allah.'"[4]

'Abd al-Razzāq narrated with his chain in his *Muṣannaf* that the Prophet ﷺ used to teach the children of Banū Hāshim to say "All praise is for Allah, Who has never had [any] offspring (until the end of the verse)" seven

(1) *Al-Isrā'*, 111; *Aḥmad* (15634).

(2) *Al-Isrā'*, 111.

(3) Bayhaqī in *al-Asmā' wa al-Ṣifāt* (216).

(4) *Abū Ya'lā* (6671); *Ṭabarānī* (1045).

آخرُ آيةٍ من سورةِ الإسراء

روى الإمامُ أحمدُ بإسنادِهِ أنَّ النبيَّ ﷺ قال: «آيةُ العزِّ: {وَقُلِ الْحَمْدُ لِلَّهِ الَّذِي لَمْ يَتَّخِذْ وَلَدًا وَلَمْ يَكُن لَّهُ شَرِيكٌ فِي الْمُلْكِ وَلَمْ يَكُن لَّهُ وَلِيٌّ مِّنَ الذُّلِّ وَكَبِّرْهُ تَكْبِيرًا}[1]»[2]. وروى ابنُ أبي الدُّنيا والبيهقيُّ في (الأسماءِ والصِّفاتِ) بإسنادِهما أنَّ النبيَّ ﷺ قال: «ما كَرَبَني أمرٌ إلَّا تمثَّلَ لي جبريلُ عليه السّلامُ، فقال لي: يا محمّدُ قل: توكَّلتُ على الحيِّ الذي لا يموتُ، {الْحَمْدُ لِلَّهِ الَّذِي لَمْ يَتَّخِذْ وَلَدًا وَلَمْ يَكُن لَّهُ شَرِيكٌ فِي الْمُلْكِ وَلَمْ يَكُن لَّهُ وَلِيٌّ مِّنَ الذُّلِّ وَكَبِّرْهُ تَكْبِيرًا}[3]»[4]. وروى أبو يَعلى وابنُ السُّنِّيِّ عن أبي هريرةَ رضي الله عنه قال: خرجتُ أنا ورسولُ اللهِ ﷺ، فأتى على رجلٍ رثِّ الهيئةِ، فقال: «أيْ فلانُ ما بلَغَ بك ما أرى مِنَ السَّقمِ والضُّرِّ؟ ألا أعلِّمُكَ كلماتٍ تُذهِبُ عنك السَّقمَ والضُّرَّ، قل: توكَّلتُ على الحيِّ الذي لا يموتُ {الْحَمْدُ لِلَّهِ الَّذِي لَمْ يَتَّخِذْ وَلَدًا}[5]»، إلى تمامِ الآيةِ، ثمّ أتى عليه رسولُ اللهِ ﷺ - أي بعدَ حينٍ - وقد حَسُنَتْ حالتُهُ، فقال: مَهْيَمْ؟ فقال: لم أزلْ أقولُ الكلماتِ التي علَّمْتَني يا رسولَ اللهِ ﷺ[6]. وروى عبدُ الرَّزّاقِ في (مصنَّفِهِ) بإسنادِهِ أنَّ النبيَّ صلى اللهُ عليه وآلِهِ وسلَّمَ كان يُعلِّمُ الغلامَ من بني هاشمٍ إذا أفصحَ سبعَ

---

(١) الإسراء: ١١١.

(٢) أخرجه أحمد (١٥٦٣٤).

(٣) الإسراء: ١١١.

(٤) أخرجه البيهقي في (الأسماء والصفات) (٢١٦).

(٥) الإسراء: ١١١.

(٦) أخرجه أبو يعلى (٦٦٧١)، والطبراني (١٠٤٥).

times once they could speak.(1) Ibn Jarīr, Ibn Abī Shaybah, and Ibn al-Sunnī have narrated something similar.

SŪRAH AL-KAHF

Abū al-Dardā' ﷺ narrated that the Prophet ﷺ said, "Whoever memorizes the first ten verses of *Sūrah al-Kahf* will be protected against Dajjāl (the Antichrist)."(2)In another narration of Muslim: "...from the end of *Sūrah al-Kahf*."

In the narration of Nasā'ī, "Whoever recited the last ten verses of *Sūrah al-Kahf* will be protected from the tribulation of Dajjāl."(3)

Abū Sa'īd al-Khudrī ﷺ narrated that the Prophet ﷺ said, "Whoever recites *Sūrah al-Kahf* on Friday will have a light that shines for them between two Fridays."(4) Nasā'ī narrated it.

Ibn 'Umar ﷺ narrated that the Messenger of Allah ﷺ said, "Whoever recites *Sūrah al-Kahf* on Friday, a light rises from underneath their feet all the way until the sky and it will shine him for them on the Day of Judgement. And they are forgiven (minor sins) between two Fridays."(5)

Ḥāfiẓ al-Mundhirī said, "Ibn Mardawayh narrated it in his exegesis with a chain that is acceptable."

Ibn Mardawayh narrated on the authority of Sayyidah 'Ā'ishah i, as a hadith attributed to the Prophet ﷺ, "Shall I not inform you of a *sūrah* whose greatness fills the expanse between the Heavens and the Earth, and the one who writes it also gets the same reward? Whoever recites it on Friday will be forgiven from that Friday until the next, and three more days. Whoever recites the last five verses of it when going to sleep, Allah

---

(1) *'Abd al-Razzāq* (7976).

(2) *Muslim* (809)

(3) *Abū Dāwūd* (4323).

(4) *Bayhaqī* (6209).

(5) Ibn Mardawayh in his exegesis, as cited by al-Mundhirī in *al-Targhīb wa al-Tarhīb*, vol. 1, p. 298.

مرّاتٍ {الْحَمْدُ لِلَّهِ الَّذِي لَمْ يَتَّخِذْ وَلَدًا} [1] الآيةَ[2]. وروى نحوَ ذلك ابنُ جريرٍ، وابنُ أبي شَيبةَ، وابنُ السّنّيّ.

سورةُ الكهف

عن أبي الدَّرداءِ رَضِيَ اللَّهُ عَنْهُ أنَّ النبيَّ ﷺ قال: «مَن حَفِظَ عشرَ آياتٍ أوَّلَ سورةِ الكهفِ عُصِمَ مِنَ الدَّجالِ»[3] رواه مسلمٌ. وفي روايةٍ له: «مِن آخِرِ سورةِ الكهفِ». وفي روايةِ النَّسائيِّ: « مَن قرأَ العشرَ الأواخِرَ من سورةِ الكهفِ عُصِمَ من فتنةِ الدَّجالِ»[4]. وعن أبي سعيدٍ الخدريِّ رَضِيَ اللَّهُ عَنْهُ أنَّ النبيَّ ﷺ قال: «مَن قرأَ سورةَ الكهفِ في يومِ الجُمَعَةِ أضاءَ له مِنَ النّورِ ما بينَ الجُمُعَتَينِ»[5] رواه النَّسائيُّ.

وعن ابنِ عمرَ رَضِيَ اللَّهُ عَنْهُمَا قالَ: قال رسولُ اللهِ ﷺ: «مَن قرأَ سورةَ الكهفِ في يومِ الجُمُعَةِ سطعَ له نورٌ من تحتِ قدمِهِ إلى عَنانِ السَّماءِ يضيءُ له يومَ القيامة، وغُفِرَ له ما بينَ الجُمُعَتَينِ»[6]. أي: من الصَّغائر. قال الحافظُ المنذريُّ: رواهُ ابن مَرْدَوَيْه في (تفسيرِهِ)، بإسنادٍ لا بأسَ به. وروى ابنُ مَرْدَوَيْه عن السَّيدةِ عائشةَ رَضِيَ اللَّهُ عَنْهَا مرفوعاً: «ألَا أُخبِرُكُم بسورةٍ مِلْءُ عظمَتِها ما بينَ السَّماءِ والأرضِ، ولكاتِبِها من الأجرِ مثلُ ذلك،

---

(١) الإسراء: ١١١.

(٢) أخرجه عبد الرزاق (٧٩٧٦).

(٣) أخرجه مسلم (٨٠٩).

(٤) أخرجه أبو داود (٤٣٢٣).

(٥) أخرجه البيهقي (٦٢٠٩).

(٦) أخرجه ابن مَرْدَوَيْه في (التفسير) كما في (الترغيب والترهيب) للمنذري (١/٢٩٨).

will wake them up whenever they wish."[1] It is the *Sūrah* of the People of the Cave, as stated in *al-Fatḥ al-Kabīr*.

(1) Al-Muttaqī al-Hindī in *Kanz al- 'Ummāl* (2398).

وَمَن قرَأَها يومَ الجُمُعَةِ غُفِرَ له ما بينَه وما بينَ الجُمُعةِ الأخرى وزيادةُ ثلاثةِ أيامٍ، وَمَن قرأ الخمسَ الأواخرَ منها عند نومِهِ بَعَثَهُ اللهُ أيَّ الليلِ شاء»[1] سورةُ أصحابِ الكهفِ كما في (الفتحِ الكبيرِ).

---

(١) ذكره المتقي الهندي في (كنز العمال) (٢٣٩٨).

SŪRAH ṬĀHĀ

Dārimī and others narrated on the authority of Abū Hurayrah ﷺ that the Messenger of Allah ﷺ said, "Indeed, Allah Most Blessed and Most High recited *Sūrah Ṭāhā* and Yāsīn 2000 years before creating the Heavens and the Earth.

When the Angels heard the Qur'an they said, 'Glad tidings for the ummah to whom this will be sent down.

Glad tidings for the hearts that carry this. Glad tidings for the tongues that recite this.'"(1)

SŪRAH AL-SAJDAH (ALIF LĀM MĪM)

Jābir ﷺ narrated that the Prophet ﷺ would not sleep until he had recited *Alif Lām Mīm* (*Sajdah*) and *Blessed is the One in Whose Hands rests all authority* (*Sūrah al-Mulk*).(2)

Tirmidhī and Nasā'ī narrated it.

---

(1) Ibn ʿAdī in al-Kāmil fī al-Ḍuʿafā', vol. 1, p. 352.

(2) *Tirmidhī* (3404).

سورةُ طه

روى الدارميُّ وغيرُه عن أبي هريرةَ رَضِيَ اللَّهُ عَنْهُ أنَّ النبيَّ صَلَّى اللَّهُ عَلَيْهِ وَآلِهِ وَسَلَّمَ قال: «إنَّ اللهَ تَبَارَكَ وَتَعَالَى قرأَ طه ويس قبل أن يخلَقَ السَّمواتِ والأرضَ بألفي عام، فلمّا سَمِعَتِ الملائكةُ القرآنَ قالت: طوبى لأمّةٍ ينزلُ عليها هذا، وطوبى لأجوافٍ تَحمِلُ هذا، وطوبى لألسنةٍ تتكلَّم بهذا»[1].

سورة السَّجدةِ {الم}

عن جابرٍ رَضِيَ اللَّهُ عَنْهُ أنَّ النبيَّ صَلَّى اللَّهُ عَلَيْهِ وَآلِهِ وَسَلَّمَ: (كان لا ينامُ حتّى يقرأَ {الم تَنْزِيل} السَّجدةَ، و{تَبَارَكَ الَّذِي بِيَدِهِ المُلْكُ}) [2]. رواه الترمذيُّ والنَّسائيُّ.

---

(١) أخرجه ابن عدي في (الكامل في الضعفاء) (٣٥٢/١).

(٢) أخرجه الترمذي (٣٤٠٤).

SŪRAH YĀSĪN

It is narrated on the authority of Anas ﷺ that the Prophet ﷺ said, "Indeed, everything has a heart, and the heart of the Qur'an is Yāsīn. Whoever recites Yāsīn, Allah will record for them the reward of reciting the Qur'an ten times excluding Yāsīn."(1) Tirmidhī and Dārimī narrated it.

Abū al-Shaykh narrated on the authority of Ibn ʿAbbās ﷺ, as a hadith attributed to the Prophet ﷺ, "Whoever recites Yāsīn at night will receive ten times more reward than at other times. And whoever recites it at the beginning of the day and presents it before their need, their need will be fulfilled."(2) This is as cited in *Kanz al-ʿUmmāl.*

Bayhaqī narrated on the authority of Maʿqil ibn Yasār ﷺ that the Prophet ﷺ said, "Whoever recites Yāsīn seeking the pleasure of Allah will be forgiven all their previous sins, so recite it upon your deceased."(3)

Jundub ﷺ narrated that the Messenger of Allah ﷺ said, "Whoever recites Yāsīn at night, seeking the pleasure of Allah Most High, will be forgiven."(4) Mālik narrated it and Ibn Ḥibbān in his *Ṣaḥīḥ*. The narration of Aḥmad on the virtue of *Sūrah al-Baqarah* has already passed.

THE VIRTUE OF THE ḤAWĀMĪM

Abū al-Shaykh narrated in *al-Thawāb* from Anas ﷺ, as a hadith attributed to the Prophet ﷺ, "The Ḥawāmīm (i.e., the *sūrahs* beginning with *Ḥa Mīm*) are the silk brocade (*dībāj*) of the Qur'an."

Ḥākim narrated it in *al-Mustadrak* on the authority of Ibn Masʿūd ﷺ as a *mawqūf* narration, as stated in *al-Jāmiʿ al-Ṣaghīr.*

Ibn Mardawayh narrated on the authority of Samurah ibn Jundub ﷺ, as

---

(1) *Tirmidhī* (2887).

(2) Al-Muttaqī al-Hindī in *Kanz al-ʿUmmāl* (2693).

(3) Bayhaqī in *Shuʿab al-Īmān* (643).

(4) Suyūṭī in al-Durr al-Manthūr, vol. 5, p. 38.

سورةُ يس

روي عن أنسٍ رَضِيَ اللَّهُ عَنْهُ أنَّ النبيَّ صَلَّى اللَّهُ عَلَيْهِ وَآلِهِ وَسَلَّمَ قال: «إنَّ لكلِّ شيءٍ قلباً، وقلبُ القرآنِ يس، ومَن قرأ يس كتبَ اللهُ له بقراءَتِها قراءةَ القرآنِ عشرَ مرّات دون يس»[1]. رواه الترمذيُّ والدارميُّ. وروى أبو الشّيخِ عن ابنِ عبّاسٍ رَضِيَ اللَّهُ عَنْهُمَا مرفوعاً: «مَن قرأ يس في ليلةٍ أُضعِفَ على غيرها عشراً، ومَن قرأَها في صَدرِ النَّهارِ وقدَّمها بين يدي حاجَتِهِ قُضِيَتْ»[2] كما في (كنز العمال). وروى البيهقيُّ عن مَعقِلِ بنِ يَسارٍ أنَّ النبيَّ صلى الله عليه وآله وسلم قال: «مَن قرأَ يس ابتغاءَ وجهِ اللهِ غَفرَ اللهُ ما تقدَّمَ مِن ذنبِهِ، فاقرَؤُوها عندَ موتاكُم»[3]. وعن جُندُبٍ رَضِيَ اللَّهُ عَنْهُ قال: قال رسولُ الله صَلَّى اللَّهُ عَلَيْهِ وَآلِهِ وَسَلَّمَ: «مَن قرأَ يس في ليلةٍ ابتغاءَ وجهِ اللهِ تعالى غُفِرَ له»[4]. رواه مالكٌ وابنُ حِبّانَ في (صحيحِه)، وتقدَّمَتْ روايةُ أحمدَ في فضلِ سورةِ البقرةِ.

فضلُ الحواميم

روى أبو الشَّيخِ في (الثَّوابِ) عن أنسٍ رَضِيَ اللَّهُ عَنْهُ مرفوعاً: «الحواميمُ دِيباجُ القرآن». ورواهُ الحاكمُ في (المستدرَك) عن ابنِ مسعودٍ رَضِيَ اللَّهُ عَنْهُ موقوفاً، كما في (الجامعِ الصَّغيرِ).

---

(١) أخرجه الترمذي (٢٨٨٧).

(٢) ذكره المتقي الهندي في (كنز العمال) (٢٦٩٣).

(٣) أخرجه البيهقي في (شعب الإيمان) (٦٣٤).

(٤) ذكره السيوطي في (الدر المنثور) (٧/ ٣٨).

a hadith attributed to the Prophet ﷺ, "The Ḥawāmīm are a garden from the gardens of Paradise."(1)

Bayhaqī narrated on the authority of Khalīl ibn Murrah as a *mursal* narration attributed to the Prophet ﷺ, "The Ḥawāmīm are seven and the doors of Jahannum are also seven.

Each Ḥa Mīm will come and stand at one of these doors and say, 'O Allah, do not admit through this door those who used to believe in me and recite me.'"(2)

ḤA MĪM DUKHĀN

It is narrated on the authority of Abū Hurayrah ؓ that the Prophet ﷺ said, "Whoever recites Ḥa Mīm Dukhān on the night of Friday will be forgiven."(3) Nasā'ī narrated it.

In one narration, "Whoever recites Ḥa Mīm Dukhān at night, 70000 Angels seek forgiveness for them until morning."(4)

Tirmidhī narrated it.

SŪRAH AL-RAḤMĀN

Bayhaqī and Daylamī narrated on the authority of Sayyidah Fāṭimah ؓ that the Prophet ﷺ said, "The person who recites (*Sūrah) Al-Ḥadīd*, al-Wāqi'ah and al-Raḥmān is called 'inhabitant of Paradise' in the kingdom of the Heavens and the Earth."(5)

This is as cited in *al-Fatḥ al-Kabīr* and other works.

---

(1) *Daylamī* (2816).

(2) *Bayhaqī* (461).

(3) *Tirmidhī* (2889).

(4) *Tirmidhī* (2888).

(5) Bayhaqī in *Shu 'ab al-Īmān*, vol. 2, p. 976.

وروى ابنُ مَرْدَوَيْه عن سَمُرَةَ بنِ جُندبٍ مرفوعاً: «الحواميمُ روضةٌ من رياضِ الجنّةِ»[1].

وروى البيهقيُّ عن الخليلِ بنِ مُرَّةَ مرسَلًا مرفوعاً: «الحواميمُ سبعٌ، وأبوابُ جهنَّمَ سبع، تجيءُ كلُّ حاميمٍ منها تقفُ على بابٍ من هذه الأبوابِ، تقول: اللَّهمَّ لا تُدخِلْ هذا البابَ مَن كان يؤمنُ بي ويقرَؤُني»[2].

حم الدُّخان

رويَ عن أبي هريرةَ رَضِيَ اللَّهُ عَنْهُ أنَّ النبيَّ صَلَّى اللَّهُ عَلَيْهِ وَآلِهِ وَسَلَّمَ قال: «مَن قرأَ {حم} الدُّخان ليلةَ الجُمُعَةِ غُفِرَ له»[3]. رواه النسائي. وفي روايةٍ: «مَن قرأَ {حم} الدُّخانَ في ليلةٍ أصبحَ يستغفرُ له سبعونَ ألف مَلَكٍ»[4]. رواه الترمذي.

سورةُ الرَّحمن

روى البيهقيُّ والدَّيلميُّ عن السَّيدةِ فاطمةَ عليها السَّلامُ ورضي الله عنها وعنا بها عن النبيِّ صلى الله عليه وآله وسلم قال: «قارئُ الحديدِ - أي: سورةِ الحديدِ - و{إِذَا وَقَعَتِ الوَاقِعَةُ} و{الرَّحْمَنُ} يُدعى في ملكوتِ السَّماواتِ والأرضِ ساكنَ الفردوسِ»[5].

---

(١) أخرجه الديلمي (٢٨١٦).

(٢) أخرجه البيهقي (٤٦١).

(٣) أخرجه الترمذي (٢٨٨٩).

(٤) أخرجه الترمذي (٢٨٨٨).

(٥) أخرجه البيهقي في (شعب الإيمان) (٢/٩٧٦).

SŪRAH AL-WĀQI'AH

"Teach your womenfolk *Sūrah al-Wāqi'ah*, because it is the *sūrah* of wealth."[1] Daylamī narrated it in *al-Firdaws* on the authority of Anas ﷺ, as a hadith attributed to the Prophet ﷺ.

THE MUSABBIḤĀT

Irbāḍ ibn Sāriyah ﷺ narrated that the Prophet ﷺ used to recite the musabbiḥāt every night before going to sleep and that he used to say, "In them is a verse greater than 1000 verses."[2] This is narrated by the authors of the *Sunan* collections.

There is a difference of opinion regarding this verse. Ibn Kathīr said it is the saying of Allah Most High at the beginning of *Sūrah al-Ḥadīd*: "He is the First and the Last, the Most High and Most Near, and He has [perfect] knowledge of all things."[3] Others said it is the last three verses of *Sūrah al-Ḥashr*.

Imam Aḥmad narrated on the authority of Ma'qil ibn Yasār ﷺ that the Prophet ﷺ said, "Whoever says in the morning, 'I seek refuge with Allah – the All-Hearing, All-Knowing – against Satan, the accursed' three times, then recites the last three verses of *Sūrah al-Ḥashr*, Allah appoints 70000 Angels to pray for them until the evening and if they die on that day they die as a martyr. And whoever says this in the evening will receive the same."[4]

Ibn Abbas ﷺ said, "If you experience any whispering in your heart, say, 'He is the First and the Last, the Most High and Most Near, and He has [perfect] knowledge of all things.' Whoever repeats this will have this whispering go away from him."

---

(1) *Daylamī* (4005).

(2) *Tirmidhī* (3406).

(3) *Al-Ḥadīd*, 3.

(4) *Tirmidhī* (2922); *Aḥmad* (20306).

كما في (الفتح الكبير) وغيرِه.

سورةُ الواقعة

«علِّموا نساءَكم سورةَ الواقعةِ؛ فإنَّها سورةُ الغِنى»[1]. رواه الدَّيلميُّ في (الفردوس) عن أنسٍ رَضِيَ اللهُ عَنْهُ مرفوعاً.

المُسَبِّحات

عن العِرباضِ بنِ ساريةَ رَضِيَ اللهُ عَنْهُ أنَّ النبيَّ صَلَّى اللهُ عَلَيْهِ وَآلِهِ وَسَلَّمَ: كان يقرأُ المسبِّحاتِ كلَّ ليلةٍ قبلَ أنْ يَرْقُدَ، يقول: «فيهنَّ آيةٌ خيرٌ من ألفِ آيةٍ»[2]. رواه أصحابُ السُّنن.

واختُلفَ في هذه الآيةِ: فقال ابنُ كثيرٍ: هي قولُه تعالى في أوَّلِ سورةِ الحديد: {هُوَ الْأَوَّلُ وَالْآخِرُ وَالظَّاهِرُ وَالْبَاطِنُ وَهُوَ بِكُلِّ شَيْءٍ عَلِيمٌ}[3]، وقال غيرُه: هي أواخرُ سورةِ الحشرِ.

وروى الإمامُ أحمدُ عن مَعقِلِ بنِ يَسارٍ رَضِيَ اللهُ عَنْهُ عنِ النبيِّ صَلَّى اللهُ عَلَيْهِ وَآلِهِ وَسَلَّمَ قال: «مَن قال حينَ يُصبِحُ - ثلاثَ مرّاتٍ - أعوذُ باللهِ السَّميعِ العليمِ من الشَّيطانِ الرَّجيمِ، ثمَّ قرأَ ثلاثَ آياتٍ من آخِرِ سورةِ الحشرِ: وكَّلَ اللهُ به سبعينَ ألف مَلَكٍ يُصلّونَ عليه حتّى يُمسيَ، وإنْ ماتَ في ذلك اليومِ ماتَ شهيداً، ومَن قالَها حين يمسي كان بتلكَ المنزلةِ»[4].

---

(١) أخرجه الديلمي (٤٠٠٥).

(٢) أخرجه الترمذي (٣٤٠٦).

(٣) الحديد: ٣.

(٤) أخرجه الترمذي (٢٩٢٢)، وأحمد (٢٠٣٠٦).

SŪRAH TABĀRAK

Abū Hurayrah ﷺ narrated that the Messenger of Allah ﷺ said, "There is a *sūrah* of 30 verses in the Qur'an which interceded for its reciter until they were forgiven. [It is:] *Blessed is the One in Whose Hand lies all authority.*"(1) This is narrated by the authors of the *Sunan* collections.

Ḥākim narrated on the authority of Abū Hurayrah ﷺ, as a hadith attributed to the Prophet ﷺ, "Indeed, a *sūrah* from the Book of Allah which is only 30 verses long interceded for a man, and thus took him out of Hellfire and entered him into Paradise."(2)

Ibn ʿAbbās ﷺ narrated on the authority of the Prophet ﷺ who said, "It (i.e., *Sūrah al-Mulk*) is the Protector (*al-Māni ʿah*) and it is the Saver (*al-Munji'ah*) which saves from the punishment of the grave."(3)

Anas ﷺ narrated on the authority of the Prophet ﷺ said, "A *sūrah* of the Qur'an which is only 30 verses long argued on behalf of its reciter until it entered them into Paradise. It is [*Sūrah*] *Tabārak*."(4) Ḍiyā' al-Maqdisī narrated it, and Ṭabarānī narrated it in *al-Awsaṭ*, as stated in *al-Jāmi ʿ al-Ṣaghīr*.

Ibn Masʿūd ﷺ said, "At the time of the Messenger of Allah ﷺ, we used to call it (i.e., *Sūrah al-Mulk*) the Protector. It is a *sūrah* in the Book of Allah Most High that whoever recites it at night has performed an abundant and good action."(5) Ṭabarānī narrated it in *al-Kabīr* and *al-Awsaṭ*, and its narrators are reliable.

Nasā'ī narrated on the authority of Ibn Masʿūd ﷺ who said, "Whoever recites *Sūrah al-Mulk* every night, Allah Almighty and Exalted will protect them thereby from the punishment of the grave. At the time of the

(1) Abū Dāwūd (1400); Tirmidhī (2891).

(2) *Ḥākim* (2076).

(3) *Tirmidhī* (2890).

(4) Ṭabarānī in *al-Mu ʿjam al-Awsaṭ* (3654).

(5) *Majma ʿ al-Zawā'id* of al-Haythamī, vol. 7, p. 130.

وقال ابنُ عبّاسٍ رضي اللهُ تعالى عنهما: إذا وجدتَ في نفسِكَ الوَسوسةَ فقُلْ: {هُوَ الْأَوَّلُ وَالْآخِرُ وَالظَّاهِرُ وَالْبَاطِنُ وَهُوَ بِكُلِّ شَيْءٍ عَلِيمٌ}[1]؛ فمَن كرَّرها ذهبَتْ عنه الوسوسةُ.

سورةُ تبارك

عن أبي هريرةَ رَضِيَ اللَّهُ عَنْهُ قال: قال رسولُ اللهِ صَلَّى اللَّهُ عَلَيْهِ وَآلِهِ وَسَلَّمَ: «مِنَ القرآنَ سورةٌ ثلاثونَ آيةً، شَفَعتْ لرجلٍ حتّى غُفِرَ له: {تبَارَكَ الَّذِي بِيَدِهِ المُلْكُ}»[2] رواهُ أصحابُ السُّنن. وروى الحاكمُ عن أبي هريرةَ رَضِيَ اللَّهُ عَنْهُ مرفوعاً: «إنَّ سورةً من كتابِ اللهِ تعالى ما هي إلّا ثلاثون آيةً، شَفَعَتْ لرجلٍ فأخرجتْهُ من النّارِ وأدخلَتْهُ الجنّةَ»[3]. وعن ابنِ عبّاسٍ رَضِيَ اللَّهُ عَنْهُمَا عن النبيِّ صَلَّى اللَّهُ عَلَيْهِ وَآلِهِ وَسَلَّمَ قال: «هي - أي: سورةُ تبارك - المانعةُ، وهي المُنجيةُ تُنجي من عذابِ القبرِ»[4]. وعن أنسٍ رَضِيَ اللَّهُ عَنْهُ عن النبيِّ صَلَّى اللَّهُ عَلَيْهِ وَآلِهِ وَسَلَّمَ قال: «سورةٌ من القرآنِ ما هي إلا ثلاثونَ آيةً، خاصَمَتْ عن صاحبِها حتى أدخلتْهُ الجنّةَ، وهي: {تبارك}»[5]. رواه الضِّياءُ المقدسيُّ، والطبرانيُّ في (الأوسط) كما في (الجامع الصغير). وعن ابنِ مسعودٍ رضي اللهُ عنه قال: (كُنّا نُسمّيها - يعني: {تبَارَكَ الَّذِي بِيَدِهِ المُلْكُ} - في عهدِ رسولِ اللهِ صلى

---

(١) الحديد: ٣.

(٢) أخرجه أبو داود (١٤٠٠)، والترمذي (٢٨٩١).

(٣) أخرجه الحاكم (٢٠٧٦).

(٤) أخرجه الترمذي (٢٨٩٠).

(٥) أخرجه الطبراني في (المعجم الأوسط) (٣٦٥٤).

Messenger of Allah ﷺ, we used to call it the Protector. It is a *sūrah* in the Book of Allah Most High that whoever recites it at night has performed an abundant and good action."[1]

ʿAbd ibn Ḥumayd narrated in his *Musnad* that Ibn ʿAbbās said to a man, "Shall I not gift you a hadith which will make you happy?" He said, "Yes, of course." He said, "Recite *Sūrah al-Mulk*, and teach it to your family, all your children, the children of your household, and your neighbours. It is the Saver and the Disputer (Mujādilah), which will dispute and argue for its reciter in the presence of its Lord on the Day of Judgement. It will ask Him to save this person from the punishment of the Fire and to save its reciter from the punishment of the grave. The Messenger of Allah ﷺ said, 'I wish it was in the heart of every Muslim in my ummah.'"[2] Ṭabarānī also narrated it, as stated in *Majma ʿ al-Zawā'id*. In the narration of Ḥākim: "I wish it was in the heart of a believer", as stated in Mundhirī's *al-Targhīb wa al-Tarhīb*.

A QUR'ANIC AND PROPHETIC INVOCATION

ʿAbdullāh ibn Aḥmad narrated in *Zawā'id al-Musnad* with a sound chain from Ubayy ibn Kaʿb who said, "I was with the Prophet ﷺ when a Bedouin came and said, 'O Prophet of Allah, I have a brother who is ill.' He ﷺ asked, 'What is his illness?' He said, 'He is possessed.' The Prophet ﷺ said, 'Bring him to me.' So he placed him in front of him and the Prophet ﷺ then read upon him: *Sūrah al-Fatihah*; the first four verses of *Sūrah al-Baqarah*; these two verses: 'Your God is only one God';[3] Āyah al-Kursī; the last three verses of *Sūrah al-Baqarah*; the verse of *Āl 'Imrān*: 'Allah [Himself] is a Witness that there is no god [worthy of worship] except

(1) Mundhirī's *al-Targhīb wa al-Tarhīb*. Vol. 2, p. 368.

(2) *Ṭabarānī* (11616).

(3) *Al-Baqarah*, 163.

اللهُ عليه وآله وسلم: المانعة، وإنّها في كتابِ اللهِ تعالى، سورةٌ مَن قرأها في ليلةٍ فقد أكثرَ وأطيبَ)[1].

رواه الطبرانيُّ في (الكبير) و (الأوسط) ورجالُهُ ثِقاتٌ. وروى النَّسائيُّ عن ابنِ مسعودٍ رضي الله عنه قال: (مَن قرأ سورةَ {تَبَارَكَ الَّذِي بِيَدِهِ الْمُلْكُ} كلَّ ليلةٍ منعَهُ اللهُ عزَّ وجلَّ بها من عذابِ القبرِ، وكنّا في عهدِ رسولِ اللهِ صلى اللهُ عليه وآلِهِ وسلَّمَ نُسمّيها المانعةَ، وإنّها في كتابِ اللهِ عزَّ وجلَّ سورةٌ مَن قرأها في كلِّ ليلةٍ فقد أكثرَ وأطابَ)[2]. وروى عبدُ بنُ حُميدٍ في (مسنَدِهِ) عن ابنِ عباسٍ رَضِيَ اللهُ عَنْهُمَا أنّهُ قال لرجلٍ: ألا أُتحِفُكَ بحديثٍ تفرحُ به؟ قال: بلى قال: اقرأْ {تَبَارَكَ الَّذِي بِيَدِهِ الْمُلْكُ} وعلِّمها أهلَكَ وجميعَ ولَدِكَ، وصبيانَ بيتِكَ وجيرانَكَ؛ فإنَّها المنجيةُ، والمجادِلةُ تجادِلُ وتُخاصِمُ يومَ القيامةِ عند ربِّها لقارِئِها، وتطلبُ له أن يُنجِيَهُ من عذابِ النّارِ، ويُنجّي بها صاحبَها من عذابِ القبرِ، وقال رسولُ اللهِ صَلَّى اللهُ عَلَيْهِ وَآلِهِ وَسَلَّمَ: «لَودِدتُ أنّها - سورةَ تبارك - في قلبِ كلِّ إنسانٍ من أُمّتي». ورواهُ الطبرانيُّ أيضاً كما في (مجمع الزوائد)، وفي روايةِ الحاكمِ: «وَدِدْتُ أنّها في قلبِ مؤمنٍ»[3]. كما في (ترغيبِ المنذريِّ).

تعويذةٌ قرآنيّةٌ نبويّةٌ

أخرج عبدُ اللهِ بنُ أحمدَ في (زوائدِ المسنَدِ) بسندٍ حسنٍ عن أُبَيِّ بنِ كعبٍ رَضِيَ اللهُ عَنْهُ قال: كنتُ عند النبيّ صَلَّى اللهُ عَلَيْهِ وَآلِهِ وَسَلَّمَ، فجاء أعرابيٌّ فقال: يا نبيَّ اللهِ إنَّ لي أخاً وبه وجعٌ، قال: «وما وجَعُه»؟ قال: لَمَمٌ - أي: جنون - ، قال: «فأْتِني به، فوضَعَهُ بينَ يديه فعوَّذَهُ

---

(١) ذكره الهيثمي في (مجمع الزوائد) (١٣٠/٧).

(٢) ذكره المنذري في (الترغيب والترهيب) (٣٦٨/٢).

(٣) أخرجه الطبراني (١١٦١٦).

Him...';[1] a verse from al-Aʿrāf: 'Indeed, your Lord is Allah...';[2] the last part of *Sūrah al-Mu'minūn*: 'Exalted is Allah, the True King...';[3]a verse from *Sūrah al-Jinn*: 'Now, we believe that] our Lord – Exalted is His Majesty...';[4] ten verses from al-Ṣāffāt; three verses from the end of *Sūrah al-Ḥashr*; *Sūrah al-Ikhlāṣ*; and the *mu ʿawwidhatān* (i.e., *Sūrah al-Falaq* and *Sūrah al-Nās*). The man then stood as though he never had any illness."[5]

THE VIRTUE OF RECITING SŪRAH AL-BAYYINAH

Ḥāfiẓ Abū Nuʿaym narrated in *Asmā' al-Ṣaḥābah* with his chain from Fuḍayl ﷺ who said he heard the Messenger of Allah ﷺ say, "Indeed, Allah listens to the recitation of *Sūrah al-Bayyinah* and then says, 'Rejoice, My slave. By My Honour, I shall settle you in Paradise until you are pleased.'"[6]

Ḥāfiẓ Abū Mūsā al-Madīnī and Ibn al-Athīr narrated on the authority of Maṭar al-Muzanī (or al-Mudalī) that the Prophet ﷺ said, "Indeed, Allah listens to *Sūrah al-Bayyinah* and then says, 'Rejoice, My slave. By My Honour, I shall not forget you at any stage in this world and the Hereafter, and I shall settle you in Paradise until you are pleased.'"[7]

The Prophetic hadiths also mention that Allah Most High commanded the Prophet ﷺ to recite this *sūrah* to Ubayy ibn Kaʿb ﷺ. Imam Aḥmad narrated with his chain on the authority of Abū Ḥayyah al-Anṣārī ﷺ that when *Sūrah al-Bayyinah* was revealed, Jibrīl said, "O Messenger of Allah, your Lord commands you to recite it to Ubayy." The Prophet ﷺ said to Ubayy ﷺ, "Jibrīl has commanded me to recite this *sūrah* to you." Ubayy

(1) *Āl 'Imrān*, 18.

(2) *Al-A 'rāf*, 54.

(3) *Al-Mu'minūn*, 116.

(4) *Al-Jinn*, 3.

(5) *Aḥmad* (20670).

(6) Al-Muttaqī al-Hindī in *Kanz al- 'Ummāl* (2711).

(7) Ibn Kathir's exegesis, vol. 4, p. 348.

النبيُّ ﷺ بفاتحةِ الكتاب، وأربعِ آياتٍ من أوَّلِ سورةِ البقرةِ، وهاتينِ الآيتينِ {وَإِلَٰهُكُمْ إِلَٰهٌ وَاحِدٌ} [١] وآيةِ الكرسيّ، وثلاثِ آياتٍ من آخِرِ سورةِ البقرةِ، وآيةٍ من آلِ عمرانَ {شَهِدَ اللَّهُ أَنَّهُ لا إِلَهَ إِلا هُوَ} [٢]، وآيةٍ من الأعرافِ {إِنَّ رَبَّكُمُ اللَّهُ} [٣]، وآخرِ سورةِ المؤمنونَ {فَتَعَالَى اللَّهُ الْمَلِكُ الْحَقُّ} [٤]، وآيةٍ من سورةِ الجنّ {وَأَنَّهُ تَعَالَى جَدُّ رَبِّنَا} [٥]، وعشرِ آياتٍ من الصَّافّاتِ، وثلاثِ آياتٍ من آخِرِ سورةِ الحشرِ، و{قُلْ هُوَ اللَّهُ أَحَدٌ} [٦]، والمعوِّذتَينِ، فقام الرَّجلُ كأنّهُ لم يَشكُ قطُّ وجعاً[٧]. كذا في (المسنَد).

ما جاء في فضلِ تلاوةِ سورةِ البيّنةِ

روى الحافظُ أبو نُعيمٍ في كتابِهِ (أسماءِ الصَّحابةِ) بإسنادِهِ عن فُضَيلٍ رَضِيَ اللهُ عَنْهُ قال: سمعتُ رسولَ اللهِ ﷺ يقول: «إنَّ اللهَ تعالى لَيسمَعُ قراءةَ {لَمْ يَكُنِ الَّذِينَ كَفَرُوا}[٨]، فيقولُ: أبشِرْ عبدي، فوعِزَّتي لأُمَكِّنَنَّ لك في الجنّةِ حتّى ترضى»[٩]. ورواهُ الحافظ

(١) البقرة: ١٦٣.

(٢) آل عمران: ١٨.

(٣) الأعراف: ٥٤.

(٤) المؤمنون: ١١٦.

(٥) الجن: ٣.

(٦) الإخلاص: ١.

(٧) أخرجه أحمد (٢٠٦٧٠).

(٨) البينة: ١.

(٩) ذكره المتقي الهندي في (كنز العمال) (٢٧١١).

ﷺ said, "I have been mentioned there (i.e., in the Higher Assembly), O Messenger of Allah?" The Prophet ﷺ said, "Yes", upon which Ubayy ﷺ cried.[1]

In a narration of Aḥmad, it is narrated on the authority of Ubayy ibn Ka'b ﷺ that the Messenger of Allah ﷺ said, "I have been commanded to recite such-and-such *sūrah* to you." He said, "O Messenger of Allah, I have been mentioned there?" He said, "Yes", and then said to him, "O Abū al-Mundhir, are you happy about that?" He replied, "Why would I not be when Allah says, 'Say, [O Prophet,] "In Allah's grace and mercy let them rejoice. That is far better than whatever [wealth] they amass."'[2]"[3]

Ḥāfiẓ Ibn Kathīr ﷺ said, "The Prophet ﷺ recited this *sūrah* to him to make him firm and increase in faith, because he had criticized a person (i.e., 'Abdullāh ibn Mas'ūd ﷺ) for reciting part of the Qur'an differently to the way the Messenger of Allah ﷺ had taught him. So, he raised this with the Messenger of Allah ﷺ who made them both recite and then said to both of them, 'You have read correctly.' Ubayy ﷺ said, 'I started having doubts at first, as I used to in [pre-Islamic] ignorance. The Messenger of Allah ﷺ struck me on my chest and I began dripping with sweat – as though I am seeing Allah – out of fear.' The Messenger of Allah ﷺ told him that Jibrīl had come to him and said, 'Your Lord commands you to teach your ummah the Qur'an in one way (*ḥarf*).' The Prophet said, 'I ask Allah for His protection and forgiveness.' He said, 'In two ways (*aḥruf*).' This continued until he said, 'Your Lord commands you to teach your ummah in seven ways.' This is according to what has come in authentic hadiths in that regard."

(1) *Aḥmad* (15674).

(2) *Yūnus*, 58.

(3) *Aḥmad* (15675)

أبو موسى المَدينيُّ، وابنُ الأثيرِ عن مطرٍ المُزَنِيِّ أو المُدَلِيِّ عن النبيِّ صلى الله عليه وآله وسلم: «إنَّ اللهَ يسمعُ قراءةَ ﴿لَمْ يَكُنِ الَّذِينَ كَفَرُوا﴾[1]، ويقولُ: أبشِرْ عبدي، فوعزَّتي لا أنساكَ على حالٍ من أحوالِ الدُّنيا والآخرةِ، ولأُمَكِّنَنَّ لك من الجنّةِ حتّى ترضى». كذا في (تفسيرِ ابنِ كثيرٍ)[2]. وقد جاءتِ الأحاديثُ النبويّةُ في أنَّ اللهَ تعالى أمَرَ النبيَّ ﷺ أن يقرأَ هذه السّورةَ على أُبَيِّ بنِ كعبٍ رَضِيَ اللهُ عَنْهُ؛ فقد روى الإمامُ أحمدُ بسندِهِ عن أبي حيّةَ الأنصاريِّ رَضِيَ اللهُ عَنْهُ قال: لمّا نزلَتْ ﴿لَمْ يَكُنِ الَّذِينَ كَفَرُوا مِنْ أَهْلِ الْكِتَابِ﴾[3] إلى آخرِها، قال جبريلُ: يا رسولَ اللهِ إنَّ ربَّكَ يأمُرُكَ أن تُقرِئَها أُبَيّاً، فقال النبيُّ صلى اللهُ عليه وآلهِ وسلَّمَ لأُبَيٍّ: «إنَّ جبريلَ أمَرَني أنْ أُقرِئَكَ هذه السُّورةَ»، قال أُبَيٌّ: وقد ذُكِرْتُ ثَمَّ - أي: هناك في الملأِ الأعلى- يا رسول الله؟ فقال: «نعم»، قال: فبكى أُبَيٌّ رَضِيَ اللهُ عَنْهُ[4]. وفي روايةٍ للإمامِ أحمدَ عن أُبَيِّ بنِ كعبٍ رَضِيَ اللهُ عَنْهُ قال: قال رسولُ اللهِ ﷺ: «إنّي أُمِرتُ أن أقرأَ عليك سورةَ كذا وكذا، قلتُ: يا رسولَ اللهِ وقد ذُكِرْتُ هناك؟ قال: «نعم»، فقال لي: «يا أبا المُنذِرِ فرحتَ بذلك»؟ قلتُ: وما يمنعني؟ واللهُ يقول: ﴿قُلْ بِفَضْلِ اللَّهِ وَبِرَحْمَتِهِ فَبِذَٰلِكَ فَلْيَفْرَحُوا هُوَ خَيْرٌ مِّمَّا يَجْمَعُونَ﴾[5]. قال الحافظُ ابنُ كثيرٍ رَحِمَهُ اللهُ تَعَالَى: وإنّما قرأَ عليه النبيُّ صلى اللهُ عليه وآلهِ وسلَّمَ هذه السُّورةَ؛ تثبيتاً له وزيادةً لإيمانِهِ، فإنّهُ كان قد أنكرَ على إنسانٍ - وهو: عبدُ اللهِ بنِ مسعودٍ - قراءةَ شيءٍ

---

(١) البينة: ١.

(٢) ينظر (تفسير ابن كثير) (٤/٣٤٨).

(٣) البينة: ١.

(٤) أخرجه أحمد (١٥٦٧٤).

(٥) يونس: ٥٨.

THE SPECIALITIES OF RECITING SŪRAH AL-KĀFIRŪN AND THE SUBSEQUENT SŪRAHS WHEN ON A JOURNEY

Abū Ya'lā and Ḍiyā' al-Maqdisī narrated on the authority of Jubayr ibn Muṭ'im ﷺ that the Prophet ﷺ said to him, "O Jubayr, when you go on a journey, do you want to be from those in the best condition and with the most provisions amongst your companions?

Read these five *sūrahs*: *Sūrah al-Kāfirūn*, *Sūrah al-Naṣr*, *Sūrah al-Ikhlāṣ*, *Sūrah al-Falaq*, and *Sūrah al-Nās*. Start every *sūrah* with the *basmalah* and finish with the *basmalah*."[1] This is as stated in *al-Fatḥ al-Kabīr*.

THE ENCOURAGEMENT TO RECITE SŪRAH AL-IKHLĀṢ AND ITS VIRTUE

Abū Hurayrah ﷺ narrated that the Messenger of Allah ﷺ said, "Gather together, because I am going to recite one-third of the Qur'an to you." So, those who could did so. The Prophet ﷺ then came out and recited *Sūrah al-Ikhlāṣ* and went back inside. People said to one another, "We think some news has come to him from the Heavens and that is why he has gone back in." The Prophet of Allah ﷺ then came out again and said, "I told you I am going to recite one-third of the Qur'an to you. Know that it is equivalent to one-third of the Qur'an."[2] Muslim narrated it.

Abū al-Dardā' ﷺ narrated that the Prophet ﷺ said, "Are any of you unable to recite one-third of the Qur'an?" They said, "How can one recite a third of the Qur'an?" He said, "*Sūrah al-Ikhlāṣ* is equivalent to one-third of the Qur'an."[3]

---

(1) *Itḥāf al-Khiyarah al-Maharah* (5684).

(2) *Muslim* (812).

(3) *Muslim* (811).

من القرآنِ على خلافِ ما أقرأَهُ رسولُ الله ﷺ، فرفَعَهُ إلى رسولِ اللهِ ﷺ فاستقرَأَهما، وقال لكلٍّ منهما: «أصبتَ». قال أُبَيٌّ: فأخذَني من الشكِّ أوَّلًا؛ إذ كنتُ في الجاهلية، فضرب رسولُ الله ﷺ في صدري، قال أُبَيٌّ: فَفِضْتُ عرقاً، وكأنَّما أنظر إلى اللهِ فَرَقاً، وأخبرَهُ رسولُ اللهِ ﷺ أنَّ جبريلَ أتاه، فقال: (إنَّ اللهَ يأمرُكَ أنْ تُقرِئَ أُمَّتَكَ القرآنَ على حرفٍ)، فقلت: «أسألُ اللهَ معافاتَهُ ومغفرتَهُ»، فقال: على حرفينِ، فلم يزل حتى قال: إنَّ اللهَ يأمُرُكَ أن تُقرِئَ أُمَّتَكَ القرآنَ على سبعةِ أحرفٍ[1]، كما جاءتِ الأحاديثُ الصّحيحةُ في ذلك. مُلَخَّصاً.

من خصائصِ تلاوةِ {قل يا أيها الكافرون} فما بعدَها في السَّفر

روى أبو يَعلى، والضّياءُ المقدسيُّ عن جُبَيرِ بنِ مُطعِمٍ رضي الله عنه أنَّ النبيَّ ﷺ قال له: «أتحبُّ يا جُبَيرُ إذا خرجتَ سَفَراً أن تكونَ من أمثلِ أصحابِكَ هيئةً، وأكثرِهم زاداً؟ اقرأْ هذهِ السُّورَ الخمسَ: {قُلْ يَا أَيُّهَا الْكَافِرُونَ}، و{إِذَا جَاءَ نَصْرُ اللَّهِ وَالْفَتْحُ}، و{قُلْ هُوَ اللَّهُ أَحَدٌ}، و{قُلْ أَعُوذُ بِرَبِّ الْفَلَقِ}، و{قُلْ أَعُوذُ بِرَبِّ النَّاسِ}، وافتَحْ كلَّ سورةٍ بـ{بِسْمِ اللَّهِ الرَّحْمَنِ الرَّحِيمِ} واختِمْ بـ{بِسْمِ اللَّهِ الرَّحْمَنِ الرَّحِيمِ}»[2]، كما في (الفتحِ الكبير).

التَّرغيبُ في قراءةِ {قُلْ هُوَ اللهُ أَحَدٌ} وفضلُها

عن أبي هريرةَ رضي الله عنه قال: قال رسولُ اللهِ ﷺ: «احشُدوا فإنِّي سأقرأُ عليكم ثُلُثَ

---

(١) أخرجه أحمد (١٥٦٧٥).

(٢) ذكره في (إتحاف الخيرة المهرة بزوائد المسانيد العشرة) (٥٦٨٤).

It is narrated on the authority of Muʿādh ibn Anas ﷺ from the Messenger of Allah ﷺ who said, "Whoever recites 'Say, [O Prophet,] "He is Allah – One [and Indivisible]"' until the end ten times, Allah will build for them a palace in Paradise." ʿUmar ibn al-Khaṭṭāb ﷺ said, "In that case, we will acquire a lot, O Messenger of Allah." The Messenger of Allah ﷺ said, "Allah can grant even more and better."(1) Aḥmad narrated it.

Sayyidah ʿĀ'ishah ﷺ narrated that the Prophet ﷺ sent a man on an expedition who would lead his companions in prayer and conclude [the recitation] with *Sūrah al-Ikhlāṣ*. When they returned, they mentioned this to the Prophet ﷺ. He said, "Ask him why he does that." He said, "Because it is the description of the Most Compassionate, and I love to recite it." The Prophet ﷺ said, "Tell him that Allah also loves him."(2) Bukhārī and Muslim narrated it.

---

(1) *Aḥmad* (15610).

(2) *Muslim* (813).

القرآنِ»، فحشَدَ مَن حشَدَ - أي: فاجتَمعوا - قال: ثمَّ خرجَ النبيُّ ﷺ فقرأَ {قُلْ هُوَ اللَّهُ أَحَدٌ} ثمَّ دخَلَ، فقال بعضُنا لبعضٍ: إنّا نرى هذا خبراً جاءَهُ من السَّماء، فذلك الذي أدخَلَهُ، ثمَّ خرج نبيُّ الله ﷺ، فقال: «إنّي قُلتُ لكم: سأقرأُ عليكم ثُلُثَ القرآنِ، ألا إنَّها تَعدِلُ ثُلُثَ القرآنِ»[1]. رواه مسلم. وعن أبي الدَّرداءِ رضي الله عنه عن النبيِّ ﷺ قال: «أيعجِزُ أحدُكُمْ أن يقرأَ في ليلةٍ ثُلُثَ القرآن»؟ قالوا: وكيف يقرأُ ثُلُثَ القرآنِ؟ قال: «{قُلْ هُوَ اللَّهُ أَحَدٌ} تعدلُ ثُلُثَ القرآنِ». وفي روايةٍ: «إنَّ اللهَ عزَّ وجلَّ جزَّأَ القرآنَ ثلاثةَ أجزاء، فجعل {قُلْ هُوَ اللَّهُ أَحَدٌ} جزءاً من أجزاءِ القرآنِ»[2] رواه مسلمٌ. وروي عن معاذِ بن أنسٍ رضي الله عنه عن رسولِ اللهِ ﷺ قال: «مَن قرأَ {قُلْ هُوَ اللَّهُ أَحَدٌ} حتّى يختِمَها عشرَ مرّاتٍ بنى اللهُ له قصراً في الجنّةِ»، فقال عمرُ بنُ الخطّابِ رضي الله عنه: إذاً نستكثرُ يا رسولَ اللهِ؟ فقال رسولُ اللهِ عليه الصلاة والسَّلامُ: «اللهُ أكثرُ وأطيبُ»[3] رواه أحمدُ. وعن السيّدةِ عائشةَ رضي الله عنها أنَّ النبيَّ ﷺ بعثَ رجلاً على سريّةٍ، وكان يقرأُ لأصحابِهِ في صلاتِهم فيختِمُ بـ: {قُلْ هُوَ اللَّهُ أَحَدٌ}، فلمّا رجَعوا ذكروا ذلك للنبيِّ ﷺ فقال: «سَلوهُ لأيِّ شيءٍ يصنعُ ذلك»، فسألوهُ، فقال: لأنّها صفةُ الرَّحمنِ وأنا أحبُّ أن أقرأَ بها، فقال النبيُّ ﷺ: «أخبروهُ أنَّ اللهَ يحبُّهُ»[4]. رواهُ البخاريُّ ومسلمٌ.

---

(١) أخرجه مسلم (٨١٢).

(٢) أخرجه مسلم (٨١١).

(٣) أخرجه أحمد (١٥٦١٠).

(٤) أخرجه مسلم (٨١٣).

RECITING SŪRAH AL-IKHLĀṢ BEFORE SLEEPING

Tirmidhī narrated on the authority of Anas ﷺ that the Prophet ﷺ said, "Whoever intends to sleep on their bed at night and lies down on their right side, then recites *Sūrah al-Ikhlāṣ* 100 times, the Lord Most Blessed and Most High will say to them on the Day of Judgement, 'O My slave, enter Paradise from your right.'"[1]

THE VIRTUE OF RECITING SŪRAH AL-IKHLĀṢ FREQUENTLY

Tirmidhī narrated on the authority of Anas ﷺ that the Prophet ﷺ said, "Whoever recites 'Say [O Prophet]: He is Allah – One [and Indivisible]' 200 times daily, the sins of 50 years will be erased from them unless they owed a debt."[2]

Bayhaqī narrated on the authority of Anas ﷺ that the Prophet ﷺ said, "Whoever recites 'Say [O Prophet]: He is Allah – One [and Indivisible]' 200 times, Allah will forgive 200 years of their sins."[3]

(1) *Tirmidhī* (2898).

(2) *Tirmidhī* (2898).

(3) Bayhaqī in *Shu'ab al-Īmān* (2316).

قراءةُ سورةِ الإخلاصِ قبلَ النَّومِ

روى الترمذيُّ عن أنسٍ رضي اللهُ عنه أنَّ النبيَّ ﷺ قال: «مَن أرادَ أن ينامَ على فراشِهِ من اللّيلِ، فنامَ على يمينِهِ ثمَّ قرأَ: {قُلْ هُوَ اللَّهُ أَحَدٌ} مائةَ مرّةٍ، إذا كان يومُ القيامةِ يقولُ له الرَّبُّ تبارك وتعالى: «يا عبدي ادخُلْ على يمينِكَ الجنّةَ»[1].

فضلُ الإكثارِ من تلاوةِ {قُلْ هُوَ اللَّهُ أَحَدٌ}

روى الترمذيُّ عن أنسٍ رضي الله عنه أنَّ النبيَّ ﷺ قال: «مَن قرأَ كلَّ يومٍ مائتي مرّةٍ {قُلْ هُوَ اللَّهُ أَحَدٌ} مُحِيَ عنه ذنوبُ خمسينَ إلّا أن يكونَ عليه دَين»[2].

وروى البيهقيُّ عن أنسٍ رضي الله عنه عن النبيِّ صلى اللهُ عليه وآلِهِ وسلَّمَ أنّهُ قال:

(١) أخرجه الترمذي (٢٨٩٨).

(٢) أخرجه الترمذي (٢٨٩٨).

Ṭabarānī and Daylamī narrated, as a hadith attributed to the Messenger of Allah ﷺ, "Whoever recites 'Say [O Prophet]: He is Allah – One [and Indivisible]' 100 times in prayer or out of prayer, Allah will record freedom from the Fire for them."(1)

Bayhaqī and Ibn ʿAdī narrated on the authority of Anas ؓ that the Prophet ﷺ said, "Whoever recites 'Say [O Prophet]: He is Allah – One [and Indivisible]' 100 times, 50 years of sins are forgiven, as long as they refrain from four traits: bloodshed, [usurping] wealth, the sexual organs (i.e., unlawful intercourse), and intoxicants."(2)

Ḥudhayfah ؓ narrated, as a hadith attributed to the Prophet ﷺ, "Whoever recites 'Say [O Prophet]: He is Allah – One [and Indivisible]' 1000 times has purchased their soul from Allah (i.e., freed themselves from the Fire)."(3) Khiyārī narrated it in his *Fawā'id*, as stated in *al-Jāmiʿ al-Ṣaghīr* and other works.

RECITING SŪRAH AL-IKHLĀṢ WHEN ENTERING THE HOME

Ṭabarānī narrated on the authority of Jarīr ibn ʿAbdillāh ؓ that the Messenger of Allah ﷺ said, "Whoever recites 'Say [O Prophet]: He is Allah – One [and Indivisible]' when entering their home, it will remove poverty from the members of this house and their neighbours."(4)

RECITING SŪRAH AL-IKHLĀṢ TEN TIMES AFTER THE PRAYER

Ibn ʿAsākir narrated on the authority of Ibn Abbās ؓ, as a hadith

(1) *Majmaʿ al-Zawā'id* of al-Haythamī, vol. 7, p. 148.

(2) Suyūṭī in *al-Jāmiʿ al-Ṣaghīr* (8931).

(3) Suyūṭī in *al-Jāmiʿ al-Ṣaghīr* (8953).

(4) Ṭabarānī in *al-Muʿjam al-Kabīr* (2419).

«مَن قرأَ {قُلْ هُوَ اللَّهُ أَحَدٌ} مائتي مرّةٍ غَفَرَ اللهُ له ذنوبَ مائتي سنةٍ»[1]. وروى الطبرانيُّ والدَّيلميُّ مرفوعاً: «مَن قرأَ {قُلْ هُوَ اللَّهُ أَحَدٌ} مائةَ مرّةٍ في الصَّلاةِ، أو غيرِها كتبَ اللهُ له براءةً من النّارِ»[2].

وروى البيهقيُّ وابنُ عَدِيٍّ عن أنسٍ رَضِيَ اللهُ عَنْهُ عن النبيِّ صَلَّى اللهُ عَلَيْهِ وَآلِهِ وَسَلَّمَ قال: مَن قرأَ {قُلْ هُوَ اللَّهُ أَحَدٌ} مائةَ مرّةٍ غُفِرَ له خطيئةُ خمسينَ عاماً ما اجتنبَ خِصالاً أربعاً: الدِّماءَ، والأموالَ، والفُروجَ، والأشربةَ»[3]. وعن حذيفةَ رَضِيَ اللهُ عَنْهُ مرفوعاً: «مَن قرأَ {قُلْ هُوَ اللَّهُ أَحَدٌ} ألفَ مرَّةٍ فقد اشترى نفسَهُ من اللهِ تعالى، - أي: أعتقَ رقبَتَهُ من النّارِ -»[4] رواهُ الخياريُّ في (فوائده)، كما في (الجامع الصغير) وغيرِه.

تلاوةُ سورةِ الإخلاصِ عند دخولِ المنزلِ

روى الطبرانيُّ عن جَرِيرِ بنِ عبدِ اللهِ رَضِيَ اللهُ عَنْهُ قال: قال رسولُ اللهِ صَلَّى اللهُ عَلَيْهِ وَآلِهِ وَسَلَّمَ: «مَن قرأَ {قُلْ هُوَ اللَّهُ أَحَدٌ} حين يدخلُ منزلَهُ نَفتِ الفقرَ عن أهلِ ذلك المنزلِ والجيرانِ»[5].

تلاوةُ سورةِ الإخلاصِ عشرَ مرّاتٍ بعدَ الصّلاة

روى ابنُ عساكرَ عن ابنِ عبّاسٍ رضي الله تعالى عنهما مرفوعاً: «ثلاثٌ مَن كُنَّ فيه أو

---

(١) أخرجه البيهقي في (الشعب) (٢٣١٦).

(٢) ذكره الهيثمي في (مجمع الزوائد) (١٤٨/٧).

(٣) ذكره السيوطي في (الجامع الصغير) (٨٩٣١).

(٤) ذكره السيوطي في (الجامع الصغير) (٨٩٥٣).

(٥) أخرجه الطبراني في الكبير (٢٤١٩).

attributed to the Prophet ﷺ, "Whoever has three things in them, or even one of them, let them marry the gorgeous-eyed maidens wherever they want: a person who is entrusted with a trust due to their fear of Allah Almighty and Exalted; a person who pardons their murderer;[1] and a person who recites *Sūrah al-Ikhlāṣ* ten times after every prayer."[2] He has also narrated it from Jābir ﷺ, as a hadith attributed to the Prophet ﷺ, as stated in *al-Jāmiʿ al-Ṣaghīr*.

THE VIRTUE OF RECITING THE MUʿAWWIDHATĀN AND THEIR SPECIALITIES

Imam Bukhārī narrated on the authority of Sayyidah ʿĀ'ishah ﷺ that when the Prophet ﷺ would retire to bed every night, he would put his palms together, blow into them, and recite into them *Sūrah al-Ikhlāṣ*, *Sūrah al-Falaq*, and *Sūrah al-Nās*. He would then wipe as much as he could of his body using his hands, beginning with his head, face, and front of his body. He would do this three times."[3] The authors of the *Sunan* collections narrated this.

This act of wiping is proof for seeking blessings and cure through them, as pointed out by Ḥāfiẓ Ibn Kathīr and others. It is also proof for the permissibility of wiping for the sake of acquiring blessings, cure, and mercy through the Words and Names of Allah Most High.

Imam Muslim and others narrated on the authority of ʿUqbah ibn ʿĀmir ﷺ that the Messenger of Allah ﷺ said, "Do you not see verses that were sent down last night and nothing like them has ever been seen? *Sūrah al-Falaq* and *Sūrah al-Nās*."[4]

---

(1) Translator's Note: Munāwī says this means the murdered forgives their murderer before passing away.

(2) Suyūṭī in *al-Jāmiʿ al-Ṣaghīr* (3424).

(3) *Bukhārī* (5017).

(4) *Muslim* (814).

واحدةٌ منهنَّ فليتزوَّجْ من الحورِ العينِ حيثُ شاءَ: رجلٌ ائتُمِنَ على أمانةٍ مخافةَ اللهِ عزَّ وجلَّ، ورجلٌ خلَّى عن قاتِلِه - أي: عفا عن قاتِلِه، كما في روايةٍ - ورجلٌ قرأَ في دُبرِ كلِّ صلاةٍ {قُلْ هُوَ اللَّهُ أَحَدٌ} عشرَ مرّاتٍ»[1]. ورواهُ عن جابرٍ رَضِيَ اللهُ عَنْهُ أيضاً مرفوعاً كما في (الجامعِ الصَّغيرِ).

فضلُ تلاوةِ المعوِّذتَينِ وخصائصُهما

روى الإمامُ البخاريُّ عن السيدةِ عائشةَ رَضِيَ اللهُ عَنْهَا أنَّ النبيَّ صَلَّى اللهُ عَلَيْهِ وَآلِهِ وَسَلَّمَ: (كان إذا أوى إلى فراشِهِ كلَّ ليلةٍ جمع كفَّيهِ، ثمَّ نفثَ فيهما، وقرأَ فيهما: {قُلْ هُوَ اللَّهُ أَحَدٌ}، و{قُلْ أَعُوذُ بِرَبِّ الْفَلَقِ}، و{قُلْ أَعُوذُ بِرَبِّ النَّاسِ}، ثم يمسحُ بهِما - أي: بيديه - ما استطاعَ مِن جسدِهِ، يبدأُ بهما على رأسِهِ ووجهِهِ، وما أقبَلَ مِن جسدِهِ صلى اللهُ عليه وآلِهِ وسلَّمَ، يفعلُ ذلكَ ثلاثَ مرّاتٍ)[2]. ورواهُ أصحابُ السُّنن.

وفي هذا التمسُّحِ دليلٌ على التبرُّكِ والاستشفاءِ بهنَّ، كما نبَّهَ على ذلك الحافظُ ابنُ كثيرٍ وغيرُه، وفيه دليلٌ على جوازِ التمسُّحِ تبرُّكاً واستشفاءً واسترحاماً بكلماتِ اللهِ تعالى وأسمائِهِ.

وروى الإمامُ مسلمٌ وغيرُهُ عن عُقبةَ بنِ عامرٍ رَضِيَ اللهُ عَنْهُ قال: قال رسولُ اللهِ صَلَّى اللهُ عَلَيْهِ وَآلِهِ وَسَلَّمَ: «ألم ترَ آياتٍ أُنزِلَتِ الليلةَ لم يُرَ مثلُهنَّ؟ {قُلْ أَعُوذُ بِرَبِّ الْفَلَقِ}، و{قُلْ أَعُوذُ بِرَبِّ النَّاسِ}»[3].

---

(١) ذكره السيوطي في (الجامع الصغير) (٣٤٢٤).

(٢) أخرجه البخاري (٥٠١٧).

(٣) أخرجه مسلم (٨١٤).

Imam Aḥmad narrated on the authority of ʿUqbah ibn ʿĀmir ﷺ that the Messenger of Allah ﷺ said, "Recite the *muʿawwidhatān*, because you will never recite anything like them."[1]

Imam Mālik narrated on the authority of Ibn Shihāb from ʿUrwah from Sayyidah ʿĀ'ishah ﷺ that whenever the Messenger of Allah ﷺ would complain (of illness or pain), he would recite the *muʿawwidhatān* upon himself and blow. Sayyidah ʿĀ'ishah ﷺ said, "When his illnessbecame worse, I used to recite the *muʿawwidhāt*[2] upon him but wiped over him with his hands, out of hope for their blessings."[3] Bukhārī and Muslim narrated it.

The authors of the *Sunan* collections narrated on the authority of Abū Saʿīd al-Khudrī ﷺ that the Messenger of Allah ﷺ would seek refuge from the jinn and people's evil eye. When the *muʿawwidhatān* were revealed, he adopted them and left everything besides them.[4]

Imam Aḥmad narrated on the authority of ʿUqbah ibn ʿĀmir ﷺ that the Messenger of Allah ﷺ said to him, "Shall I inform you of the best thing with which those who seek refuge have sought refuge?" He said, "Yes, of course." He said, "*Sūrah al-Falaq* and *Sūrah al-Nās*."[5]

Nasā'ī narrated on the authority of ʿUqbah ibn ʿĀmir ﷺ who said, "I followed the Messenger of Allah ﷺ whilst he was riding. I placed my hands on his feet and said, 'Teach me *Sūrah Hūd* or *Sūrah Yūsuf*.' He said, 'You will never read anything more beneficial in the sight of Allah Most High than *Sūrah al-Falaq*." Ibn Kathīr has cited it thus in his exegesis.

(1) *Aḥmad* (17366).

(2) Translator's note: i.e., the *muʿawwidhatān* and *Sūrah al-Ikhlāṣ*.

(3) *Bukhārī* (5016); *Muslim* (2192).

(4) *Tirmidhī* (2058).

(5) *Nasā'ī* (5432); *Aḥmad* (17389).

وروى الإمامُ أحمدُ عن عُقبةَ بنِ عامرٍ رَضِيَ اللهُ عَنْهُ قال: قال رسولُ اللهِ صَلَّى اللهُ عَلَيْهِ وَآلِهِ وَسَلَّمَ: «اقرأْ بالمعوِّذتَينِ؛ فإنَّك لن تقرأَ بمثلِهما»[1].

وروى الإمامُ مالكٌ عن ابنِ شهابٍ، عن عروةَ، عن السيدةِ عائشةَ رَضِيَ اللهُ عَنْهَا: أنَّ رسولَ اللهِ صَلَّى اللهُ عَلَيْهِ وَآلِهِ وَسَلَّمَ كان إذا اشتكى- أي: مرضاً أو وجعاً- يقرأُ على نفسِهِ بالمعوِّذتَينِ وينفُثُ، قالت السيدةُ عائشةُ رضي عنها: فلمّا اشتدَّ وجعُهُ صَلَّى اللهُ عَلَيْهِ وَآلِهِ وَسَلَّمَ كنتُ أقرأُ عليه بالمعوِّذاتِ، وأمسحُ بيده عليه؛ رجاءَ بركتِها)[2]. ورواهُ البخاريُّ وغيرُه. وروى أصحابُ السُّننِ عن أبي سعيدٍ الخدريِّ رَضِيَ اللهُ عَنْهُ (أنَّ رسولَ اللهِ صَلَّى اللهُ عَلَيْهِ وَآلِهِ وَسَلَّمَ: كان يتعوَّذُ من الجانِّ، وأُعيُنِ الإنسانِ، فلمّا نزلتِ المعوِّذتانِ أخذ بهما، وتركَ ما سواهُما)[3].

وروى الإمامُ أحمدُ عن عُقبةَ بنِ عامرٍ رَضِيَ اللهُ عَنْهُ أنَّ رسولَ اللهِ صَلَّى اللهُ عَلَيْهِ وَآلِهِ وَسَلَّمَ قال له: «ألا أخبرُكَ بأفضلَ ما تعوَّذَ به المتعوِّذون؟ قال: بلى. فقال: «{قُلْ أَعُوذُ بِرَبِّ الْفَلَقِ}، و{قُلْ أَعُوذُ بِرَبِّ النَّاسِ}»[4]. وروى النَّسائيُّ عن عُقبةَ بنِ عامرٍ رَضِيَ اللهُ عَنْهُ قال: تبعتُ رسولَ اللهِ صلى اللهُ عليه وآلِهِ وسلَّمَ عنه وهو راكبٌ، فوضعتُ يدي على قدميه، فقلتُ: أَقرِئني سورةَ هودٍ أو سورةَ يوسُفَ، فقال: «لن تقرأَ شيئاً أنفعَ عندَ اللهِ تعالى من: «{قُلْ أَعُوذُ بِرَبِّ الْفَلَقِ}»[5] هكذا أورَدَهُ ابنُ كثيرٍ في (تفسيره).

---

(١) أخرجه أحمد (١٧٣٦٦).

(٢) أخرجه البخاري (٥٠١٦)، ومسلم باختلاف (٢١٩٢) يسير.

(٣) أخرجه الترمذي (٢٠٥٨).

(٤) أخرجه النسائي (٥٤٣٢)، وأحمد (١٧٣٨٩).

(٥) أخرجه النسائي (٥٤٣٩)، وأحمد (١٧٤٥٥).

RECITING THE MU'AWWIDHĀT AFTER THE OBLIGATORY PRAYERS

Imam Aḥmad narrated on the authority of 'Uqbah ibn 'Āmir ﷺ who said, "The Messenger of Allah ﷺ ordered me to recite the *mu'awwidhāt* after every prayer."[1] Abū Dāwūd, Tirmidhī, and others narrated it.

RECITING THE MU'AWWIDHĀT SEVEN TIMES AFTER THE FRIDAY PRAYER

Ibn al-Sunnī narrated on the authority of Sayyidah 'Ā'ishah ﷺ that the Prophet ﷺ said, "Whoever recites *Sūrah al-Ikhlāṣ*, *Sūrah al-Falaq*, and *Sūrah al-Nās* seven times after the Friday prayer, Allah will grant them refuge against evil until the next Friday."[2] Abū Sa'īd al-Qushayrī narrated in *al-Arba'īn* on the authority of Anas ﷺ, as a hadith attributed to the Prophet ﷺ, "Whoever recites, after the imam concludes the Friday prayer and before changing their place, the Opening Chapter, *Sūrah al-Ikhlāṣ*, *Sūrah al-Falaq*, and *Sūrah al-Nās* seven times each, their past and future sins will be forgiven."[3]

---

(1) *Abū Dāwūd* (1523); *Aḥmad* (17417).

(2) Ibn al-Sunnī in *'Amal al-Yawm wa al-Laylah* (375).

(3) Suyūṭī in *al-Jāmi' al-Ṣaghīr* (8955).

قراءةُ المعوِّذاتِ وراءَ الصَّلواتِ المكتوبات

روى الإمامُ أحمدُ عن عُقبةَ بنِ عامرٍ رَضِيَ اللهُ عَنْهُ قال: (أمَرَني رسولُ اللهِ صَلَّى اللهُ عَلَيْهِ وَآلِهِ وَسَلَّمَ أنْ أقرأَ بالمعوِّذاتِ في دُبُرِ كلِّ صلاةٍ)[1]. ورواهُ أبو داودَ والترمذيُّ وغيرُهما.

قراءةُ المعوِّذاتِ سبعاً سبعاً بعد صلاةِ الجُمُعَةِ

روى ابنُ السُّنّي عن السيدة عائشةَ رَضِيَ اللهُ عَنْهَا عن النبيِّ صَلَّى اللهُ عَلَيْهِ وَآلِهِ وَسَلَّمَ أنّه قال: (مَن قرأَ بعد صلاةِ الجُمُعَةِ: {قُلْ هُوَ اللَّهُ أَحَدٌ}، و{قُلْ أَعُوذُ بِرَبِّ الْفَلَقِ}، و{قُلْ أَعُوذُ بِرَبِّ النَّاسِ}، سبعَ مرّاتٍ أعاذهُ اللهُ بها من السّوءِ إلى الجُمُعَةِ الأُخرى»[2]. وروى أبو سعيدٍ القُشَيريُّ في (الأربعين) عن أنسٍ رَضِيَ اللهُ عَنْهُ مرفوعاً: «مَن قرأَ إذا سلَّمَ الإمامُ يومَ الجُمُعَةُ قبل أن يَثني رِجليه: فاتحةَ الكتابِ، و{قُلْ هُوَ اللَّهُ أَحَدٌ}، و{قُلْ أَعُوذُ بِرَبِّ الْفَلَقِ}، و{قُلْ أَعُوذُ بِرَبِّ النَّاسِ} سبعاً سبعاً غُفِرَ له ما تقدَّمَ من ذنبِهِ وما تأخَّرَ»[3].

---

(١) أخرجه أبو داود (١٥٢٣)، وأحمد (١٧٤١٧).

(٢) أخرجه ابن السني في (عمل اليوم والليلة) (٣٧٥).

(٣) ذكره السيوطي في (الجامع الصغير) (٨٩٥٥).

RESPECTING THE MUṢḤAFS

Allah Most High said, "This is truly a noble Qur'an, in a well-preserved Record, touched by none except the purified [Angels]. [It is] a Revelation from the Lord of all worlds."(1)

Allah Most Glorified has informed that this Qur'an is noble, i.e., it is honoured and revered. This is why nobody in the Higher Assembly can touch it besides the Angels and these lofty holy souls, as they are purified, clean, and immaculate. And the Qur'an deserves this honour, because "[it is] a Revelation from the Lord of all worlds."

He Most High said, "Ḥa Mīm. By the clear Book! Certainly, We have made it a Qur'an in Arabic so perhaps you will understand. And indeed, it is – in the Master Record with Us – highly esteemed, rich in wisdom."(2)

In these noble verses, Allah Most High explained and proclaimed to His slaves the dignity of this Noble Qur'an in the Higher Assembly, and its nobility and loftiness. That is so the people on Earth also exalt it, esteem it, and revere it – in following with how the Higher Assembly honour and revere their Lord's Book.

He Most High said, "But no! This [Revelation] is truly a reminder. So let

---

(1) *Al-Wāqi'ah*, 77-80.

(2) *Zukhruf*, 1-4.

تعظيمُ المصاحفِ

قال اللهُ تعالى: {إِنَّهُ لَقُرْآنٌ كَرِيمٌ (٧٧) فِي كِتَابٍ مَّكْنُونٍ (٧٨) لَّا يَمَسُّهُ إِلَّا الْمُطَهَّرُونَ (٧٩) تَنزِيلٌ مِّن رَّبِّ الْعَالَمِينَ} [(١)]. فقد أخبرَ سبحانه أنَّ هذا القرآنَ كريمٌ، أي: مُكرَّمٌ مُعظَّمٌ، ومِن ثَمَّ لا يمسُّه في الملأِ الأعلى إلّا الملائكةُ، وتلك الأرواحُ العاليةُ القدسيّةُ؛ لأنّهم مطهَّرونَ أصفياءُ أنقياءُ، وحُقَّ له ذلك؛ لأنّهُ {تَنزِيلٌ مِّن رَّبِّ الْعَالَمِينَ}. وقال تعالى: {حم (١) وَالْكِتَابِ الْمُبِينِ (٢) إِنَّا جَعَلْنَاهُ قُرْآنًا عَرَبِيًّا لَّعَلَّكُمْ تَعْقِلُونَ (٣) وَإِنَّهُ فِي أُمِّ الْكِتَابِ لَدَيْنَا لَعَلِيٌّ حَكِيمٌ} [(٢)].

وفي هذه الآياتِ الكريمةِ بيانٌ من اللهِ تعالى، وإعلامٌ منه لعبادِهِ بشرفِ هذا القرآنِ الكريمِ في الملأِ الأعلى، ومجدِهِ ورفعةِ شأنِهِ؛ وذلك لِيُشرِّفَهُ أهلُ الأرضِ ويُعظِّموه ويكرموه، مقتدينَ بالملأِ الأعلى في تمجيدِهم وتعظيمِهم لكتابِ ربِّهم.

---

(١) الواقعة: ٧٧-٨٠.

(٢) الزخرف: ١-٤.

whoever wills be mindful of it. It is [written] on pages held in honour – highly esteemed, purified – by the hands of Angel-scribes, honourable and virtuous."(1)

He Most Glorified explained that the pages of this Noble Qur'an are honoured and esteemed in the Higher Assembly. They are purified from every impurity, addition, deletion, and discrepancy. They are in the hands of the Angels who are emissaries between Allah Most High and His creation. These Angels have noble characteristics, traits, and habits, and they are righteous in their deeds, actions, and statements. Glad tidings for those who resemble them – in their exalting, revering, and honouring this Noble Book, and in their characteristics, actions, and acts of worship. He ﷺ said, "The proficient reciter of the Qur'an will be with the honourable and virtuous Angel-scribes (*safarah*)."(2) O Allah, make us amongst them.

Thus, this Qur'an has a great status and an honourable rank, because it is "a Revelation from the Lord of all worlds" upon the best of the first and the last. Moreover, the one bringing it down is the Trustworthy Spirit – the possessor of loftiness, command, a high rank, and leadership. Allah Most High informed of that in His saying, "Indeed, this [Qur'an] is the Word of [Allah delivered by Gabriel,] a noble Messenger-Angel, full of power, held in honour by the Lord of the Throne, obeyed there [in Heaven], and trustworthy."(3)

When Jibrīl – held in honour, obeyed, and trustworthy – would descend with the verses of Allah Most High, a large convoy of noble Angels would accompany him. They would surround the Speech of the All-Knowing Sovereign which he was coming down with – out of esteem, reverence, veneration, and honour.

It has already passed in the hadith narrated by Imam Aḥmad on the authority of Maʿqil ibn Yasār ؓ that the Messenger of Allah ﷺ said, "Al-

---

(1) *ʿAbasa*, 11-16.

(2) *Bukhārī* (4653); *Muslim* (798).

(3) *Al-Takwīr*, 19-20.

وقال تعالى: {كَلَّا إِنَّهَا تَذْكِرَةٌ (١١) فَمَن شَاءَ ذَكَرَهُ (١٢) فِي صُحُفٍ مُّكَرَّمَةٍ (١٣) مَّرْفُوعَةٍ مُّطَهَّرَةٍ (١٤) بِأَيْدِي سَفَرَةٍ (١٥) كِرَامٍ بَرَرَةٍ}[1].

فبيَّنَ سبحانه أنَّ صُحُفَ هذا القرآنِ الكريمِ مُكرَّمَةٌ مرفوعةُ المكانةِ في الملأ الأعلى، مُطهَّرَةٌ من كلِّ دنسٍ، وزيادةٍ، ونقصٍ، وخَلَلٍ، وأنّهُ بأيدي الملائكةِ الذين هم سَفرةٌ بين اللهِ تعالى وبين خلقِهِ، وهم كرامُ الأخلاقِ والخصالِ والشِّيَمِ، بَرَرَةُ الأفعالِ والأعمالِ والأقوالِ، فطوبى لِمَن تشبَّهَ بهم في تمجيدِهم وتعظيمِهم وتكريمِهم لهذا الكتابِ الكريمِ، وفي أخلاقِهم وأعمالِهم وعباداتِهم، قال ﷺ: «الذي يقرأُ القرآنَ وهو ماهِرٌ به مع السَّفَرَةِ الكرامِ البَرَرَةِ»[2]. الحديث كما تقدَّمَ. اللَّهمَّ اجعلنا منهم.

فهذا القرآنُ شأنُهُ عظيمٌ ومقامُه كريمٌ؛ لأنّهُ {تَنزِيلٌ مِّن رَّبِّ الْعَالَمِينَ}[3] على أفضلِ الأوَّلينَ والآخِرينَ، والنّازِلُ به هو الرُّوحُ الأمينُ، ذو المكانةِ والسِّيادةِ والرُّتبةِ العاليةِ والقيادةِ، كما أخبرَ اللهُ تعالى عن ذلك في قوله: {إِنَّهُ لَقَوْلُ رَسُولٍ كَرِيمٍ (١٩) ذِي قُوَّةٍ عِندَ ذِي الْعَرْشِ مَكِينٍ (٢٠) مُّطَاعٍ ثَمَّ أَمِينٍ}[4].

فكان هذا المكينُ جبريلَ عليه السلام المطاعَ الأمينَ، إذا نزل بآياتِ اللهِ تعالى نزل معه موكِبٌ حافلٌ من الملائكةِ الكرامِ عليهم السلام، يَحُفونَ بما نزل به من كلامِ المَلِكِ العلّامِ؛ إجلالاً وإعظاماً وتهيُّباً وإكراماً. وقد تقدَّمَ في الحديثِ الذي رواه الإمامُ أحمدُ عن مَعقِلِ بنِ يسارٍ رضي الله عنه أنَّ رسولَ اللهِ ﷺ قال: «البقرةُ سَنامُ القرآنِ وذروتُه، نزل مع

---

(١) عبس: ١١-١٦.

(٢) أخرجه البخاري (٤٦٥٣) ومسلم (٧٩٨).

(٣) الواقعة: ٨٠.

(٤) التكوير: ١٩-٢١.

Baqarah is the peak of the Qur'an and its pinnacle. With every verse, 80000 Angels came down." [1] That was only to manifest its esteem, to revere its status, and to demonstrate its virtue and honour.

Likewise, the Prophet ﷺ informed – as narrated by Ṭabarānī and others – that when *Sūrah al-An ʿām* was revealed, 70000 Angels came down to escort it whilst they were loudly glorifying and praising [Allah].[2]

In the narration of Ḥākim in *al-Mustadrak* on the authority of Jābir ﷺ, when *Sūrah al-An ʿām* was revealed, the Messenger of Allah ﷺ said *Subḥān Allāh* and then said, "This sūrah was escorted by so many Angels that they filled the horizon."[3] Ḥākim said it is authentic according to the criteria of Muslim.

In a narration of Ibn Mardawayh on the authority of Anas ﷺ, the Prophet ﷺ said, "Sūrah al-Anʿām came down with a convoy of Angels that filled the horizon. They were loudly glorifying and the ground was shaking with them." Anas ﷺ said, "The Messenger of Allah ﷺ then started to say, 'Glory be to Allah, the Great. Glory be to Allah, the Great.'"[4]

Furthermore, for the sake of one phrase – the saying of Allah Most High "except those with valid excuses"[5] – Jibrīl ﷺ came down with a convoy of Angels to convey that to the Prophet ﷺ. Bukhārī narrated on the authority of Zayd ibn Thābit ﷺ who said, "The Messenger of Allah ﷺ dictated to me: 'Those who stay at home are not equal to those who fight in the cause of Allah.' Ibn Umm Maktūm ﷺ came whilst he was dictating it to me and said, 'O Messenger of Allah – by Allah – if I could fight, I would do so.' He was blind, so Allah Most High revealed upon the Messenger of Allah: 'except those with valid excuses.'"[6]

---

(1) *Aḥmad* (20300).

(2) Abū Nuʿaym in *al-Ḥilyah*.

(3) Isḥāq ibn Rāhwayh in *al-Musnad* (2298).

(4) Ṭabarānī in *al-Muʿjam al-Awsaṭ* (178).

(5) *Al-Nisā'*, 95.

(6) *Bukhārī* (4592).

كلِّ آيةٍ منها ثمانونَ مَلَكاً»[1]. الحديثَ. وما ذلك إلّا لتفخيمِ أمرِها، وتعظيمِ شأنِها، وبيانِ فضلِها وكرامتِها. كما أخبرَ النبيُّ ﷺ أنَّ: «سورةَ الأنعامِ لمّا نزلَتْ نزلَ معها سبعونَ ألفِ مَلَكٍ يُشيِّعونُها لهم زَجَلٌ بالتَّسبيحِ والتَّحميدِ»[2]. كما رواه الطَّبرانيُّ وغيرُه. وفي روايةِ الحاكمِ في (المستدرَكِ) عن جابرٍ رضي الله عنه قال: لمّا نزلت سورةُ الأنعامِ سبَّحَ رسولُ اللهِ ﷺ ثمَّ قال: «لقد شيَّعَ هذه السُّورةَ من الملائكةِ ما سدَّ الأُفُقَ»[3]. قال الحاكمُ: صحيح على شرطِ مسلمٍ. وفي روايةِ ابنِ مَرْدَوَيْه عن أنسٍ رضي الله عنه عن النبيِّ ﷺ قال: «نزلتْ سورةُ الأنعامِ معها موكِبٌ من الملائكةِ سدَّ ما بينَ الخافِقَينِ، لهم زَجَلٌ بالتَّسبيحِ، والأرضُ بهم ترتَجُّ»، قال أنسٌ رضي الله عنه: وجعلَ رسولُ الله ﷺ يقول: «سبحانَ اللهِ العظيمِ، سبحانَ اللهِ العظيمِ»[4]. ومن أجلِ حرفٍ - أي طَرَفِ جملةٍ - وهو قولُ اللهِ تعالى: {غَيْرُ أُولِي الضَّرَرِ} نزل جبريلُ ومعه موكبٌ من الملائكةِ يُلقي ذلك على النبيِّ صلى الله عليه وسلم، كما روى البخاريُّ عن زيدِ بنِ ثابتٍ رضي الله عنه أنَّهُ قال: «أملى عليَّ رسولُ اللهِ ﷺ {لَّا يَسْتَوِي الْقَاعِدُونَ مِنَ الْمُؤْمِنِينَ وَالْمُجَاهِدُونَ فِي سَبِيلِ اللَّهِ}[5]، فجاءَهُ ابنُ أمِّ مكتومٍ وهو يُمليها عليَّ، فقال: يا رسولَ اللهِ، واللهِ لو أستطيعُ الجهادَ لجاهدتُ، وكان أعمى رضي الله عنه، فأنزل اللهُ تعالى على رسولِ اللهِ ﷺ:

---

(١) أخرجه أحمد (٢٠٣٠٠).

(٢) أخرجه أبو نعيم في (حلية الأولياء) (٥١/٣).

(٣) أخرجه إسحق بن راهويه في (المسند) (٢٢٩٨).

(٤) أخرجه الطبراني في (المعجم الأوسط) (٦٤٤٧).

(٥) النساء: ٩٥.

So, look at the honour of the Noble Qur'an with Allah Most High: Jibrīl – the trustworthy and honoured – comes down for the sake of part of a verse, and then look at the respect of this Noble Qur'an that is binding upon the creation of Allah Most High. Therefore, it is an emphasized right upon every Muslim that they revere and respect this Qur'an.

RESPECT OF THE NOBLE QUR'AN REQUIRES A NUMBER OF THINGS:

Amongst them is respecting the muṣḥaf, because it contains the pages on which it is written, and it has comprised it and compiled it. Ibn Abī Dāwūd narrated in *al-Maṣāḥif* from Ibrāhīm al-Taymī that in the era of the Companions ﷺ, it used to be said, "Respect the *muṣḥafs*."

Part of respecting the muṣḥaf is to keep it raised and not to place it on the ground. This is because this Qur'an is noble, and the Record in which it is written and which has compiled it is also honoured and revered, as Allah Most High informs, "This is truly a noble Qur'an, in a well-preserved Record."[1] This well-preserved Record is the Preserved Tablet – most holy and most revered. Allah Most High said, "In fact, this is a glorious Qur'an, recorded in a Preserved Tablet."[2]

Therefore, the books and pages on which the words of the Noble Qur'an are written are honoured and revered, due to their comprising and compiling the Qur'an. A book and its pages are considered noble, revered and honourable according to what they comprise and what is written on them – and there is nothing more noble, more revered, and more honourable than the verses of Allah Most High and its words. Hence, it is incumbent to respect the pages which compile them.

That being the case, to place a book on the floor is not considered respectful or reverent to that book, as is apparent and obvious. In fact, placing a book on the floor gives the exact opposite impression. Is it not

(1) *Al-Wāqi 'ah*, 77-78.

(2) *Al-Burūj*, 21-22.

{غَيْرُ أُولِي الضَّرَرِ} (1). فانظرْ في كرامةِ هذا القرآنِ الكريمِ على اللهِ تعالى؛ حتى إنَّ جبريلَ الأمينَ المكينَ ينزلُ من أجلِ بعضِ آيةٍ، ثمَّ انظرْ في واجبِ إكرامِ هذا القرآنِ الكريمِ عند خلقِ اللهِ تعالى. فحقٌّ حقيقٌ على كلِّ مسلمٍ أن يُجِلَّ هذا القرآنَ ويُعظِّمَهُ.

وتعظيمُ القرآنِ الكريمِ يتطلَّبُ عِدّةَ أمورٍ:

منها: تعظيمُ المصحفِ لِما فيه من الصُّحُفِ التي رسَمَتْهُ، واحتوتْ عليه وجمعتْهُ، وقد روى ابنُ أبي داودَ في كتابِ (المصاحفِ) عن إبراهيمَ التيميِّ قال: كان - أي: في عصرِ الصَّحابةِ رضي الله عنهم - يُقالُ: عظِّموا المصاحفَ. اهـ. ومن تعظيمِ المصحفِ وتكريمِهِ: أن يُرفَعَ ولا يُوضَعَ على الأرضِ؛ وذلك لأنَّ هذا القرآنَ كريمٌ، وهو الكتابُ الذي كُتِبَ فيه وجمَعَهُ مُكرَّمٌ ومُعظَّمٌ، كما أخبرَ اللهُ تعالى عن ذلك في قوله: {إِنَّهُ لَقُرْآنٌ كَرِيمٌ (٧٧) فِي كِتَابٍ مَّكْنُونٍ} (2) وهذا الكتابُ المكنونُ هو اللَّوحُ المحفوظُ المُقدَّسُ المُعظَّمُ، قال اللهُ تعالى: {بَلْ هُوَ قُرْآنٌ مَّجِيدٌ (٢١) فِي لَوْحٍ مَّحْفُوظٍ} (3). فالكتابُ والصُّحفُ التي كُتِبَ فيها كلماتُ القرآنِ الكريمِ مُكرَّمَةٌ مُعظَّمةٌ؛ لِما حوتْهُ وجمَعَتْهُ، وإنَّ الكتابَ والصُّحفَ تَشْرُفُ وتَعْظُمُ وتَكْرُمُ على حسبِ ما احتوتْ عليه وكُتِبَ فيها، ولا أشرفَ ولا أمجدَ وأعظمَ من آياتِ اللهِ تعالى وكلماتِهِ، فيجبُ تعظيمُ الصُّحُفِ الجامعةِ لها. وإذا كان الأمرُ كذلك: فإنَّ وضعَ الكتابِ على الأرضِ لا يُعَدُّ من بابِ التَّكريمِ ولا التَّعظيمِ لذلك الكتابِ كما هو ظاهرٌ معلومٌ بالبَداهة، بل وضعُ الكتابِ على الأرضِ يُؤْذِنُ بعكس

---

(١) أخرجه البخاري (٤٥٩٢).

(٢) الواقعة: ٧٧-٧٨.

(٣) البروج: ٢١-٢٢.

obvious that a person who wants to respect your letter to them will lift it up on their hands? At times, they may even raise it to a high, respectful place. And if they were to put the letter you sent them on the floor in front of you when you visit them, you would find this offensive.

Accordingly, placing the muṣḥaf on the floor can never be considered respectful. The Sacred Law ordains that the muṣḥaf be honoured, because it is truly a noble Qur'an in a well-preserved Record, and because it is highly esteemed and rich in wisdom, in the Master Record with the Lord of Honour and Power. Thus, honouring the muṣḥaf is by lifting and keeping it raised off the floor, not by placing it on there.

THE MUṢḤAF IS TO BE REVERED AND HONOURED – EVEN IF IT WEARS OUT AND ITS PAGES SPLIT

It states in *al-Durr al-Mukhtār*, "If the muṣḥaf reaches a state in which it cannot be read, it will be buried, in the same manner as a Muslim."

It states in *Radd al-Muḥtār*, "In other words, the muṣḥaf will be placed in a clean cloth and buried in a place that is not degrading or trampled. In *al-Dhakhīrah*: It should be buried in a niche (*laḥd*) and not a trench (*shaqq*), because it (i.e., a trench) requires soil to be thrown on top of it, and this is somewhat degrading – unless a covering is placed over the muṣḥaf so that the soil does not get to it; that is also good."

It states in *Shir ʿah al-Islām* that when the muṣḥaf becomes tattered and its writing becomes worn out, it will be wrapped in a clean cloth and buried in a clean place which no filth can reach and which nobody will trample. It states in *Shir ʿah al-Shir ʿah* and in *Sharḥ al-Nuqāyah* that a page on which the name of Allah Most High is written – and similarly the names of the Prophets and Angels – and which is no longer needed will be placed in running water or buried in clean land. It will not be burnt. Imam Muhammad has alluded to this in *al-Siyar al-Kabīr*. It states in *al-Dhakhīrah*, "This (i.e., the opinion of Imam Muhammad) is the position we adopt." In *al-Sirājiyyah*, it states that it will be buried or burnt. It states likewise in *al-Fatāwā al-Tātarkhāniyyah*. It states in *al-Qunyah*, "It is not

ذلك، ألا ترى من البديهيِ أنَّ مَن أراد أن يحترمَ كتابَكَ رفعه بينَ يديه، بل ربَّما رفعَهُ على موضعٍ مرتفعٍ مكرَّمٍ، ولو وضع كتابَكَ المُرسَلَ إليه على الأرضِ أمامَكَ حين يقدُمُ إليه لكَبُرَ ذلك عليك. إذاً وضعُ المصحفِ على الأرضِ ليس تكريماً للمصحفِ قطعاً، وإنَّ الشَّرعَ يأمرُ بتكريمِهِ؛ لأنّهُ قرآنٌ كريمٌ في كتابٍ مَكْنونٍ، ولأنّهُ في أمِّ الكتابِ عند ربِّ العِزّةِ لعليٌّ حكيمٌ، بل من التَّكريمِ له أن يُرفَعَ عن الأرضِ، ولا يوضَعَ عليها.

المصحفُ يعظَّمُ ويُكرَّمُ ولو بَلِيَتْ أو تشقَّقتْ صُحُفُه

قال في (الدُّرِ المختارِ): المُصحفُ إذا صارَ بحالٍ لا يُقرأُ فيه يُدفَنُ، كالمسلمِ. اهـ.

قال في (ردِّ المحتار): أي: يُجعَلُ المصحفُ في خِرقةٍ طاهرةٍ، ويُدفَنُ في محلٍّ غيرِ ممتهَنٍ لا يُوطَأُ. قال: وفي (الذَّخيرة): وينبغي أن يُلحَدَ له، ولا يُشَقَّ له؛ لأنّهُ - أي: الشِّقُ - يحتاجُ إلى إهالةِ التُّرابِ عليه، وفي ذلك نوعُ تحقيرٍ، إلا إذا جَعَلَ فوقَ المصحفِ سقفاً، بحيثُ لا يَصِلُ التّرابُ إليه فهو حسنٌ أيضاً.

وفي (شِرعةِ الإسلامِ): وإذا بَلِيَ المصحفُ واندرَسَ ما فيه فإنّهُ يُلَفُّ في خِرقةٍ طاهرةٍ، ويُدفَنُ في مكانٍ طيّبٍ لا يصيبُهُ قَذَرٌ، ولا يطأُهُ أحدٌ. اهـ.

وقال في (شِرعةِ الشرعةِ): وفي (شرحِ النّقاية): ورقةٌ كُتِبَ فيها اسمُ اللهِ تعالى، وكذلك أسماءُ الأنبياءِ والملائكةِ، واستُغنِيَ عنها، تُلقى في الماءِ الجاري، أو تُدفَنُ في أرضٍ طاهرةٍ، ولا تُحرَقُ بالنَّارِ، أشار إليه الإمامُ محمّدٌ في (السِّيَرِ الكبيرِ).

قال في (الذخيرة): وبه - أي: بقول الإمامِ محمّدٍ - نأخذُ. اهـ.

وفي (السِّراجيّة): تُدفَنُ أو تُحرَقُ، وكذلك في (الفتاوى التاترخانية). اهـ.

قال: وفي (القُنيةِ): لا يجوزُ في المصحفِ الخَلَقِ - أي: الذي بَلِيَتْ أو تشقَّقَتْ صحُفُه الذي لا يَصلحُ للقراءةِ فيه - لا يجوز أن يُجلَّدَ به القرآنُ. اهـ.

permissible to use a worn-out muṣḥaf (i.e., one that has tattered and whose pages have split making it illegible) to make the cover of another muṣḥaf." In other words, it is not permissible to use its pages as a cover for another muṣḥaf.

So, take a lesson and be mindful – O intelligent one – because the muṣḥaf contains the Speech of Allah Most High. Moreover, the merit of Allah's Speech over all other speech is like the merit of Allah Most High over His creation – as already stated in the noble hadiths. And whoever honours the Speech of Allah Most High is honouring Allah Most High.

Sharḥ al-Shirʿah, citing al-Bazzāziyyah, states that it is impermissible to stretch one's feet towards the muṣḥaf – unless the muṣḥaf is raised so that the place of the muṣḥaf and the feet are not parallel to each other. In that case, it will not be disliked. Similarly, if it is hanging on a peg and he stretches his feet towards the ground because the muṣḥaf is on a higher place, he will not be parallel to it. This has been cited with a slight change.

In the same vein we say that the jurists have explicitly stated it is disliked to stretch one's feet towards the *qiblah* (the direction of the Kaʿbah). The proof for this is that the direction of the *qiblah* is esteemed and sacred, as it is the direction in which the slave turns towards their Lord in their prayers, worship, and supplications. He Most Glorified manifests Himself to His slaves during their prayers, supplications, worship, and their circumambulation (ṭawāf) in their *qiblah*. He ﷺ said, as related in the *Sunan* of Tirmidhī and others, "When you pray, do not turn around, because Allah keeps His Face directly in front of His slave's face as long as they are praying."[1]

In the *Sunan* of Abū Dāwūd and other works, it is narrated on the authority of Jābir ﷺ that the Prophet ﷺ said, "Who amongst you would like Allah to turn away from them? When any of you stand in prayer, Allah Most High is in front of them. Therefore, they should not spit in front of themselves or to their right, but rather spit to their left under

(1) *Tirmidhī* (3102).

أي: لا يجوزُ أن تُجعلَ صُحُفُهُ جِلداً لمصحفٍ آخرَ.

فاعتبِرْ وادَّكِر أيُّها العاقلُ؛ فإنَّ المصحفَ فيه كلامُ اللهِ تعالى، وإنَّ فضلَ كلامِ اللهِ تعالى على سائرِ الكلامِ كفضلِ اللهِ تعالى على خلقِهِ، كما تقدَّمَ في الحديثِ الشريف.

ومَن أكرمَ كلامَ اللهِ تعالى فقد أكرمَ اللهَ تعالى.

ونُقِلَ في (شرحِ الشِّرعةِ) عن (البزازيّة): أنّهُ لا يجوزُ مَدُّ الرِّجلِ إلى المصحفِ إلّا أن يكونَ المصحفُ مرفوعاً، بحيثُ لا تقعُ المُحاذاةُ بين موضِعِ المصحفِ وبين الرِّجلِ، قال: فإنّهُ لا يُكرَهُ حينئذٍ، وكذلك لو كان مُعلَّقاً في وَتَدٍ ومدَّ رِجلَه إلى الأسفل؛ لأنَّ المصحفَ على العلوِّ فلم يُحاذِهِ. اهـ. بتصرُّفٍ قليلٍ.

وبهذه المناسبةِ نقول: قد نصَّ الفقهاءُ على كراهةِ مدِّ الرِّجلِ إلى القبلةِ، والدليلُ على ذلك أنَّ جهةَ القبلةِ معظَّمةٌ ومحترَمةٌ؛ لأنَّها الجهةُ التي يُقبِلُ فيها العبدُ على ربِّهِ في صلواتِهِ وعباداتِهِ ودعواتِهِ، وإنه يتجلّى سبحانه على عبادهِ في صلواتِهم ودعواتِهم وعباداتِهم وطوافِهم في قِبلتِهم. قال ﷺ كما في (سننِ الترمذيّ) وغيرِه: «فإذا صلَّيتُم فلا تلتفِتوا؛ فإنَّ اللهَ ينصبُ وجهَهُ لوجهِ عبدِهِ ما دام في صلاتِهِ»[1]. الحديثَ.

وفي (سننِ أبي داودَ) وغيرِها عن جابرٍ رضي الله عنه أنَّ النبيَّ ﷺ قال: «أيُّكم يحبُّ أن يُعرِضَ اللهُ عنه؟ إنَّ أحدَكم إذا قام يُصلّي فإنَّ اللهَ تعالى قِبَلَ وجهِهِ فلا يبصُقْ قِبَلَ وجهِهِ، ولا عن يمينِه، وليبصُقْ عن يسارِهِ تحتَ رِجلِهِ اليُسرى»[2]. الحديث.

فجانِبُ القِبلةِ مكرَّمٌ ومحترَمٌ شرعاً؛ ولذلك نهى رسولُ اللهِ ﷺ عن استقبالِ القِبلةِ واستدبارِها حالةَ البولِ أو التَّغَوُّطِ؛ تكريماً لها وتعظيماً؛ لأنَّ حالةَ التَّبوُّلِ والتغوُّطِ

---

(١) أخرجه الترمذي (٣١٠٢).

(٢) أخرجه أبو داود (٤٨٥).

their left foot instead."[1] Thus, the direction of the *qiblah* is honourable and sacred according to the Sacred Law. This is why the Messenger of Allah ﷺ forbade facing the *qiblah* or turning one's back towards it whilst urinating or defecating, due to the honour and reverence of the *qiblah*. The state of urinating or defecating is not one of honour and reverence, and so it is inappropriate to face the *qiblah* in this state.

Bukhārī and Muslim narrated on the authority of Abū Ayyūb al-Anṣārī ؓ that the Prophet ﷺ said, "When you go to relieve yourself, do not face the *qiblah* or turn your back towards it, but rather turn to the east or west."[2] Abū Ayyūb ؓ said, "When we came to the Levant and found that the lavatories were built facing the *qiblah*, we would turn away from it and seek Allah's forgiveness."

All of this clearly proves that the direction of the *qiblah* is honourable and revered according to the Sacred Law. This is why the gathering which faces the *qiblah* enjoys superiority, eminence, and honour over other gatherings, as has come in the Prophetic hadiths. Ḥāfiẓ al-Mundhirī has cited in *al-Targhīb*, in the chapter on sitting facing the *qiblah*, on the authority of Abū Hurayrah ؓ that the Prophet ﷺ said, "Indeed, everything has a superior, and the most superior of gatherings is that which faces the *qiblah*."[3] Ṭabarānī has narrated it with a sound chain.

It is narrated on the authority of Ibn ʿUmar ؓ that the Messenger of Allah ﷺ said, "The most honourable gathering is that which faces the *qiblah*."[4] Ṭabarānī narrated it in *al-Awsaṭ*.

It is narrated on the authority of Ibn ʿAbbās ؓ that the Messenger of Allah ﷺ said, "Indeed, everything has an eminence, and the most eminent gathering is that which faces the *qiblah*."[5] Ṭabarānī narrated it.

---

(1) *Abū Dāwūd* (485).

(2) *Bukhārī* (144); *Muslim* (264).

(3) Ṭabarānī in *al-Muʿjam al-Awsaṭ* (2354).

(4) Ṭabarānī in *al-Muʿjam al-Awsaṭ* (8361).

(5) *Ḥākim* (7706).

ليست مكرَّمةً ولا معظَّمةً، فلا ينبغي أن يستقبلَ القِبلةَ وهو على تلك الحالةِ.

روى البخاريُّ ومسلمٌ عن أبي أيوبَ الأنصاريّ رَضِيَ اللهُ عَنْهُ أنَّ النبيَّ صَلَّى اللهُ عَلَيْهِ وَآلِهِ وَسَلَّمَ قال: «إذا أتيتُم الغائطَ فلا تستقبِلوا القِبلةَ، ولا تستدبِروها، ولكنْ شرّقوا أو غرّبوا»[1].

قال أبو أيوبَ: فلمّا قدِمنا الشّامَ وجَدْنا مراحيضَ قد بُنِيَتْ قِبَلَ القِبلةِ، فنَنْحَرِفُ عنها ونستغفرُ اللهَ تعالى.

وفي هذا كلِّه دليلٌ صريحٌ في أنَّ جانبَ القِبلةِ معظَّمٌ ومحترَمٌ شرعاً؛ ولذلك كان المجلسُ الذي استُقبِلَ به القِبلةَ له السِّيادةُ على غيرِهِ، وله الشَّرفُ على غيرِهِ، وله الكرامةُ على غيرِهِ، كما جاء في الأحاديثِ النَّبويَّةِ، كما أوردَ ذلك الحافظُ المنذريُّ في (التَّرغيب) في الجلوسِ مستقبِلَ القِبلةِ فقال: وعن أبي هريرةَ رَضِيَ اللهُ عَنْهُ قال: قال رسولُ اللهِ صَلَّى اللهُ عَلَيْهِ وَآلِهِ وَسَلَّمَ: «إنَّ لكلِّ شيءٍ سيّداً، وإنَّ سيّدَ المَجالِسِ قبالةُ القِبلةِ»[2]. رواه الطَّبرانيُّ بإسنادٍ حسنٍ.

قال: وروي عن ابنِ عمرَ رَضِيَ اللهُ عَنْهُمَا قال: قال رسولُ اللهِ صَلَّى اللهُ عَلَيْهِ وَآلِهِ وَسَلَّمَ: «أكرمُ المجالسِ ما استُقبِلَ به القِبلة»[3] رواه الطَّبرانيُّ في «الأوسط».

وروي عن ابنِ عبّاسٍ رضي الله تعالى عنهما قال: قال رسولُ اللهِ صَلَّى اللهُ عَلَيْهِ وَآلِهِ وَسَلَّمَ: «إنَّ لكلِّ شيءٍ شَرفاً، وإن أشرفَ المجالِسِ ما استُقبِلَ به القبلة»[4]. رواهُ الطَّبرانيُّ.

فهذه الأحاديثُ تدلُّ على شَرَفِ جانِبِ القِبلةِ وكرامتِهِ وسيادتِهِ، وإذا كان الأمرُ

---

(١) أخرجه البخاري (١٤٤)، ومسلم (٢٦٤).

(٢) أخرجه الطبراني في الأوسط (٢٣٥٤).

(٣) أخرجه الطبراني في الأوسط (٨٣٦١).

(٤) أخرجه الحاكم (٧٧٠٦).

Thus, these hadiths prove the eminence, honour, and superiority of the *qiblah*. When that is the case, stretching one's feet towards the *qiblah* is neither respectful or honourable, nor the appropriate etiquette it deserves. It is an obvious fact that stretching one's feet towards elders, nobles, leaders, and dignitaries is considered offensive, disparaging, and a breach of decorum.

The hadiths have affirmed eminence, superiority, and honour for the direction of the *qiblah* – so take heed and maintain respect. The direction of the *qiblah* is esteemed and revered, because it is the direction the slave faces their Lord in prayer and acts of worship – as already mentioned – just as it is the direction the slave faces when supplicating and beseeching Him.

Tirmidhī, Nasā'ī, and Aḥmad narrated – and the wording is Aḥmad's – on the authority of ʿUmar ibn al-Khaṭṭāb ﷺ who said, "When Revelation would come down to the Messenger of Allah ﷺ, a sound like the buzzing of bees could be heard near his face. So, we waited a little, after which he faced the *qiblah*, lifted his hands, and said, 'O Allah, increase us and do not decrease us, honour us and do not humiliate us, grant us and do not deprive us, and prefer us and do not prefer [others] over us, and be pleased with us and please us.' Then he ﷺ said, 'Ten verses have been revealed to me; whoever establishes them will enter Paradise.' He then recited, 'Successful indeed are the believers'[1] until he completed all ten verses."[2]

In conclusion, the *qiblah* is esteemed and revered according to the Sacred Law, and the person facing it must adopt esteem and reverence for it.

PEOPLE USED TO KISS THE MUṢḤAF AND WIPE IT ON THEMSELVES

Dārimī narrated with an authentic chain that ʿIkrimah ibn Abī Jahl ﷺ –

(1) *Al-Mu'minūn*, 1.

(2) *Tirmidhī* (3173).

كذلك فليسَ مدُّ الرِّجل للقِبلةِ تشريفاً لها ولا تكريماً لها، ولا أدباً لائقاً بجانبِ القِبلةِ؛ فإنَّ من المعلوماتِ البدهيّةِ أنَّ مدَّ الرِّجل إلى العُظماءِ، أو الأَشرافِ، أو السّاداتِ، أو الأفاضلِ يُعتَبَرُ إساءةً وتهاوناً وخروجاً عن حدودِ الأدبِ، وقد أثبتَتْ أحاديثُ النّبيّ عليه الصلاة والسلامُ الشَّرفَ والسّيادةَ والكرامةَ لجانبِ القِبلةِ، فاعتبِرْ والزَمِ الأدبَ، فجانِبُ القِبلةِ معظَّمٌ و محترَمٌ؛ لأنّهُ متَّجَهُ العبدِ إلى ربّهِ في صلواتِهِ وعباداتِهِ كما تقدَّمَ، كما أنَّه متّجَهُ العبدِ إلى ربِّهِ في دعواتِهِ وابتهالِه.

وقد روى الترمذيُّ والنَّسائيُ والإمامُ أحمدُ - واللفظُ له - عن عمرَ بنِ الخطّابِ رضي الله عنه قال: (كان إذا نزلَ على رسولِ الله ﷺ الوحيُ يُسمَعُ عند وجهِهِ كدويِّ النَّحلِ، فلبِثْنا ساعةً، فاستقبلَ القِبلةَ ورفعَ يديه، وقال: «اللّهم زِدنا ولا تَنقُصْنا، وأكرِمْنا ولا تُهِنّا، وأعطِنا ولا تَحرِمنا، وآثِرْنا ولا تُؤثِرْ علينا، وارضَ عنّا وأرضِنا»، ثمَّ قال ﷺ: «لقد أُنزِلَ عليَّ عشرُ آياتٍ مَن أقامَهنَّ دخلَ الجنّةَ»، ثمَّ قرأَ {قَدْ أَفْلَحَ الْمُؤْمِنُونَ}[1] حتّى ختَمَ العشرَ[2].

فالقِبلةُ معظَّمةٌ شرعاً ومحترَمَةٌ، والمتوجّهُ إليها ينبغي أن يتَّصِفَ بصفةِ المحترِمِ والمعظِّمِ لها.

كانوا يُقبّلونَ المصحفَ ويتمسَّحونَ به

روى الدارميُّ بإسنادٍ صحيحٍ أنَّ عكرمةَ بنَ أبي جهلٍ - الحيُّ ابنُ الميّتِ رَضِيَ اللهُ عَنْهُ - كان يضعُ المصحفَ على وجهِهِ، ويقول: (كتابُ ربّي)، أي: هذا كتابُ ربّنا أنزلَهُ إلينا

(١) المؤمنون: ١.

(٢) أخرجه الترمذي (٣١٧٣).

the living, son of the dead – used to place the muṣḥaf on his face and say, "The Book of my Lord." In other words, this is the Book of our Lord which He has sent to us through our Messenger and master Muhammad ﷺ. If someone were to receive a book from an eminent person, it would only be appropriate that they read it. So, what can be said of the great Qur'an, sent down from the Lord of the Great Throne to our master Muhammad ﷺ who possessed great character?

It states in *al-Durr al-Mukhtār* that Ibn 'Umar ؓ used to take hold of the muṣḥaf every morning, kiss it, and say, "My Lord's edict. My Lord's publication." 'Uthmān ibn 'Affān ؓ used to kiss the muṣḥaf and wipe it on his face.

بواسطةِ رسولِنا سيّدِنا محمّدٍ ﷺ. أي: ومَن جاءه كتابٌ من عظيمٍ فينبغي له أن ينظرَ فيه، فكيف بالقرآنِ العظيمِ النّازلِ مِن عندِ ربِّ العرشِ العظيمِ على سيّدِنا محمّدٍ ﷺ ذي الخُلُقِ العظيمِ؟ ونقلَ في (الدُّرِّ المختارِ) أنَّ ابنَ عمرَ رَضِيَ اللَّهُ عَنْهُمَا كان يأخذُ المصحفَ كلَّ غداةٍ، ويقبّلهُ ويقول: (عهدُ ربّي، ومنشورُ ربّي عزَّ وجلَّ). وكان عثمانُ بنُ عفّانَ رَضِيَ اللَّهُ عَنْهُ يقبِّلُ المصحفَ ويمسحُهُ على وجهِهِ. اهـ.

THEY USED TO LIKE LOOKING INTO THE MUṢḤAF IN THE MORNING

Ḥalīmī reported in *Shu'ab al-Īmān* that Yūnus ibn 'Ubayd said, "Looking into the muṣḥaf was the tradition of the predecessors."

Awzā'ī said, "They used to like looking into the muṣḥaf."

The author of *al-Qūt* said, "Many of the Companions used to read from the muṣḥaf and they would like that not a single day passes by them except that they had looked into the muṣḥaf. 'Uthmān ibn 'Affān ended up ripping two *muṣḥafs* due to frequently reading from them."

They also used to like leaving the muṣḥaf as part of their inheritance. This is a form of revering and honouring the muṣḥaf, as an intelligent person leaves that which is dear, cherished, and beloved to them in inheritance, and passes it on to those whom they love. Moreover, they wanted the reward of the person who recites from the muṣḥaf after them to continue for them.

Ibn Mājah narrated with a sound chain, as well as Bayhaqī and others, on the authority of Abū Hurayrah that the Messenger of Allah said, "Amongst the actions and good deeds a believer will continue to receive after their death are sacred knowledge they taught and spread; a pious child they left behind; a copy of the Qur'an they left in inheritance; a masjid they constructed; a lodge they built for travellers; a stream they

كانوا يستحبّونَ النَّظرَ في المصحفِ إذا أصبَحوا

نقل الحليميُّ في (شُعَبِ الإيمانِ) عن يونسَ بنِ عُبيدٍ رحمه الله تعالى أنّهُ قال: كان خُلُقاً للأَوَّلينَ النَّظرُ في المصحفِ. وقال الأوزاعيُّ رضي الله عنه: كان يُعجبُهم النَّظرُ في المصحفِ. اهـ. وقال صاحبُ (القوت): كان كثيرٌ من الصَّحابةِ رضي الله عنهم يقرؤونَ في المصحفِ، ويستحبّونَ ألّا يخرجَ يومٌ إلّا وقد نظروا في المصحفِ. قال: وخَرَّقَ عثمانُ بنُ عفّانَ رضي الله عنه مصحفَينِ؛ مِن كثرةِ درسِهِ فيهِما. اهـ.وقال العلّامةُ الفاسيُّ رحمه الله: كان الأئمّةُ والصّالحونَ من السَّلفِ أوَّلَ ما يبدؤونَ به إذا أصبَحوا النَّظرَ في المصحف، وكانوا يأمرون مَنِ اشتكى بصرَهُ أن ينظرَ في المصحفِ. اهـ. كانوا يستحبّونَ توريثَ المصحفِ، وفي ذلك نوعٌ من التَّعظيمِ للمصحفِ والتَّكريمِ له؛ لأنَّ شأنَ العاقلِ أن يُورِّثَ ما هو عزيزٌ عليه كريمٌ لديه محبوبٌ إليه، يورِّثُهُ لِمَن يحبُّه، ولأجل أن يجريَ عليه أجرُ القارئِ فيه من بعدِه. فقد روى ابنُ ماجه بإسنادٍ حسنٍ، والبيهقيُّ وغيرُهما عن أبي هريرةَ رضي الله عنه قال: قال رسولُ الله صلى الله عليه وآله وسلم: «إنَّ ممّا يلحَقُ المؤمنَ من عملِهِ وحسناتِهِ بعد موتِه علماً علَّمهُ ونشَرَهُ، وولداً صالحاً تركَهُ، أو مُصحفاً ورَّثهُ، أو مسجداً بناه، أو بيتاً لابنِ

set flowing; or charity they took out from their wealth whilst they were healthy – these things will continue reaching them after their death."[1]

BEING SINCERE TO THE BOOK OF ALLAH MOST HIGH IS INCUMBENT AND IT HAS ITS REQUIREMENTS

Imam Muslim narrated on the authority of Tamīm al-Dārī ﵁ that the Prophet ﷺ said, "The religion is to be sincere." He said this three times. They asked, "To whom, O Messenger of Allah?" He ﷺ said, "To Allah, His Book, His Messenger, the leaders of the Muslims, and the common people amongst them."[2]

Ṭabarānī narrated from the hadith of Ḥudhayfah ibn al-Yamān ﵁ that the Prophet ﷺ said, "Whoever is not concerned with the affairs of the Muslim is not from them. Whoever does not spend the morning and evening being sincere to Allah, His Messenger, His Book, their leader, and the common Muslims is not from them."[3]

Therefore, being sincere to the Book of Allah Most High is amongst the most important and greatest obligations of the religion, and the most difficult in terms of accountability before Allah Most High.

Being sincere to the Book of Allah Most High has a number of requisites. Ḥāfiẓ Ibn Rajab al-Ḥanbalī has cited Imam Muhammad ibn Naṣr al-Marwazī's work, *Ta'ẓīm Qadr al-Ṣalāh*, and related what the scholars amongst the Pious Predecessors said about the requirements of being sincere to the Book of Allah Most High: "As for sincerity to the Book of Allah Most High, it is to love it intensely, esteem its rank because it is the Speech of the Creator Almighty and Exalted, have an intense yearning to understand it, pay great attention to contemplating it, and to pause when reciting it to seek the meanings of one's Master's Book, in order

(1) *Ibn Mājah* (242).

(2) *Muslim* (55).

(3) Ṭabarānī in *al-Mu'jam al-Awsaṭ* (471).

السَّبيلِ بناه، أو نهراً أجراه، أو صدقةً أخرجَها من مالِهِ في صحّتِهِ، وحياتِهِ تلحقُهُ مِن بعدِ موتِه»[١].

النَّصيحةُ لكتابِ اللهِ تعالى واجبةٌ ولها مطالِبُها

روى الإمامُ مسلمٌ عن تميمٍ الداريِّ رَضِيَ اللهُ عَنْهُ أنَّ النبيَّ صلى اللهُ عليه وآلِهِ وسلَّمَ قال: «الدِّينُ النّصيحةُ» - ثلاثاً -، قلنا: لِمَن يا رسولَ الله؟ قال: «للهِ، ولكتابِهِ، ولرسولِهِ، ولأئمّةِ المسلمينَ، وعامَّتِهم»[٢].

ورواه الطبرانيُّ من حديثِ حذيفةَ بنِ اليَمانِ رَضِيَ اللهُ عَنْهُ عن النبيِّ صَلَّى اللهُ عَلَيْهِ وَآلِهِ وَسَلَّمَ قال: «مَن لا يهتَمُّ بأمرِ المسلمينَ فليس منهم، ومَن لم يُمسِ ويُصبحْ ناصحاً للهِ، ولرسولِهِ، ولكتابِه، ولإمامِه، ولعامّةِ المسلمينَ فليس منهم»[٣].

فالنصيحةُ لكتابِ اللهِ تعالى من أهمِّ واجباتِ الدِّينِ، وأعظمِها، وأشدِّها مسؤوليةً عند اللهِ تعالى، والنَّصيحةُ لكتابِ اللهِ تعالى لها متطلَّباتٌ عديدةٌ:

وقد نقلَ الحافظُ ابنُ رجبٍ الحنبليّ رَحِمَهُ اللهُ تَعَالَى عن الإمامِ محمّدِ بنِ نصرٍ المروزيّ في كتابِه (تعظيمِ قدرِ الصّلاة) عن أهلِ العلمِ من السَّلفِ الصّالحِ في مطالبِ النّصيحةِ لكتابِ اللهِ تعالى قولَهم: وأمّا النّصيحةُ لكتابِ اللهِ تعالى: فشِدَّةُ حبّهِ، وتعظيمُ قدرِهِ؛ إذ هو كلامُ الخالِقِ عزَّ وجلَّ، وشدّةُ الرَّغبةِ في فهمِهِ، وشدَّةُ العنايةِ في تدبُّرِه، والوقوفُ عند

---

(١) أخرجه ابن ماجه (٢٤٢).

(٢) رواه مسلم (٥٥).

(٣) أخرجه الطبراني في (المعجم الأوسط) (٤٧١).

to understand it from Him or to implement it for His sake after having understood it from Him.

It is similar to a sincere slave who wishes to understand the counsel of the person advising them. If they receive a letter from them, they look to understand it, so that they can fulfil what they have written to them therein. Similarly, a person who is sincere to the Book of their Lord looks to understand it, so that they can – for the sake of Allah – carry out what he has commanded them as He loves and as pleases Him. Thereafter, they disseminate what they have understood amongst the slaves, and they constantly study it with love, inculcating its characteristics and adopting its manners."

Ḥāfiẓ Ibn Rajab ﵀ then reports the statement of Abū ʿAmr ibn al-Ṣalāḥ ﵀, "Sincerity to the Book of Allah Most High is to believe in it, revere it, deem it pure (from all unbecoming matters), recite it properly, comply with its commands and prohibitions, seek to understand its knowledge and its similitudes, invite towards it, and defend it against the distortions of the extreme and the attacks of the heretics."

Amongst the necessary requirements of sincerity to the Book of Allah Most High is to commit oneself to acting upon it – with the belief that it is the Truth that clarifies all rights and obligations. He Most High said, "We have sent down the Qur'an in truth, and with the truth it has come down."(1) One must also believe that it is the decisive Word which distinguishes between truth and falsehood. He Most High said, "By the sky with its recurring cycles, and the earth with its sprouting plants! Surely this [Qur'an] is a decisive Word, and is not to be taken lightly."(2)

Here, He Most Glorified and Most High swears by the sky and its recurring cycles of rain that grant life to the souls and bodies. Then, He swears by the earth, splitting open with plants and giving forth fruits and good things as nourishment for all creatures that eat. He swore an oath by

(1) *Al-Isrā'*, 105.

(2) *Al-Ṭāriq*, 11-14.

تلاوتِهِ لطلبِ معاني كتابِ مَولاهُ أنْ يفهمَهُ عنه، أو يقومَ به له - أي: لله تعالى - بعدَما يفهَمُهُ عنه.

وكذلك النّاصحُ من العبادِ يفهمُ وصيّةَ مَن ينصحُهُ إنْ وردَ عليه كتابُ مَنْ عُنِيَ بفهمِهِ؛ ليقومَ بما كتبَ فيه إليه، فكذلك النّاصحُ لكتابِ ربِّهِ، يُعنَى بفهمِهِ؛ ليقومَ للهِ بما أمرَهُ به كما يحبُّ ربُّنا ويرضى، ثم ينشرَ ما فَهِمَ في العبادِ، ويُديمَ دراستَهُ بالمحبَّةِ له، والتخلُّقِ بأخلاقِهِ، والتأدُّبِ بآدابِهِ.

ثم نقلَ الحافظُ ابنُ رجبٍ عن أبي عمرِو بنِ الصَّلاحِ رحمه اللهُ تعالى قولَه: والنَّصيحةُ لكتابِ اللهِ تعالى: الإيمانُ به، وتعظيمُه، وتنزيهُه، وتلاوتُه حقَّ تلاوتِه، والوقوفُ مع أوامرِهِ ونواهيه، وتفهُّمُ علومِه وأمثالِه، وتدبُّرُ آياتِه، والدُّعاءُ إليه، وذبُّ تحريف الغالينَ وطعن الملحدينَ عنه اهـ.

ومن واجباتِ النَّصيحةِ لكتابِ اللهِ تعالى: التزامُ العملِ به، معتقداً أنَّهُ الحقُّ المبيِّنُ لجميعِ الحقوقِ والواجباتِ، قال تعالى: {وَبِالْحَقِّ أَنزَلْنَاهُ وَبِالْحَقِّ نَزَلَ}[1] الآية.

ومعتقِداً أنَّهُ هو القولُ الفاصلُ بين الحقِّ والباطلِ، قال تعالى: {وَالسَّمَاءِ ذَاتِ الرَّجْعِ (١١) وَالْأَرْضِ ذَاتِ الصَّدْعِ (١٢) إِنَّهُ لَقَوْلٌ فَصْلٌ (١٣) وَمَا هُوَ بِالْهَزْلِ}[2].

وفي هذا يُقسِمُ سُبْحَانَهُ وَتَعَالَى بالسَّماءِ ورَجْعِها بالمطرِ الذي به حياةُ النُّفوسِ والأجسامِ، وبالأرضِ وصَدْعِها بالنباتِ وإخراجِها الثَّمراتِ والخيراتِ التي بها الأقواتُ لكلِّ مُقتاتٍ، أقسمَ بذلك على حقيّةِ هذا القرآنِ الكريمِ الذي به حياةُ الأرواحِ والقلوبِ، فقال سبحانه: {إِنَّهُ لَقَوْلٌ فَصْلٌ} أي: هو الذي يفصلُ بين الحقِّ والباطلِ، فيميّزُ هذا

---

(١) الإسراء: ١٠٥.

(٢) الطارق: ١١-١٤.

this to prove the veracity of this Noble Qur'an that grants life to the souls and hearts. He Most Glorified said, "Surely this [Qur'an] is a decisive Word." In other words, it is that which distinguishes between truth and falsehood, separating them from one another. Furthermore, it judges between people in their mutual differences. This includes affirming the fact that it is most assuredly the truth and not false, and that it is serious in its entirety and not a joke. Hence, there is no joke, falsehood, vainness, or frivolity therein. Rather, all of it is true, real, decisive, and accurate.

He Most High said, "*Alif Lām Rā*. [This is] a Book whose verses are well perfected and then fully explained. [It is] from the One [Who is] All-Wise, All-Aware."(1) The Prophet ﷺ also said, as mentioned previously, "It is a decisive Word; it is not a joke."(2) Hence, it is impermissible to take the verses of Allah Most High lightly. He Most High said, "Do not take Allah's verses lightly. Remember Allah's favours upon you as well as the Book and wisdom He has sent down for your guidance. Be mindful of Allah, and know that Allah has [perfect] knowledge of all things."(3)

As for the prohibition of taking Allah's verses lightly, it includes a number of things:

Firstly, it includes using Qur'anic words and phrases in the context of jokes, lightheartedness, laughing, and entertainment, as the heretics do in their gatherings.

Secondly, it includes not giving due importance to the Qur'an's commands and prohibitions. So, when the verses of the Qur'an comprising commands or prohibitions are related to them, they do not care. Neither do they have any interest in what Allah Most High has encouraged nor are they apprehensive of that against which Allah Most High has cautioned. It is as though the verses of the Qur'an are trivialities in this person's eyes, or merely amusement and play. They fail to observe the truth,

---

(1) *Hūd*, 1.

(2) *Al-Jinn*, 1-2.

(3) *Al-Baqarah*, 231.

تِلاوَةُ القُرآنِ المَجيدِ

من هذا، وهو الذي يفصلُ بين النّاسِ فيما اختلَفوا فيه، وذلك يتضمَّنُ إثباتَ أنَّه هو الحقُّ وليس بالباطلِ، وأنَّه الجِدُّ كلُّ الجِدّ، وليس بالهزلِ، فلا هزلَ فيه، ولا باطَلَ، ولا عبثَ، ولا لعبَ؛ بل هو كلُّهُ حقٌّ وحقيقةٌ وفصلٌ وإحكامٌ.

قال تعالى: {الر كِتَابٌ أُحْكِمَتْ آيَاتُهُ ثُمَّ فُصِّلَتْ مِن لَّدُنْ حَكِيمٍ خَبِيرٍ} (١).

وقال ﷺ كما تقدَّمَ في الحديثِ: «هو الفَصلُ ليس بالهزلِ» (٢)، فلا يجوزُ أن تُتَّخَذَ آياتُ اللهِ تعالى هزواً؛ قال تعالى: {وَلَا تَتَّخِذُوا آيَاتِ اللَّهِ هُزُوًا وَاذْكُرُوا نِعْمَتَ اللَّهِ عَلَيْكُمْ وَمَا أَنزَلَ عَلَيْكُم مِّنَ الْكِتَابِ وَالْحِكْمَةِ يَعِظُكُم بِهِ وَاتَّقُوا اللَّهَ وَاعْلَمُوا أَنَّ اللَّهَ بِكُلِّ شَيْءٍ عَلِيمٌ} (٣).

والنَّهيُ عن اتِّخاذِ آياتِ اللهِ هزواً يتناولُ أموراً:

أوَّلاً: سَوقُ بعضِ الكلماتِ القرآنيَّةِ في مساقاتِ الهزلِ، أو المُزاحِ، أو الضَّحِكِ، أو العَبَثِ، كما يفعلُهُ الزَّنادقةُ في مجالِسِهم.

ثانياً: عدمُ الاهتمامِ بأوامرِ القرآنِ ونواهيه، بحيثُ إذا وردَتْ عليه آياتُ القرآنِ، وفيها الأوامرُ، أو النَّواهي لم يعبأُ بذلك، ولم يرغَبْ فيما رغَّبه اللهُ تعالى، أو لم يَرهَبْ ما حذَّرَ اللهُ تعالى منه، وكأنَّ آياتِ القرآنِ في نظرِهِ أباطيلُ، أو لهوٌ ولَعِبٌ، ولا يرى فيها الحقَّ والحقيقةَ، والجِدَّ والقولَ الفصلَ، وفصلَ الخطابِ، قال تعالى فيهم: {وَإِذَا عَلِمَ مِنْ آيَاتِنَا شَيْئًا اتَّخَذَهَا هُزُوًا أُولَٰئِكَ لَهُمْ عَذَابٌ مُّهِينٌ} (٤).

---

(١) هود: ١.

(٢) أخرجه الترمذي (٢٨٥٠).

(٣) البقرة: ٢٣١.

(٤) الجاثية: ٩.

reality, earnestness, decisive speech, and sound judgement they contain. Regarding them, He Most High said, "And whenever they learn anything of Our Revelations, they make a mockery of it. It is they who will suffer a humiliating punishment."[1]

Thirdly, it includes being deceptive with the texts of the Noble Qur'an, by turning them away from their meanings stated in the *Sunnah*, or as transmitted from the Companions, or the Pious Predecessors who acquired them from the first of this ummah. Such a person turns these texts towards what they themselves desires, and thus tampers with rulings, legalizes unlawful matters, and so forth. It is as though the Qur'anic verses are playthings at this person's disposal to exploit however they desire and want.

Fourthly, it includes not having trust and conviction in the matters of the Unseen and major incidents of which the Noble Qur'an informs, and considering their occurrence to be farfetched. An example of this is that which Ibn al-Mundhir and Ibn Abī Ḥātim narrated on the authority of Qatādah ﵀ who said, "Whilst the Messenger of Allah ﷺ was marching towards Tabuk, he saw some hypocrites ahead of him saying, 'Does this man anticipate he will conquer the palaces and fortresses of the Levant? It is impossible, absolutely impossible!' Allah informed His Prophet about this, so he ﷺ said, 'Detain this group of riders for me.' He then came to them and said, 'You said such-and-such.' They replied, 'O Prophet of Allah, we were only talking idly and joking around.' So, the saying of Allah Most High, 'If you question them, they will certainly say, "We were only talking idly and joking around." Say, "Was it Allah, His Revelations, and His Messenger that you ridiculed?"'[2] came down."[3]

Therefore, the prohibition in His saying "do not take Allah's verses lightly" necessitates that a person's approach to the Qur'an be extremely

---

(1) *Al-Jāthiyah*, 9.

(2) *Al-Tawbah*, 65.

(3) Ṭabarī in his exegesis (16928).

ثالثاً: الاحتيالُ على نصوصِ القرآنِ الكريمِ؛ بأنْ يصرِفَها عن معانيها الواردةِ في السُّنّةِ، أو عن الصَّحابةِ، أو عن السَّلفِ الصَّالحِ الذين تلقَّوها عن صدرِ هذه الأمَّةِ - يصرفُ تلك النصوصَ إلى ما تهواهُ نفسُهُ فيتلاعبُ في الأحكامِ ويُحلِّلُ الحرامَ، إلى ما وراءَ ذلك -، وكأنَّ نصوصَ الآياتِ القرآنيّةِ لُعبةٌ بين يديه يُقلّبُها كما يهوى ويريد.

رابعاً: عدمُ الثّقةِ واليقينِ بما أخبرَتْ عنه آياتُ القرآنِ الكريمِ من أمورٍ غَيبيّةٍ، أو حوادثَ كبرى يستبعدُ ذلك من الوقوعِ، وذلك مثلَ ما رواهُ ابنُ المنذرِ، وابنُ أبي حاتمٍ عن قتادةَ قال: بينَما رسولُ الله صلى اللهُ عليه وآلِهِ وسلَّمَ في غزوتِهِ إلى تبوكَ إذ نظرَ إلى أُناسٍ بين يديه من المنافقينَ يقولون: أيرجو هذا الرَّجلُ أن تُفتَحَ له قصورُ الشَّامِ وحصونُها؟! هيهاتَ هيهاتَ! فأطلعَ اللهُ نبيَّهُ على ذلك فقال ﷺ: «احبِسوا عليَّ هؤلاءِ الرَّكبِ»، فأتاهم فقال عليه الصلاة والسلام: «قلتُم كذا وكذا، قالوا: يا نبيَّ اللهِ إنَّما كنّا نخوضُ ونلعبُ! فنزل قولُه تعالى: {وَلَئِن سَأَلْتَهُمْ لَيَقُولُنَّ إِنَّمَا كُنَّا نَخُوضُ وَنَلْعَبُ قُلْ أَبِاللَّهِ وَآيَاتِهِ وَرَسُولِهِ كُنتُمْ تَسْتَهْزِئُونَ}[1] [2].

فالنّهيُ في قولِه تعالى: {وَلَا تَتَّخِذُوا آيَاتِ اللَّهِ هُزُوًا} [3] يقضي أن يكونَ موقفُ الإنسانِ مع القرآنِ موقفَ الجادِّ الحازمِ الجازمِ المهتمِّ كلَّ الاهتمامِ بالتمسُّكِ بكتابِ اللهِ تعالى والملتزِمِ بآياتِه.

قال تعالى: {وَالَّذِينَ يُمَسِّكُونَ بِالْكِتَابِ وَأَقَامُوا الصَّلَاةَ إِنَّا لَا نُضِيعُ أَجْرَ

---

(١) التوبة: ٦٥.

(٢) ذكره الطبري في (تفسيره) (١٦٩٢٨).

(٣) البقرة: ٢٣١.

serious, prudent, and of utmost care to firmly abide by the Book of Allah Most High and commit to adhere to its verses.

He Most High said, "As for those who firmly abide by the Book and establish prayer – surely We never discount the reward of the reformers."(1) Allah, the Greatest, has spoken the truth.

The compilation of this book and its transcription have been completed on 29th Ramadan 1401 AH.

We ask Allah Most High for acceptance, and that He benefit the slaves thereby. Indeed, He alone is the All-Hearing, All-Knowing. May Allah Most High send blessings on the Imam of the Prophets and Messengers, the master of all the children of Ādam, at all times – and upon his family and his Companions – and may He send peace forever and ever.

All praise is for Allah, Lord of all worlds.

---

(1) *Al-A'rāf*, 170.

الْمُصْلِحِينَ} [1] صدق اللهُ العظيم.

هذا وقد تمَّ جَمْعُ هذا الكتابِ ونسخُهُ في التّاسعِ والعشرينَ من رمضانَ المباركِ (١٤٠١) هـ.

نسألُ اللهَ تعالى القَبولَ، وأن ينفعَ به العبادَ إنّهُ هو السَّميعُ العليمُ، وصلى الله تعالى على إمامِ الأنبياءِ والمرسلينَ، وسيّدِ ولدِ آدمَ أجمعين، في كلِّ وقتٍ وحينٍ، وعلى آله وصحبه وسلَّمَ تسليماً أبدَ الآبِدين.

والحمدُ للهِ ربِّ العالمين

---

(١) الأعراف: ١٧٠.

www.ingramcontent.com/pod-product-compliance
Lightning Source LLC
Chambersburg PA
CBHW030429010526
44118CB00011B/559
9781087903781